Masters of Small Worlds

MASTERS

of

SMALL
WORLDS

*Yeoman Households,
Gender Relations,
and the Political Culture
of the Antebellum
South Carolina
Low Country*

STEPHANIE McCURRY

OXFORD UNIVERSITY PRESS
New York   Oxford

Oxford University Press

Oxford   New York
Athens   Auckland Bangkok   Bombay
Calcutta   Cape Town   Dar es Salaam   Delhi
Florence   Hong Kong   Istanbul   Karachi
Kuala Lumpur   Madras   Madrid   Melbourne
Mexico City   Nairobi   Paris   Singapore
Taipei   Tokyo   Toronto

and associated companies in
Berlin   Ibadan

First published in 1995 by Oxford University Press, Inc.,
198 Madison Avenue, New York, New York 10016

First issued as an Oxford University Press paperback, 1997

Oxford is a registered trademark of Oxford University Press

Library of Congress Cataloging-in-Publication Data
McCurry, Stephanie.
Masters of small worlds :
yeoman households, gender relations, and the political culture
of the antebellum South Carolina Low Country /
Stephanie McCurry.
p.   cm.   Includes bibliographical references (p.   ) and index.
ISBN 0-19-507236-7;   0-19-511795-6 (pbk.)
1. South Carolina—History—1775–1865.
2. Political culture—South Carolina—History—19th century.
3. Social classes—South Carolina—History—19th century.
4. Sex role—South Carolina—History—19th century.
5. Slavery—South Carolina—History—19th century.
I. Title.   F273.M48   1995   975.7'03—dc20   94-16869

9 8 7 6 5 4 3 2

Printed in the United States of America
on acid-free paper

To Steven

Preface

This is a book about power and the complex channels in which it worked in slave society in the United States; about the yeomanry and the web of relations within which they were enmeshed; and about women as historical actors and gender as a conceptual category in the history of the antebellum South. But the book is, of course, also something far more modest, for it focuses on a particular class and region: the yeomanry in the South Carolina Low Country.

To date, most studies of the southern yeomanry have looked to up-country regions in which yeoman farmers were the dominant demographic presence, even, some have argued, the dominant social and political presence. I was interested, in contrast, in studying the yeomanry in a plantation-belt setting in which relations between yeoman heads of households and more powerful planter ones were direct and immediate, matters of everyday, face-to-face negotiation, and in which those negotiations were conducted in full recognition of the importance of the enslaved black majority that surrounded them. Nowhere was this more palpably the case than in the South Carolina Low Country, where the very presence of a yeomanry, although perfectly evident on the manuscript census, had long been overlooked and even denied and where the size of the black majority and the immense wealth and power of the planter class had long provided the central, if not exclusive, dynamic of historical interpretation. Nowhere, then, did the inclusion of a yeomanry promise more dramatic historiographical consequences than in this, the vanguard of the Confederacy.

But precisely because of the qualities that recommended it as an exciting site for study, the choice of the South Carolina Low Country posed inevitable questions of representativeness or typicality. And indeed, it was in many respects a unique place. Like every locale, the Low Country had its distinctive features. Yet, in ways I try to demonstrate, the Low Country also evinced clear kinship (demographic, social, political) with other parts of the black-belt South, and thus its historical experience can shed much broader light. This, then, is my hope: that the questions raised here and the perspectives offered, although grounded in analysis of a particular place, will prove suggestive for historians of the antebellum south and even of the United States.

Although this book originated in a driving interest in the yeomanry and the politics of secession, as time went on and other dimensions of the problem became apparent my interests became as much analytical as narrative. And while it is difficult now to recall all of the paths taken on this intellectual journey, a few are sufficiently important to the book to mention here. Most important, perhaps, is the conviction I came to that relations of power *within* yeoman households were every bit as important in the analysis of the antebellum South as those between yeoman and planter household heads on which historians have customarily focused; that the assumptions and values that governed the yeomanry's political choices were engendered in the household itself—in the relations of power that engaged those men most directly; and, finally, that domestic dependencies had critical public meanings, if only we could discern them. I have tried, then, to eschew conventional historiographical boundaries, particularly those that separate the public from the private sphere and the history of women and gender from that of "high" politics and political ideology. After all, in the slave South the defense of domestic institutions and domestic relations was a matter of primary political significance, and high politics was the politics of the household and the so-called private sphere.

I have brought the same perspective to the analysis of the political economy of yeoman households. Because the question of "independence" has assumed a pivotal interpretive role in virtually every study of the antebellum yeomanry, it is imperative, as I see it, to inquire into the relations of power and dependency out of which that vaunted yeoman independence was produced and reproduced. That inquiry starts in the household, with the fundamental matter of the organization of work by race and gender, and it proceeds to the churches, those critical institutions of yeoman, and indeed lowcountry, culture and politics. For as I discovered in the course of my research, it was in evangelicalism, in its familial discourse, in its image of Christian society as a perfected family, and especially, in the daily dispensation of gospel discipline in local congregations, that yeoman men and women gave clearest articulation to usually unspoken assumptions about the nature and workings of power and authority—including their gendered dimensions.

Although ambitious, my goal in writing this book has been to redraw the complex web of gender, class, and race relations within which lowcountry farmers were enmeshed and to locate in it the meaning of their political sensibilities and fateful political decisions. To do so involved making the boundaries of the body politic themselves a subject of historical analysis—inquiring into the ways in which the exclusion of slaves and women defined slavery republicanism, for example, as distinct from the "democracy" emergent in the free-labor North—and, most difficult of all, challenging the assumptions, still widespread in the historiography, about the natural exclusion of women from political life and political history. In one sense, then, I wanted to see what difference the inclusion of women and gender would make to the mainstream political narrative of antebellum history and of the yeomanry's role in secession and the coming of the Civil War. In the course of my work, I became intrigued by the possibility of a gendered political history, one that expanded the cast of political actors to embrace the disfranchised as well as the enfranchised, the excluded as well as the included, and to move beyond the boundaries of the body politic prescribed by contemporary southern white men, within which so much southern history has remained confined. In the end, then, I hope to show that a focus on relations of power within the household, on domestic dependencies and their public meanings, produces a very different perspective on the yeomanry's politics, one that challenges the now customary insistence on its egalitarian impulse.

My success in this endeavor remains for the reader to judge; my intellectual debts, however, are already perfectly evident. My ability to come to such a perspective on the yeomanry and on gender and political culture was made possible by the hard work and exciting advances in a number of fields over the past thirty years: by the pathbreaking and politically energized scholarship on slavery and slave society that dominated the field of American history in the 1960s and 1970s; by the innovative history of rural America, the development of capitalism, and the importance of republican political traditions that captured scholarly attention and inspired heated political battle in the late 1970s and 1980s; by the transformative influence of women's history, which since its brilliant resurgence in the 1960s has virtually redefined the way some of us do history; and, most recently, by an emergent history of gender relations that promises to bring the concerns of feminist historians to bear on the main narratives of American political history. This project has involved for me a fruitful traveling between these various fields.

San Diego
July 1994

S. McC.

Acknowledgments

I had great company along the way. It is with great pleasure and no small sense of relief that I acknowledge here the many individuals and institutions that helped me in my work. First and foremost, I would like to thank my teachers: Craig Simpson of the University of Western Ontario in whose class it all began, Eugene D. Genovese, Stanley Engerman, and Elizabeth Fox-Genovese. My colleagues in the history department at the University of California, San Diego, Michael Meranze, Eric Van Young, Julie Saville, and Rachel Klein along with the other members of the Graduate Seminar in Southern History, provided the best possible environment in which to write this book. Rachel has proven the truest of friends as well, the kind who is there when it counts to offer a careful reading, incisive criticism, and unstinting support. Michael Johnson, now of Johns Hopkins and a sadly missed member of the seminar, provided support in a variety of ways, including as a commentator on a very early conference paper. Other colleagues at UCSD and elsewhere provided important sounding boards for various parts of the argument or expert advice on key matters. I would especially like to thank Masao Miyoshi, Thomas Dublin, Catherine Clinton, Nancy Hewitt, Edward Ayers, Steven Stowe, Christine Stansell, Peter Coclanis, and, for last-minute cautions, Eric Foner. For excellent assistance in research, I would like to thank Thomas Summerhill, Bonnie-Heather Merrick, Trenton Hizer and, for his expertise on the numbers, Michael Gorman.

Some individuals saw this project in almost as many versions as I did. Drew Faust read the dissertation, the book manuscript, at least one journal article, and any number of conference papers and always, to my amazement, was interested. Her advice made an immeasurably better book of the dissertation, and her encouragement was as valuable to the graduate student as it remains to the associate professor. Lacy Ford has been my good friend and spirited interlocutor since my first days in Columbia, South Carolina. His eleventh hour reading of my manuscript and the painstaking care with which he did it are only the most recent evidences of his personal and scholarly generosity. Only he will ever know—and this is a threat—the embarrassing errors from which he saved me. Elizabeth Colwill saw it all with me from the State University of New York at Binghamton to San Diego. Her own wonderful work on gender and political culture in the French Revolution was a wellspring of new ideas and a tantalizing reminder of the scholarly worlds that awaited beyond the yeomanry and the South Carolina Low Country.

There was as well, of course, the kind of institutional support without which no work gets done. When I first began my research in Columbia, South Carolina, I found a comfortable home and stimulating intellectual company in the Institute for Southern Studies. For that I thank the director Walter B. Edgar. The American Council of Learned Societies provided critical leave time through their program of fellowships for recent recipients of the Ph.D. UCSD also afforded me leave from teaching through both the sabbatical leave and the affirmative action programs. At UCSD I had, as well, valuable institutional support from Michael Bernstein, the department chair, and Stanley Chodorow, the Dean of Humanities. Sheldon Meyer of Oxford University Press provided the perfect combination of patience and encouragement needed to see this project into print.

I would also like to express my appreciation to the staffs of the Library of Congress, the Southern Historical Collection, the South Carolina Department of Archives and History, the South Carolina Historical Society, the Perkins Library and Rare Book Library both at Duke University, the Baker Business Library at Harvard University, the National Archives, and the South Caroliniana Library where I did much of the research for this book. Like the many others who have worked in the Caroliniana, I owe a great debt of gratitude to the excellent staff, especially Henry Fulmer, the manuscript librarian, and Allen H. Stokes, the director. Their knowledge of the collections and engagement in the various projects under way in the library are rare indeed. That my work in the Caroliniana is now completed is one of my few regrets at having finished the project.

Some debts are more personal and more longstanding even, remarkably, than the book. To my parents, Margaret and Sylvester McCurry who opened up a world of possibilities for all of their children, and to my sisters and brother, Deirdre McCurry, Timothy McCurry, Roisín Doria, Ursula McCurry, and Gráinne McCurry, who helped keep it all in perspective, I offer my heartfelt thanks and a promise—to talk about something else for a change.

Most of all, I would like to thank Steven Hahn, to whom this book is dedicated. Two outsiders to the South—one Yankee, one Irish—we were brought together by the unlikely subject of the southern yeomen, and by fate in the form of the Southern Historical Association. Much more has kept us together. Steve has been my intellectual partner in the writing of this book, tolerating my obsession with a subject to which he had already devoted considerable energy; encouraging me to trust my instincts and to do it my own way; sustaining my flagging spirit with his own great passion for the work we both have chosen. For the past ten years we have made our life together. His brilliant company has made work a pleasure and life much, much more than work. For all of it I thank him.

Finally, I would like to acknowledge Declan, the very mention of whose name makes me smile. His imminent arrival presented an unnegotiable deadline for completion of the manuscript; his presence since has proven the most joyful reward.

Abbreviations

DU   Manuscript Division, Perkins Library, Duke University, Durham, North Carolina

LC   Library of Congress, Washington, D.C.

NA   National Archives, Washington, D.C.

SCDAH   South Carolina Department of Archives and History, Columbia, South Carolina

SCHS   South Carolina Historical Society, Charleston, South Carolina

SCL   South Caroliniana Library, University of South Carolina, Columbia, South Carolina

SHC   Southern Historical Collection, University of North Carolina, Chapel Hill, North Carolina

Contents

Tables

Masters of Small Worlds

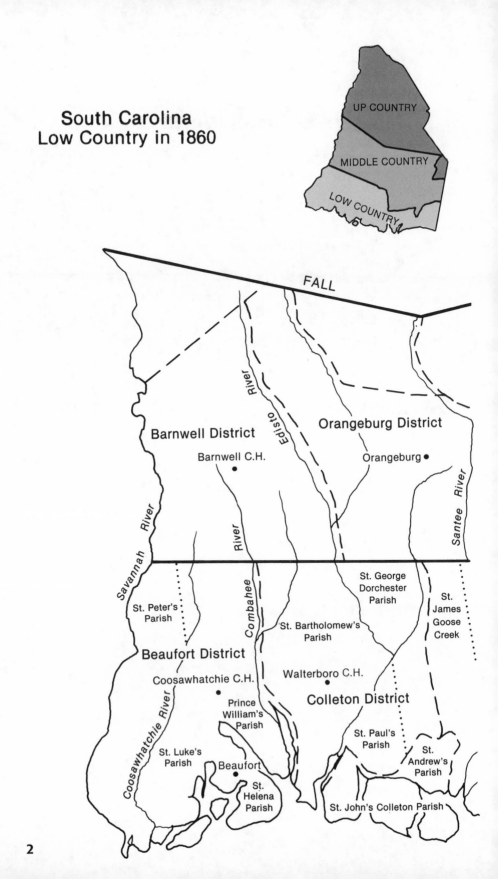

South Carolina
Low Country in 1860

UP COUNTRY

MIDDLE COUNTRY

LOW COUNTRY

FALL

River

Edisto River

Barnwell District

Orangeburg District

Barnwell C.H.

Orangeburg

Savannah River

River

Santee River

Combahee

St. George
Dorchester
Parish

St.
James
Goose
Creek

St. Peter's
Parish

St. Bartholomew's
Parish

Beaufort District

Coosawhatchie River

Coosawhatchie C.H.

Walterboro C.H.

Colleton District

Prince
William's
Parish

St. Luke's
Parish

Beaufort

St. Paul's
Parish

St.
Andrew's
Parish

St.
Helena
Parish

St. John's Colleton Parish

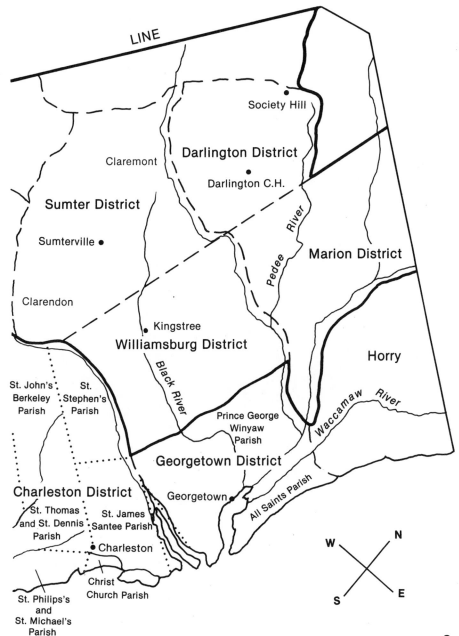

- ········ Parishes
- — — — Districts
- • Cities, towns, and villages

LINE

Society Hill

Darlington District

Claremont

Darlington C.H.

Sumter District

Pedee River

Marion District

Sumterville •

Clarendon

Kingstree

Williamsburg District

Horry

Black River

St. John's
Berkeley
Parish

St.
Stephen's
Parish

Prince George
Winyaw
Parish

Waccamaw River

Georgetown District

Charleston District

Georgetown •

All Saints Parish

St. Thomas
and St. Dennis
Parish

St. James
Santee Parish

• Charleston

Christ
Church Parish

St. Philips's
and
St. Michael's
Parish

W   N

S   E

chapter 1

Boundaries of Power

I

Sometime in the fall of 1855 near Adams Run in Colleton District, Ralph Elliott, the son of a very wealthy planter, and a yeoman neighbor named Price came to blows over Price's relationship to the slaves on Elliott's PonPon plantation. Convinced that the "vulgar" Price had been engaged in illegal trading with the PonPon slaves, Elliott had "knocked him down," an insult Price had answered with two pistol shots in Elliott's face that were "so close as to burn him with the powder" but that missed their mark and "shot through his hat."[1] The yeoman Price had refused to play slave to Elliott's master.

Lowcountry planters had always been touchy about the matter of illegal trading with slaves, regarding it as an "evil . . . which strikes at the vitals of our domestic Institution." They were usually content to harass slaves and allegedly incendiary strangers. But in the 1850s, with sectional tensions heightened, planters turned their formidable police powers on the vulnerable white men of their own communities.[2] It was a risky

1. William Elliott to Wife, Paris, September 20, 1855, Elliott-Gonzales Papers, SHC. The PonPon plantation was one of eight William Elliott owned in Beaufort and Colleton districts, and Ralph appears to have gained legal title to it sometime between the mid-1850s and 1860 when he represented the parish (St. Paul's, Colleton) in the state legislature. See Walter B. Edgar, ed., *Biographical Directory of the South Carolina House of Representatives*, vol. 1 (Columbia, S. C.: University of South Carolina Press, 1974), p. 384.

2. "Petition by Citizens of Barnwell District for more serious punishment of whites convicted of trafficking with slaves . . . ," Petitions to the Legislature, 1850, General Assembly Records, SCDAH. For the law on trading with slaves, see H. M. Henry, *The Police Control of the Slave in South Carolina* (1914; reprint ed., New York: Negro Universities Press, 1968), pp. 28–51, 79–94. Patterns in the irregular enforcement of the law revealing a similar tendency to target the "internal enemy" in the early 1830s can be traced in Grand Jury Presentments, 1820–1865, General Assembly Records.

and sometimes explosive strategy. For yeoman farmers such as Price, who became the objects of planter suspicion, were also touchy—about the rights and respect due them as freemen in a slave society.[3] And as the younger Elliott was soon to learn, yeomen brought to the struggle with planters considerable means, both legal and customary, with which to compel recognition of the social and political identity to which they laid passionate claim.

The neophyte Ralph thought his case against Price to be open and shut. The man had shot at him. His more experienced father had no such illusions, however, and proceeded to instruct him in the complex cartography of power in lowcountry Carolina. The paramount legal issue, William Elliott informed his son, was not whether Price was guilty of shooting at him but whether Ralph had been justified in his attack on Price in the first place. And that, he explained, depended entirely on the location of the assault: "If you had attacked him in his house, he would escape punishment on the plea that his house was his castle and that you had invaded him—but if the case happened as you write—and you can prove it—he must smart for it."[4] William Elliott thereby exposed a key spatial dimension of class and gender relations in the slave South: the virtually unlimited right of an independent man to mastery over his own household and the property that lay within its boundaries. In so doing, Elliott also delivered a pointed lesson in the politics of lowcountry households.

In South Carolina, as in other slave states, the household was a spatial unit, defined by the property to which the owner held legal title and over which he exercised exclusive rights. But it was much more than that. In societies in which land constituted the chief means of subsistence, title to land historically incorporated claims over the persons and the labor of those dependent on it. The household was thus a social unit as well. Indeed, in antebellum South Carolina households were the constituent units of society, organizing the majority of the population—slaves of both sexes and all ages and free women and children—in relations of legal and customary dependency to the propertied male head, whether yeoman or planter.[5] The integrity William Elliott accorded to lowcoun-

3. Price was a landowner and farmer. See William Elliott to Ralph Elliott, Beaufort, July 12, 1856, Elliott-Gonzales Papers. Such accusations were, however, more commonly made of marginal "poor white" men: tenants, peddlers, grog shop keepers, petty traders, and boatmen.

4. William Elliott to Ralph Elliott, Paris, October 1, 1855, Elliott-Gonzales Papers. The legal decision in the case is not recorded in the collection, but there is subsequent indication that Price sold out and moved away from the neighborhood. See William Elliott to Ralph Elliott, Beaufort, July 12, 1856, Elliott-Gonzales Papers. A similar episode is recounted in Lacy K. Ford, Jr., *Origins of Southern Radicalism: The South Carolina Upcountry, 1800-1860* (New York: Oxford University Press, 1988), p. 67.

5. For an illuminating discussion of household property and labor relations, see Elizabeth Blackmar, *Manhattan for Rent, 1785–1850* (Ithaca, N.Y.: Cornell University Press, 1989), pp. 1–71; for a social and spatial definition of rural households, see Christopher

try households was therefore inseparable from the particular relations of power they embodied.

It is not hard to see the planters' hands in the construction of the household as a world unto itself. After all, it was the security of slave property that provoked Ralph Elliott in the first place. But neither was the yeoman Price an unarmed man in the struggle that ensued. As a free man and a proprietor, he invoked the same principle in his own defense. Out of the materials of the slave regime and planter prerogatives, ante-bellum yeoman farmers wrested their claims to authority over independent households. In the Low Country, the household grounded their own claims to masterhood.

II

Power and authority clearly had spatial grounding in antebellum South Carolina. Yet there was nothing self-evident about the definition of the household or its boundaries. Rather, the prevailing customary and legal boundaries were worked out through almost incessant contestation in every neighborhood in the region and, subsequently, in the courts and the legislature. That William Elliott so adroitly identified the significance of seemingly narrow issues of property law was no coincidence. As an avid sportsman, early conservationist, and author of *Carolina Sports by Land and Water,* he followed struggles over boundaries closely and reflected deeply on property rights and class relations, particularly as they pertained to the rituals and practice of hunting. Yet Elliott was more than chronicler and critic. In an earlier phase of his political career, as an elected representative from St. Helena Parish, he had been instrumental in shaping property law in the state and in giving definition to the

Clark, *The Roots of Rural Capitalism: Western Massachusetts, 1780–1860* (Ithaca, N.Y.: Cornell University Press, 1990), p. 21. Other historians have identified the household as the constituent unit of antebellum southern society. See particularly Elizabeth Fox-Genovese, "Antebellum Southern Households: A New Perspective on a Familiar Question, " *Review* 7 (Fall 1983), pp. 215–53 and *Within the Plantation Household: Black and White Women of the Old South* (Chapel Hill: University of North Carolina Press, 1988), pp. 37–99; Steven Hahn, *The Roots of Southern Populism: Yeoman Farmers and the Transformation of the Georgia Upcountry, 1850–1890* (New York: Oxford University Press, 1983); Gavin Wright, *The Political Economy of the Cotton South: Households, Markets, and Wealth in the Nineteenth Century* (New York: W. W. Norton, 1978). The conceptual focus on households in rural society originated in the debate over the development of capitalism in the late colonial and the early national periods and was influenced particularly by the work of Michael Merrill, "Cash Is Good to Eat: Self-Sufficiency and Exchange in the Rural Economy of the United States," *Radical History Review,* no. 4 (Winter 1977), pp. 42–71; James Henretta, "Families and Farms: Mentalité in Preindustrial America," *William and Mary Quarterly,* 3d. series, vol. 35, no. 1 (January 1978), pp. 3–32; and Christopher Clark, "Household Economy, Market Exchange and the Rise of Capitalism in the Connecticut Valley, 1800–1860," *Journal of Social History* 13, no. 2 (Winter 1979), pp. 19–89.

household and the master's domain.[6] In his various incarnations as legislator, author, planter litigant, and correspondent, William Elliott left a
clear trail through the complex thicket of power and its spatial dimensions in the Low Country.

As befitted a man tainted, or so his political enemies charged, with
the "reputed sin of federalism," William Elliott evinced a life-long concern for the sanctity of private property in lowcountry society.[7] Yet
Carolina Sports, his best-known publication, has been read primarily as a
text on common rights, as proof of the persistence in the antebellum
South of the right to hunt on unenclosed land, a custom that had been
eradicated in the Northeast, as in England in an earlier period, with the
capitalist transformation of the countryside.[8] And in his indictment of
this practice and his advocacy of "laws conservative of game," Elliott did
give powerful testimony to the tenacious hold of common rights in state
law and lowcountry custom. But his primary purpose in *Carolina Sports*
was to press for a greater recognition of the exclusive rights that adhered to private property in a republic. If customary respect for common rights was one side of the regional coin—and Elliott no doubt

6. William Elliott, *Carolina Sports by Land and Water: Including Incidents of Devil-Fishing,
Wild-Cat, Deer and Bear Hunting, Etc.* (1846; reprint ed., New York: Arno Press, 1967).
Elliott himself articulated the political purpose of his sporting stories. See William Elliott
to William Plummer, Jr., n.d. [1847], Elliott-Gonzales Papers; Elliott, *Carolina Sports,* pp.
109–12. In addition to the correspondence, see Lewis Pinckney Jones, "William Elliott,
South Carolina Non-Conformist," *Journal of Southern History* 17, no. 3 (August 1951),
pp. 361–81.

7. J. Hamilton to William Elliott, Walterboro, November 21, 1822, Elliott-Gonzales
Papers. Elliott did indeed belong to a minority of proslavery Unionist planter politicians
whose Unionism was of a distinctly aristocratic cast. Elliott remained a dedicated Unionist
throughout Nullification and the first secession crisis; he embraced secession only in 1859.
See William Elliott, *Address to the People of St. Helena's Parish* (Charleston: William Estill,
Printer, 1832); Elliott, *The Letters of Agricola* (Greenville, S.C.: Office of the Southern
Patriot, 1852); and Mrs. Elliott to Caroline Elliott, n.d. [1859], Elliott-Gonzales Papers. For
an interesting discussion of lowcountry Unionists as old Federalists, see Lacy K. Ford, Jr.,
"James Louis Petigru: The Last South Carolina Federalist," in Michael O'Brien and David
Moltke-Hansen, eds., *Intellectual Life in Antebellum Charleston* (Knoxville: The University of
Tennessee Press, 1988), pp. 152–85.

8. Steven Hahn, "Hunting, Fishing, and Foraging: Common Rights and Class Relations
in the Post-Bellum South," *Radical History Review,* no. 26 (1982), pp. 37–64; J. Crawford
King, "The Closing of the Southern Range: An Exploratory Study," *Journal of Southern
History* 48, no. 1 (February 1982), pp. 53–70. On the Northeast, see Morton Horowitz, *The
Transformation of American Law, 1780–1860* (Cambridge, Mass.: Harvard University Press,
1977); Gary Kulik, "Dams, Fish, and Farmers: Defense of Public Rights in Eighteenth-
Century Rhode Island," in Steven Hahn and Jonathan Prude, eds., *The Countryside in the Age
of Capitalist Transformation: Essays in the Social History of Rural America* (Chapel Hill:
University of North Carolina Press, 1985), pp. 25–50. On England, see E. P. Thompson,
Whigs and Hunters: The Origin of the Black Act (New York: Pantheon Books, 1975); Jane
Humphries, "Enclosures, Common Rights, and Women: The Proletarianization of Fami-
lies in the Late 18th and Early 19th Centuries," *The Journal of Economic History* 50, no. 1
(March 1990), pp. 17–42.

exaggerated its currency—then the "religious" respect for "the rights of property . . . in our community," as he put it, was decidedly the other.[9]

In many ways Elliott's text was an extended consideration of the problem of defining boundaries between privately owned land to which proprietors had exclusive claim and land still private but to which the community customarily claimed use rights. The problem bore directly on the parameters of the household, and it plagued not only Elliott but the state's jurists and juries as well, crowding court dockets and legislative petition rolls throughout the antebellum period.[10] For Elliott the problem was simple enough. A man's land "for which he pays taxes to the state—is no longer his (except in a qualified sense) unless he encloses it. In other respects, it is his neighbors' or anybody's." The extent of common rights was too great for Elliott's taste, that much was clear, but he acknowledged nonetheless a sure demarcation of their limits and of the beginnings of private property. What jury would convict, he noted, "if the trespass was not committed by entering his own enclosure"? Trespass, and consequently the boundary of private property had, at least by 1846, found clear definition. The only thing as certain as the community's jealous regard for common rights to hunt, fish, and forage stock on unenclosed land was, as Elliott admitted, its jealous regard for that property bounded by the fence: "[I]t is the broad common law maxim that everything upon a man's land is his own . . . and he can thus shut it out from his neighbor without wrong to him."[11] The only spatially and temporally fixed boundary of private property that free South Carolinians could agree to observe was drawn by the fences that surrounded the cultivated fields and dwelling houses of plantations and farms. Proprietors' rights followed their fences. The household was coterminous with the "enclosure."

Lowcountry communities had not always recognized the fence as such an impermeable boundary, for *Carolina Sports* fixed a mid-antebellum moment in an ongoing debate over competing claims and the boundaries devised to settle them. It had acquired that meaning as part of a process, anchored in statute and elaborated in case law, in which common rights were constrained within ever narrower limits. Elliott may have been frustrated with what he regarded as the still too circumscribed domain of private property, but he knew from experience that common rights could not be vanquished entirely. He also knew that by 1846 the legal ground had shifted critically in the direction of proprietors' rights and that the fence had figured centrally in that transition. In fact, Elliott

9. Elliott, *Carolina Sports*, pp. 170–72.

10. Extant court records and petitions to the legislature sustain the conclusion that this was the single most frequent source of community conflict by the 1840s and 1850s. See Petitions to the Legislature, 1820–1865, General Assembly Records, and the trespass cases cited below.

11. Elliott, *Carolina Sports*, pp. 167–69.

had been the chief proponent of the 1827 Fence Act, a key statutory component of the definition of private property and the household that came to prevail throughout the antebellum period. That law represented a sea change in attitudes towards property and class relations from the colonial law it overturned.[12] It also—and Elliott must have known this—became the legal referent for a relentless assault on common rights that persisted until the Civil War.

In the legislative session of 1827, as most representatives were absorbed in heated discussion of "the constitutionality of the Tariff," Elliott introduced a bill "to amend the law concerning fences." At one level the proposed legislation was not very different from the law it amended, a 1694 statute that mandated six-foot fences around "corn and other provisions." At another level, however, the difference could not have been more profound. The clear purpose of the seventeenth-century act was to protect stock owners from "evilly minded" subsistence farmers. Poor farmers were accused of "keeping low and ill-Fences" with the express intent of enticing foraging "horses, neat cattle and other stock" into their provision grounds where they "set canes and use[d] other dangerous . . . means" to trap them. The "good, strong and sufficient Fence six feet high" required by law was thus designed to protect property rights in stock, one of the young colony's most valuable market goods.[13] The open range and common rights to land dominated the landscape imagined by the early colonial law; fences demarcated exceptional and delimited spaces in an otherwise open terrain.

Antebellum law encoded a markedly different landscape. By 1827 it was not only crops and landowners' rights that Elliott and the legislature sought to protect but, more specifically, staple crops and planters'

---

12. William Elliott to Ann Elliott, Columbia, November 16, 1827, Elliott-Gonzales Papers. For the 1827 Fence Act, see David J. McCord, ed., *The Statutes at Large of South Carolina*, vol. 6 (Columbia, S.C.: A. S. Johnson, 1839), pp. 331–32. As late as 1855, under the pseudonym "Venator," Elliott advocated the restriction of common right to hunt on unenclosed land despite the fact that he knew it to be a profoundly unpopular postion. See "A Friend and Fellow Parishioner of St. Paul's" to William Elliott, Charleston, June 15, 1855, Elliott-Gonzales Papers.

13. William Elliott to Ann Elliott, Columbia, November 26, 1827, Elliott-Gonzales Papers. For the 1694 law, see Thomas Cooper, M.D.-L.L.D., ed., *The Statutes at Large of South Carolina*, vol. 2 (Columbia, S.C.: A. S. Johnston, 1837), pp. 81–82. There was one other minor act before the Civil War, a 1785 Hog Act that affected only the towns of Beaufort and Georgetown. See Thomas Cooper, M.D.-L.L.D., ed., *The Statutes at Large of South Carolina*, vol. 4 (Columbia, S.C.: A. S. Johnston, 1838), p. 673. On the importance of stock as a marketable surplus that was part of a distinct period of class formation in colonial South Carolina, see Rachel N. Klein, *Unification of a Slave State: The Rise of the Planter Class in the South Carolina Backcountry, 1760–1808* (Chapel Hill: University of North Carolina Press, 1990), pp. 9–46; Converse Clowse, *Economic Beginnings in Colonial South Carolina* (Columbia, S.C.: University of South Carolina Press, 1971); and Lewis C. Gray, *History of Agriculture in the Southern United States to 1860,* 2 vols. (Gloucester, Mass.: Peter Smith, 1958), 1: 41-59.

interests. Fences five feet in height or navigable water courses were required to enclose fields in which were "growing or ungathered any grain, cotton or vegetable production, raised for market or domestic consumption. . . . " Common rights to forage stock and to hunt, though recognized outside enclosures, found absolute limits at the fence. Any "breaking and entering" constituted a "trespass" and entitled the landholder to collect damages from the stockowner. Although fences remained, the tables had been turned.[14] Legislators' predominant interest in securing valuable market crops against depredation had led them to define carefully the boundaries of property reserved for exclusive use; it had compelled them, that is, to define the terrain of private property. There was nothing new, certainly, about the patterns of land use described in the antebellum Fence Act. But it codified the antebellum lowcountry as a plantation landscape, dominated by fenced enclosures and proprietors' rights, in which the open range was the delimited space that remained between independent households.

The 1827 Fence Act provided more than a solid foundation for proprietors' rights. It proved to be an expansive one as well. As antebellum jurists faced dockets crowded with right-of-way and trespass cases, they repeatedly invoked that law to circumscribe common rights, etching the fence deeply in the legal cartography of power. In the process, they gave increasingly distinct shape to the household, secured its legal integrity as an inviolable private space, and rendered the authority of the master over it virtually absolute.

The juridical retreat from common rights was slow and steady. The significance of the ground surrendered to proprietors was, however, encapsulated in the judgments handed down in two trespass cases, one in 1818 and the other in 1846. In the earlier case, *M'Conico* v. *Singleton,* which involved Singleton's right to hunt on M'Conico's unenclosed land despite the latter's express prohibition, the presiding judge expressed astonishment that such an action had even been brought. Not only was "[t]he right to hunt on unenclosed lands . . . clearly established; but if it were doubtful," he continued, "I should still be strongly inclined to support it." The judge offered sound political reason: Having rightly rejected standing armies as "dangerous to our free institutions," South Carolina and the rest of the states had embraced a militia system in its stead. Carolina's freemen, accustomed by right to use the forest as a common, learned "in the pursuit of game . . . the dexterous use . . . of fire arms" and the skills of militiamen. Common rights and public good, he concluded, must take precedence over "the mere will and caprice of any individual." The very survival of the republic depended on it. His

14. McCord, ed., *Statutes at Large of South Carolina*, vol. 6, pp. 331–32. The closing of the range in South Carolina began in 1866 with the introduction of county-level stock laws. See Hahn, "Hunting, Fishing, and Foraging," pp. 43–50.

was an ardent and principled judicial defense of common rights—and the last antebellum South Carolinians were to hear.[15]

By 1846 nearly thirty years of chipping away at common rights had shifted judicial presumption entirely toward proprietors and their preemptory rights over all the land to which they held legal title. The 1846 case, *Fripp* v. *Hasell et al.*, also involved the defendant's right to hunt on unenclosed land, in this case an island. Explicitly rejecting the precedent of *M'Conico* and invoking the provisions of "our fence act which declares a deep navigable stream equal to a fence," Judge Evans concluded, so the court reporter said, "with opinions leading him to maintain very strongly the proprietary rights of the landlord against the inroads of the hunter."[16] The means by which the ascendancy of private property had been accomplished—with reference to the fence and the boundaries of the enclosure—had profound meaning for the household and the respect accorded it by law and custom in the antebellum period.

As judges imposed increasingly restrictive conditions on customary claims ("right-of-way" through privately owned land, for example), they did so by literal interpretation of the Fence Act. Indeed, the fence could quite reasonably stand as the preeminent symbol of private property in antebellum South Carolina; as a movable boundary it was also a fitting one. In one key case, *Rowland* v. *Wolfe,* presiding Judge Josiah Nott insisted that John Wolfe was entirely within his rights when he enclosed with a fence and thus rendered impassable a "settlement road" through his property that had been used by his neighbors for "upwards of thirty years." Despite the fact that twenty years' uninterrupted use had formerly served as the measure for a "grant of right," Nott insisted that "[a] privilege thus enjoyed can never be claimed as right."[17] The customary claims of the community were already, by 1827, losing their earlier ability to configure the landscape. Not only did the fence mark the absolute boundary of private and common land but the power to locate the fence, and to relocate it, was coming to rest squarely in the hands of propri-

15. *Christopher M'Conico* v. *John Singleton*, Columbia, May 1818, in *Reports of Cases Argued and Determined in the Supreme Court of South Carolina*, Book 4 (St. Paul: West Publishing Co., 1921), pp. 65–66. Only one case between 1818 and 1846 could be interpreted as a defense of common rights, and even that case also entrenched the principle that such "rights" existed only at the sufferance of the proprietor. See *E. D. Law* v. *J. Nettles*, Darlington, Spring Term, 1831, in H. Bailey, *Reports of Cases Argued and Determined in the Court of Appeals of South Carolina*, vol. 2 (Charleston: A. E. Miller, 1834), pp. 447–48.

16. *Hamilton Fripp* v. *W. M. Hasell et al.*, Charleston, January-February Term, 1847, in *Reports of Cases Argued and Determined in the Supreme Court of South Carolina*, Book 13 (St. Paul: West Publishing Co., 1918), pp. 76–77.

17. *H. J. Rowland* v. *John Wolfe*, Spartanburg, Fall Term, 1827, in H. Bailey, *Reports of Cases Argued and Determined in the Court of Appeals of South Carolina*, vol. 1 (Charleston: A. E. Miller, 1833), pp. 56–59. For earlier definitions of right of way, see *R. I. Turnbull* v. *William Rivers*, February Term, 1825, in David J. McCord, *Reports of Cases Argued and Determined in the Court of Appeals of South Carolina*, vol. 3 (Columbia, S.C.: Doyle and Sweeny, 1826), pp. 131–41; and *Thomas McKee* v. *Elizabeth Garrett*, Edgefield, Fall Term, 1829, in Bailey, *Reports of Cases*, vol. 1, pp. 341–42.

etors. The "security of the landowner" assumed the republican mantle. By the end of the antebellum period, common rights, beaten back into privileges or courtesies, were virtually impossible to sustain at law. When in a rare 1858 case the court did uphold a jury decision in favor of community "right of way" through private land on the grounds that it was "unenclosed" by the 1827 definition, a jeremiad accompanied it in the form of the dissenting opinion. "To . . . appropriate to the public use the property of the citizen," Judge Munro wrote in stunned disbelief, is "to abandon the rights of the property of the honest landowner as a prey to the lawless rapacity of squatter sovereignty."[18]

South Carolina's republican freeholders had acquired exclusive claims to the property within the fence. Just as important, they had come to embody the expanded prerogatives that property conferred. "Until inclosed, or appropriated in some other way to the owners' exclusive use," Judge John Belton O'Neall ruled in 1831, "he is regarded as permitting it [land] to be used as a common for hunting, pasture, and militia training." But once enclosed, he concluded ominously, a proprietor has "the right to be as churlish as he pleases with his own."[19] As the boundaries of households and proprietors' rights were ever more vigilantly guarded at law, public recognition of masters' legitimate power over those households and the diverse property within them deepened in proportion.

III

Notions of property "rights" as boundaries to the intrusions of community and state had been central to American constitutional thought and legal theory since at least the Revolution. Such notions were not peculiar to the slave South. But as the definitions of property and of labor relations diverged in the North and the South during the postrevolutionary period, so the household came to embody both disparate relations and structural positions in sectional political economy. As a consequence, the conception of the rights that legitimately attached to property and the limits that they established acquired very different social meaning.[20]

In South Carolina, as in the other slave states, the enduring commitment to slave property put its stamp on every aspect of property and labor relations, especially on the powers arrogated by household heads.

18. *William H. Heyward* v. *Robert Chisolm*, Charleston, January Term, 1858, in *Reports of Cases Argued and Determined in the Supreme Court of South Carolina*, Book 18 (St. Paul: West Publishing Co., 1918), pp. 84–88.

19. O'Neall quotation is from *E. D. Law* v. *J. Nettles*, Darlington, Spring Term, 1831, in H. Bailey, *Reports of Cases*, vol. 2, pp. 447–48.

20. On the conception of rights as legal boundaries, see Jennifer Nedelsky, "Law, Boundaries, and the Bounded Self," *Representations* 30 (Spring 1990), pp. 162–89. On the divergent character of households North and South, see Fox-Genovese, "Antebellum Southern Households."

Title to land in rural societies had historically incorporated claims over dependents enmeshed in a range of customary and legal relations, from kinship to contract to chattel. In antebellum South Carolina, those traditional claims were elaborated through and accentuated by the particular requirements of slave society and its labor discipline. And although they reflected the distinctive relations of plantation households, the principles that governed the relations of masters and dependents spoke to all independent households, yeoman as well as planter.[21]

As antebellum legislators and jurists ruled on the unassailable rights of proprietors, they did so with full recognition of the powers and authority conferred. The rights of "freemen"—the term privileged in legal discourse—were vigilantly guarded at law, as befitted a society that called itself republican, and they were indissociable from those which accompanied property ownership. "There is no authority given by the patrol law or any law of the state," one appellate court judge explained in a trespass case, "to enter the dwelling house of a free man of the country, . . . and take from thence his arms or other property." That "extraordinary power," he concluded, stood "in opposition to the common rights of the citizen."[22] Even the state's obvious interest in public security did not often justify transgression of the boundaries of the enclosure. Among a freeman's most fundamental rights was the enjoyment of virtually unlimited authority over the property within his own enclosure.

Property, however, took many forms in South Carolina, as it did in the rest of the slave South. The spatial grounding of freemen's rights thus had critical social and political ramifications. The almost medieval language jurists commonly used in their decisions, in references to "churlish proprietors" and "descendants of the 'Barons bold'," for example, suggested the relations of power that property law supported and fences enclosed.[23] Indeed, the law elided distinctions between forms of property, rendering a man's control over his enclosure synonymous with his control over the familial and extrafamilial dependents within it. In one case, Judge Nott explained that assault and battery was justified if the defendant could prove that the victim "had traduced his character, had insulted his wife or daughter, or that he had found him within his

21. Blackmar, *Manhattan For Rent*, pp. 1–71; Hahn, *Roots of Southern Populism*, pp. 29–31; Elizabeth Fox-Genovese and Eugene D. Genovese, "Yeoman Farmers in a Slaveholders' Democracy," in *Fruits of Merchant Capital: Slavery and Bourgeois Property in the Rise and Expansion of Capitalism* (New York: Oxford University Press, 1983), pp. 249–71; Fox-Genovese, "Antebellum Southern Households," pp. 215–53.

22. *John Porteous* v. *Joseph Hazel and Joseph Jenkins*, Charleston, May Term, 1824, in William Harper, *Reports of Cases Determined in the Constitutional Court of South Carolina*, 2d ed., vol. 1 (Columbia, S.C.: State Printer, 1841), pp. 332–33.

23. *Law* v. *Nettles*, in Bailey, *Reports of Cases*, vol. 2, pp. 447–48; *State* v. *Thomas Dawson*, Coosawhatchie [Beaufort District], Spring Term, 1835, in W. R. Hill, *Reports of Cases at Law Argued and Determined in the Court of Appeals of South Carolina*, vol. 3 (Columbia, S.C.: A. S. Johnston, 1841), pp. 100–23.

enclosure attempting to steal his goods or to excite his negroes to insurrection." A free man had the right to defend what was his own. He was
justified in injuring anyone who attempted to dispossess him of his land
and goods, just as "a parent may justify a battery in defence of the wife
or the child."[24] Where the boundaries of households were inviolable,
property rights and power over dependents were inextricable. By law
and custom in the South Carolina Low Country, adult freemen, heads of
households, were constituted as masters.

There can be little doubt that the construction of the household as an
independent and impenetrable domain primarily reflected planters' interests in the security of slave property, even against, in some cases, their
yeoman or poor white neighbors. The planters' admittedly ineffectual
efforts to isolate their slaves from the larger lowcountry community,
slave and free, required that boundaries be clearly demarcated and that
their neighbors be compelled to observe them. To David Gavin, a Colleton planter, such respect was the sine qua non of good neighborliness.
"He had his faults," Gavin wrote of his "only near neighbor," the yeoman James Pendarvis, but "I do not believe he ever carried on illicit
traffick with my negroes, and that is saying a good deal." More than
most southern slaveholders perhaps, lowcountry planters worried about
potential transgressions of their households and authority. William
Elliott's principled conservative stewardship of proprietors' rights comes
into clearer focus in the context of his own struggles to police the boundaries of his plantations. After years of acrimony over title to a piece of
swamp land that lay between their plantations, Elliott's neighbor—none
other than his old political enemy, Robert Barnwell Rhett—warned him
to settle the case out of court. "Some things are worse than litigation,"
Rhett wrote in the ominous tone of much planter correspondence of
1850. "Amongst them is a teasing, harassing, and dangerous difference
as to the rights between neighbours. We are both of us heads of families," he reminded Elliott, "surrounded with inflamable materials which
may not be hard to kindle."[25] The reference could not have been lost on
Elliott.

Take his story "The Firehunter." Elliott's commitment to conserving
the manly sport of hunting as an elite ritual distinguished in every meaningful respect from the common man's practice of hunting for subsistence certainly suggests his class sensibilities. But his attack on common
rights to hunt on unenclosed land renders them explicit. Common rights

24. *A. S. Rhodes* v. *Lydia Bunch et al.*, Charleston, February Term, 1825, in McCord,
Reports of Cases, vol. 3, pp. 66–71; *John Marsh* v. *Iverson L. Brookes and Others*, Edgefield,
Spring Term, 1834, in W. R. Hill, *Reports of Cases Argued and Determined in the Court of
Appeals of South Carolina*, vol. 2 (Columbia, S.C.: Printed and Published at the Telescope
Office, 1835), pp. 427–30.

25. David Gavin Diary, February 11, 1859, SHC; R. B. Rhett to William Elliott, March
11, 1850, Elliott-Gonzales Papers. The case did go to trial, more than once, in fact. See
William Elliott to Phoebe Elliott, Oak Lawn, March 25, 1852, Elliott-Gonzales Papers.

constituted, in his inflated rhetoric, nothing less than "the principle of the anti-rent excitement . . . at work with us." "[I]n a country peculiarly situated as ours is," it was a questionable policy to limit and narrow proprietors' rights. Common rights all but invited the violation of legitimate property in land, stock, and slaves. In "The Firehunter," an overseer pursues a deer into his employer's fallow pea field despite the latter's explicit request that the deer be conserved for his private sport. When, in the dark of night, hunting with a flaming torch as only dishonorable men do, the firehunter mistakes one of his employer's horses for the deer and shoots it dead, he is propelled into a spiral of deception that allies him with a slave, his social subordinate. The first transgression, justified as a freeman's legitimate right in common, thus unhinges social hierarchy, dissolves social distinction, and unleashes social disorder, with tragic consequences for innocent slaves and hapless white men.[26] Elliott's transparent morality tale weds the prerogatives of property and power to the inviolate boundaries of the household and invests in that union the very fate of social order in slave society.

There can be no doubt that slavery gave shape to plantation households. Its reach, however, did not end there. For notwithstanding the fact that planters desired, in part, to repel the intrusions of other classes of free men, they could not simultaneously establish the requisite legal and customary basis of household integrity and masters' authority without making more general claims. Rooted in notions of property rights, those claims extended inexorably to the household of every free and propertied man. Slavery thereby gave shape to yeoman households as well, to their legal boundaries, and, most important, to the gender and class relations that prevailed within them.

There was a price exacted from planters for the power they claimed as masters of households. It was one William Elliott had acknowledged his obligation to pay in the conflict between his son Ralph and their yeoman neighbor Price. For when jurists ruled on the rights of proprietors they made no distinction between yeomen and planters. Nor could they within the conventions of republican discourse. The relevant term in their vocabulary, as in political discourse, was "freemen," among whose ranks lowcountry yeomen, however poor, proudly numbered themselves. Thus, when yeoman proprietors sought to restrain over-

26. Quotations are from Elliott, *Carolina Sports*, pp. 291, 287. For "The Firehunter," see pp. 139–49. All of Elliott's sporting stories reveal homoerotic subtexts, which is not surprising given the highly ritualistic homosocial culture of hunting. See particularly the story "A Business Day at Chee-Ha," pp. 109–37. For an interesting discussion of the class and racial dimensions of antebellum hunting, see Stuart A. Marks, *Southern Hunting in Black and White: Nature, History, and Ritual in a Carolina Community* (Princeton, N.J.: Princeton University Press, 1991), pp. 15–38. For an illuminating protrait of the lowcountry elite's socially exclusive hunting "clubs" and their political significance, see Samuel Gaillard Stoney, ed., "The Memoirs of Frederick A. Porcher," *South Carolina Historical and Genealogical Magazine*, vols. 44–48 (April 1943 to January 1947), 45, no. 1 (January 1944) pp. 36–38.

weening state officials or neighboring planters, they reached for precisely the same materials out of which planters had constructed the independence and integrity of their household domains.

In 1835, when the yeoman farmer Thomas Dawson of St. Peter's Parish in Beaufort District resisted the power of William Buckner, a small planter and the local commissioner of roads, to seize some of his "good pine timber" for road repairs, he won not only a verdict of trespass but an impassioned judicial articulation of "power and its abuses" and "the liberties of citizens." It was just such "encroachments upon private property and personal rights" that had occasioned the Magna Carta, Judge Richardson proclaimed, and Carolina's "decendants of the 'Barons bold'" held their "liberties" no less dear. "No man can be legally convicted of any offence, for opposing the abuse of official authority, whenever such abuse reaches his person or property," the judge ruled. Dawson was entitled, in fact obligated, to defend both with the knife. On the protection of this yeoman freeman's right to resist "tyranny . . . [and] despotic power" rested nothing less than the fate of the republic itself.[27]

Although the rigorously observed boundaries of lowcountry households and the prerogatives of proprietors did not reflect, in the first instance at least, the particular needs of yeoman farmers, the claim of yeomen as property holders and heads of households to those legal and customary principles could not be denied. Moreover, as small farmers in a plantation region, yeomen were, like Dawson and Price, particularly vulnerable to planter violation of their households in the alleged interest of slave discipline, public interest, or gentlemanly sport. Their stake in a system that conceived of freemen's rights as bounded by the property they owned may even have deepened in proportion to their vulnerability to planter power. Yeoman may well have constituted themselves loyal guardians of the venerable tradition of common rights, as William Elliott charged. But it was ultimately ownership of property—not access to it—that distinguished them from the vast majority of other lowcountry adults—slaves and free women—who endured the status of dependents. It was on the venerable tradition of private property rights, then, that lowcountry yeomen drew for their own political identity and language, including the language with which to protect their precarious position as small farmers in a world of large planters.

So when "[s]undry citizens" of Lexington District sought to defend their rights as property holders against invasive neighborhood planters, they adopted the self-conscious pose of "free men" and "free-holders."

---

27. *State* v. *Thomas Dawson*, in Hill, *Reports of Cases* vol. 3, pp. 100-23. The profiles of Thomas Dawson and William Buckner were derived from the tax list of 1824, the only such record of household propertyholdings that exists for the Low Country prior to the 1850 census. The characterizations offered in the text are thus only approximations, based as they are on records ten years previous to the event. See South Carolina Lower Division Tax Returns, [St. Peter's Parish, Beaufort District], 1824, Records of the Comptroller General, SCDAH.

Describing themselves as representatives of "the poorer sort . . . compelled by necessity to work their farms and attend to [their] stock," these
yeoman citizens petitioned the General Assembly for relief from the
depredations of the "wealthy citizens of our community [who] keep a
numerous quantity of dogs and can spare the time for the amusement of
. . . [chasing] a famished deer over a dozen of the free-holds of petitioners," killing, mangling, and driving off their stock. Private property
in stock, they concluded, was "lost to their owners" in consequence of
this planter abuse of common rights.[28] Yeomen thereby held planters
firmly to their own standards—to respect for the boundaries of private
property and the authority of a man to rule over his own enclosure.

Yeoman farmers fully comprehended the terms of lowcountry politics, the terms on which they could contest planter or state power. Thus,
there was nothing haphazard about the posture adopted by a group of
Darlington farmers in their efforts to scuttle a new road project in their
neighborhood. Property, they knew, anchored citizens' rights. "The
road ill invade persnel [sic] rights," they proclaimed righteously. And
circumventing the fact that the proposed road ran through mostly unenclosed land, they argued, as they knew they had to, that "by crossing
through the lands of your petitioners" it violated their legitimate interests in their enclosed fields, "depreciating value and adding much to the
labor necessary to keep their fences up."[29] The public interest in this
road, they insisted with the confidence born of a sanctioned posture, did
not supersede the "persnel rights" that belonged to men of property.
Yeomen held planter legislators hostage to the very principle that they
had made the cornerstone of republican society. Plain folk were not
naive. They made their case with full recognition of the disparate power
property conferred on lowcountry free men. "[I]f you think it is right to
take a mans rights a way from him in this free state South Caroliny and
not pay him for it it is in you Gentlemen what you will do," a desperate
farmer wrote to the General Assembly. "Lieving the matter with you to
deside," he ventured the opinion that such an appropriation represented "unlegal forse" and asked only "a fare chance" from them "as
free men and wise men and as honest men and thinking men and as
friends to both rich and pore men." Resignation thinly disguised distrust
and righteous anger. This Darlington yeoman knew his "rights."[30]

As the principles on which planters claimed exclusive authority over

28. "Petition of Sundry Citizens of Lexington District for a Law Controlling Hunters on
their Lands," Petitions to the Legislature, 1825, General Assembly Records. Elliott acknowledged that planter sportsmen regularly pursued their deer into farmers' enclosures,
claiming it was no trespass but rather "hunter's law." See Elliott, *Carolina Sports*, pp. 170–
71.

29. "Petition of Sundry Citizens of Darlington District Respecting the Opening of a
New Public Road," Petitions to the Legislature, 1843, General Assembly Records.

30. "Petition of Sundry Citizens of Darlington District Against the Opening of a New
Road," Petitions to the Legislature, 1844, General Assembly Records.

their households became more deeply entrenched in state law and low-country custom, yeoman farmers gained greater leverage in struggles over the integrity of their own households. Like the "sundry citizens" of Lexington and Darlington districts, lowcountry yeomen constituted themselves ardent advocates of the system that empowered them as propertied men. No matter that in doing so they entrenched planter prerogatives firmly in the same ground. For in the South Carolina Low Country, governance of a household and command of its dependent members were the coordinates of a freeman's public identity. In forcing planters to concede their rights as propertied men, yeomen also extracted their identity as masters, at least of the small worlds within their enclosures.

IV

Equally masters of independent households, yeomen and planters were anything but equals in the South Carolina Low Country. A larger world lay outside the fence. Beyond that boundary where authority was clearly recognized lay vast expanses of privately owned but unenclosed land. On that liminal ground—neither fully private nor fully public—independent men of widely disparate economic and political power met. And in ongoing struggles for control and authority over right-of-way, trespass, trading with slaves, and the general definition of common land, yeomen found it hard to prevail.

Even at the end of the antebellum period, after decades of agricultural expansion, fully three-quarters of privately owned land in the South Carolina Low Country remained unenclosed, uncultivated, and subject to common claims.[31] Notwithstanding that impressive figure, however, especially in interior lowcountry districts, the last antebellum decade had seen a process of accelerated enclosure and heightened conflict over community access to formerly "common" land. In the 1820s

31. In 1850 more than 80 percent of privately owned acreage remained unimproved in both the coastal and the interior districts of the Low Country. By 1860 this figure had shrunk to about 75 percent in the interior, although it had not decreased at all along the coast. It is interesting to note by way of contrast that a greater percentage (31 percent) of the privately owned acreage in upcountry districts had been improved and enclosed by 1850, perhaps reflecting the fact that those districts were, on the whole, smaller with respect to total acreage than were lowcountry ones. Statistics were calculated from the following: United States Census Office, *Seventh Census of the United States, 1850* (1853; reprint ed., New York: Arno Press, 1976), p. 345; *Agriculture of the United States in 1860; Compiled from the Original Returns of the Eighth Census Under the Direction of the Secretary of the Interior By Joseph C. G. Kennedy* (Washington: Government Printing Office, 1864), p. 128. It is difficult to find reliable figures for the period before 1850. Robert Mills commented simply that "most" of the land in lowcountry districts was unimproved in 1826. See Robert Mills, *Statistics of South Carolina, Including A View of its Natural, Civil, and Military History, General and Particular* (1826; reprint ed., Spartanburg, S.C.: The Reprint Company, 1972), p. 367.

and 1830s, lowcountry farmers and planters had inundated the legislature with petitions demanding the improvement of river navigation and the opening of new "public" roads to facilitate the marketing of traditional and new surpluses (especially short-staple cotton). Despite the fact that the development of new roads often involved encroachment on privately owned unenclosed land, counter petitions and opposition by local landowners were rare indeed. By the 1840s and '50s, demands for improved access to markets had not abated, but petitions were delivered to legislators amid a welter of opposing opinions and claims testifying to deep community conflict over the proposed roads. Indeed, by the 1840s it was common to find citizen petitions opposing new public roads as an infringement of their property rights or protesting the shutting up, as they put it, of an existing "public" road by a local landowner who had enclosed the formerly common land through which the road ran.[32]

Jurists too were deluged with the litigation that such intractable community conflicts produced. In this context the fence came to function as the absolute boundary of private property. One exasperated judge commented in 1841 that "in the olden time" efforts to foreclose development were unheard of "because every one was glad to have a road run through his particular land."[33] By the 1840s and '50s, however, the shared market orientation of all lowcountry farmers and planters had produced contradictory desires: for more roads, bridges, ferries, and generally greater access to market towns on the one hand, and for more land under fence and in cultivation on the other. Heightened conflict over the engrossment of unenclosed land, and thus over the definition of private and public land outside the enclosure, was the result.

In the Low Country, such conflicts had many dimensions. Not infrequently they involved planter adversaries quarreling or litigating over what constituted the "public" interest in the placement of a new road or the necessity of keeping an old one open.[34] But the conflicts also showed the marks of class. Struggles over customary right-of-way to rivers, fer-

---

32. Petitions to the Legislature, 1820–1860, General Assembly Records.

33. *State* v. *Thomas Dawson*, in Hill, *Reports of Cases*, vol. 3, p. 115.

34. For examples of intra-elite conflict see the following: "Petition of Sundry Inhabitants of St. Peter's Parish Proposing a New Road to Red Bluff Landing" and "Petition of Sundry Inhabitants of St. Peter's Parish Opposing the Proposed New Road to Red Bluff Landing," Petitions to the Legislature, 1824; "Petition of Sundry Citizens of St. Peter's Parish Opposing Proposed New Road," Petitions to the Legislature, 1831; "Petition of three citizens of Prince Williams Parish, Beaufort District, Viz. Mrs. Eliza McPherson, James Cuthbert, and Richard H. Bacot to Erect Gates on Public Road," Petitions to the Legislature, 1850; "Petition of William A. Sinkler of Charleston District to Shut Up Public Road," Petitions to the Legislature, 1850; "Petition of R. J. McFadden of Williamsburg District Protesting Route of New Public Road Through a Part of His Land," Petitions to the Legislature, 1853; "Petition of Sundry Citizens of St. James, Goose Creek Opposing Opening of a New Public Road," Petitions to the Legislature, 1857; "Petition of Sundry Citizens of Barnwell District Praying for New Route for Proposed Public Road," and "Petition of Sundry Citizens of Barnwell District Requesting Continuance of Approved Route of New Public Road," Petitions to the Legislature, 1858; all in General Assembly Records.

ries, landing docks, main thoroughfares, and thereby to market typically pitted yeoman farmers against neighboring planters; in these conflicts the scale was tipped mightily in favor of planters.[35] As the case law on trespass revealed, authority to determine the boundary between private and public property lay ultimately with those who held legal title to the land in question. That single principle all but determined the outcome. In the Low Country, judging from the landholding patterns in one coastal parish, fully 80 percent of the unenclosed land in 1850 was owned by planters.[36]

However weakened, customary notions of common rights retained legitimacy, and the distinction between private and public space was never fully realized. In fact, the household, as it was bounded by the fence, emerged as the only clearly defined private space. But if the household was a private space, it was not by any means a private "sphere" in the conventional bourgeois sense of that term. Nor, by contrast, was the area beyond the fence a clearly public space or public "sphere."[37] Rather, it was liminal land, subject to common claims and

35. "Petition of Sundry Citizens of Prince William's Parish, Beaufort District Praying for a New Road," Petitions to the Legislature, 1831; "Petition of Sundry Citizens of Sumter District for New Road into the Santee Swamp," Petitions to the Legislature, 1845; "Petition of Sundry Citizens of St. Stephen's and St. James, Santee, Charleston District Praying for New Public Landing on the Santee River," Petitions to the Legislature, 1849; "Petition of Sundry Citizens of Marion District Respecting Closing of Public Road," Petitions to the Legislature, 1852; "Petition of Sundry Citizens of Edisto Island, Colleton District, Requesting a New Landing," Petitions to the Legislature, 1855; "Petition of Sundry Citizens of St. James, Goose Creek Opposing the Opening of a New Public Road," Petitions to the Legislature, 1857; "Petition of Sundry Citizens of St. Matthew's Parish, Orangeburg District Opposing the Proposed Route for a New Road," Petitions to the Legislature, 1857; "Petition of Sundry Citizens of Darlington District Praying for Reopening of Public Road to Ferry," Petitions to the Legislature, 1859; "Petition of Sundry Citizens of St. John's, Berkeley, and St. James, Goose Creek Praying for New Road Through the Wassamasaw Swamp," Petitions to the Legislature, 1859; all in General Assembly Records.

36. The figure was calculated for St. Peter's Parish, Beaufort District, from the Federal Manuscript Census, South Carolina, [Beaufort District], Schedules of Slaves and Agriculture, 1850, 1860, NA. The 1860 data, which suggests that planters owned only about 70 percent of the unimproved land in the parish, appears to be in error. The census reports that farmers who owned between 50 and 99 improved acres held an average of 1,066 unimproved acres, a figure more than four times larger than the 1850 one. It is unlikely that yeoman control of unenclosed land increased so dramatically or that planter control decreased in the last antebellum decade.

37. In the historiography of antebellum America, the terms "private" and "public" sphere carry specific meanings that are inseparable from the relations and ideology of "domesticity" that characterized the former and of a capitalist free-labor economy that accompanied the latter. Few of these conditions, as described by Habermas (whose work theoretically underpins much of the recent discussion), pertained in the antebellum South. For Habermas, a modern "public sphere" is by definition a category of bourgeois society. For it took shape, he argues, in the context of social revolution in which "activities and dependencies" formerly contained within household economy "emerged from this confinement into the public sphere." Jürgen Habermas, *The Structural Transformation of the Public Sphere: An Inquiry into a Category of Bourgeois Society*, trans. Thomas Burger with the assistance of Frederick Lawrence (Cambridge, Mass.: MIT Press, 1989), p. 19 and passim.

thus not clearly demarcated as public or as private. By its very liminality, the vast expanse of unenclosed land that extended between some low-country households emerged as the predominant terrain of conflict between yeomen and planters. On that ground outside the fence, masters of households did not meet as equals. For the very principle in which yeomen anchored their identity as masters—the uncontested right of a man to authority over his own property—left them few political resources with which to protect their particular interests as small farmers in the land of great planters. In a society in which rights and power proceeded directly from property ownership, yeoman farmers, all too often, found themselves simply overmatched by those who owned far more and far more valuable property.

V

Most societies display social patterns in the spatial arrangement of households. The South Carolina Low Country was no exception. Households were not scattered randomly across the open country but were arranged in clusters, referred to by yeomen and planters alike as "settlements."[38] Those settlements, moreover, evinced a common social identity that in no small measure grew out of their particular location in the variegated landscape of the region. In the Low Country, as in many black-belt districts, land quality and value were inextricably tied to location. Not only did planters engross the vast majority of land; they engrossed the best quality land as well. The region thus exhibited a distinct social geography of class and race, one that was already well established by the beginning of the antebellum period and did not change meaningfully before the onset of the Civil War. Yeoman households had their characteristic places within it. Just as power relations within households showed distinct spatial dimensions, so too did the disparate power of yeoman and planter masters.[39]

To use these terms for the antebellum South, where labor was negotiated not primarily through a market but rather through older forms of compulsion and discipline contained largely within independent households, is to invite confusion and to risk obscuring the most distinctive features of this modern slave society. For further discussion on this point, see Eugene D. Genovese, *The Political Economy of Slavery: Studies in the Economy and Society of the Slave South* (New York: Vintage Books, 1965); Fox-Genovese, *Within the Plantation Household,* pp. 37–99.

38. The term was used by the Charleston planter Frederick Porcher in Stoney, ed., "Memoirs of Porcher," *South Carolina Historical and Genealogical Magazine,* 45, no. 1 (January 1944), p. 36, and by numerous yeoman farmers and small planters who gave testimony to agents of the Southern Claims Commission after the Civil War. See, for example, Claim of Felix W. Tuten, Beaufort, Southern Claims Commission Records [hereafter SCCR] RG 233 [Disallowed Claims], NA; Claim of William Peeples, Beaufort, SCCR, RG 233, and Claim of Ellender Horton, Beaufort, SCCR, RG 217, [Allowed Claims], File 8006, NA.

39. For an exploration of gender, space, and power within yeoman households, see Ch. 2 below. For exemplary treatments of the gendered uses of public space see Christine

By the beginning of the nineteenth century, the "face of the country," as former Governor John Drayton put it, revealed the already considerable cosmetic effect of human industry.[40] Coastal districts, especially, had been reconfigured by huge amounts of capital in the persons of slave laborers used to reclaim for cultivation formerly impenetrable river swamps. Nonetheless, patterns of settlement and cultivation still traced the contours of a finely veined landscape.

"So much land reclaimed from the sea," the Low Country, or, in geological terms, the coastal plain, presented an undulating terrain of river valleys alternating with high sandy ridges. The coastal districts were intricately dissected by inlets, rivers, and creeks, bordered on each side by fertile swamps or marshes; those within forty miles or so of the sea were washed by the tidal flow that caused the rivers to spill over their banks and onto the swampy land beyond. Although dotted here and there with "knolls or small rising grounds," the fertile river swamp land was generally low-lying. Between the river valleys, however, swamps gradually gave way to upland ridges of sandy soil, called sand hills or pine barrens after their landmark vegetation. These uplands were relatively infertile on the whole, although even they were sprinkled with "swamps, green savannahs, and small knolls and ridges of vegetable loam" that were productive pockets of land. With river swamps traversing sand ridges at random but close intervals, the Low Country presented a complex landscape. To William Elliott it was a sportsman's paradise. As he gloated to the "city sportsmen" of Long Island and Jersey game preserves, "a chase which . . . never took us five miles from our winter homes" provided a challenging course "over roads, piney ridge, marsh, swamp, knolls, thickets, rivers, woods, and 'old fields'." This scape of river swamps and sand ridges repeated in paisley pattern across the face of the coastal Low Country and, in a modified form, across the interior districts as well.[41]

Interior districts were separated from coastal parishes by a range of sand hills, extending across the coastal plain from the Savannah River on

Stansell, *City of Women: Sex and Class in New York, 1789–1860* (New York: Alfred A. Knopf, 1986), esp. pp. 193–216; Kathy Peiss, *Cheap Amusements: Working Women and Leisure in Turn-of-the-Century New York* (Philadelphia: Temple University Press, 1986); Mary Ryan, *Women in Public: Between Banners and Ballots, 1825–1880* (Baltimore: Johns Hopkins University Press, 1990). On the antebellum South, see Fox-Genovese, *Within the Plantation Household*, and Jean E. Friedman, *The Enclosed Garden: Women and Community in the Evangelical South, 1830-1900* (Chapel Hill: University of North Carolina Press, 1985).

40. John Drayton, *A View of South Carolina as Respects her Natural and Civil Concerns* (1802; reprint ed., Spartanburg, S.C.: The Reprint Company, 1972), p. 6. For an outstanding treatment of the environmental history of the Low Country, see Peter A. Coclanis, *Shadow of A Dream: Economic Life and Death in the South Carolina Low Country, 1670–1920* (New York: Oxford University Press, 1989), pp. 27–47.

41. Drayton, *A View of South Carolina*, pp. 6–16, esp. p. 7; William Gilmore Simms, *The Geography of South Carolina* (Charleston: Babcock, 1843), pp. 2, 10–11, 34–142, esp. p. 44; Elliott, *Carolina Sports*, pp. 107–08, esp. p. 92, 127. This passage also draws heavily on Mills, *Statistics of South Carolina*, pp. 130–33, and the descriptions of individual districts, pp. 358–765.

the southwest to the Pee Dee River on the northeast, about eighty miles from the sea. From there to the river falls, where the Upcountry properly began, a "comparatively open" version of the coastal pattern prevailed, with rivers and adjacent swampy low ground alternating with sand ridges rising as high as two hundred feet. The sandy high ground, though typically barren, was, like the coastal pine barrens, cut through by fertile veins of soil, and wherever the sluggish rivers traced their course they left rich alluvial soil in their wake. There was no shortage of rich cultivable land in interior districts. Although the interior claimed no tidal swamp land, every district in the Low Country encompassed in varying degrees almost the full regional range of soil types, from the "richest vegetable and marine mould to the most barren and unproductive sands."[42] Interspersed in close proximity within neighborhoods, these lands characteristically sustained different classes of producers. The social structure of the Low Country had a discrete geography.

As yeoman farmers later explained to federal officials, their antebellum "settlements" or clusters of farms were situated in particular niches within larger "neighborhoods" or "sections" of parishes and districts. Two sites recurred in the stories they told: the "forks" of the swamps and the "Sand Hills." These constituted the essential coordinates of the social patterns of yeoman landownership.[43]

One neighborhood in St. Peter's Parish, Beaufort District, came into special focus in yeoman depositions. Abner Ginn's and Joseph Rosier's small farms adjoined in the Coosawhatchie Swamp "section" of the parish, and Ginn's land also adjoined that of his yeoman kinfolk. The "neighborhood about the swamp" was a diverse one, embracing wealthy planters and free black farmers as well as yeomen like Ginn and Rosier. Their "settlement," however, was situated on high ground, "on a Hammock formed by branches of Coosawhatchie Swamp" and thus on land that could be cultivated without an expensive and labor-intensive process of reclamation. The hammock itself and the swamp that surrounded it established clear boundaries between the yeoman settlement and the nearest plantation one, which lay "a few miles back" on the Coosawhatchie River. There, on the river swamp land flowed by the tide, plantation households had clustered for decades, as even a cursory glance at Robert Mill's map of the parish in 1825 confirms. Not far away from Ginn's and Rosier's yeoman settlement, also nestled in the forks of the swamps, was a free black settlement called "Steepbottom," one of three in Beaufort

42. Elliott, *Carolina Sports*, p. 156; Simms, *Geography of South Carolina*, pp. 2, 34–142, esp. p. 44; Drayton, *A View of South Carolina*, pp. 9–10, 114–44; Mills, *Statistics of South Carolina*, pp. 130–33, 358–765. On the proximity of river swamp and sand ridges in the region, see Frederick Law Olmsted, *The Cotton Kingdom*, ed. Arthur M. Schlesinger (New York: Random House, 1984), pp. 159, 161, 167, 169, 181.

43. For a few examples of such testimony, see the following: Claim of Elizabeth Airs, Beaufort, SCCR, RG 217, File #9364; Claim of Felix W. Tuten, Beaufort, SCCR, RG 233; Claim of Ezekiel Stokes, Beaufort, SCCR, RG 217, File #6662.

District that sheltered a community of small landholders, a black yeomanry of sorts.[44] Ginn and Rosier emphasized the "isolated location" of
their households, and no doubt the swamp was difficult to traverse.
But James Ruth and John Morree, slaves from the neighboring plantations of Nathaniel Ruth and Jerry Youmans, provided a more accurate
perspective on settlement patterns within the Coosawhatchie Swamp
section, explaining that they had worked regularly for Ginn and Rosier, as
Ruth put it, "at night in my own time." They had readily covered the
distance of three-quarters of a mile in one case and two miles in another
between their plantations and Ginn's and Rosier's farms.[45] The boundaries between those distinct settlements were not chiefly a measure of
distance.

Similar settlement patterns prevailed all over the Low Country. In
coastal and interior districts alike, yeoman households clustered in the
forks of the swamps or on the sand ridges, while plantation households
hugged the banks of the rivers and reached back into the reclaimed
parts of the swamps beyond. As in the Coosawhatchie section, yeoman
and planter settlements existed in close proximity. Felix Tuten and William Peeples identified another yeoman settlement in St. Peter's Parish
as "our own Sand Hill settlement," presumably to distinguish it from the
neighboring plantation households that extended into the sand ridge
but were located on the river. Especially in the interior districts it was not
unusual for large plantations to embrace both low-lying river land and
high sandy pine land. But even in coastal districts, pine land bordered
swamp, leaving distances of as little as two miles between the two. After a
particularly devastating cholera outbreak on his Savannah River rice
plantation in 1854, Louis Manigault determined to buy some land nearby in the healthier "piney woods" to use as cholera camps. To illustrate
the proximity of the camps, he drew his father a map that graphically
depicted the complexity of the lowcountry terrain in a way a government
soil map never could. That map located the pine land in one place a
mere half mile away from tidal swamp fields. Such a bird's-eye view of a
small area explains how it was possible for a yeoman like Benjamin
Sellers to own a farm "in the pine land about four miles above the
Hobonny place," Edward Middleton's Combahee River rice plantation,
and to work as overseer on that plantation, sleeping "one night at one

44. Claim of Abner Ginn, Beaufort, SCCR, RG 217, File #10076; Claim of Joseph
Rosier [Rozier], Beaufort, SCCR, RG 217, File #5671; Claim of Lavinia Cohen, Beaufort,
SCCR, RG 217, File #9370; Claim of William Russell, Beaufort, SCCR, RG 217, File
#20749; Claim of Ellender Horton, Beaufort, SCCR, RG 217, File #8006. See the map of
Beaufort District in Robert Mills, *Mills' Atlas: Atlas of the State of South Carolina* (1825;
reprint ed., Easley, S.C.: Southern Historical Press, 1980), n.p. Confirmation of Ginn's and
Rosier's yeoman status was provided by the Federal Manuscript Census, South Carolina,
[Beaufort District], Schedules of Population, Slaves, and Agriculture, 1850, 1860.

45. In addition to the claims of Abner Ginn and Joseph Rosier, see the testimony of
Ruth and Morree offered to support their own claims. Claim of James Ruth, Beaufort,
SCCR, RG 217, File #8016; Claim of John Moree [Morree], SCCR, RG 217, File #6881.

place and one night on the other."[46] The settlement pattern of Ginn's and Rosier's Coosawhatchie section was not unique, for neither was the topography of St. Peter's Parish. In both interior and coastal districts, yeoman and plantation settlements were distinct; they were not removed.

This was a point Frederick Porcher made inadvertently in characterizing "our society" in the Santee Swamp section of St. John's, Berkeley and in Pineville, a village in the "Pinelands that skirt the swamps" to which local planters resorted for their health in the summer. "Our Society was unique," Porcher insisted, claiming at once that it consisted "entirely of planter's families, all of whom occupied the same social position" and that "the line of demarcation between them and the others was so distinctly drawn that there were none who stood sometimes upon one side, and sometimes upon the other." The "others," his editor felt compelled to clarify, were "the small farmers of the pinelands" with whom Porcher and his sort "lived intimately only in such settlements as Pineville." But of course, as Porcher had already acknowledged, there were also small farmers, "others," in the Santee Swamp section of the parish where his home plantation was situated. "The truth was," Porcher admitted, "of those other people I knew nothing, and fear was the result of ignorance." Of invisibility and contempt, too, he might have added.[47] Encouraged by the terrain and the topographical boundaries it presented, social distance typically outpaced geographical distance.

The social meaning of the disparate sites of yeoman and planter households was not fully apparent in physical location alone; it was embedded in the specific interrelationship of location, soil type, crop culture, and land value that pertained in the Low Country and in the history of the region itself. Tax collectors were, for obvious reasons of state, especially attentive to such matters of classification and assessed value. Their records—extant for only a number of parishes and for one antebellum year, 1824—when read with an eye to land type and location represent a cartography of power of the early antebellum lowcountry.

In Beaufort District, which contained St. Peter's Parish—to return to Abner Ginn's and Joseph Rosier's turf—half of the roughly 1.3 million parish acres in 1826 were rich swamp lands, and the other half were highlands of sand bottomed on clay. Those two basic categories, how-

46. Claim of Felix W. Tuten, Beaufort, SCCR, RG 233; Claim of William J. Peeples, Beaufort, SCCR, RG 233; Louis M. Manigault to Charles Manigault, Pulaski House, Savannah, Georgia, December 26, 1854, Louis Manigault Papers, William R. Perkins Library, DU; Claim of Edward Middleton, SCCR, RG 217, File #10351.

47. Stoney, ed., "Memoirs of Porcher," *South Carolina Historical and Genealogical Magazine*, 44, no. 2 (April 1943), p. 80; 44, no. 3 (July 1943) pp. 135–37; 45, no. 1 (January 1944), pp. 32, 36–37. For a discussion of Pineville and other resorts in the healthier sea islands, pine barrens, sand ridges, and out-of-state areas to which lowcountry planters migrated during the summer fever season, see Laurence Fay Brewster, *Summer Migrations and Resorts of South Carolina Low Country Planters* (Durham, N.C.: Duke University Press, 1947).

ever, concealed a complex hierarchy of land value shaped by other natural factors such as proximity to the sea but also, and perhaps more important, by the forces of capital and human industry, which had already reclaimed almost three-quarters of the fertile swamp land for cultivation. Parish land ranged in value from twenty-six dollars per acre to a mere twenty cents per acre for purposes of tax assessment. Established by the tax statute of 1815, those values by 1824 already bore little resemblance to actual market values—especially of the best lands—but they still provided an accurate map of the relative distribution, geographic and social, of diverse parish lands.[48] That map explicated the patterns of settlement indicated by Ginn and Rosier and established that the patterns were time-honored ones by 1860.

If there was any doubt about the intimate relation of space and power in the Low Country, it was dispelled by the tax collector's record. Fully 95 percent of the land parish yeomen owned was high pine land; valued at only twenty cents per acre, it was without a doubt the least desirable. The mostly poor, sandy soil was suitable only for the cultivation of provision crops and, in low yields, short-staple cotton. Much of it was used as range for stock. A few more fortunate farmers, probably those who lived on hammock farms in the forks, also owned some swamp land. Valued at only one dollar per acre, however, that land was typically unreclaimed swamp, which meant that it had not been cleared, drained, and embanked in the labor and capital-intensive process that would have transformed it into the most fertile land in the state. Unimproved, it chiefly provided a rich range on which to forage livestock and to gather lumber, shingles, and other cypress forest products. It was precisely this combination of land types—high, somewhat sandy land and unimproved swamp—that made up the household property of Abner Ginn and of Joseph Rosier in 1860. "The farm contains 562 acres," Ginn said proudly, "100 acres of which is cultivable lands, the rest in wood and swamp." So endowed, Ginn and Rosier were rightly described as among the "better off poor men" of St. Peter's Parish. Only the merest handful of yeoman households included, in addition, small amounts of reclaimed swamp land that could yield rich returns in cotton and provisions. And even that was assessed at only three or four dollars an acre, confirming that it was inland swamp land that lay beyond the tidal flow. Yeoman settlements clustered on the poorest land in the parish, bounded by the forks of the swamps and the sandy ridges that rose between them. Not one was to be found on the rivers.[49]

48. Mills, *Statistics of South Carolina*, p. 367; Simms, *Geography of South Carolina*, pp. 38–39; Thomas Cooper and David J. McCord, *The Statutes at Large of South Carolina*, 10 vols. (Columbia, S.C.: A. S. Johnston, 1836–1841), 6: 7–10. According to Robert Mills, the best land in Beaufort, although assessed at $26 per acre, commanded $50 to $60 per acre in the market in 1826. See Mills, *Statistics of South Carolina*, pp. 372, 209.

49. The assessed value of land owned by yeoman farmers was calculated from the 385 individual tax returns collected for St. Peter's Parish in 1824. Yeoman households were

The lands on the rivers within forty miles of the sea, called tidal swamp lands, were universally acknowledged to be "the best lands in this state." Once cleared, "well drained and banked," they sustained the Low Country's signature crops: rice and long-staple or sea-island cotton. In 1824 those tidal swamp lands were, at least in St. Peter's Parish, exclusively the property of planter households. Almost nine-tenths of that land, valued alternately at $26, $17, and $8.50 per acre—the three highest categories of assessment—was owned by substantial planters, men who also owned twenty or more (and usually many more) slaves. The rest was held by the estates, probably, of deceased planters and (in only two cases) by men who appeared to be small planters. Planters also had a virtual monopoly on inland swamp land, which lay further up the river beyond the tide mark and which, when reclaimed, proved fertile ground for the cultivation of short-staple cotton and provisions. Unlike the unreclaimed swamp land owned by a few fortunate yeoman farmers, this was valued at from thirteen dollars to four dollars per acre, reflecting the capital investment involved in improving it; 85 percent of that land, the second best in the state, was owned by planters in 1824.[50]

The particular social geography of St. Peter's Parish, while better documented than that of most other lowcountry parishes and districts, was a variation of a regional pattern. In every coastal district of the Low Country, the site of plantation settlements revealed that planter wealth was not just a function of the extent of households, of the amount of land they enclosed, but of the quality and value of that land as well. All over the rice-growing areas of the coast, for example, the value of farms-per-improved-acre increased steadily from those that grew minimal amounts of rice (or none) to those that grew more than 1 million pounds annually. Part of the increase in value reflected the capital invested in rice-cleaning mills and other equipment; more important, it revealed that "the largest plantations generally occupied the most valuable rice lands." In interior districts, the largest plantations also enclosed the most

---

identified from the tax lists, using a combination of the total number of improved acres assessed (up to 150) and of slaves (0–9): South Carolina Lower Division Tax Returns, [St. Peter's Parish, Beaufort District], 1824, Records of the Comptroller General; Cooper and McCord, *Statutes at Large of South Carolina*, vol. 6, pp. 7–10; Claim of Abner Ginn, Beaufort, SCCR, RG 217, File #10076; Claim of Joseph Rosier, Beaufort, SCCR, RG 217, File #5671. The description of his farm operation that Ginn offered to Southern Claims Commission officials conformed even in the details to that reported on the manuscript census for 1860. See Federal Manuscript Census, South Carolina, [Beaufort District], Schedule of Agriculture, 1860.

50. Drayton, *A View of South Carolina*, pp. 110, 116. Again, planters were identified on the tax list by two statistics: total number of improved acres for which they were assessed (150 and greater) and slaveholdings (20 or more). Planter engrossment of tide and inland swamp land was calculated from the assessments reported in individual tax returns. South Carolina Lower Division Tax Returns, [St. Peter's Parish, Beaufort District], 1824, Records of the Comptroller General; Cooper and McCord, *Statutes at Large of South Carolina*, vol. 6, pp. 7–10.

valuable lands within their fences. In St. Matthew's Parish in Orangeburg District, an 1840 survey confirmed the general pattern that the "size of the estates decreased in proportion as they were removed from the rivers."[51] The social geography of St. Peter's Parish was anything but unique within the state.

The example of the Low Country, in fact, casts an even wider net. At least in its general outlines, this social geography characterized every black-belt region in the antebellum South. As in the South Carolina Low Country, yeoman and planter households were intermingled on every census tract in every black-belt county, but so, in local variations of the lowcountry landscape, was fertile and poor soil. Although yeoman and planter households may have existed in close proximity, there was nothing more random about the arrangement of yeoman settlements in black-belt cotton counties than there was in St. Peter's Parish. Planter settlements were situated on the most valuable land; yeoman settlements, no matter how proximate, occupied physically and socially distinct sites.[52]

In the South Carolina Low Country, as in much of the plantation South, the planters' often vast holdings included every kind of land, from the cheapest pine land to the most valuable swamp land. Not infrequently an individual plantation traversed the river swamps into the sand ridges that lay beyond. But the heart of plantation settlements, in interior as well as coastal districts, lay on the rivers and their adjacent lands. The yeomanry was thereby rendered at once present and yet in some sense invisible to those who, for good reason, identified—and continue to identify—river plantation settlements as the essence of Low Country society and history. If fences were the boundaries of the masters' power, making yeomen and planters equally authorities over the domains within, then the immensely disparate resources that the fences enclosed and that the masters commanded marked a geography of inequality.

By 1824, when tax collectors mapped the social geography of the

---

51. Dale Evans Swan, *The Structure and Profitability of the Antebellum Rice Industry, 1859* (New York: Arno Press, 1975), p. 103, and Table IV–14, p. 133; Marjorie S. Mendenhall, "A History of Agriculture in South Carolina, 1790–1860: An Economic and Social Study" (Ph.D. Diss., University of North Carolina, 1940), p. 218. See also Alfred Glaze Smith, *Economic Readjustment of an Old Cotton State: South Carolina, 1820-1860* (Columbia, S.C.: University of South Carolina Press, 1958), p. 46.

52. Fabian Linden, "Economic Democracy in the Slave South: An Appraisal of Some Recent Views," *Journal of Negro History* 31 (April 1946), pp. 140–89; Gavin Wright, "'Economic Democracy' and the Concentration of Agricultural Wealth in the Cotton South, 1850–1860," *Agricultural History* 44, no. 1 (January 1970), pp. 64–99. Linden's article was a pointed refutation of Frank L. Owsley's argument that yeomen claimed a share of the landed wealth of the Old South proportional to their majority share of the free white population. Owsley had insisted that planters did not monopolize the best land. See Frank L. Owsley, *Plain Folk of the Old South* (Baton Rouge: Louisiana State University Press, 1949), pp. 10, 52 and passim.

Low Country, its formative years already represented the stuff of history. In the patriarchal landscape of St. Peter's Parish two features dominated: plantations, predictably on rivers, and villages, named no less predictably for leading planter families that had staked their claim in the eighteenth century.[53] There was little if anything new about the regional pattern of plantation settlement in the antebellum period. By 1820 the Low Country—coastal districts, certainly, but most of the interior too—was aptly characterized as a mature plantation society. And as Abner Ginn's and Joseph Rosier's description of their neighborhood in 1860 suggests, although the intervening years saw a process of intensification of established patterns, the spatial dimensions of class and power did not change significantly until the dislocations resulting from the Civil War.

VI

The Low Country had never been innocent of wealth and power, not even at the moment of its founding: neither in the internal relations of households nor in the relations between households, and surely not in the relations that had historically existed between the Low Country and other sections of the colony and state. The development of plantation society in South Carolina followed a distinct regional pattern. And although by the beginning of the antebellum period planters and plantations had extended their reach over all but the most remote mountain corners of the state, sectional boundaries yet retained political meaning and grafted disparate power onto the state constitution itself. The eighteenth-century dominance of the Low Country maintained a vital presence in antebellum politics.

Geographically, South Carolina is composed of three different regions. The Low Country, defined geologically by the coastal plain, is itself divided into upper and lower sections and extends from the coast to the fall line. The Upcountry, a piedmont area of gently rolling red clay hills undergirded by a granite, gneiss, and schist rock formation, extends from the fall line to the foot of the mountains. Finally, the mountains, part of the Blue Ridge chain, peek into the extreme northwest corner of the state. The coastal plain covers more than two-thirds of the entire territory.[54]

53. See, for example, the map of Beaufort District, which reveals the district landscape to have been dominated by plantations and villages named after planter families. See *Mills' Atlas*, n.p. The concept of a patriarchal landscape as an area in which the very social institutions marked on the map convey and buttress the power of elite male household heads was suggested by the analysis of Allen Tullos, in *Habits of Industry: White Culture and the Transformation of the Carolina Piedmont* (Chapel Hill: University of North Carolina Press, 1989), pp. 24–39, esp. 25.

54. Drayton, *A View of South Carolina*, pp. 6–16; Mills, *Statistics of South Carolina*, pp. 130–60; Simms, *Geography of South Carolina*, pp. 2–14; Edmund Ruffin, *Report on the Commencement and Progress of the Agricultural Survey of South Carolina for 1843*, (Columbia,

The principal political sections of the state in the antebellum period conformed to the rough geographical division between piedmont and coastal plain. The Upcountry long evinced a separate identity. Settled from the North during the great migration of the mid-eighteenth century and encumbered by the difficulties of transporting goods to coastal markets, it exhibited only the embryonic outlines of plantation society by the time of the Revolution. The Low Country, by contrast, was settled from the coast starting in the late seventeenth century, and by the mid-eighteenth century settlement already extended well into the "Middle Country," as the area between the parishes and the fall line came to be known. By the Revolution, the Low Country was not only a mature plantation society with a black majority, it was one whose glory days already lay in the past.[55]

The development of plantation society and the spread of slavery throughout the Middle Country was sufficiently advanced by 1802 that the Low Country could reasonably be perceived as extending fully to the fall line. Although meaningful distinctions persisted within the Low Country and provided not a little of the challenge of politics within the state, by the opening of the antebellum period the fall line had emerged as the major sectional boundary, and the middle districts had become part of the Low Country proper.[56] The sectional divisions of the antebellum years, and especially the political dominance of the Low Country, had deep roots in the colonial history of the state.

Born from the commercial expansion of Western Europe, the South Carolina Low Country was, from the first, caught in the web of an emergent world market. Under the auspices of the British Board of

---

S.C.: A.M. Pemberton, 1843) pp. 22–23, 30–31, 45; Ulrich B. Phillips, *Life and Labor in the Old South* (Boston: Little, Brown, 1929), pp. 3–13; Coclanis, *Shadow of a Dream*, pp. 144–49.

55. The definitive treatment of the development of plantation society in the South Carolina Backcountry is Klein, *Unification of a Slave State*, esp. pp. 7, 9–46, 238–68. The general discussion in this paragraph and in what follows draws on an outstanding body of work on South Carolina in the colonial and the early national periods. In addition to Klein, see Peter Wood, *Black Majority: Negroes in Colonial South Carolina From 1670 Through the Stono Rebellion* (New York: Alfred A. Knopf, 1974); Daniel C. Littlefield, *Rice and Slaves: Ethnicity and the Slave Trade in Colonial South Carolina* (Baton Rouge: Louisiana State University Press, 1981); Coclanis, *Shadow of a Dream;* and Ford, *Origins of Southern Radicalism.*

The pattern of development can be traced from the following early-nineteenth century and antebellum accounts: Drayton, *A View of South Carolina*, p. 11; Mills, *Statistics of South Carolina*, pp. 173–76, and the histories of settlement of each district, pp. 348–771; Simms, *Geography of South Carolina*, pp. 30–143.

56. F. A. Michaux quoted in Klein, *Unification of a Slave State*, p. 252. There remains some disagreement among historians about how to define the Low Country and, more specifically, about whether the middle or interior districts should be considered part of that region in the antebellum period. As early as the beginning of the nineteenth century, however, David Ramsay, one of South Carolina's first historians, insisted that they should for reasons of culture (especially settlement) and political economy, and he specifically listed Orangeburg, Sumter, Darlington, and Marion. See the discussion in Mendenhall, "A History of Agriculture in South Carolina," pp. 27–28, 34–35.

Trade and of proprietors already experienced in the ventures of joint stock companies, the colony was immediately oriented to plantation development by a mercantilist policy that supported settlers in the search for a staple. The colony's first settlers, Barbadian planters and their slaves, combined with the proprietary system of land grants to lend a plantation cast even to the Low Country's earliest years.[57]

Mercantilist dreams were not long in fulfillment. Within twenty years of settlement, rice, the staple on which lowcountry fortunes were made, had already eclipsed the colony's first exports—furs and slaves from the Indian trade and naval stores and provisions. By 1699 rice had given the colony its first favorable balance of trade. Grown initially on inland fresh water swamps, rice was perfectly suited to lowcountry climate and soil conditions and, after the collapse of the Royal Africa Company's monopoly on the slave trade in 1698, to its rapidly expanding force of slave labor. Demand matched supply, for the transformation of northwest Europe in the early modern period created new markets for supplemental foodstuffs such as rice, and South Carolina quickly became a major supplier.[58] Exports grew from 250,000 pounds in 1699 to a staggering 66 million pounds by 1770. Even after the introduction of indigo into the economy in the 1740s, rice alone continued to account for more than half the value of the colony's exports.[59]

The colonial and the early national—not the antebellum—years formed the Low Country's golden age. From 1725 to 1775 the Low Country was, by many measures, the richest region in British North America, its fortunes made by rice, or, more accurately, by slaves. As early as 1708, when the overwhelming majority of settlers still clustered in parishes along the coast, South Carolina alone among the British

57. On the European context, see Immanuel Wallerstein, *The Modern World System,* 2 vols. (New York: Academic Press, Inc., 1974); Ralph Davis, *The Rise of the Atlantic Economies* (Ithaca, N.Y.: Cornell University Press, 1974); Jan De Vries, *The Economy of Europe in an Age of Crisis, 1600–1750* (Cambridge: Cambridge University Press, 1976); Robert Brenner, "The Social Basis of English Commercial Expansion," *Journal of Economic History* 32 (1972), pp. 361–84, and Brenner, "The Civil War Politics of London's Merchant Community," *Past and Present* 58 (February 1973), pp. 361–84. On South Carolina specifically, see Coclanis, *Shadow of a Dream,* pp. 13–26; Richard S. Dunn, "The English Sugar Islands and the Founding of South Carolina," *South Carolina Historical Magazine* 72 (April 1971), pp. 81–93; M. Eugene Sirmans, *Colonial South Carolina: A Political History, 1663–1763* (Chapel Hill: University of North Carolina Press, 1966), pp. 3–5, 15–31: David L. Coon, "The Development of Market Agriculture in South Carolina, 1670–1785" (Ph.D. Diss., University of Illinois, 1972), pp. 38–64; Petty, *Growth and Distribution of Population,* pp. 17, 198.

58. A. S. Salley, *The True Story of How the Madagascar Gold Seed Rice was Introduced into South Carolina,* in E. Milby Burton, ed., *Contributions from the Charleston Museum* (Charleston, 1936), p. 51; Coclanis, *Shadow of a Dream,* pp. 52–78; Sirmans, *Colonial South Carolina,* pp. 23–24, 57, 60; Robert M. Weir, *Colonial South Carolina: A History* (New York: KTO Press, 1983), pp. 141–45; Petty, *Growth and Distribution of Population,* pp. 27–30; Coon, "Development of Market Agriculture," pp. 95, 135–44.

59. Coclanis, *Shadow of a Dream,* pp. 70–84; Petty, *Growth and Distribution of Population,* pp. 28–29.

North American colonies had a black majority population. By the Revolution, fully 80 percent of the lowcountry population was black and enslaved. Nothing more dramatically conveyed the rapid development of plantation society.[60]

Other characteristic features of plantation society were evident well before the Revolution. The Low Country was not simply North America's richest colony, it was also the most inegalitarian. Social inequality was, of course, most visibly racial. Virtually all of the black population—the lowcountry majority, that is—was enslaved and propertyless and, indeed, constituted the property of wealthier others. But the distribution of wealth even among the white minority in lowcountry parishes revealed a degree of concentration in the 1720s that would not be reached in New York or Philadelphia until the 1760s or 1770s. By the mid-eighteenth century, when the top 10 percent of wealthholders owned more than half of the wealth, the Low Country already manifested the highly skewed distribution of wealth that would become a characteristic of plantation regions all over the South in the antebellum period.[61]

Plantation development traced its own uneven course within the Low Country, extending gradually, usually along the rivers, south into Beaufort on the Georgia line, into the upper reaches of coastal parishes, and into that extensive inland area beyond the original nineteen parishes, known for most of the eighteenth century simply as the Backcountry. Although the Backcountry retained a coherent sectional identity until the end of the century when inland areas finally won representation in the state legislature, it was already sufficiently differentiated internally by the 1750s to allow for distinctions between the districts below the fall line in which plantation slavery had taken firm hold and those above in which it had not yet done so. Thus, while the term Middle Country was not commonly used until the end of the century, by mid-century those townships that became the antebellum districts of Barnwell, Orangeburg, Sumter, Darlington, Williamsburg, and Marion had extensive plantations fanning out from the rivers, a discernible planter class, and much higher concentrations of slaves than Upcountry areas. By

60. Wood, *Black Majority*, pp. xiv, 131; Petty, *Growth and Distribution of Population*, pp. 24–28, 55–58, 198; Peter Coclanis and Lacy K. Ford, Jr., "The South Carolina Economy Reconstructed and Reconsidered: Structure, Output, and Performance, 1670–1985," in Winifred B. Moore, Jr., and Joseph F. Tripp, eds., *Developing Dixie: Modernization in a Traditional Society* (Westport, Conn.: Greenwood Press, 1988), p. 7; Coclanis, *Shadow of a Dream*, pp. 90–91.

61. The data on the distribution of wealth and concentration of slaveholdings are from Coclanis, *Shadow of a Dream*, pp. 79–91, 97–98, 149–51. The increasing concentration of wealth in the middle of the eighteenth century owed, in no small measure, to the shift in rice production from inland swamp to tidal swamp culture. The latter system required intensive capitalization in slaves and equipment; economies of scale were realized only with a labor force of about 30 slaves and $25,000 of nonhuman capital. In addition to Coclanis, see Swan, *Structure and Profitability of the Antebellum Rice Industry*, pp. 96–104.

the turn of the nineteenth century a number even had black majorities, and by 1820 fully 54 percent of the population of the middle districts was black.[62] Solidly in the black belt by the opening of the antebellum period, the Middle Country had also been incorporated, albeit imperfectly, into the political economy and culture of the Low Country. The political unification of South Carolina was generated out of the same process.

Throughout the colonial period and the early years of statehood, coastal planters, suspicious of the yeoman-dominated backcountry, had exercised a virtual stranglehold on political power. In the 1760s the entire Backcountry had only two representatives in the colonial legislature, and despite repeated calls for political parity in the aftermath of the Revolution, coastal planters refused to preside over the diminution of their own power. In the second state constitution of 1790, the Low Country again defeated backcountry efforts to apportion representation on the basis of white population and managed to reproduce its colonial dominance in the new republic. Although they contained only about one-fifth of the white population of the state, the coastal parishes retained control over both houses of the legislature.[63] Resentment continued to build in the Backcountry, especially in its Upcountry districts where the great majority of the state's white population resided, effectively deprived of political representation. But just as the spread of slavery remade the Middle Country in the image of the Low Country, so did the formation of a planter class in the Upcountry in the latter half of the eighteenth century—a process massively accelerated by the first cotton boom of the late 1790s—create the conditions by which the lowcountry elite was finally reconciled to a conservative solution to sectional political struggle.[64]

By 1808, when backcountry political leaders finally mustered the two-thirds majority required for a constitutional convention or legisla-

62. On the emergence of the Middle Country, and for statistics on slaveholdings, 1750s–1810, see Klein, *Unification of a Slave State,* pp. 7, 21–24, 248–57. According to the population statistics provided by Robert Mills, the middle country districts of Williamsburg, Orangeburg, and Sumter had black majority populations in 1800. See Mills, *Statistics of South Carolina,* pp. 348–71. The black population in 1820 is calculated from the compendium in *Ninth Census of the United States, 1870* (Washington, D.C. 1872), vol. 1, pp. 60–61. See Mills, *Statistics of South Carolina,* pp. 348–71. For one example of the early-nineteenth-century use of the term *Middle Country,* see Drayton, *A View of South Carolina,* p. 11.

63. Klein, *Unification of a Slave State,* pp. 41, 145–48; Mark D. Kaplanoff, "Making the South Solid: Politics and the Structure of Society in South Carolina, 1790–1815" (Ph.D. Diss., Cambridge University, 1979).

64. On the development of plantation society in the Upcountry, see Klein, *Unification of a Slave State,* pp. 14–15, and passim; Ford, *Origins of Southern Radicalism,* pp. 5–19 and passim; and Ford, "Self-Sufficiency, Cotton, and Economic Development in the South Carolina Upcountry, 1800–1860," *Journal of Economic History* 45, no. 2 (June 1985), pp. 261–62; Mendenhall, "History of Agriculture in South Carolina," pp. 93–132; Kaplanoff, "Making the South Solid."

tive act to reapportion representation, much had changed in the Middle Country and the Upcountry. Indeed, what made compromise possible was that the upcountry planter leadership, itself threatened by the democratic republicanism of their predominantly yeoman districts, had come to share lowcountry planter politicians' concern with making the state, and particularly their own districts, safe for slavery. They shared with their lowcountry allies, in other words, a common conservative republican vision. The polity they imagined would guarantee independent men the rights due them in a republic, but it would also guarantee the members of the planter elite their natural position of political dominance. That was precisely what the compromise of 1808 promised, and that was precisely what it delivered. Lowcountry planters had nothing to fear. For while the Upcountry finally won a clear majority in both houses, owing to a new system of apportionment based on a combination of population and taxable property, control of the legislature remained safely in the hands of black-belt representatives, upcountry and lowcountry both. In a not insignificant part of the calculus of compromise, the Low Country with its unparalleled concentration of wealth retained a disproportionate grip on the levers of state.[65]

The compromise of 1808 was the foundation of South Carolina's antebellum political culture. It paved the way for the amendment of 1810, the last significant constitutional reform enacted before the Civil War, which in an apparently progressive spirit introduced white manhood suffrage to South Carolina well before most northern states ventured to do the same.[66] The compromise thus perpetuated and entrenched the political power of the Low Country and ensured that sectional boundaries retained political meaning. But in what constituted one of the most compelling problems in the antebellum history of the state, it also laid the groundwork for the peculiar combination of white manhood suffrage and planter rule that defined lowcountry political culture in the antebellum period and that had such monumental consequences for the rest of the nation.

VII

By the beginning of the antebellum period, the South Carolina Low Country was already a mature plantation society. The next forty years would see the intensification and elaboration of established social patterns in the crucible of cultural and political conflict. Within the Low Country, the gender relations in yeoman households, the class relations between yeoman and planter masters, and the regional distinctions between coastal and interior districts in a society configured around the

65. Klein, *Unification of a Slave State*, pp. 262–68; Kaplanoff, "Making the South Solid," pp. 52–58, 60–64, 96–117, 208–13; Ford, *Origins of Southern Radicalism*, pp. 103–13.
66. Ford, *Origins of Southern Radicalism*, p. 108.

relations of masters and slaves, gained ever more political salience. As South Carolina struggled toward a coherent position in national politics, those gender, class, race, and regional relations were among the most powerful forces shaping the state's political culture.

The spatial dimensions, or boundaries, of power—within households, between households, and within and between regions—provide an imaginary landscape on which to begin to reconstruct the complex web of social relations in which yeoman farmers were enmeshed in the South Carolina Low Country and in which their politics were so unpredictably engendered.

chapter 2

Producing Independence

I

Historians never find it easy to cross the threshold of the household and look inside. For the most part, they have stayed outside, witnessing the struggle for independence by yeoman heads of household from the vantage point of the federal census taker or local merchant. Yet that independence, and its attendant public meanings, was produced, quite literally, out of the relations of power and dependency that prevailed within the household's boundaries. To write this history of the household one must follow the master home.

The obstacles are considerable everywhere, but particularly in the case of the South Carolina Low Country. For there the very existence of a class of yeoman farmers has been denied, almost without exception, by modern historians. Hostage to a powerful tradition of regional representation that extends from the antebellum period to the present day, historians of the Low Country have found it impossible to see even the outlines of yeoman households, let alone to cross the thresholds. Rendering the yeomanry visible is, then, the first and necessary step toward a history of yeoman households, their relations of power, and the production of independence.

II

Historical visibility is everywhere related to social power. In the Low Country, with its special social geography, however, planter visibility appeared as a part of nature's design. With planter households situated prominently on river fronts and yeoman ones tucked away behind often impassable swamps, it is little wonder that yeomen figure so marginally in accounts of the region. But there is more to the enduring representation of the Low Country than topographical logic or even social geography. Regions are not "inert fact[s] of nature . . . merely there" but geographical and cultural entities created out of complex fields of social forces. By the midantebellum period, the idea of the Low Country as a bounded and distinctive place had already emerged, with an "imaginative geography" configured essentially, not incidentally, around the absence of a yeomanry. It was not just the dominance of planters but the social nonexistence of a class of sturdy yeoman farmers that figured in the discursive construction of the Low Country.[1]

In the antebellum period the contradictory social forces of the modern western world converged on South Carolina, staging the region as an ideological battleground. In the struggle that ensued, the Low Country was clearly and irrevocably defined as an aristocratic enclave in the body of the American democratic republic. South Carolina was slave society writ large. The question of origins is an elusive one, for that representation existed before it was so inscribed in the extensive travel literature of the period, its most obvious textual expression. By the time Frederick Law Olmsted in 1854 characterized "the government and society of the South [as] the most essentially aristocratic in the world," his readers already knew that the "despotic power" of South Carolina planters made the Low Country "the centre of the Southern aristocracy" and its elite "the aristocracy of the South, the slave power par excellence."[2]

Basil Hall, the British travel writer, suggested one early discursive channel (and its materialist underpinnings) when he remarked to his British readers in 1828 that "everybody must have read in the newspapers, under the head of Liverpool News, some mystical notices about 'Uplands' and 'Sea Island'."[3] Driven by capitalist assumptions and abolitionist curiosity, a good many travel writers, bourgeois "seeing-men" and women, followed the commodity trail of rice and sea-island cotton back to its source: the large plantations of the coastal parishes of South Carolina.[4] This was the Low Country that travelers and their readers expected

1. Quotations are from Edward W. Said, *Orientalism* (New York: Vintage Books, 1978), pp. 4–5, 49–50.

2. Charles E. Beveridge and Charles Capen McLaughlin, eds., *The Papers of Frederick Law Olmsted*, vol. 2 (Baltimore: Johns Hopkins University Press, 1981), p. 243; Frederick Law Olmsted, *A Journey in the Seaboard Slave States, with Remarks on their Economy* (1856; reprint ed., New York: Negro Universities Press, 1968), p. 499; James Stirling, *Letters From the Slave States* (1857; reprint ed., New York: Kraus Reprint Co., 1969), pp. 247, 319. Basil Hall had used the term "despot" as early as 1828. See Hall, *Travels in North America in the Years 1827–1828*, 3 vols. (Edinburgh: Cadell, 1829), 3: 225.

3. Hall, *Travels in North America*, vol. 3, p. 217.

4. The term is from Mary Louise Pratt, *Imperial Eyes: Travel Writing and Transculturation* (London and New York: Routledge, 1992), p. 7. Olmsted's southern travels, for example, were billed as a direct intervention in the debate over slavery by a free-soil moderate and should be read in the context of his long-standing debate with the radical abolitionist Charles Loring Brace. Beveridge and McLaughlin, eds., *Papers of Olmsted*, vol. 2, pp. 9, 82–83, 86, 243. Basil Hall visited "by invitation" a Combahee River rice plantation with more than 1,000 slaves. Hall, *Travels in the United States*, vol. 3, pp. 186–91.

to see, especially after more than thirty years of "orientalist discourse" made it possible to see no other.[5]

The process of regional definition was not wholly one-sided, however. In its geographical parameters and ideological content it reflected as well the uncanny complicity of the travelers' planter hosts and interlocutors in the debate over slavery. Jealous guardians of the power to represent their world, planters trained their visitors' sights narrowly on their beloved Low Country turf of sprawling riverfront plantations and refined town society, averting all eyes from the unsightly society of the swamps and sand hills.[6] Geographically so delimited, two opposite visions of the region converged: planters' self-representation of an aristocratic and superior republic of slaveholders and bourgeois outsiders' representation of an aristocratic, backward, and antirepublican society of slaveholders. The idea of the aristocratic Low Country took on the appearance of incontrovertible truth. It is a discursive construction that retains, even in our own time, much of its original power to conceal.

The elision of the yeomanry, in particular, revealed a precise political logic. To travel writers, whether British or American, there was a perfect symmetry between the exotic landscape of the region and its peculiar social structure. Unlike the sunny, picturesque Upcountry of "gentle glens" and "babbling waters," the Low Country was a region of "dark jungles" and "lazy, muddy" rivers, of "luxuriant magnolia and a thousand pendant vines." The tropical scene twenty miles out of Charleston, the "quivering, palpitating, pendulous moss . . . the gnarled trunks . . . heavy groining . . . strong, dark, rough, knotty branches" stimulated a "sensation . . . strange and delightful" in Frederick Law Olmsted and confirmed that this was like no other place in America.[7] Like the "budding flowerets cling[ing] around the rotting *debris* of former vegetation,"

5. Bourgeois travel literature on the antebellum South bears striking resemblance to that analyzed by Edward Said on the Near East, or "Orient." Similar dichotomies were employed to distinguish slave from free-labor society: passion/reason; laziness/industry; despotism/democracy. In this sense the discursive construction of the Low Country registered power relations between observers and observed similar to those at work in the Near East, except of course that the South was not a colony. I borrow the term, then, not to imply occident/orient oppositions but in the more general sense in which it is now used to address the power relations within which cultural discourse is produced. See Said, *Orientalism;* Pratt, *Imperial Eyes;* and J. M. Coetzee, "Idleness in South Africa," in Nancy Armstrong and Leonard Tennenhouse, eds., *The Violence of Representation: Literature and the History of Violence* (London and New York: Routledge, 1989), pp. 119–39.

6. Planters' definition of the Low Country and of its exclusive society is evident in the accounts of both Frederick A. Porcher and Francis Lieber. See Samuel Gaillard Stoney, ed., "The Memoirs of Frederick A. Porcher," *South Carolina Historical and Genealogical Magazine*, vols. 44–48 (April 1943–January 1947), 45, no. 1 (January 1944), p. 32; Francis Lieber, *Slavery, Plantations and the Yeomanry* (New York: C. S. Wescott and Co., Printers, 1863).

7. T. Addison Richards, "The Landscape of the South," *Harpers New Monthly Magazine* 6, no. 36 (May 1853), pp. 728, 731; James Silk Buckingham, *Travels in the Slave States of America*, 2 vols. (1842; reprint ed., New York: Negro Universities Press, 1968), 2: 17; Beveridge and McLaughlin, eds., *Papers of Olmsted*, vol. 2, pp. 163, 160.

brilliant plantation society fed on a decaying social body. As Harriet Martineau and others observed, the social landscape could sustain only "two classes, the servile and the imperious, between whom there is a great gulf fixed." From the circumscribed perspective of the Combahee River rice plantations and other parts of the canonical Low Country, that was indeed a reasonable conclusion, and the abolitionist eye recognized in it the instrumental logic of slavery.[8]

Where men "persist . . . in hugging so fatal a delusion as the belief in the profitableness of enforced labor," the British traveler James Stirling explained in "The Gain of Emancipation," not only are masters and slaves "debased" in consequence, the first into sensuous despotism and the latter brutish ignorance, but labor itself is degraded by association. This was patently evident in the Low Country, in a group of "unhappy persons . . . too few . . . to be called a class, who strongly exemplify the consequences of such a principle as that work is a disgrace." "No induce-ment [could] bring honest, independent men" into such a world, Harriet Martineau noted, and certainly the native climate nurtured none. Thus, upland regions of slave states, "even of the Carolinas," could sustain "an industrious yeomanry," but the Low Country had only planters, "the aristocracy of the South," their legions of slaves, and a small number of marginalized poor whites, the "crackers" or "poor white trash" despised even by slaves because they "work with their hands."[9]

Slavery corrupted everything it touched, turning a place rich in natu-ral resources into a developmental backwater, luring a refined elite into moral and sensual depravity, and, more generally, corrupting the two natural, and supposedly universal, instincts of human beings: domes-ticity and the work ethic. The confinement and ornamental role of plan-tation mistresses thereby figured prominently in bourgeois diagnostics. But it was, above all else, the absence of a solid middle class that marked the position of the Low Country on the scale of civilization somewhere closer to Bengal than to Birmingham or Boston.[10] This was the social

8. Richards, "Landscape of the South," p. 730; Harriet Martineau, *Society in America* (1837; reprint ed., Garden City, N.Y.: Anchor Books, 1962), pp. 217, 219; Hall, *Travels in North America*, vol. 3, p. 186.

9. Stirling, *Letters From the Slave States*, pp. 248–49, 319; Martineau, *Society in America*, p. 219. For a classic description of lowcountry planters as sensuous despots, see Beveridge and McLaughlin, eds., *Papers of Olmsted*, vol. 2, pp. 244–45, 253.

10. Women writers were particularly critical of slavery's corruption of women's natural domestic instincts, although male writers commented on it as well, especially with respect to the maternal instinct and the gender division of labor. See Martineau, *Society in America*, pp. 217–18, 230–32, 291–92; Fredrika Bremer, *Homes of the New World*, 3 vols. (London: Arthur Hall, Virtue and Company, 1853), 2: 283; Frederick Law Olmsted, *The Cotton Kingdom*, ed. Arthur M. Schlesinger (New York: Random House, 1984), p. 71; Olmsted, *Seaboard Slave States*, pp. 505–08; Beveridge and McLaughlin, eds., *Papers of Olmsted*, vol. 2, p. 253. Virtually every writer commented on the absence of a middle class, the corruption of the work ethic, and the backwardness of the slave South in the scale of development. See especially Stirling, *Letters From the Slave States*, pp. 221, 247–51, 319, 344; Olmsted, *Cotton Kingdom*, 67–71, 91, *Seaboard Slave States*, pp. 451–61, 506–16; Beveridge and McLaughlin, eds., *Papers of Olmsted*, vol. 2, pp. 240–45, 247–54.

logic of slavery carried to its extreme. There could be no yeomanry
there. In the vision of the capitalist vanguard,[11] the essential definition
of the region was configured around the impossibility of such a social
class.

The obviously nonelite whites glimpsed off the beaten track could,
then, only be "poor whites," no matter how much land or how many
slaves they owned. And that is precisely how they appear in the travel
literature of the period. The obvious contradictions of such a view were
easily submerged by the force of the logic itself, as Frederick Law
Olmsted's accounts of his repeated encounters with lowcountry plain
folk show.

By the time he went to South Carolina in the winter of 1853–1854,
travel writers were in disrepute, and Olmsted had trouble finding planter guides to the Low Country he had, as he put it, "set out to see."[12] The
ensuing need to fill up his contracted-for pages with accounts of extra-
neous things no doubt explains why, when he was en route from Marion
Court House to Charleston, his attention was seized by an "elderly countryman with a young woman and three little children" who boarded the
train somewhere in Orangeburg District.[13]

Intrigued by their primitive appearance (the man was dressed in "a
long-skirted, snuff-colored coat of very course homespun") and folksy
speech, Olmsted learned that the man was a local farmer bound for
home at the "next deeper" [depot]. He and his family "owned no Negroes . . . and did not hire any" but "made their own crap" of maize,
sweet potatoes, and cowpeas on the 125 acres of mostly "common . . .
upland," which, along with a little swampland, constituted their holding.
Historians could not offer a better profile of a lowcountry or middle
country yeoman farmer if they assembled a composite portrait from the
manuscript census. In Olmsted's eyes, however, the Orangeburg man
was not an industrious yeoman but a primitive peasant, whose agricultural techniques bore greater resemblance to those of a Chinese rural
laborer than to those of an improving capitalist farmer such as himself.
Not only did the old man not know where New York was or what land

11. Pratt, *Imperial Eyes*, p. 144. Pratt uses this term to connote the intimate relationship
between imperial and literary design in the production of colonial or newly independent
Latin American states for a literate, urban, European readership. Her analysis of travel
writing about Latin America and South Africa and of its implication in the expansion of
capitalism is brilliantly suggestive of travel writing about the slave South in the antebellum
period. The laziness and indolence attributed to the lower classes of the indigenous population in all such writing is only the most obvious example. See Pratt, *Imperial Eyes*, p. 45,
and, for an earlier and equally suggestive analysis, Coetzee, "Idleness in South Africa."

12. Beveridge and McLaughlin, eds., *Papers of Olmsted*, vol. 2, p. 11. As Olmsted complained to his friend Charles Loring Brace, "As to domestic life or negro plantation life, I
can not see it." Planters "are jealous of observation of things that would tell against slavery." Beveridge and McLaughlin, eds., *Papers of Olmsted*, vol. 2, p. 210, and see as well
pp. 2, 9–11, 82–83, 86, 243.

13. Olmsted published a number of versions of this encounter: in *Seaboard Slave States*,
pp. 398–401, and in *Cotton Kingdom*, pp. 67–71. My discussion is based on the lat· ··
text.

values were in that free labor state, but he had no idea about improved agriculture and boasted pathetically of a new plow that Olmsted disparaged as "constructed on the same principles as those of the Chinese." And, in the predictable pairing of such frameworks, the old man confirmed the backwardness of slave society when he alighted from the train and "strode ahead, like an Indian or a gypsy man," while his daughter was left to "carr[y] in her arms two of the children and a bundle, [as] the third child held to her skirts." He was as ignorant of improved womanhood as he was of improved farming.

Olmsted's obvious elision of the yeomanry as a social class in the Low Country was rendered explicit a few days (or a few pages) later. Confronted with fifty similar white people at a rural church in "the rice district," he readily categorized them as "[t]he Crackers," although, as he admitted, "I was told that some of them owned a good many negroes, and were by no means so poor as their appearance indicated."[14] But such discrete information was no match for a perspective nurtured by more than thirty years of debate. Olmsted made sense of what he saw. The Orangeburg yeoman notwithstanding, he saw only poor whites in the Low Country.[15] In the crossfire of the battle over slavery the yeomanry were literally written out.[16]

The idea of the aristocratic Low Country has proved a powerful, and powerfully blinding, one, indeed. It did not die with Frederick Law Olmsted and the last generation of planter masters. Rather, it has survived into our own time by virtue of the same unlikely convergence between the self-representation of the planter elite or their descendants in the Lost Cause and the reports of outsiders who are still guided through the Low Country by that elite or their texts. The power of that representation is a measure not only of the dead weight of the past but of the contemporary power of a small elite to define its region and its history. Perhaps it owes simply to endurance, to the outlasting of antislavery adversaries, or perhaps to the commercial power of a sanitized aristocratic past in the tourist economy of the present-day Low Country.[17] But there can be little doubt that the latter-day planters have

14. Olmsted, *Cotton Kingdom*, p. 91. There are a number of versions of this story, too. See *Cotton Kingdom*, pp. 86–96, and *Seaboard Slave States*, pp. 451–61.

15. Olmsted's language was formulaic: In the Low Country "the degradation of all labor . . . by slavery" had resulted in "a distinct separation of classes into the ignorant and uncultivated." The Low Country thus was more arrested aristocracy than robust republic. See Beveridge and McLaughlin, eds., *Papers of Olmsted*, vol. 2, p. 253, and Olmsted, *Seaboard Slave States*, p. 516.

16. There was room for only one yeoman in Olmsted's world: He had used the pen name (and self-conferred honorific) "YEOMAN" since the days of his first republican essay into aristocratic dens. See Beveridge and McLaughlin, eds., *Papers of Olmsted*, vol. 2, p. 17.

17. On tourism and the contemporary lowcountry economy, see the incisive analysis of Peter A. Coclanis, *The Shadow of a Dream: Economic Life and Death in the South Carolina Low Country, 1670–1920* (New York: Oxford University Press, 1989), pp. 154–58.

triumphed over their progressive critics and interlocutors, co-opting even the travel-writing genre to perpetrate their version of the Low Country into yet another generation.

In *A Turn in the South,* a recent and well-publicized contribution to that genre, V. S. Naipaul extended the lease on the idea of the aristocratic Low Country, while exposing in his unseemly celebration of it the political necessity of its overdue demise. For Naipaul not only revisited the canonical Low Country of Lost Cause writers—and more specifically, that of Herbert Ravenel Sass—but in doing so he entrenched that same limited imaginative geography of riverfront plantations, stately oak avenues, and rustic parish churches. More significantly, though, he appropriated as his idea of the region the nostalgic "Religion of the Past" as it had been offered to him one day on a south-of-Broad piazza in conversation with Marion Sass, the thoroughly unreconstructed son of none other than Naipaul's textual guide, Herbert Ravenel Sass.[18] Those lowcountry folk, descendants of slaves and crackers, for whom the past might not yet be sufficiently past, do not figure in Naipaul's Low Country, just as they did not in Herbert Ravenel Sass's, Frederick A. Porcher's, or, for very different and far more progressive reasons, Frederick Law Olmsted's. Little wonder that historians cannot see those who have gone so long without the power to render themselves visible.

The discursive construction of the Low Country has shaped modern historical scholarship on the region in profound, although largely unacknowledged, ways. Whatever else its effects, and they are many, it has made it difficult to write a history of the white majority—the sturdy yeoman farmers who elsewhere formed the backbone of the slave republic. The idea of the Low Country has admitted no such history and no such people.

III

It is difficult to get past this version of the Low Country to the complex world of Ralph Elliott, Price, and their many other neighbors, whether yeoman, planter, slave, free black, mechanic, merchant, or minister. But it is not impossible. Shadowy signs of another lowcountry society can be discerned even in travel accounts and planter memoirs. What, for example, are we to make of the fifty "Crackers" in the rice district or the elderly Orangeburg "countryman" of Olmsted's accounts? Were they indeed, as antebellum travelers insisted and modern historians have

18. V. S. Naipaul, *A Turn in the South* (New York: Alfred A. Knopf, 1989), pp. 101–08. Naipaul acknowledges that his image of the Low Country was formed by reading the work of Herbert Ravenel Sass during his Oxford days. For a sample of Sass's writing see D. E. Huger Smith and Alice R. Huger Smith, *A Carolina Rice Plantation of the Fifties* (New York: William Morrow, 1936), and Sass, "The Low Country," in Augustine T. Smythe et al., *The Carolina Low Country* (New York: Macmillan, 1931), pp. 3–32.

assumed, part of a class of propertyless poor whites who existed on the margins of plantation society? The evident commitment of most free men to private property suggests otherwise, as does an imaginative geography configured more broadly around the parish and district boundaries observed by federal census takers.

The Low Country that comes into focus in the census takers' more prosaic portrait includes the settlements back of the swamps and in the pine land, as well as those on the rivers. Unlike the other, this Low Country was home to a class of small independent proprietors—to a yeomanry, for that is what they would have been called if encountered in any other part of the South. Indeed, it is not only the yeomanry who are rendered visible from this perspective but the complex social world in which they were enmeshed, making it possible to determine if they constituted there, as they did elsewhere in the South, the politically pivotal majority of the white population.

Distinctions among propertied white men have meaning, and especially political meaning, however, only in the context of slave society and, most concretely, of the region's substantial black majority. It is misleading to speak in historical terms of a "white majority" in reference to the South Carolina Low Country or any other black-belt region for that matter. For although the white population of the coastal and middle country districts did grow modestly over the course of the antebellum period, the yeomen, planters, merchants, overseers, laborers, and artisans who constituted it never achieved more than a minority presence among a black majority of almost 70 percent.[19] (See Table 2.1.) The distinction between slave and free, and thus (though not seamlessly) between black and white, was the single most important dimension of

19. The white population grew from 73,000 in 1820 to 106,000 by 1860. For data and sources, see Table 2.1. Historians have long commented on the floodtide of migration of free South Carolinians to the new colonies and states to the west, a population movement that began as early as the second half of the eighteenth century and reached crisis proportions (by statesmen's accounts) in the 1820s. By one historian's calculation more than 40 percent of South Carolinians born after 1800 left the state, including "droves" of "yeoman farmers." See Tommy W. Rogers, "The Great Population Exodus from South Carolina, 1850–1860," *South Carolina Historical Magazine* 68, no. 1 (January 1967), pp. 15–21. On the eighteenth century see Coclanis, *Shadow of a Dream*, p. 67. On the crisis of the 1820s, see Robert Mills, *Statistics of South Carolina, Including a View of its Natural, Civil, and Military History, General and Particular* (1826; reprint ed., Spartanburg, S.C.: The Reprint Company, 1972), p. 297.

Rogers was no doubt correct that yeoman farmers constituted the foot soldiers of the southwest migration, but the evidence hardly sustains the view that such outmigration left the Low Country a yeomanless place. For a few examples of such interpretations see Ulrich B. Phillips, *Life and Labor in the Old South* (Boston: Little, Brown, 1929), pp. 100, 105–06; Phillips, "The Origin and Growth of the Southern Black Belts," in Eugene D. Genovese, ed., *The Slave Economy of the Old South: Selected Essays in Economic and Social History* (Baton Rouge: Louisiana State University Press, 1968), pp. 96–99; Lewis C. Gray, *History of Agriculture in the Southern United States to 1860*, 2 vols. (Gloucester, Mass.: Peter Smith, 1958), 1: 444–45; Alfred Glaze Smith, *Economic Readjustment of an Old Cotton State: South Carolina, 1820–1860* (Columbia, S.C.: University of South Carolina Press, 1958), pp. 8, 23–25, 29–30.

regional social structure, and it was one that shaped every other social relation, including that between yeomen and planters.

The demographic pattern was most marked in the coastal districts of the Low Country.[20] Notwithstanding a black population that declined in proportion to the white population between 1820 and 1860, blacks still outnumbered whites in those districts by the considerable ratio of three or four to one throughout most of the period. This was the racial demography that ostensibly set the coastal Low Country apart from the rest of the state and from the South as a whole. But it was, in fact, a condition toward which the middle districts of South Carolina were unmistakably converging. As the black majority in the coastal Low Country (including Charleston and Horry) declined steadily from 79 percent to 70 percent, in the middle districts it grew steadily from 54 percent to 62 percent, reaching almost coastal proportions in Sumter and, to a lesser extent, in Williamsburg and Orangeburg, where by 1860 there were between two and three black persons for every white one.[21] (See Table 2.1.) Although the distinctions between coastal and inland Low Country did not disappear, they were significantly less pronounced by 1860. Thus, while the coastal districts continued to look unlike any other place in the South with the possible exception of the leading cotton parishes of Louisiana, the Low Country as a whole, and the middle districts in particular, bore a striking resemblance to the rest of the Cotton South.[22] To the extent that it retained a distinction of degree, the Low Country case

20. Two districts, Charleston and Horry, represent significant departures from the general coastal lowcountry pattern. Until the late antebellum period when the turpentine industry established a foothold there, Horry was a poor and sparsely populated district barely penetrated by the plantation economy. Charleston was a different case, owing in large part to the impact of the city on district demography. The only district in the state with an urban center and an immigrant population, Charleston's white population was both larger and more socially diverse than that of other coastal districts. (See Appendix, Table I.) On Charleston's immigrant population, see Ira Berlin and Herbert G. Gutman, "Natives and Immigrants, Free Men and Slaves: Urban Workingmen in the Antebellum South," *American Historical Review* 88, no. 5 (December 1983), pp. 1175–1200.

21. See also Appendix, Table I.

22. For more complete data by district, see Appendix, Table I. For comparative data on Louisiana, see Roger W. Shugg, *Origins of Class Struggle in Louisiana* (1939; reprint ed., Baton Rouge: Louisiana State University Press, 1968), pp. 317–18, and Fabian Linden, "Economic Democracy in the Slave South: An Appraisal of Some Recent Views," *Journal of Negro History* 31 (April 1946), pp. 140–89. For comparison with other parts of the cotton South, including upcountry South Carolina, see Gavin Wright, *The Political Economy of the Cotton South: Households, Markets, and Wealth in the Nineteenth Century* (New York: W. W. Norton, 1978), pp. 18–22; William L. Barney, "Towards the Civil War: The Dynamics of Change in a Black Belt County," in Orville V. Burton and Robert C. McMath, Jr., eds., *Class, Conflict, and Consensus: Antebellum Southern Community Studies* (Westport, Conn.: Greenwood Press, 1982), pp. 147–48; Steven Hahn, *The Roots of Southern Populism: Yeoman Farmers and the Transformation of the Georgia Upcountry, 1850–1890* (New York: Oxford University Press, 1983), pp. 19–20; Lacy K. Ford, Jr., *Origins of Southern Radicalism: The South Carolina Upcountry, 1800–1860* (New York: Oxford University Press, 1988), pp. 44–45; Guion Griffis Johnson, *A Social History of the Sea Islands with Special Reference to St. Helena Island, South Carolina* (Chapel Hill: University of North Carolina Press, 1930), p. 106.

Table 2.1 Racial Composition of the Lowcountry Population, 1820–1860

	1820			1850			1860		
	White	Black	% Black	White	Black	% Black	White	Black	% Black
Coastal districts	33,794	127,649	79.1	45,645	133,763	74.6	53,734	127,602	70.4
Middle districts	39,620	46,081	53.7	50,652	79,442	61.1	52,293	84,245	61.7
Lowcountry total	73,414	173,667	70.3	96,297	213,205	68.9	106,027	211,847	66.6

Sources: *Ninth Census of the United States, 1870* (Washington, D.C., 1872), Vol. I, pp. 60–61; *Seventh Census of the United States, 1850* (Washington, D.C., 1853), pp. 338–39; *Eighth Census of the United States, 1860* (Washington, D.C., 1864), Vol. I, p. 452.

simply serves to underscore an inescapable point: that the demographic predominance of black slaves is the crucial context for every other calculation and inquiry with respect to slave society in general and the plantation South in particular.

Race marked the most significant class divide within lowcountry society, but by no means the only one. Although the black population was indeed overwhelmingly enslaved, social inequality was so pervasive that it escaped the neat boundaries of race and, although less frequently acknowledged, gender within which historians have so often attempted to contain it.[23] The minority white population evinced enormous social complexity with respect to the control of productive property, and not only because of the palpable inequality between women and men that most historians regard as irrelevant to social analysis. Not at all the stripped-down world of great planters, slaves, and a few marginalized poor whites, white society in the rural Low Country included small planters with fewer than twenty slaves, great ones with more than one hundred slaves, and planter-merchants with all manner of property; tenant farmers, laborers, overseers, and all kinds of poor whites; and, as elsewhere in the South, a substantial class of yeoman farmers.

Various definitions of the yeomanry have been presented over the years, ranging from nonslaveholding farmers to small slaveholding ones.[24] But the best conceptual definition is the one lowcountry yeomen

23. Since the days of U. B. Phillips and Frank Owsley, southern historians have argued about the political significance of social divisions among whites and about the meaning of the distribution of wealth. Few, however, have conceptualized the problem in terms of class relations. Notable exceptions include Eugene D. Genovese, "Yeoman Farmers in a Slaveholders' Democracy," *Agricultural History* 49 (April 1975), pp. 331–42, and Hahn, *Roots of Southern Populism*. For the centrality of class relations to the study of slave society see also Barbara J. Fields, "Ideology and Race in American History," in J. Morgan Kousser and James M. McPherson, eds., *Region, Race, and Reconstruction: Essays in Honor of C. Vann Woodward* (New York: Oxford University Press, 1982), pp. 143–78, and Fields, "Slavery, Race, and Ideology in the United States of America," *New Left Review* 181 (May/June 1990), pp. 95–118. The usual containment of social inequality within the boundaries of race is evident in the still ascendant "herrenvolk democracy" school. The classic statement remains George Fredrickson, *The Black Image in the White Mind: The Debate on Afro-American Character and Destiny, 1817–1914* (New York: Harper and Row, 1971), pp. 61–71. But for a more recent example specific to South Carolina, see Ford, *Origins of Southern Radicalism*, in which he argues that "the widespread ownership of productive property among households in the region effectively calmed any gnawing popular anxiety over the uneven distribution of wealth" and that, politically, planters were "supplicants for [the] favor, almost captive to [the] will of common whites." Quotations are on pp. 50, 373 respectively.

24. Compare, for example, the definitions employed by Owsley, Hahn, and Ford. Owsley eschewed the term "yeoman" for the broader one of "plain folk" or "farmers," within which social category he embraced "small slaveholding farmers" (owners of 1 to 10 slaves), nonslaveholding farmers, herdsmen (in frontier, pine barrens, and mountain areas), and tenant farmers; see Frank L. Owsley, *Plain Folk of the Old South* (Baton Rouge: Louisiana State University Press, 1949), pp. 8–9. Steven Hahn defined the yeomanry in the Georgia Upcountry as those farmers who owned fewer than 200 acres of improved land and few (typically 5 or fewer) or no slaves; see Hahn, *Roots of Southern Populism*, pp. 27–33. Ford too defined yeomen as those landowners who owned 5 or fewer slaves; see Ford, *Origins of Southern Radicalism*, p. 71.

themselves offered to federal officials after the Civil War in explaining what, precisely, had distinguished them "from the higher class of planters" in their neighborhoods. We were "self-working farmers," one after another proclaimed, by which they meant to differentiate themselves by the character of their labor; by the plain fact that they worked the land with their own hands. Unlike planters whose ownership of slaves was sufficient to render their labor, and that of their families, managerial, yeoman farmers and their families composed the primary labor supply of their households.

In this respect the ownership of slaves, whatever its other meanings, was not the fundamental dividing line between yeoman and planter. Ezekiel Stokes was a slaveholder and still a "self-working farmer." "He had but few slaves himself," a neighbor observed, "and those he has [*sic*] were but three or four for help, and he and his family worked with his slaves in the field." It took more than a few slaves to transform a farmer's productive role into a purely supervisory one or to relieve his wife and children of the necessity of regular farm labor.[25] Clearly a combination of factors—the amount of land to be worked; the number, age, and sex of family members; and the number, age, and sex of slaves—determined who were "self-working farmers."[26]

In St. Peter's Parish in Beaufort District, which runs parallel to the Savannah River from the coast to the Barnwell District line, that class of independent proprietors can be discerned, albeit with some quantitative translation, among the complex white population recorded in the late antebellum reports of federal census takers. Distinguished on the lower end from poor whites by the ownership of real property, yeomen are necessarily less clearly distinguished on the upper end from small planters whose ownership of slaves was enough to make their labor chiefly managerial. The issue is not simply the number of slaves household heads owned but more precisely the amount of labor the owners thereby acquired in addition to that of family members. Surprising as it might seem, farmers could well have owned as many as nine slaves and still have found themselves dependent on family members even for field labor.

The reason lies in the striking pattern in the age and sex of the slaves small slaveholders typically owned. There were considerably more women slaves than men in the households of small slaveholders, and, no doubt as a consequence, there were almost as many children and young

25. Claim of Ezekiel Stokes, Beaufort, Southern Claims Commission Records [hereafter SCCR], RG 217, File #6662, NA. The term *self-working farmer* was used in other depositions. See Claim of Nancy Sandifer, Barnwell, SCCR, RG 217, File #10079; Claim of William R. Tuten, Beaufort, SCCR, RG 233: Claim of Felix W. Tuten, Beaufort, SCCR, RG 233; Claim of Sarah Ann Harvey, Beaufort, SCCR, RG 233; Claim of Ann Mew, Beaufort, RG 217, File #6659; Claim of Ellender Horton, Beaufort, SCCR, RG 217, File #8006.

26. To date none of the studies of the yeomanry consider either the age or the sex of the slaves yeomen owned.

Table 2.2 Sex and Age Composition of Yeoman Slaveholdings,
St. Peter's Parish, Beaufort District, 1850

	Distribution of Slaves in Slaveholdings				
No. Slaves in Holding	% Adult Females	% Adult Males	% Children	% Total Female*	No. Households
1†	60	20	20	70	9
2	21	21	58	58	7
3	43	20	37	67	10
4	28	33	40	50	9
5	29	16	55	57	12
6	28	22	50	50	3
7	30	23	47	52	9
8	31	22	47	53	4
9	34	18	48	60	7
Totals	32	21	47	56	70

Source: Federal Manuscript Census, South Carolina [Beaufort District], Schedules of Population, Slaves and Agriculture, 1850, NA.

*Denotes percentage of slaves in a slaveholding household who were female adults and female children.

†Shows percentage of slaveholdings with one slave that were composed of either one adult male slave, one adult female slave, one male child, or one female child. In this case, 60 percent of slaveholders who owned one slave owned an adult female, and 70 percent owned either an adult female or a female child.

adolescents as there were adults.[27] In St. Peter's Parish in 1850, for example, six of ten farmers who owned only one slave owned an adult woman. Those who owned five slaves owned usually two or three children, one or two adult women, and at most, although not always, one male adult slave. Even those who owned nine slaves owned, on average, four or five children, three or four adult women, and at most one or two adult men. (See Table 2.2.)

The overrepresentation of women among the adult slave population and the significant proportion of children shaped the labor force commanded by yeoman slaveholders and the necessity of performing field labor that continued to press upon the household head and his family. For although slave women undoubtedly worked, as one put it, "like a man" at all manner of farm tasks, including field work, and although they might well have contributed more labor than that signified by the usual plantation designation "three-quarter hand," they did not usually match the productive output of adult male slaves. In harvesting short-staple cotton, where farmers and planters experienced the seasonal labor bottleneck that dictated the amount of cotton they could plant, a woman slave typically picked 80 percent as much as a male slave on an average

27. Although necessarily imprecise, the age categories employed in this analysis are an attempt to represent labor categories. Those of child (1–8 years; 9–13 years) and adolescent (14–18) are, moreover, an attempt to represent the particular case of adolescent girls' age of menarche and thus of their potentially double labor, reproductive and productive.

day; those women who were pregnant or had infants or young children to care for probably picked less. Slave children did not work regularly in the fields until they were about ten years old, and then they were assigned tasks as "one-quarter hands."[28]

Yeoman farmers had their own reasons for preferring women slaves to men, if they had to make a choice. The lower market price of women slaves involved a lower initial capital investment that, although risky, promised a higher return in the long run. In women slaves yeoman farmers may have settled for less by way of immediate profit in field labor and a marketable staple, while laying claim to a kind of labor they could never extract from male slaves: reproductive labor.[29] This was the strategy that yeoman slaveholders pursued, perhaps partly of necessity. But the overrepresentation of women and children meant that even the man who owned nine slaves was still by all accounts, a "self-working farmer," whose regular calculus of production on the one hundred-odd acres he would typically have cultivated included his own manual labor and, most likely, that of his sons, daughters, and even, on occasion, his wife. It was not that it made no difference whether a yeoman farmer owned no slaves or some, whether he owned one, five, or nine. It was just that the capacity to leave his own hands unsoiled was not one of the differences.

In quantitative terms, therefore, "self-working farmers" were those who owned fewer than 150 acres of improved land and fewer than ten

---

28. Jacqueline Jones, *Labor of Love, Labor of Sorrow: Black Women, Work, and the Family, from Slavery to the Present* (New York: Vintage Books, 1985), p. 18. For the usual designation of women and children as three-quarter and one-quarter hands respectively, see George P. Rawick, ed., *The American Slave: A Composite Autobiography* (Westport, Conn.: Greenwood Publishing Co., 1972), vol. 3, *South Carolina Narratives*, part 4, pp. 116–18, 102–05, 273–75. The discussion of the productive output of female as compared to male slaves is drawn from John Campbell, "The Gender Division of Labor, Slave Reproduction, and the Slave Family Economy on Southern Cotton Plantations, 1800–1865," (Ph.D. Diss., University of Minnesota, 1988), pp. 55–75. Studies of slave women, although growing in number, have yet to do justice to the rich material on the gender division of labor contained in farm and plantation records. For one example of a plantation book that lists hands by gender and task, that includes evidence of women plowing, and that complicates easy generalizations about the employment and designation of hands by gender (women were counted as full "hoe hands"), see James Henry Hammond, Plantation Records, August 7, 1850 (nearest date cited), James Henry Hammond Papers, in Kenneth Stampp, ed., Records of Antebellum Southern Plantations From the Revolution Through the Civil War, Series A, Part 1, Reel 5. Other studies of slave women's work include Deborah Gray White, *Arn't I a Woman? Female Slaves in the Plantation South* (New York: W. W. Norton, 1985), and Elizabeth Fox-Genovese, *Within the Plantation Household: Black and White Women in the Old South* (Chapel Hill: University of North Carolina Press, 1988).

29. The overrepresentation of women slaves among yeomen slaveholdings is not peculiar to the South Carolina Low Country, as Michael Johnson and David Rankin have confirmed in a representative sample of the South for the early national period. For the data and some preliminary analysis, see Johnson and Rankin, "Southern Slaveholders, 1790–1820: A Census" (Paper presented at the Annual Meeting of the Southern Historical Association, New Orleans, November 1990).

Table 2.3 Occupations of Free Household Heads,
St. Peter's Parish, Beaufort District, 1850–1860

	1850		1860	
Occupation	*No.*	*%*	*No.*	*%*
Farmer and planter*	265	61.1	301	58.1
Overseer and manager	42	9.7	55	10.6
Merchant	7	1.6	17	3.3
Professional	17	3.9	28	5.4
Artisan and skilled worker	25	5.8	45	8.7
Laborer	63	14.4	56	10.8
Other	15	3.5	16	3.1
Total	434	100.0	518	100.0
Not reported	85		68	

Sources: Federal Manuscript Census, South Carolina [Beaufort District], Schedule of Population, 1850, 1860.

*Includes heads of household reporting two occupations if the first listed is "farmer" or "planter."

slaves. The number of households that actually fit this description—that is, the size of the lowcountry yeomanry—turns on the pattern of land and slave ownership that prevailed among the heads of rural households. It would be difficult to overstate the weight that this question has come to bear in historical analysis. For it is now frequently and compellingly argued that whites in the Old South were obsessed with the idea of slavery, defined its opposite as independence, and founded a social order and political ideology on the widespread ownership of property in land and, to a lesser extent, slaves—that is, with the exception of enclaves such as lowcountry South Carolina, which evinced more of an aristocratic aspect.[30] Yet in the overwhelmingly rural and agricultural society of St. Peter's Parish, in which more than six of every ten free household heads were farmers or planters and another three were farm laborers, overseers, or managers—in which, in other words, fully nine of ten inhabitants participated directly in the farming economy in 1850—

30. This interpretation of white society in the antebellum South is now widely accepted, although it incorporates a number of different political perspectives on the nature of republican political ideology. In his discussion of upcountry Georgia, for example, Steven Hahn refers to a "preindustrial republicanism," the "republicanism of petty producers," which "linked freedom and independence with control over productive resources" and tied the yeomanry into a radical republican tradition; see Hahn, *Roots of Southern Populism*, pp. 2, 10. Lacy Ford refers to a "country-republicanism" to evoke the association with "Revolutionary era political ideals," although not of the radical republican variety; Ford, *Origins of Southern Radicalism*, pp. 51–52. For other interpretations see J. Mills Thornton III, *Politics and Power in a Slave Society* (Baton Rouge: Louisiana State University Press, 1978), and J. William Harris, *Plain Folk and Gentry in a Slave Society: White Liberty and Black Slavery in Augusta's Hinterlands* (Middletown, Conn.: Wesleyan University Press, 1985).

the extent of landownership was anything but anomalous.[31] (See Table 2.3.) Indeed, in 1850 and again in 1860, two-thirds of the household heads and fully eight of every ten farm operators owned their own land. Not just planters, then, but most free men in the parish had managed to secure their independence from the labor market and employers. (See Table 2.4.) By current definition, the Low Country was as much a republican society as any other area of the slave South.[32]

To a greater extent than their counterparts elsewhere, moreover, white men in St. Peter's Parish secured that personal and household independence through ownership of the South's other characteristic form of productive property. Almost half of the household heads and almost three-quarters of farm operators in the parish owned at least one slave in 1850. Although the proportion decreased during the decade of the 1850s, it nonetheless matched the distribution of chattel property in other black-belt regions and exceeded that of the Cotton South as a whole, where, on the eve of the Civil War, one-quarter of white families and only one-half of farm operators fell into the ranks of slaveholders.[33] (See Table 2.4.) Low Country landholders were more often slaveholders, too.

If property was broadly distributed, however, it was anything but

31. Of the free household heads in 1850, 12 percent were free blacks, about one-third of whom owned real property and one-fifth of whom owned and operated farms. Tucked away in the swamps of the Low Country, then, was a black yeomanry of sorts. Moreover, 16 percent of free households heads were women, although it goes without saying that, as for the free black farmers, property ownership did not secure their status as republican citizens.

The remaining one-tenth of household heads not directly involved in the agricultural economy were merchants and physicians, preachers and lawyers, schoolteachers and artisans, virtually all of whom met demands that issued chiefly from the agricultural sector. The most distinctive local wrinkle in the social fabric of the parish was a greater proportion of overseers and managers than was typical of the cotton South (9.7 percent of household heads compared to 1.2 percent in the South Carolina Upcountry in 1850, for example), more merchants and professionals, and more rural laborers, although the number of the latter was probably exaggerated in 1850 by census takers who failed to distinguish laborers from tenants. For comparison with the cotton South, see, for example, Ford, *Origins of Southern Radicalism*, pp. 47–50, and Hahn, *Roots of Southern Populism*, pp. 20–23.

32. Similar rates of land ownership prevailed in other regions of the antebellum South. See Ford, *Origins of Southern Radicalism*, p. 48; Hahn, *Roots of Southern Populism*, pp. 21–24; Harris, *Plain Folk and Gentry*, pp. 20–23; Owsley, *Plain Folk of the Old South*, pp. 16, 155–95; Blanche H. Clark, *The Tennessee Yeomen, 1840–1860* (Nashville: Vanderbilt University Press, 1942), pp. 27–29; William L. Barney, *The Secessionist Impulse: Alabama and Mississippi in 1860* (Princeton, N.J.: Princeton University Press, 1974), p. 38.

33. Relevant comparisons are to be found in Ford, *Origins of Southern Radicalism*, p. 45; Hahn, *Roots of Southern Populism*, pp. 24–26; Wright, *Political Economy of the Cotton South*, pp. 27–28; Gavin Wright, "'Economic Democracy' and the Concentration of Agricultural Wealth in the Cotton South, 1850–1860," *Agricultural History* 44, no. 1 (January, 1970), p. 79; Owsley, *Plain Folk of the Old South*, pp. 182, 209. In the extent of slave ownership as in racial demography, the Low Country appears to bear closest structural resemblance to leading Louisiana cotton parishes. See Shugg, *Origins of Class Struggle in Louisiana*, p. 151.

Table 2.4 Land and Slave Ownership, St. Peter's Parish,
Beaufort District, 1850–1860

	A. FREE HOUSEHOLD HEADS					
	Land			Slaves		
	Owners	*Nonowners*	*% Own*	*Owners*	*Nonowners*	*% Own*
1850	340	179	65.5	252	267	48.6
1860	374	204	64.7	255	323	44.1
	B. FARM OPERATORS					
1850*	308	1	99.7	224	85	72.5
1860	246	59	80.7	200	105	65.6

Source: Federal Manuscript Census, South Carolina [Beaufort District], Schedules of Population, Slaves
and Agriculture, 1850, 1860.

*Landless farmers appear to have been unreported in the 1850 census or reported as laborers.

evenly distributed among rural proprietors. It was here—not in the
ownership of land but in the distribution of it—that the contradictory
character of lowcountry society was most clearly displayed. For the Low
Country had one of the most inegalitarian distributions of real wealth in
the South, and perhaps in the country, during the antebellum period. In
plantation regions like the South Carolina Upcountry, for example, the
richest tenth of real propertyholders in the 1850s generally owned about
55 percent of the real wealth; in the Low Country, judging by St. Peter's
Parish, they owned a remarkable 70 percent.[34] (See Table 2.5.) And
while the top quarter of real propertyholders claimed about 90 percent
of the wealth, the bottom half claimed less than 5 percent. In general,
the trend was toward greater concentrations of wealth over time.[35]

34. Ford, *Origins of Southern Radicalism,* pp. 48–51. For comparison with other parts of
the South, see Wright, "'Economic Democracy' and the Concentration of Agricultural
Wealth," pp. 76–85, and Wright, *Political Economy of the Cotton South,* pp. 25–27; Barney,
"Towards the Civil War," p. 147; Hahn, *Roots of Southern Populism,* pp. 23–24; Linden,
"Economic Democracy in the Slave South," p. 163. The distribution of wealth and its
meaning for yeoman-planter relations is explored more fully in the following chapter.

35. Also see Appendix, Table II, for the greater concentration of wealth in 1860 when
calculated in terms of real and personal property. The growing concentration of wealth in
the parish during the 1850s is partially obscured by census takers who failed to report the
value of absentee planters' property and reported instead the much lesser wealth of managers or overseers. In 1850 census takers reported 17 absentee planters and listed their
average real wealth as in excess of $40,000. In 1860, by contrast, 24 absentee planters were
recorded, but their real wealth was listed as 0, this notwithstanding the fact that they
owned on average in excess of 550 acres and 60 slaves. This inconsistency in the census
takers' method probably explains the apparent decline in the proportion of real wealth
owned by the richest tenth of property owners between 1850 and 1860. For evidence of the
progressive concentration of real wealth in the Low Country more generally during the
decade, see Coclanis, *Shadow of a Dream,* pp. 149–54.

Table 2.5 Distribution of Real Wealth among Real Propertyholders, St. Peter's Parish, Beaufort District, 1824–1860 (by decile of real wealth)

	1824		1850		1860*	
Decile	Total Real Wealth	% Share Real Wealth	Total Real Wealth	% Share Real Wealth	Total Real Wealth	% Share Real Wealth
Top decile	$195,092	70.0	$1,336,000	71.4	$2,940,520	64.0
Second	38,678	13.9	239,000	12.8	747,800	16.3
Third	19,600	7.0	119,150	6.4	340,300	7.4
Fourth	10,141	3.6	68,300	3.7	198,800	4.3
Fifth	5,917	2.1	41,500	2.2	137,875	3.0
Sixth	3,684	1.3	26,300	1.4	94,050	2.0
Seventh	2,467	0.9	16,850	0.9	66,625	1.5
Eighth	1,656	0.6	11,105	0.6	38,760	0.8
Ninth	1,085	0.4	7,740	0.4	22,600	0.5
Tenth	481	0.2	4,305	0.2	9,660	0.2
Total	278,801	100.0	1,870,250	100.0	4,596,990	100.0
NUMBER	325		340		374	

Sources: South Carolina Lower Division Tax Returns [St. Peter's Parish, Beaufort District], 1824, Records of the Comptroller General, SCDAH; Federal Manuscript Census, South Carolina [Beaufort District], Schedule of Population, 1850, 1860.

*Farm value was substituted for the total value of real property if the latter was missing. The distribution is less skewed owing to the census taker's failure to report propertyholdings of most absentee owners, recording instead the holdings of managers and overseers.

Only slightly more than one rural proprietor in ten (13 percent) owned the land and slaves (at least five hundred acres of improved land and at least one hundred slaves) necessary to admit them to the planter elite in 1850. Their ranks did not grow proportionally during the following decade, but in 1860 they still accounted for fewer than two in every ten (18 percent) rural proprietors. Yet these are the men regarded as emblematic of the Low Country's peculiar social structure. There were, of course, other, less wealthy planters in the parish, men who owned between 150 and 500 acres of improved land and more than ten and usually more than twenty slaves. They constituted another three or at most four rural proprietors in ten.

The conclusion, although perhaps unexpected, is nonetheless clear. The majority of rural proprietors in St. Peter's Parish in 1850, slightly more than five in ten, were yeoman farmers. These were men who owned no more than 149 acres of improved land and nine slaves, although most did not command even such modest resources. About half made their living with fewer than fifty acres of improved land and with no slaves at all, while those who did own slaves owned at most one or two.

Table 2.6 Farms and Plantations in St. Peter's Parish, Beaufort District, 1850–1860

Category (Imp. Acres)	1850			1860		
	No. Farms	% All Farms	Avg. No. Slaves	No. Farms	% All Farms	Avg. No. Slaves
1–24	28	9.1	0.7	31	10.2	4.1
24–49	55	17.8	1.6	54	17.7	1.4
50–99	49	15.9	4.6	37	12.1	6.1
100–149	30	9.7	15.0	30	9.9	5.7
Yeoman totals	162	52.5	4.8	152	49.8	2.6
150–199	20	6.5	22.8	19	6.2	14.3
200–299	44	14.2	28.5	44	14.4	21.0
300–499	44	14.2	55.8	36	11.8	34.3
Planter totals	108	34.9	38.6	99	32.4	24.6
500+	39	12.6	101.9	54	17.7	71.5
Great planter totals	39	12.6	101.9	54	17.7	71.5

Sources: Federal Manuscript Census, South Carolina [Beaufort District], Schedules of Slaves and Agriculture, 1850, 1860.

Even the most substantial yeoman farmers and their families, moreover, still faced the necessity of putting their shoulder to the plow. These were the self-working farmers of lowcountry South Carolina. In 1860 they were still there, and they were still the single largest class of rural proprietors. (See Table 2.6.) The "aristocratic" Low Country had its yeoman "majority" after all.

The South Carolina Low Country was a unique place. What place, indeed, is not? But the Low Country's uniqueness did not reside in an idiosyncratic social structure. With its large black majority and its rice and long-staple cotton plantations, St. Peter's Parish exemplified the social formation long associated with the region. And if St. Peter's Parish had a white population with a yeoman majority, then there is little reason to doubt that the same was true of other coastal parishes and of interior lowcountry districts as well. The social formation that prevailed in St. Peter's Parish was not unique, and neither was that of the Low Country. Rather, it was an accentuated version of the characteristic black-belt pattern: a large black majority, a broad-based but highly unequal distribution of real wealth among free household heads, and a white population the majority of which was yeoman farmers. The stark dimensions of the social inequality that prevailed in the Low Country— the size of the black majority, the incredible wealth of the planter elite— only served to cast in bold relief the complex social web within which all black-belt yeomen were embedded.

IV

Yeomen were defined, above all else, by the social relations of the household, and particularly by the necessity of family labor. Yet as Frederick
Law Olmsted acknowledged in private correspondence, it was no easy
matter to observe the internal workings of southern households, or, as
he put it, their "domestic life." "[I] have been able no more than to
glance at the outside of things, occasionally getting peeps in through
accidental openings," he complained.[36] In a sense, historians can hope
for no more, especially when it comes to the yeomanry, who left behind
few of the texts that have allowed entrance into planter households:
diaries, account books, correspondence, pamphlets, and narratives by
former slaves, to name only the most obvious. There are, however, still a
few apertures through which the workings of yeoman households and
the production of independence can be glimpsed.

To begin with, the very process of yeoman household formation was
a complex and extended one. Most of the white men in the Low Country
acquired the much-valued status of landowner and head of independent
household over the course of a lifetime. For planters' sons it was not easy
to lay claim to that identity; for yeoman sons, the route to manhood was
an extended and difficult one indeed.[37] Judging by the census returns
for St. Peter's Parish in the late antebellum period, the route could, and
usually did, last into middle age. Even the youngest group of landholders in the parish, those who owned small farms of fewer than fifty
cultivated acres, were, on average, forty years old in 1850. By 1860 it
took longer to come into possession of a farm, no matter how modest.
More prosperous farmers, those who owned 100 to 149 acres of improved land, were older men; in 1850 and again in 1860, they were
closer to fifty years old. Clearly the yeomanry's acquisition of property
came slowly and with age. Only the wealthiest yeoman slaveholders
proved any exception to the pattern, and even though they were significantly younger than their nonslaveholding counterparts, in 1860 they
were still, on average, forty years old. (See Table 2.7.)

Yeomen knew dependence intimately. They experienced many
forms of it, not just as adolescents and young adults in their fathers'
households but in the extended period that followed between the formation of separate households, usually upon marriage, and the acquisition of title to land. The process could take more than ten years, for men
and women married, typically, at twenty-four and twenty years of age
respectively. At marriage, a moment of at least symbolic independence,
most young men (and virtually all young women) evidently left their
fathers' households, for few households included any children older

36. Beveridge and McLaughlin, eds., *Papers of Olmsted*, vol. 2, p. 213.
37. On the extended passage to manhood of planter sons see Steven M. Stowe, *Intimacy
and Power in the Old South: Ritual in the Lives of the Planters* (Baltimore: Johns Hopkins
University Press, 1987).

Table 2.7 Yeoman Households, St. Peter's Parish, Beaufort District, 1850–1860 (by farm size)

Category (Imp. Acres)	No. Households	Age Household Head	No. of Children*	Age Oldest Child	Age Youngest Child	No. Households with Others†
A. NONSLAVEHOLDING YEOMEN, 1850						
1–24	23	42.1	2.9	10.9	2.0	4
25–49	36	38.1	3.3	14.8	2.0	2
50–99	19	49.2	3.6	18.8	6.6	1
100–149	4	47.8	3.5	21.7	6.0	0
B. SLAVEHOLDING YEOMEN, 1850						
1–24	5	35.2	3.4	9.5	2.0	0
25–49	17	44.6	2.9	10.8	2.5	3
50–99	23	39.9	3.7	15.2	3.0	2
100–149	10	47.4	2.8	18.1	4.0	0
C. NONSLAVEHOLDING YEOMEN, 1860						
1–24	22	38.7	3.6	11.6	3.0	3
25–49	39	44.6	3.8	13.3	4.5	6
50–99	12	39.2	4.6	15.5	2.0	2
100–149	10	50.2	5.7	22.3	5.0	1
D. SLAVEHOLDING YEOMEN, 1860						
1–24	7	39.7	3.0	13.5	1.0	2
25–49	12	46.4	1.8	16.4	8.0	1
50–99	17	45.7	3.4	14.8	4.0	4
100–149	11	40.9	4.5	15.1	1.3	1

Source: Federal Manuscript Census, South Carolina [Beaufort District], Schedules of Population, Slaves and Agriculture, 1850, 1860.

*Neither the 1850 nor the 1860 census records the relationships of household members. This category therefore represents those household members with the same surname who were neither the household head nor the spouse. Some were clearly relatives rather than members of the immediate family, but the figure provides a reasonable estimate.

†This category indicates the number of households containing at least one individual with a different surname than that of the household head.

than twenty-two years of age. Very few of those young married men could expect to own land immediately, however. Of the twenty couples who married in St. Peter's Parish in 1859, only four already owned land, and two of the bridegrooms were wealthy widowers, while another was a young merchant and physician, obviously a planter's son. Only one could have been a yeoman farmer. The other sixteen bridegrooms owned no land whatsoever but had established separate households nonetheless in various capacities as overseers, farm laborers, tenants, or farmers on their fathers' land. It was not uncommon for those who would ultimately own their own farms to suffer through a period of tenancy, renting land from local planters and other yeomen, as did the man who "cropped" on the small Barnwell farm that belonged to widow Low and her daughters.[38] Such men could at least function as family farmers of sorts, appearing on the census not infrequently as if they owned, rather than rented, the land on which they lived. Others were forced into more explicitly dependent positions. Political rhetoric aside, lowcountry planters' account books make it abundantly clear that white men provided all manner of hired labor on plantations, from overseeing the entire operation or assisting a head overseer on an annual contract to taking on laboring jobs on a seasonal basis to building and repairing fences for a daily wage.[39] Through a variety of strategies, then, yeomen negotiated the dangerous distance between household formation and the acquisition of title to land by purchase, inheritance, or, as is likely, a combination of the two. And while it is difficult to know precisely how the yeomanry reproduced itself as a social class, the relationship between age, wealth, and the composition of the household points to one crucial dimension of the process. A man's claim to land, and to greater amounts of it, increased not with his age so much as with the number and age of his dependents.

38. Age at marriage statistics and propertied status of newly married couples was derived from the Federal Manuscript Census, South Carolina [Beaufort District], Schedule of Population, 1860; John H. Cornish Diary, January 9, 1847, SHC.

39. With respect to the variety of labor white men performed on plantations and the range of contract or wage terms on which they did it, the best single source is Anonymous, Plantation Journal, "Fair Mount" Plantation, Barnwell District, January 15, 1839 (hired overseer, apparently on annual contract), May 14, 1839 (hired man to dig well), January 7, 1840 (hired laborer to make fence), March 26, 1840 (hired neighbor on as hand, apparently seasonally), SCL. For one intriguing but unusual example of a white laborer hired to work in the fields alongside slaves, see James Vidal to Mr. H. Cranston, Charleston, August 16, 1850, Cranston Family Papers, SCHS. Louis Manigault hired both an overseer and a "sub overseer." See Louis Manigault to his Father, Gowrie, January 8, 1854, February 27, 1854, Louis Manigault Papers, Perkins Library, DU. For examples of the terms of overseers' contracts, see Joseph Palmer, Account Book, January 1, 1827, n.d. [1829], SCL; Receipt of Seth Dupuis, January 1, 1846, Lawton Family Papers, SCL; John Berkley Grimball Diary, November 23, 1832, November 26, 1832, SHC. And for insights into the character of relations between planters and yeoman overseers, see Robert Marshall to Col. Richard Manning, November 29, 1824, Williams-Chesnut-Manning Families Papers, SCL; John Berkley Grimball Diary, December 7, 1832, July 4, 1834, November 28, 1855.

In yeoman households most dependents were, by definition, family members, but even those households that included slaves evinced the same basic pattern. The more children a man had and the older they were, the greater the amount of land he cultivated. (See Table 2.7.) The logic was unmistakable. On family farms, children were "flesh, blood, and labor supply."[40] So, in an even more literal sense, were wives, for few kinds of labor were more important to the yeoman household economy than women's reproductive labor. The predominantly agricultural slave states of the South persisted in more traditional demographic patterns even as the birth rate was dropping dramatically in the increasingly urban free-labor states of the Northeast. While bourgeois women in the North employed a variety of birth control practices to reduce the number of children they bore from an average of 6.4 to 4.9 between 1800 and 1850 and in the next generation to a thoroughly modern 2.9 children per family, southern white women continued to bear large numbers of children until the end of the nineteenth century, when an average family still had six.[41] Family strategy, and the gender relations and ideologies that undergirded it, were, in both cases, crucial to class formation and reproduction. The imperatives, however, could not have been more distinct. The emergence and consolidation of bourgeois society in the Northeast demanded fewer children and a more extended (and thus a more labor- and capital-intensive) upbringing, while the reproduction of slave society continued to demand large numbers of children for agricultural labor on plantations and family farms.[42] In the yeoman households of the South Carolina Low Country, the reproductive labor of wives, and in some cases that of slave women, paved the route to household independence.

40. Mary P. Ryan, *Cradle of the Middle Class: The Family in Oneida County, New York, 1790–1865* (New York: Cambridge University Press, 1981), p. 26.

41. J. Potter, "The Growth of Population in America, 1700–1860," in D. V. Glass and D. E. C. Eversley, eds., *Population in History: Essays in Historical Demography* (London: Edward Arnold Ltd, 1965), pp. 631–88; Judith Walzer Leavitt, "Under the Shadow of Maternity: American Women's Responses to Death and Debility Fears in Nineteenth-Century Childbirth," *Feminist Studies* 12, no. 1 (Spring 1986), pp. 129–54; Robert V. Wells, *Revolutions in Americans' Lives: A Demographic Perspective on the History of the Americans, Their Families, and Their Society* (Westport, Conn.: Greenwood Press, 1982), pp. 91–149; Robert V. Wells, "Women's Lives Transformed: Demographic and Family Patterns in America, 1600–1970," in Carol Ruth Berkin and Mary Beth Norton, eds., *Women of America: A History* (Boston: Houghton Mifflin, 1979), pp. 16–37. Dates cited refer to women who married within those years.

42. The best single source on bourgeois family strategy remains Ryan, *Cradle of the Middle Class*, pp. 54–59 and passim. See also Jeanne Boydston, *Home and Work: Housework, Wages, and the Ideology of Labor in the Early Republic* (New York: Oxford University Press, 1990). On the family strategy of southern yeomen and their attempts to establish the next generation as independent farmers, see Hahn, *Roots of Southern Populism*, pp. 47–48 and passim.

On birth control and the increasing role of surgical abortion in the antebellum Northeast, see James C. Mohr, *Abortion in America: The Origins and Evolution of National Policy, 1800–1900* (New York, 1978), and the classic essay by Carroll Smith-Rosenberg, "The

It could not have been otherwise. The productive capabilities of every yeoman farmer, but most obviously those who did not own slaves, were framed by the particular logic of land and labor that prevailed on family farms. In St. Peter's Parish, those who owned small farms had fewer and younger children than their more prosperous neighbors. In 1850 men who cultivated fewer than fifty improved acres and who were about forty years old had, typically, three children, the youngest of whom was a toddler about two years old and the oldest, at best, an adolescent, eleven to fifteen years old. By contrast, those yeomen who owned the largest farms (100–149 improved acres) and who were closer to fifty years old had, on average, four children, the youngest of whom was about six and the oldest, twenty-two. The pattern was intensified in 1860 as the disparity in both the number of children and the age of the eldest increased even further. Without slaves, yeoman farmers headed households in which the number of dependents increased only as they grew older. And since family members provided the only labor, with the possible exception of slaves hired sporadically to work on their own time, it is not surprising that young men with young families cultivated small farms and that they slowly expanded acreage as their children grew up and contributed more labor. Beginning with the wife, the possibility of household independence grew in direct proportion to the number of dependents the household head commanded.

The same was true of yeoman slaveholders, except, of course, that their dependents were not exclusively family members. Among their ranks the same hierarchy prevailed. The most prosperous farmers, those who cultivated the most land, had the greatest number of children and the oldest ones. This was itself powerful evidence that they were still, despite the ownership of slaves, bound by the land and labor logic of family farms. The difference, then, was one of degree, not kind. Nonetheless, while the majority of yeoman slaveholders owned fewer than five slaves, only two of whom were likely to have been adults, the labor provided did make a difference, especially for those with young families, in the amount of land they could cultivate. Although the pattern is by no means consistent, on the whole slaveholding yeomen had larger numbers of dependents, commanded more labor, and operated larger farms than their nonslaveholding counterparts of the same age. (See Table 2.7.) In the most literal sense, then, for yeomen no less than for planters, independence was produced out of the customary relations of power and dependency that prevailed within the household.

Abortion Movement and the AMA, 1850–1880," in her *Disorderly Conduct: Visions of Gender in Victorian America* (New York: Oxford University Press, 1985), pp. 217–44. On women's knowledge of mechanical and herbal contraceptive practices in the rural South, see Charles Rosenberg, ed., *Gunn's Domestic Medicine* (Knoxville: University of Tennessee Press, 1986), especially the introduction and pp. 291–320, and Lewis E. Atherton, *The Southern Country Store, 1800–1860* (Baton Rouge: Louisiana State University Press, 1949), pp. 66–84.

But if the command of dependents established the yeomanry's claim to independence and to its attendant rights at home and abroad, then the distinctions between nonslaveholding and slaveholding yeomen point as well to the social inequality that those same relations embedded at the heart of lowcountry society. For in terms both of the number and the kind of dependents they governed, the power of yeoman masters was no match for that of their planter neighbors. The characteristic inequalities of southern society thus were rooted in the household itself, confounding customary divisions between public and private spheres. Within the boundaries of the household, however, on their own land, in daily governance of wives, children, and, in some cases, slaves, yeomen both produced the material basis of independence and practiced its considerable prerogatives.

V

Having successfully negotiated the path to manhood, yeomen understandably practiced a cautious kind of household economy designed to protect their hard-won independence and to enhance their chances of reproducing it in the next generation. It is difficult to know the daily substance of that economy and especially the division of labor around which it was organized. But the ossified statistical remnants of yeoman households (the census records of social composition, farm value, crop mix, and agricultural production) do retain significant traces of the workings of once vibrant farm households, or at least of the face they turned to the world outside the fence.

Take Abner Ginn, for example.[43] Ginn was a fifty-four-year-old farmer who lived with his wife and nine children near Nix Crossroads in the middle part of St. Peter's Parish in Beaufort District, about nine miles from where he was born. His was a yeoman settlement in the high land of the Coosawhatchie Swamp, and many of his neighbors—Longs, Smiths, Allens, and Stones—were "self-working farmers" like himself. Others, however, such as Edmund Martin, were scions of the South's richest planter families who lived in one of the many plantation settlements that dotted the river nearby. Also fifty-four years old, Edmund Martin was head of a household that included 250 slaves in addition to his six children. His land alone was worth thirty thousand dollars in 1850. Ginn's entire 560-acre farm, by contrast, was worth only about

43. The case of Abner Ginn is drawn from the following sources: Claim of Abner Ginn, Beaufort, SCCR, RG 217, File #10076; Claim of Elizabeth Airs, Beaufort, SCCR, RG 217, File #9364; Claim of Joseph Rosier, Beaufort, SCCR, RG 217, File #5671. The evidence from the Southern Claims Commission Records was supplemented with data on Ginn and his neighbors drawn from the Federal Manuscript Census, South Carolina [Beaufort District], Schedules of Population, Slaves, and Agriculture, 1850 and 1860, NA.

$1,000, for most of the land was unimproved wood and swampland used to forage cattle. He had managed to clear and cultivate only sixty acres of it by 1850. The record of Ginn's farming operation contained in a number of different sources is an interesting one, for it suggests the broad outlines of the productive strategy lowcountry yeomen typically pursued, and it hints at the division of labor on which it was based.

Abner Ginn never owned slaves, but like other nonslaveholders in the neighborhood he often hired a slave man to work on his off-time, splitting rails, digging fence posts, cutting shingles, or doing whatever else needed to be done. When, for example, Ginn hired James Ruth, a slave who lived two miles away on the plantation of his master, Nathaniel Ruth, Ruth would walk into the swamp on Saturday night and work on Ginn's place on Saturday night and Sunday.[44] But for his daily work-force, Abner Ginn could count only on himself, his wife, and his children. And since six of their children were still under ten years of age in 1850, the burden of the labor fell on the parents, their two adult daughters, and their sixteen-year-old son, the only person Ginn formally counted as a laborer when he reported his affairs to the census taker. The gender division of labor thus must have been an interesting one, indeed. With no slaves and only one adolescent son, Ginn had little choice but to rely on his wife and eldest daughters to help him run the three plows he regularly employed on the farm. Although the particular arrangements have to remain a matter of speculation, by dint of hard work Ginn and his family managed to produce the basic subsistence requirements of the household and a modest surplus for market.

The Ginn's did not live high off the hog. Their foodcrops, although plentiful, were not very diversified. Lowcountry yeomen stuck to basics. In 1850 Ginn grew three hundred bushels of corn and one hundred bushels of sweet potatoes, no small feat given the low yields common on his predominantly sandy soil.[45] He grew no wheat or rye, peas or beans, no Irish potatoes and apparently no fruit, although he did produce twenty pounds of butter and some homemade sugar and syrup. He took full advantage of the rich swampland that encompassed his little farm, however, and like many of his neighbors ranged sizable herds of live-stock, including twenty-five beef cattle and seventy-five swine, as well as the fifteen dairy cows from which, presumably, he got buttermilk. The

---

44. The Southern Claims Commission Records are, as some historians have already acknowledged, a rich source of information about the informal economy of southern slave society. To my knowledge, however, slaves' sale of their labor to local yeoman farmers remains a largely unexplored dimension of that informal economy. See, for example, Philip D. Morgan, "The Ownership of Property by Slaves in the Mid-Nineteenth Century Low Country," *Journal of Southern History* 49, no. 3 (1983), pp. 399–434; Philip D. Morgan, "Work and Culture: The Task System and the World of Low Country Blacks, 1700–1880," *William and Mary Quarterly*, 3d series, vol. 39 (October 1982), pp. 563–93.

45. On yields per acre in the Low Country, see Marjorie S. Mendenhall, "A History of Agriculture in South Carolina, 1790–1860: An Economic and Social Study" (Ph.D. Diss., University of North Carolina, 1940), p. 57.

corn, sweet potatoes, pork, and, to a lesser extent, beef were the staples of the Ginn family diet and household economy. Food crops were the obvious priority in this household, although, like most nonslaveholding yeomen in the Low Country, Ginn did grow a little cotton in 1850—two bales, to be precise.[46]

Ginn's experience typified another pattern of lowcountry yeomen: He became wealthier as he aged or, more accurately, as his children aged, provided more labor, and permitted him to bring more land into cultivation. During the 1850s Ginn expanded production considerably. He improved another forty acres and diversified his crop selection a little, adding wheat, rye, and even rice to the mix, a luxury facilitated, no doubt, by the additional acreage. He also diversified his livestock holdings, reducing the number of cattle and swine but adding three horses, which made the value of his livestock at $1,140 nearly equal to the value of the land. Sometime during the decade Ginn made an important purchase, a bay stallion worth three hundred dollars, which, as he would later explain, he "seldom used for work, but stood around the neighborhood in the seasons and made from two hundred to three hundred dollars and more too." Of such small steps was social mobility made in yeoman settlements.

By 1860, with the additional land and labor, Ginn also expanded his acreage in cotton and produced three bales instead of two. This was an exceedingly modest cotton crop, especially in the Low Country, but one fairly typical of nonslaveholders. Slaveholding yeomen usually produced more cotton, but then they had both more labor and, usually, more land. Ginn's neighbor William Airs, who owned nine slaves and worked 130 acres, produced four bales of cotton in 1850; a decade later, after purchasing an additional slave, he produced eleven bales. With ten slaves in 1860, Airs also raised a substantial rice crop (fifty-four bushels), suggesting that he was one of the few yeoman slaveholders who made it into the ranks of the region's class of small planters. Few yeomen, nonslaveholders or otherwise, ever grew that much cotton or rice, but, like Abner Ginn, the vast majority of them did grow some of each. Most of the products of Ginn's farm were probably consumed by his large family, but some doubtless found their way to market: most, but not necessarily all, of the cotton, along with an assortment of other surplus products, from lard, corn, beef, butter, and chickens to feathers, hides, shingles, and homespun cloth or "jeans," as it was sometimes called.

Abner Ginn's strategy was fairly clear. By combining a primary commitment to self-sufficiency in basic foodstuffs with a modest investment in staple crops, he attempted to meet most of the subsistence needs of the household from its own production. The strategy worked. Ginn not only held onto his land in the last antebellum decade but increased the

46. On the diet of southern yeomen, see Sam Bowers Hilliard, *Hog Meat and Hoecake: Food Supply in the Old South* (Carbondale: Southern Illinois University Press, 1972).

production and the value of the farm, as well. Long years of effort had
made him by 1860 what one local planter later called "a well-off poor
man" and secured his place, and perhaps that of his son, as one of the
"hard-working yeomanry of the South." As the record suggests, the
credit did not go exclusively to this "self-working farmer."

Ginn's strategy was not unique but was pursued by his yeoman neighbors in the Coosawhatchie settlement and by his counterparts throughout the Low Country. Like Abner Ginn, they were not averse to producing for the market. Every yeoman household participated in informal
local exchange networks with other yeoman and planters, as well as in
more formal exchange relations with merchants. But they did subordinate crops grown primarily for market to food crops in their production
priorities, and they aspired to self-sufficiency in an effort to avoid incur-
ring debts they could not repay.[47] Maintaining the household required
regular forays into the marketplace, if only to make the money to pay
the taxman. But caution was exercised to ensure that whatever happened, whether cotton and rice sold high or low, whether corn and pork
were cheap or dear, the household's basic needs would be met and the
land itself kept beyond the reach of the sheriff's hammer.

To this end, lowcountry yeomen committed significantly more of
their limited resources in land and labor to foodcrops than to cotton or
other staple crops. Indeed, surprising as it might seem in a region that
had been in the grip of world staple markets since the middle of the
eighteenth century, lowcountry yeomen grew proportionately more
food and less cotton than their upcountry counterparts.[48] Every yeoman
farmer grew substantial amounts of corn, and the size of the crop increased, as one would expect, with the size of the farm. Thus, small
farmers who had fewer than 50 improved acres grew, on average, 173
bushels of corn, while those who had 100 to 149 improved acres grew,
on average, 435 bushels. The same was true of sweet potatoes, the other
basic food crop. Together these crops did not equal in absolute terms the
quantity produced by yeomen on comparable farms in the Upcountry,
and the latter produced a greater variety of grains and vegetables in
addition. But lowcountry farmers' crop mix had its own regional characteristics, notably far larger herds of livestock and a little of the pearly
grain that had made the Low Country rich and famous. (See Table 2.8.)

Like Abner Ginn, most yeomen took advantage of the vast expanses
of unimproved and unenclosed land to range large herds of swine,
cattle, and sheep. Upcountry yeomen's swine herds averaged about
twenty-five head. In the Low Country, even the poorest yeomen with
holdings of fewer than fifty acres had herds roughly that size (they had,
on average, twenty-four hogs), and the herds got bigger as farmers got

47. In other words, lowcountry yeomen practiced a version of the "safety-first" farming analyzed by Gavin Wright. See Wright, *Political Economy of the Cotton South*, pp. 55–88.

48. For the upcountry comparison to the data that follow, see Ford, *Origins of Southern
Radicalism*, pp. 59, 70–78.

Table 2.8 Agricultural Production on Yeoman Farms,
St. Peter's Parish, Beaufort District, 1850
(mean values)

Category	Farm Size by Improved Acres		
	1–49	*50–99*	*100–149*
Number of farms	81	42	14
Bales of cotton	1.1	2.1	6.1
Pounds of rice	1118.6	1260.7	3159.6
Bushels of corn	173.0	244.2	434.6
Bushels of sweet potatoes	108.6	118.5	275.0
Number of swine	24.0	45.0	53.9

Source: Federal Manuscript Census, South Carolina [Beaufort District], Schedules of Slaves and Agriculture, 1850.

wealthier. Thus, farmers with fifty to ninety-nine improved acres had, typically, herds of forty-five hogs in 1850, and the most prosperous yeomen had slightly more (fifty-four on average). Obviously, lowcountry yeomen made the most of their customary right to use the rich and extensive swamp and forest land that surrounded their settlements, and the herds of livestock the range supported contributed significantly to their efforts at self-sufficiency.[49]

Perhaps the most striking thing about lowcountry yeomen's farming operations, however, was the frequency with which they grew rice, a notoriously, or so it is usually assumed, labor- and capital-intensive crop. About half of all yeoman households grew some rice. Big farmers were more likely to grow it, but a surprising 45 percent of even the smallest farm households did so as well. In fact, on both the largest and the smallest farms yeomen grew rice as frequently as cotton. The size of the crop increased with the size of the farm, from twenty-four bushels on the smallest ones to a considerable ninety-two bushels on the largest. And while rice was certainly no match for corn, the remarkable thing is that so many households grew any at all.

Rice, after all, was a plantation crop, raised explicitly for export by a very select group of planters on the most expensive land in the region. To a far greater extent than with cotton, the commercial production of rice was a capital-intensive process, involving the labor costs of building and maintaining an elaborate system of trunks and ditches to control the flow of water over the fields.[50] Yeomen could not possibly have grown

49. For the upcountry comparison, see Ford, *Origins of Southern Radicalism*, Table 2.9, p. 59.

50. On lowcountry rice production, see Coclanis, *Shadow of a Dream;* Dale E. Swan, *Structure and Profitability of the Antebellum Rice Industry* (New York: Arno Press, 1975); David Doar, *Rice and Rice Planting in the South Carolina Low Country* (Charleston: The Charleston Museum, 1936); R. F. W. Allston, "Sea-Coast Crops of the South," *De Bow's Review* 16 (June 1854), pp. 589–615.

rice by this method, and by all indications they did not. Instead, they probably sowed it in inland swamps or used one of the various dry rice cultivation methods, both of which methods yielded less and inferior-quality grain, not competitive in the international marketplace but perfectly adequate for home consumption.[51] There are other indications that yeomen grew rice primarily as a foodstuff, including their small share of the region's total crop (5%) and the lack of comparison between the amount of rice grown by even the biggest slaveholding yeomen producers (a not inconsiderable 91 bushels) and that grown by small planters (a markedly greater 1,391 bushels).[52] While they may have traded rice among themselves or perhaps sold it to local planters for slave provisions, the rice grown on yeoman farms was produced primarily for consumption within the household.

The particular crop mix of corn, sweet potatoes, and rice, combined with large herds of hogs and beef cattle, made self-sufficiency a real possibility for all yeoman farmers, nonslaveholders as well as slaveholders. Farms of every size produced sufficient grain on average to meet the needs of household members, and most produced a modest surplus that presumably found its way to market in one form or another. Nonslaveholders produced more grain per capita than slaveholders, although the latter also produced enough on average to meet basic subsistence needs.[53] (See Table 2.9.)

For individual farmers, however, self-sufficiency was much more difficult to accomplish, at least if current econometric standards are any measure. Despite the fact that the smallest farmers devoted more of their scarce acreage to grain, only 43 percent attained self-sufficiency. Larger farmers did not do noticeably better: Only 48 percent of those who cultivated 100 to 149 acres met the goal. It was not slaveholding that made the difference, moreover, for nonslaveholders were considerably more likely to be self-sufficient in grain than either those who owned five or fewer slaves or those who owned between six and nine.[54] That only about half of lowcountry yeomen actually reached self-sufficiency in any given year reflected both the choices of individual household heads and the challenges they all faced in feeding large families on small holdings. The rate of success they did have, however, came close to that of their counterparts in the plantation districts of the Upcountry and

51. On dry rice cultivation, see Gray, *History of Agriculture,* vol. 1, pp. 279–81.

52. See Appendix, Table III.

53. For the method used to calculate rates of self-sufficiency, see the Appendix. Measures of self-sufficiency, it should be pointed out, are crude indications only. Complications in the reporting of rice production by census takers in 1860 preclude calculation of rates of self-sufficiency for that census year.

54. Rates of self-sufficiency by slaveholding are as follows: 0 slaves—54 percent; 1–5 slaves—36 percent; 6–9 slaves—45 percent; 10–20 slaves—13.8 percent; 21–50 slaves—9 percent; 51–100 slaves—12.6 percent; 101+ slaves—9.5 percent.

Table 2.9 Self-Sufficiency of Farms and Plantations,
St. Peter's Parish, Beaufort District, 1850

Category (Imp. Acres)	Number of Farms	Mean Food Production Per Capita*	% Self Sufficient†
1–49	83	24.9	43
50–99	49	24.9	39
100–149	30	24.4	47
All yeomen‡	162	24.8	43
150–199	64	14.3	20
300–499	44	13.5	16
500+	39	11.6	15
All planters	147	13.1	18

Source: Federal Manuscript Census, South Carolina [Beaufort District], Schedules of Population, Slaves and Agriculture, 1850.

*Represents corn bushel equivalents.

†Percentage of farms and plantations producing more than twenty corn bushel equivalents per capita. Calculation includes all of the rice crop for yeoman farms and 10 percent of the rice crop for plantations.

‡Includes several farms with more than nine slaves.

might well have matched it, since lowcountry yeomen were more likely to have achieved self-sufficiency in meat as well.[55] While success was by no means assured, yeoman farmers in the Low Country pursued a productive strategy that privileged food crops in pursuit of household self-sufficiency.

The cost of that strategy was immediately apparent. Most, although by no means all, yeomen grew some cotton. But they typically produced very small amounts, confirming that their priorities lay elsewhere. Cotton was the only crop grown primarily for market on yeoman farms, and farmers approached its cultivation with considerable caution. Although the caution was most pronounced among those whose resources were most scarce, all lowcountry yeomen grew less cotton in absolute and proportional terms than their counterparts in the plantation districts of the Upcountry.

To start with, a surprisingly small proportion of lowcountry yeomen grew any cotton at all. Almost 90 percent of yeomen in the lower piedmont districts of the Upcountry ventured into the cotton market, but only about 65 percent of lowcountry farmers took the chance in 1850. And those who did hedged their bets more vigilantly. While in 1850 nonslaveholding farmers in lower piedmont districts like Abbeville usu-

55. For the upcountry comparison, see Ford, *Origins of Southern Radicalism*, p. 77. Lowcountry yeomen did not, however, match the impressive rates of self-sufficiency (about 75 percent for slaveless farmers) reported by Steven Hahn for their counterparts in the Georgia Upcountry. See Hahn, *Roots of Southern Populism*, p. 32.

Table 2.10 Cotton Production
of Yeoman Slaveholders and
Nonslaveholders, St. Peter's Parish,
Beaufort District, 1850–1860

	Cotton Bales/Farm	
Number of Slaves	*1850*	*1860*
0	1.1	2.4
1–4	3.0	4.1
5–9	7.2	13.3
Totals	2.5	4.8
Number of farms	154	112

Source: Federal Manuscript Census, South Carolina
[Beaufort District], Schedules of Slaves and Agriculture, 1850, 1860.

ally produced about three bales annually, their counterparts in St. Peter's Parish produced only one. In both regions farmers expanded production of cotton as their means permitted, although in this case it was
the availability of labor, particularly slave labor, and not land that made
the difference. Slaveholding yeomen not only grew more cotton than
nonslaveholders—an average 4.3 bales compared to 1.2 in 1850—but
the largest slaveholders grew even greater amounts. Farmers who
owned five or fewer slaves produced an average cotton crop of three
bales; those who owned between six and nine slaves, grew more than
seven bales. The extent of their involvement in the cotton market was
the single most striking distinction between nonslaveholding and slaveholding yeomen in the Low Country. Perhaps the investment in slaves
and, in some cases, the debt incurred thereby, could be justified only by
a tangible return in a cash crop. But interestingly, even the cotton crops
of slaveholding yeomen did not match those of their upcountry counterparts, for there small slaveholders (1–5 slaves) grew an average of four
bales and the largest yeoman slaveholders (6–9 slaves) grew an impressive eleven bales.[56] (See Table 2.10.)

In the end, most lowcountry yeomen made the safest choice and
grew more food.[57] (See Table 2.11.) Among a class of farmers known for
their cautious approach to the marketplace, lowcountry yeomen distinguished themselves by the conservatism of their household economy.

They maintained that strategy, although with some modification,

56. For the figures on cotton production in Abbeville District, see Ford, *Origins of
Southern Radicalism*, pp. 70–72.

57. For the method of calculating the cotton-corn ratio, see the Appendix. In virtually
every part of the Upcountry, yeoman devoted more of their resources to cotton than did
their lowcountry counterparts. See Ford, *Origins of Southern Radicalism,* p. 77.

Table 2.11 Cotton/Corn Ratios
on Yeoman Farms, St. Peter's Parish,
Beaufort District, 1850–1860

Category (Imp. Acres)	1850*	1860*
1–24	1.7	0.6
25–49	3.0	2.1
50–99	3.2	5.2
100–149	6.7	8.2
Totals	4.5	5.2

Source: Federal Manuscript Census, South Carolina [Beaufort District], Schedules of Agriculture, 1850, 1860.

*Represents a ratio of pounds of cotton to bushels of corn based on an estimate of 400 pounds to the bale of cotton.

during the decade of the 1850s, as they attempted to respond to the opportunities and inevitable dangers presented by the soaring price of cotton. The poorest yeoman farmers found it impossible to seize the main chance. They had not the land, the labor, nor apparently the inclination to risk all in the cotton market. Thus, farmers who owned more than fifty acres of improved land increased the proportion of their acreage devoted to cotton, while those with fewer than fifty acres actually reduced theirs and concentrated more on food crops. In lieu, presumably, of cotton, they diversified their grain and vegetable crops, adding rice and growing more peas and beans. And for reasons that are unclear, all yeomen reduced the size of their herds, especially swine, during the 1850s, although larger farmers made the most dramatic shift away from livestock.[58]

Neither in 1850 nor 1860 were yeoman farmers' productive strategies premised on hostility to the marketplace. After all, they steadily increased investment in market crops, notably cotton, as their limited resources in land and labor permitted. Rather, it seems that they attempted to harness market opportunities to their own ends, making a priority not of cash income but of the production and reproduction of household independence more generally construed.[59] In calculating the

58. See Appendix, Table III.

59. There is no necessary contradiction between aspirations to self-sufficiency and limited market engagement. As Florencia Mallon has argued with respect to the persistence of the peasant economy in the Peruvian highlands, a cautious deployment of new forms of market activity (such as labor in the mines) sustained independent household production and staved off the domination of capital, foreign and domestic. See Mallon, *The Defense of Community in Peru's Central Highlands: Peasant Struggle and Capitalist Transition, 1860–1940* (Princeton, N.J.: Princeton University Press, 1983).

annual crop mix, they provided first and generously for subsistence and marketed, quite literally, the surplus produce. Virtually everything produced in yeoman households, including cotton, was simultaneously a subsistence and a market crop: Corn, pork, and rice could be eaten or traded; cotton could be ginned and sold or carded, spun, woven, and sewn into work clothes, curtains, mattress covers, bolts of "jeans cloth," or cotton-picking bags. Yeomen thus participated in a number of different market networks, from the lively local provisions markets (created by the almost certain failure of regional and especially plantation self-sufficiency) on the one hand to the international cotton market on the other.[60] Cotton was not the sole measure of the yeomanry's market engagement. By "safety-first farming" lowcountry yeomen, like their counterparts throughout the South, sought less to avoid the market than to retain some control over their engagement in it and, ultimately, to limit their dependence on it.

Their ability to do so owed in no small measure to the nature of the market in slave society. In the slave South the relations of production, reproduction, and consumption were all contained within independent households. Labor power was not a commodity exchanged for a wage in the marketplace, as it was rapidly becoming in the Northeast. Southern households, as a consequence, could more successfully forestall the penetration of market relations and the attendant reconfiguration of social relations than could households in the free labor states. Just as planters' interest in the inviolability of household boundaries provided yeomen unassailable ground on which to protect their own integrity as masters, so did the particular limits slavery placed on the emergence of market society buttress the fragile independence of yeoman households.[61]

60. Levels of food production on lowcountry plantations were woefully low, although no measure could claim accuracy without including the products of slaves' provision grounds. See Table 2.9 in text and Appendix, Table III, for estimates. It is almost certainly the case that lowcountry plantations provided a market for foodcrops of local and extra-regional origin, contrary to the argument of Robert E. Gallman and others; thus, the South Carolina Low Country provides an interesting case in the debate over regional self-sufficiency in the cotton South and the extent of the southern market in foodstuffs. See Robert E. Gallman, "Self-Sufficiency in the Cotton Economy of the Antebellum South, " *Agricultural History* 44, no. 1 (January 1970), pp. 5–23; Raymond C. Battaglio and John Kagel, "The Structure of Antebellum Southern Agriculture: South Carolina, A Case Study," *Agricultural History* 44, no. 1 (January 1970), pp. 25–37. Their critics include Diane Lindstrom, "Southern Dependence Upon Interregional Grain Supplies: A Review of the Trade Flows, 1840–1860," *Agricultural History* 44, no. 1 (January 1970), pp. 101–13; Stanley L. Engerman, "The Antebellum South: What Probably Was and What Should Have Been," *Agricultural History* 44, no. 1 (January 1970), pp. 127–42; Eugene D. Genovese, *The Political Economy of Slavery: Studies in the Economy and Society of the Slave South* (New York: Vintage Books, 1965), pp. 124–53; and Eugene D. Genovese, "Commentary: A Historian's View," *Agricultural History* 44, no. 1 (January 1970), pp. 143–47. The market relations of yeoman farmers will be treated more fully in the following chapter.

61. Part of a larger debate over the transition to capitalism in the United States, the particular debate over the precapitalist or capitalist nature of the economy and society of the slave South was a fabulously productive one in time and place. It has, however, become

The only meaningful measure of success was, of course, holding onto the farm. That became increasingly difficult in the 1850s as the Low Country, like the rest of the South, underwent a marked concentration of wealth in land and slaves. The effects on the yeomanry in St. Peter's Parish were twofold. Significant numbers of yeoman families left the parish during the decade, with the poorest most likely to leave. But of those who stayed the great majority managed to hold onto their land, and some, like Abner Ginn, even managed to get ahead.

Persistence rates in the parish were comparable to the rest of the plantation South, with three of ten individuals and almost eight of ten families remaining from 1850 to 1860. Wealth had everything to do with who stayed and who moved on. Almost half of the richest planters were still in the parish ten years later, but fewer than a quarter of landless men remained. Yeomen occupied a middle ground. Between one-quarter and one-half of them remained in the parish throughout the decade, and the likelihood of their doing so increased as their property holdings increased. Among those yeomen who did remain and whose households can be traced over the decade, the poorest (those with fewer than twenty-five acres) struggled and often failed (more than half lost title to their land), but fully eight out of ten held onto their land, and about half even added to their holdings. For yeomen in this lowcountry parish, mobility into the ranks of the planter class was about as common as snow in September. Only one man, and he was probably a planter's son, made such a move during the 1850s. Yeomen had to settle for more modest gains. Two out of every ten increased their holdings in slaves, and a handful, like Ginn's neighbor William Airs, who started the decade with seven or eight slaves, acquired the few more that moved them into the ranks of small planters.[62] For the most part, however, the suc-

---

stalemated, mired in fundamental and irresolvable political and ideological disagreements over the definition of capitalism itself and, particularly, the centrality of free labor to any society historically called capitalist. My views should be clear. For major contributions to the debate in its southern context, see Genovese, *The Political Economy of Slavery*, and, with Elizabeth Fox-Genovese, *The Fruits of Merchant Capital: Slavery and Bourgeois Property in the Rise and Expansion of Capitalism* (New York: Oxford University Press, 1983); Robert W. Fogel and Stanley L. Engerman, *Time on the Cross: The Economics of American Negro Slavery*, 2 vols. (Boston: Little, Brown, 1974); Hahn, *Roots of Southern Populism;* James Oakes, *The Ruling Race: A History of American Slaveholders* (New York: Vintage Books, 1982); Barbara Fields, *Slavery and Freedom on the Middle Ground: Maryland During the Nineteenth Century* (New Haven: Yale University Press, 1985); Elizabeth Fox-Genovese, *Within the Plantation Household: Black and White Women of the Old South* (Chapel Hill: University of North Carolina Press, 1988); Ford, *Origins of Southern Radicalism.*

62. See Appendix, Table IV. For persistence and social mobility rates in other parts of the South, see Linden, "Economic Democracy in the Slave South," pp. 174–84, and Hahn, *Roots of Southern Populism*, pp. 16, 47. For the Low Country in the early antebellum period, see Mark D. Kaplanoff, "Making the South Solid: Politics and the Structure of Society in South Carolina, 1790–1815" (Ph.D. Diss., University of Cambridge, 1979), pp. 22, 43. The lowcountry planter elite had the highest persistence rate in North America in the nineteenth century.

cess they achieved was the one for which they planned: to hold onto the farm, to increase its size and value, and, in the best possible world, to establish the next generation of yeoman farmers. With reasonable prospects of success, self-working farmers went about the work of producing independence.

VI

"Self-working farmer." That was the face lowcountry yeomen turned to the world beyond the fence. But it was only one profile of yeoman household economy, inseparable from the other, domestic, one. Infinitely harder to see, the domestic face turned into the household where the daily work of independence was conducted. Abner Ginn and his neighbors were not really "self-working farmers." On the contrary, the very term expressed their successful appropriation of the labor of others: the women, children, and, sometimes, slaves who peopled their households and tilled their fields. The vitality of male independence that characterized the public sphere of marketplace and ballot box was tied intimately to the legal and customary dependencies of the household.[63] Dependence was the stuff of which independence—and manhood— were made.

In yeoman households, familial and productive relations were virtually indistinguishable, and both were defined by a series of dependencies that subordinated all members to the male head. Any number of factors shaped the particular configuration of labor, including, as we have seen, the total number of household members, their sex and age, the stage in the family lifecycle, and the presence of slaves, whether hired or owned, and their sex and age. But in yeoman households the work done by wives, sons, and daughters was, by definition, crucial to the calculus of production. Even the ownership of slaves did not change the predominantly familial character of household economy. Thus, while relations between masters and slaves were part of the social dynamics of a substantial minority of yeoman households, the relations of domination and subordination characteristic of every household were, in fact, those between the sexes. Gender was thus a primary axis of power in yeoman households. It undergirded the material production of independence and framed its political meanings as well.

Abner Ginn's story hinted at the importance of women's work and at its unorthodox sphere in yeoman households. Travelers underlined the point in their shock at the discomfort and apparent disorder of yeoman homes and their disapproval of a gender division of labor that seemed to

---

63. For one study that explores the relationship between domestic hierarchies and public, political ones, see Allen Tullos, *Habits of Industry: White Culture and the Transformation of the Carolina Piedmont* (Chapel Hill: University of North Carolina Press, 1989).

weigh unnaturally on women. The bourgeois assumptions embedded in, for example, Olmsted's perspective reveal a great deal more about him than his yeoman subjects, but they do serve the purpose of dramatizing sectional difference, historicizing women's work, and cautioning against acceptance of the still powerful universal claims of bourgeois gender ideology or domesticity.

Olmsted had more than sufficient opportunity to observe the domestic arrangements of yeoman households. Lacking letters of introduction to planter families, he was forced not infrequently to seek their hospitality. He was a miserable guest. Neither yeoman homes nor their inhabitants conformed to his standards of decency and comfort. He complained incessantly about slovenly women, lazy men, and packs of towheaded children and about filthy, vermin-infested cabins, "mere square pens of logs roofed over" with a "shed of boards before the door." He longed for the comforts of home: a private room with a "clean sweet bed" in which to sleep "alone and undisturbed"; hot water in the morning with which to wash; a parlor, curtained, carpeted, and "glowing softly with the light of sperm candles or a shaded lamp"; an armchair, a "fragrant cup of tea" with refined sugar and wheat bread; and the soothing sound of a woman playing classical music or reading aloud from Shakespeare or Dickens. Instead, when he was forced into yeoman homes by the approach of nightfall, "nine times out of ten" he had to sleep in "a room with others, in a bed that stank, supplied with but one sheet if any" and to make his morning ablutions in a common washbasin that doubled as a bread bowl. He found "no garden, no flowers, no fruit, no tea, no cream, sugar, or bread, no curtains, no lifting windows, no couch and no carpets," not to mention Shakespeare or sheet music.[64]

At a purely descriptive level, Olmsted's depiction was not inaccurate. Yeomen did live mostly in crude, unchinked double log cabins with porches in front and kitchens behind and with chimneys of sticks and clay and unglazed windows. One former slave from a yeoman neighborhood in Marion District pointed out that there was little difference between her "one room pole house that wad daubed wid dirt" and the one "my white folks live in [which was] a pole house daubed wid dirt too."[65] Inventories of yeomen's household goods, moreover, confirm that they were few and basic: wood and pewter dishes, cast iron pots, more homemade stools than "seting chares," and more "shuck mattresses" than the prized feather beds that were typically the most valuable household

64. Olmsted, *The Cotton Kingdom*, pp. 160–63; Olmsted, *A Journey in the Backcountry*, pp. 393–96; Beveridge and McLaughlin, eds., *Papers of Olmsted*, vol. 2, pp. 291–311.

65. Rawick, ed., *The American Slave, South Carolina Narratives*, part 1, pp. 187–95. Yeoman cabins described by Harriet Martineau and others as "log dwelling[s], composed of two rooms, with an open passage between" bear strong resemblance to those Henry Glassie has characterized as the typical folk-house of the eastern seaboard. See Martineau, *Society in America*, p. 150; Henry Glassie, *Patterns in the Material Folk Culture of the Eastern United States* (Philadelphia: University of Pennsylvania Press, 1968).

goods yeomen owned. Luxury items such as clocks, books, and mahogany furniture were rare even in yeoman slaveholders' households. Upholstered armchairs, pianos, couches, and carpets were nowhere to be found.[66]

Olmsted's tone of moral indignation suggests, however, that something more basic than his sense of comfort was assaulted in yeoman homes. Unlike the newly privatized middle-class homes of the urban Northeast (Olmsted's point of reference), from which so-called "productive" labor had been largely expelled by the 1850s, yeoman households remained the locus of production as well as of reproduction and consumption.[67] They had not developed the familiar spatial, material, or moral arrangements of bourgeois "homes" associated with separate spheres and domesticity. Instead, house spilled out into yard and yard into house in total disregard of basic notions of order and morality such as privacy and hygiene. There was no parlor, never mind a womanly parlor culture, and the kitchen, far from representing the emotional center of domestic life, was usually an outbuilding physically separate from the dwelling house.[68] There was, of course, a customary gender division of labor in yeoman households and distinct ideas about what constituted appropriate work for men and women. But the customary arrangement of work and space that prevailed did not, as Olmsted was acutely aware, conform to bourgeois beliefs about the gender division of

66. No probate records have survived for coastal districts, but judging from the inventories of yeoman estates in Barnwell and Darlington districts, the personal property (and household goods) of nonslaveholding and slaveholding yeomen was roughly comparable in value once the value of slave property was subtracted. For the inventories of yeoman estates used in this study, see Barnwell District, Court of Probate, Inventories, Appraisements and Sales Book, 1809–1841, SCDAH; Darlington District, Court of Probate, Inventories, Appraisements and Sales Book, 1789–1840, SCDAH; and Darlington District, Court of Probate, Inventories, Appraisements and Sales Book, 1853–1859, SCDAH.

67. It should be obvious by this point that such distinctions as "productive" and "unproductive" or "domestic" work were as much ideological as anything else. As Jeanne Boydston and others have demonstrated, the notion of "productive" work underwent a process of redefinition in free labor states in precisely this period. As capitalist relations extended their grip, work was increasingly defined as that labor exchanged in the market for a wage. See Boydston, *Home and Work,* and Nancy Folbre, "The Unproductive Housewife: Her Evolution in Nineteenth Century Economic Thought," *Signs* 16, no. 3 (Spring 1991), pp. 463–84. This line of analysis, pioneered by feminist historians concerned about the consequences for women's labor in the Northeast, would be deepened by a greater attention to definitions of work and value in the household economy of the slave states.

68. The literature on bourgeois homes, domesticity, and separate spheres is now enormous, but for a few key contributions, see Barbara Welter, "The Cult of True Womanhood, 1820–1860," *American Quarterly* 18 (Summer 1966), pp. 151–74; Kathryn Kish Sklar, *Catharine Beecher: A Study in American Domesticity* (New Haven: Yale University Press, 1973); Nancy Cott, *The Bonds of Womanhood: Women's Sphere in New England, 1780–1835* (New Haven: Yale University Press, 1977); Ryan, *Cradle of the Middle Class;* Christine Stansell, *City of Women: Sex and Class in New York, 1789–1860* (New York: Alfred A. Knopf, 1986). An overdue interrogation of the spatial conception of gendered spheres has been urged by Linda Kerber, "Separate Spheres, Female Worlds, Woman's Place: The Rhetoric of Women's History," *Journal of American History* 75, no. 1 (June 1988), pp. 9–39.

labor, space, and spheres of influence. Indeed, it confounded them. Deeply invested in the universalist claims of bourgeois gender ideology, committed to the notion that gender difference was literally written on the body, Olmsted could not confront a different gender division of labor without confronting its discomfitting implications. Olmsted may have written off the yeomanry as backward and uncivilized, but his outrage implies that the challenge to his own universalist assumptions was not so easily dismissed.[69]

If Olmsted's main point was that bourgeois distinctions between public and private, work and home, men and women's spheres had no meaning in yeoman households, then his fruitless search for the "Cult of Domesticity" made one other point abundantly clear. Southern society was fashioned as distinct not simply by the external relations of households but, perhaps more fundamentally, by the relations that prevailed within them. In yeoman households, gender relations were the key to the organization of production. Independence was achieved by a gender division of labor in which women's work in the fields and in the provision of subsistence and market goods was a central, although still largely unacknowledged, part.

Women's labor has historically been obscured by the public representation of the household in the person of its male head and by definitions of work that focus on the value of market exchange.[70] Such a resolutely ungendered approach cannot even begin to explain how, for example, self-sufficiency was achieved. Yeoman farmers at least were fully aware that they could aspire to self-sufficiency in large measure because, in addition to grain, virtually everything else their families ate was grown or raised, preserved and cooked by women, and virtually everything they wore was spun and woven, dyed and sewed by women. What little milk and butter yeomen had their wives or daughters produced. "Milk cow!" a slave man said incredulously, "I nebber bid do sich a ting in my life. Dat 'oman work."[71] A farm household without a farm wife was a disadvantaged one, indeed. Even planters sought married overseers to acquire women's labor in the dairy and poultry houses and in the making of cloth and clothing.[72]

69. On the emergence of modern beliefs in the physiological grounding of gender difference, see Thomas Lacquer, *Making Sex: Body and Gender From the Greeks to Freud* (Cambridge, Mass.: Harvard University Press, 1990), esp. 149–92. For evidence that Olmsted's refrain was a common one among bourgeois travelers in other "backward" parts of the nineteenth-century world, see Pratt, *Imperial Eyes*.

70. For an interesting discussion of the history of census categories and their effect on assessments of women's work, see Folbre, "The Unproductive Housewife," and Boydston, *Home and Work*. The slave South presents an intriguing point of contrast to Folbre's argument about the gendering of use value as female in the antebellum North.

71. Anonymous, *The Old Pine Farm, or The Southern Side* (Nashville: Southwestern Publishing House, 1860), p. 93.

72. When C. C. Pinckney hired an unmarried overseer, he provided him with a "Boy and a Woman to wait on him, cook and wash, and another Woman to take care of the

The value of women's work was clear. By their industry wives and daughters ensured that nothing was purchased that could be produced at home, whatever the cost in labor and sweat. In antebellum yeoman households women contributed more than the services and skills that continue to represent the unpaid labor of wives and mothers; they contributed as well the production of goods for household consumption that had elsewhere passed into the realm of the market. "I have been down at York today," the upcountry farm wife Mary Davis Brown noted in her diary, and "I did not by much of enything."[73] In the broadest sense, then, women's "domestic" production played a critical role in limiting the extent of the home market in consumer goods in the antebellum South. If yeoman farmers escaped relations of debt and dependency with local merchants and planters, they knew that the accomplishment was as much their wives' as their own.

Women's contribution to subsistence notwithstanding, the gender division of labor in yeoman households did not conform to distinctions between domestic and market production. The reason is simple. All economy was "domestic economy," at least in comparative terms; none of the products of yeoman households was definitively a subsistence or a market crop. Even cotton, although it could not be eaten, could be marketed in the raw for cash or goods or, by virtue of women's traditional craft skills, be turned into cloth for use at home or for sale. Yeoman families kept their account balances with local merchants within manageable limits, not just with the annual influx of credit from the sale of two or three bales of cotton or a few bushels of surplus corn but also with the steady trickle of "country produce" that testified to women's ability to turn household production to market exchange. Intended chiefly for use in the household, the products of women's labor regularly appeared on the credit side of the ledger in store accounts and petty trade with local planters; presumably, they figured as well in the informal exchanges, virtually impossible to document, between yeoman households. Eggs, chickens, feathers, butter, tallow, and homespun cloth were sufficiently important to local trade to figure prominently in the advertisements of village and crossroads merchants. "I feel like eating chicken and eggs, please bring me some," one enterprising rural Orangeburg merchant bantered in an illustrated advertisement, promising in another that those who called at "Uncle Tom's Corner . . . will be certain to get

---

Dairy, his Garden, and Poultry." The terms of the overseer's contract make clear the value of women's labor and the gender division of labor customarily observed. Contract of C. C. Pinckney and William Winningham, January 20, 1855, Charles Cotesworth Pinckney and Family Papers, Series III, LC.

73. Mary Davis Brown Diary, January 13, 1857, July 29, 1857, April 25, 1858, August 7, 1858, August 31, 1858, and throughout, SCL. On the value of women's (and girls') work, see also Elizabeth Finisher to Nancy H. Cowen, August 23, 1846, and Eleibers Cowen and Martha Cowen to John Cowen, February 1846, Nancy H. Cowan Papers, Perkins Library, DU.

as much for [their] money, eggs, chickens, rags, and Raw Hides as [they] can almost anywhere else."[74] The value of such transactions usually did not approach that of the annual sale of the cotton crop, but the $23.50 that Mary Davis Brown was paid for the "web of janes cloth" she sold in 1858 must have been a significant contribution to a typical perennially cash-poor household.[75] At least one household of women, a widowed Barnwell farm wife and her daughters, managed to eke out a living by making cloth for sale, and another lowcountry woman told federal officials that she had purchased her farm with the proceeds of her "weaving." From this perspective women's work provides one of the best demonstrations that yeoman households did not exist outside the market or fully within its grasp but moved along a continuum of self-sufficiency, interdependence, and market engagement.[76]

The significance of women's work in the production of independence was not lost on contemporary politicians. In periodic prescriptions for economic reform, politicians encouraged the products of women's labor to sustain self-sufficiency at the level of the household and independence at the sectional level: Domestic economy as a proslavery strategy. "True independence is to be found in your own farms," John Belton O'Neall, a prominent jurist and agricultural reformer, exhorted suffering cotton producers in 1844. "Raise my countrymen your own hogs, sheep, cattle, horses, and mules, clothe your own household by domestic wheel and loom . . . supply your own tables with flour, po-

74. *Orangeburg Southron*, June 11, 1856, May 21, 1856. On the sale of butter to planters, see the receipts of July 2, 1841, December 4, 1841, and November 17, 1842, in Lawton Family Papers, SCL. On store accounts, see Account of Rebecca Robertson, April 18-November 21, 1821, Account of Elsey Edwards, March 7, 1821, and Account of Jane Oram, May 30-August 28, 1821, in Anonymous, Account Book, Camden and Hanging Rock, Kershaw District, SCL; Samuel K. Carrigan, Sales Book, 1859–1860, SCL; Atherton, *The Southern Country Store*, pp. 48–54, 87–91. Women's labor in exchange relations will be treated more fully in the following chapter.

75. Mary Davis Brown Diary, October 9, 1858.

76. John H. Cornish Diary, January 9, 1847, SHC; Claim of Ellender Horton, SCCR, RG 217, File #8006. This complex relation to the market was not peculiar to South Carolina but was a characteristic of rural women's work before the emergence of capitalism in the countryside and thereafter on farms that continued to rely primarily on family labor. For the comparative case, see Laurel Thatcher Ulrich, "Housewife and Gadder: Themes of Self-Sufficiency and Community in Eighteenth-Century New England," in Carol Groneman and Mary Beth Norton, eds., *"To Toil the Livelong Day": America's Women at Work, 1780–1980* (Ithaca, N.Y.: Cornell University Press, 1987), pp. 21–34; Ulrich, *Good Wives: Image and Reality in the Lives of Women in Northern New England, 1650–1750* (New York: Oxford University Press, 1982), pp. 13–14, 34–39; Nancy Grey Osterud, "'She Helped Me Hay It as Good as a Man': Relations Among Women and Men in an Agricultural Community," in Groneman and Norton, eds., *"To Toil the Livelong Day"*, pp. 89–97; John Mack Faragher, *Sugar Creek: Life on the Illinois Prairie* (New Haven: Yale University Press, 1987), pp. 101–05; Margaret J. Hagood, *Mothers of the South: Portraiture of the White Tenant Farm Woman* (Chapel Hill: University of North Carolina Press, 1939), p. 77; David Levine, *Family Formation in the Age of Nascent Capitalism* (New York: Academic Press, 1977), p. 12.

tatoes, butter, and cheese of your own crops . . . and you can bid defi-
ance to all the tariffs in the world." The centrality of women's work in
such admittedly ill-fated strategies was evident. In the midst of the Nullification Crisis, the Pendleton Farmers' Society had initiated an antitariff
campaign by obliging their members to appear at the next meeting
"dressed *entirely in the Homespun of the district.*" This gratifying acknowl-
edgement of the yeomanry's true republican style (they usually wore
homespun—planters did not) was, like O'Neall's invocation of the republican producer ideal, a tribute to women's traditional craft skills. But
the Society went further, voting to cancel the annual prizes for stock
and grain in the belief that "the encouragement of our household industry [is] the only means within our reach to avert in some measure the
inferior effects of this . . . act." Prizes were awarded only for cuts of
plain and twilled homespun of cotton or wool, for linen diapers, cover-
lets, and imitation gingham cloth, for wool and cotton stockings, and for
butter and cheese. Women thus received all of the premiums that year
in acknowledgment of their work in the production of independence.
And if yeoman women's work acquired added value in political crisis, it
was not entirely neglected in quieter times.[77] In their romantic dreams
of southern independence, politicians elevated to a sectional strategy the
gendered practices that constituted the yeomanry's usual bid for independence.

There was, however, one aspect of women's work that contemporary
southerners were entirely unwilling to acknowledge. That was their labor, and especially wives' labor, in the fields. It is an interesting historical
omission, especially in light of the inordinate attention such field work
drew from northern and European travelers. Frederick Law Olmsted,
for one, insisted that he had "in fact, seen more white native American
women at work in the hottest sunshine in a single month, and that near
mid-summer, than in all my life in the free states." It was, he added, "not
on account of an emergency, as in harvesting, either, but in the regular
cultivation of cotton and of corn [but] chiefly of cotton." His almost
anthropological interest in the subject reflected passionately held but
newly constructed truths about women's physiology and the "natural"
gender divisions of spheres and labor that pertained among the ascendant American and European bourgeoisie. Olmsted revealed as much
when he admitted that confronted with the spectacle of slave women
plowing, he had "watched with some interest to see if there was any
indication that their sex unfitted them for the occupation." Southerners
would never have held such essentialist views of gender as to separate it

77. O'Neall quoted in Ford, *Origins of Southern Radicalism*, p. 53; Pendleton Farmers'
Society Records, Minutes, October 12, 1827, October 9, 1828, August 13, 1829, SCL; Black
Oak Agricultural Society, Constitution and Proceedings, November 16, 1847, SCL. On
homespun as a powerful symbol of southern resistance invoked in local political meetings,
see *Charleston Mercury*, June 25, 1828, July 9, 1828, July 16, 1828. I would like to thank
John Campbell for bringing the Pendleton Farmers' Society Records to my attention.

so completely from slave, and thus from class and racial, status. To outsiders, however, the transgressions against white womanhood witnessed in the yeomanry's fields served to confirm the superiority of free labor society. Frances Trollope's harsh judgment of yeoman men and sympathy for their wives, those "slaves of the soil," as she put it, was thus a foreigner's gross misunderstanding of gender, race and class relations in the slave South.[78] But it captured an important truth.

Perhaps because they too remain influenced by bourgeois ideas about separate spheres and the gender division of labor, most historians have assumed that field work was men's work, except of course for slaves. In taking this position, they have inadvertently deepened a contemporary southern silence on the subject that derived from very different sensibilities about the gender conventions of slave society.[79] Contemporaries of all classes were aware that the labor yeoman farmers commanded in the field included that of their wives and daughters; most yeomen simply did not own enough slaves to free female family members from field work. In the safe confines of the Black Oak Agricultural Society, an association of largely planter citizens of St. Stephen's Parish in rural Charleston District, Samuel DuBose openly attributed the local yeomanry's success at short-staple cotton cultivation to the fact that it was "a labor in which wives and daughters may conveniently and safely share with the husband and father. While he traces the furrow, they, protected by their sun bonnets, eradicate the weeds with a light hoe." Few public men showed such poor political judgment as did DuBose in acknowledging white women's labor in the fields.[80]

The gender relations of yeoman households embodied a dangerous class divide within lowcountry society—one that race could not close. The Colleton planter David Gavin jabbed the danger spot when he noted that his neighbor William Salsberry "used to work [his older girls] in the fields like negroes." Everybody knew yeoman women and girls worked in the fields. But the yeomanry's customary gender relations had

78. Olmsted, *A Journey in the Back Country*, p. 298; Frances Trollope, *Domestic Manners of the Americans*, (1832; reprint ed., Gloucester, Mass.: Peter Smith, 1968), pp. 117, 243.

79. Many southern historians would admit that yeoman women worked in the fields during harvest. But they typically treat that activity as an exception to an otherwise clear gender division of labor, as if harvesting were a crisis or an emergency rather than a regular seasonal activity. In none of the studies cited below, however, did women's field work figure in the analysis of self-sufficiency or yeoman household economy. See Wright, *Political Economy of the Cotton South*, pp. 82–83; Hahn, *Roots of Southern Populism*, p. 30; Ford, *Origins of Southern Radicalism*, pp. 78–81. It would be interesting to know when this (mis)representation of the gender division of labor among free whites emerged in the South. Certainly no one bothered to deny that white female indentured servants worked the fields in the early colonial period, but by the antebellum period few would have publicly acknowledged such a fact. The representation of a complete racial divide between slave and free women of all classes thus appears to have emerged as part of a larger ideology of slavery.

80. Samuel DuBose, *Address Delivered at the Seventeenth Anniversary of the Black Oak Agricultural Society* (Charleston: A. E. Miller, 1858), p. 21.

to be forced into at least ideological conformity with those of the planters lest critics of slavery attempt to open up that class distinction, as, for example, Hinton Rowan Helper did in his famous *Impending Crisis of the South*.[81] In the South as in the North, gender ideology was anything but descriptive and it functioned, in part, to occlude the centrality of white women's work. The issue for yeoman men and women was less the work women actually performed in the household than the representation of it to the community at large. Yeoman wives and daughters might work in the fields from Monday to Saturday, for example, but they would not appear at church on Sunday without a proper dress and shoes.[82] Ellender Horton embodied the convention in her violation of it. She was ostracized by the respectable community of yeomen in the Coosawhatchie Swamp (Abner Ginn's settlement) not because, as her daughter explained, "[m]e and sister worked together with the colored women in the field ["We had no men servants"] and made the crop" but rather because her mother sustained unorthodox relations with local free blacks, including purportedly a past love affair with a mulatto man, the father of her four daughters. Likewise, although less dramatically, Gavin's neighbor William Salsberry had violated community conventions, not by working his daughters in the fields—all yeomen did that—but by working them "like negroes." The offense, as it turns out, was that he had disinherited his eldest daughters even though they had worked at his side to "make some of this property." Both in his lifetime and afterward Salsberry had apparently denied his three older daughters their rightful place in the community of respectable yeomen and had, as a result, invited community disapprobation of his domestic affairs.[83]

Women's work in the fields, although customary, was customarily ignored and even denied. A collusive silence surrounded one of the labor practices that most clearly distinguished yeoman farms from plan-

---

81. David Gavin Diary, September 1, 1856, SHC. Hinton Rowan Helper offered an antislavery platform grounded in a vision of an industrial South and pitched it to yeoman farmers in gendered terms as one designed to relieve poor white men of the humiliation of watching their women toil in the fields. That postemancipation South, he insisted, would "see no more plowing, or hoeing, or raking or grain-binding by white women in the southern states; employment in cotton mills and other factories would be far more profitable and congenial to them, and this they shall have within a short period after slavery shall have been abolished." Helper probably miscalculated. Instead of using gender to open up the class divide between white southern men, his vision could well have had the opposite effect, reminding yeomen that in slave society their wives and daughters at least worked for them, and were not, as they would be in cotton mills, subject to the authority of other men. See Helper, *The Impending Crisis of the South: How to Meet It* (1851; reprint ed., Cambridge, Mass.: Harvard University Press, 1968), p. 300.

82. Sister Martha Shurley said "she has neither shoes nor bonnet is the reason she has not attended [church]," and the church resolved to "purchase shoes and bonnet for her provided she cannot obtain them by her husband." Gum Branch Baptist Church, Darlington District, Minutes, August 19, 1842, SCL.

83. Claim of Ellender Horton, Beaufort, SCCR, RG 217, File #8006; Gavin Diary, September 1, 1856.

tations, that set yeoman wives and daughters apart from their planter counterparts, that dangerously eroded the social distinctions between free women and slaves, and that cut deeply into the pride of men raised in a culture of honor. Out of respect for yeoman masters and particularly for their votes, planter politicians refrained.

The gender division of labor in yeoman households had political meaning that inhered in the production of material independence and went well beyond it, supporting the construction and reproduction of the identity of "free man" and master in the head of the household. Yet historians have found it difficult to know with any certainty how yeoman farmers deployed their families' labor, especially in the fields, and have been able only to speculate about how it shaped relations with household dependents—with the slaves whose labor they owned or hired and with other subordinates, including women, in their households and black-belt communities. But one very rare treasure, a yeoman farmer's journal, permits the historian to cross the threshold of the household and take a look inside. It confirms some of the labor patterns discernible in the more intransigent public records, and, more important, it suggests how they supported the manly public identity of its author.

James F. Sloan was not a lowcountry farmer. He lived in the upcountry district of Spartanburg. But notwithstanding the differences in household economy above and below the fall line, Sloan's journals of his farm operation, one identical in size to Abner Ginn's, provide a tantalizing glance into the late antebellum world of yeoman farmers. For Sloan assiduously recorded the tasks performed by each member of his household on the sixty improved acres that he cultivated. In 1854, when his journal begins, Sloan's household consisted of himself, a thirty-four-year-old native-born South Carolinian, his second wife, Dorcas Lee Sloan, three children from his first marriage (a son, Seth, who was fifteen or sixteen years old and two daughters, Sarah-Jane and Barbara, who were about thirteen and fourteen years old respectively), and at least two other children (James Haddon and an unnamed baby girl) from his marriage with Dorcas Lee. For only one year, 1859, did that household include a slave, an adolescent girl named Manda whom Sloan hired for four dollars per month.[84]

If there was ever any doubt about the strategies by which yeoman farmers produced independence in the absence of significant numbers of slaves, Sloan's journal puts it to rest, along with any lingering notions that field labor marked an absolute class and racial divide between southern women, slave and free. Sloan put his "wimmin" to work in the fields regularly throughout the year, from at least late spring to the end of picking season in December. In June 1856, for example, while he and

84. James F. Sloan Journals, June 24, 1854 to March 27, 1861, SCL. I would like to thank Lacy Ford for bringing these journals to my attention. Sloan's property holdings are outlined in Ford, *Origins of Southern Radicalism*, pp. 78–80.

Seth (his eldest son) harrowed the cotton and corn fields, "the wimmin commenced hoeing cotton in the lot field." Prior to that, since May, the "children" had been thinning out the cotton, and in June they were joined by "the wimmin," who hoed first the corn and then the cotton fields. By July 5, Sloan noted, the "girls had finished the cotton," and by July 15 his crop was laid by. The children went to school briefly in August, but by September 15 the cotton was "right smartly open," and picking season began. Sloan did not note the length of the picking season in 1856, but in 1858 it started on September 8 and continued until November 30, during which time the "chilldren" and the "balance of the family" picked cotton while he and Seth periodically attended to other tasks.[85]

Each year the tempo of work differed slightly. In June 1857, in one tragic interruption of the seasonal cycle, Dorcas Lee Sloan took "very bad" and later that day gave birth to "a still born babe"; she stayed out of the fields for a time after that. A little more than a year later she was again absent from the fields, but this time the reason was a joyous one. "Mrs Sloan sent out and presented me with a very fine girl child," Sloan recorded with evident pride on July 7.[86] What Dorcas Lee Sloan thought we can only imagine. But given the toll on her own health of repeated pregnancies and the recent memory of having lost a baby, Mrs. Sloan no doubt shared something of the sentiment of another new upcountry mother, Mary Davis Brown, who wrote after the birth of her tenth child, Fanny: "Oh how thankful i should be fore all things to doo so well a living chile and living mother."[87]

Mrs. Sloan did not work in the fields for some time after the baby was born; in fact, it is entirely possible that her husband hired the slave girl to compensate for the field labor lost as a consequence. But yeoman women like Mrs. Sloan made a fundamental contribution to the household economy at great cost to their own health. For household independence required above all else the reproduction of the labor force. Well might yeomen boast, then, as another upcountry man did, of the recent "edition to our family," declaring himself "well satisfied" with his riches: "a fine garden . . . a nice little crop . . . a pretty little stock of hogs and Cattle . . . the Best neigbour," and children who were growing "powerful fast and Bids fare to be a smart help to me soon should they be

85. Sloan Journals, June 21, 1856, July 5, 1856, September 15, 1856, and September 8 to November 30, 1858.

86. Sloan Journals, June 4, 1857, June 5, 1857, and July 7, 1858.

87. Mary Davis Brown Diary, October 14, 1859. Although the tenth child, this was the first of Mrs. Brown's births attended by a doctor. Men typically reported news of births differently from their wives. For one example, including heartbreaking correspondence between Elizabeth Finisher and her sister Nancy Cowan about her illness during and after pregnancy, her pain at losing two children, and her husband's neglect, see Elizabeth Finisher to Nancy H. Cowen, August 23, 1846, Elizabeth Fincher to "Dearest Sister" [Nancy H. Cowan], February 11, 1849, William P. Benson to Mr. John Cowan, 1846, and William P. Benson to Mrs. John Cowan, October 12, 1830, Cowan Papers.

sparrd."[88] Children were precious assets in the relentless struggle to keep the farm.

The particular allocation of labor and tasks changed along with the family life cycle and with the presence of other dependent laborers. Yet every year Sloan's family, including his teenage daughters and, although with less regularity, his wife, worked in the fields steadily from May until December, enabling them to produce sufficient subsistence and market crops to maintain their status as a respectable yeoman family. And if, unlike some other farmers' daughters, Sloan's girls were spared the indignity of driving a plow, the farm task perhaps most clearly demarcated as masculine, it was, at least in 1859, because another young woman assumed that burden: the slave Manda, who joined Seth Sloan in the fields and matched him task for task the year round.[89] Manda's presence did not, needless to say, relieve the Sloan women of the burden of field work, never mind of housework.

It did, however, change the gender division of labor, although the point is not that the ownership of slaves relieved yeoman women of domestic drudgery but that it relieved wives of the necessity of combining it with regular field labor. Mrs. Sloan escaped the fields (if temporarily); her daughters did not. They continued to work the land with Manda and Seth. In this respect the Sloan case suggests that the deployment of female family members' labor constituted a significant difference between those yeoman households with slaves and those without. The point is confirmed by comparison with small planters' operations. The most striking distinction between the Sloan household with its one hired slave and that of David Golightly Harris (another upcountry man), who had eleven slaves of his own and access to more belonging to his planter father, was that unlike Sloan's, Harris's wife and children never worked in the fields, and his children attended school the year round.[90] This comparison is a more stark one, admittedly. But the pattern is clear. The presence of even one slave, even if hired and even if a young woman, changed the gender division of labor among family members in

88. William P. Benson to Mr. John Cowan, 1846, William Benson to Mr. John Cowan, August 13, 1841, and Elizabeth Finisher to Nancy H. Cowen, August 23, 1846, Cowan Papers.

89. On the global identification of plowing as primarily a male task, see Esther Boserup, *Women's Role in Economic Development* (London: George Allen and Universal Ltd., 1970), pp. 19–34. Such gender assumptions went so deep in antebellum perceptions that when Olmsted came upon slave women plowing in the lower South he "watched them with some interest to see if there was any indication that their sex unfitted them for the occupation." Beveridge and McLaughlin, eds., *Papers of Olmsted*, vol. 2, pp. 218–19. The idea has persisted among historians that women, even slave women, did not plow. But there is considerable evidence that slave women plowed on many plantations and that, on yeoman farms where grown sons were in short supply, wives and daughters took their turn driving the plow. On slave women, see the list of field hands by task in James Henry Hammond, Plantation Records, August 7, 1850, James Henry Hammond Papers.

90. Philip N. Racine, ed., *Piedmont Farmer: The Journal of David Golightly Harris, 1855–1870* (Knoxville: University of Tennessee Press, 1990), pp. 29–169.

yeoman households; rarely, if ever, did it entirely relieve women family members of field labor.

It is startling how easily Sloan appeared to manage the adjustment to masterhood, however temporary, of a slave. With the exception of Mrs. Sloan's withdrawal from the fields, Manda was introduced to his established labor system with little apparent disruption, extending it but not transforming it. On the first day that Sloan put Manda to work, he simply noted "Seth and Manda hauled wood and rails," and thereafter she worked alongside Seth. Sloan's was an adjustment facilitated, no doubt, by years of commanding the labor of his other dependents, the "wimmin," "girls," "boys," and "children" who peopled his journal and cultivated the fields.[91]

The gender division of labor on Sloan's farm evinced a great deal more flexibility than the relations of power that underlay it. Not all dependents were equally subordinated to the head, and not only because one was a slave. Manda did occupy a position of particular dependence within Sloan's household, but his wife and daughters did, as well. Because sons could eventually reproduce their fathers' role as heads of independent households (a chief goal of the yeomanry's strategy, after all), the patriarch's control and discipline of women's labor and the assumptions of natural authority that accompanied it had profoundly different public meaning. It sustained the vaunted independence of the male yeomanry and their claim to equality in the slave republic. Indeed, the distinct trajectories of the coming of age of Sloan's eldest son and his eldest daughter suggest the generational reproduction of gendered relations of power and their implications for the assumptions yeomen brought to public political culture. For those yeomen who were slaveowners, masterhood assumed its characteristic southern form. But for those who were not or who acquired that status only in advanced age, other domestic relations nurtured many of its prerogatives. In all households, complex structures and relations lay within and gave definition to public postures.

There can be no doubt that Sloan's eldest son, Seth, labored under his father's authority throughout the 1850s, finding himself "sent" to do specific tasks on and off the farm. But there can also be no doubt that he was being prepared to assume his father's role. Not only was Seth increasingly assigned independent jobs on the farm; he was gradually introduced to the community of independent men and that of their sons and heirs in the surrounding neighborhood. With increasing regularity, Seth Sloan took his father's place in labor exchanges with neighbors and kinsmen and on trips to the grist mill and cotton screw, country store and tavern. These were the sites of male sociability, some of which also provided the social location of electoral politics and the rituals of manhood within which they were enacted.[92] In such places yeoman sons like Seth Sloan were initiated into the culture of freemen.

91. Sloan Journals, October 14, 1859, and March 8, 1859.
92. These issues are pursued in more depth in the following chapters.

Although Seth still worked under his father, he gradually came to stand beside him as well, a coming of age perhaps ritually marked in Sloan's journal by the entry of April 6, 1859, when for the first time Seth accompanied him to court day at Spartanburg. It was almost certainly a moment of ritualistic significance when father and son first worked together cultivating cotton in the field called "Seth's patch" in April 1860. Finally, Seth became his father's surrogate in the household, commanding dependents in his absence. Thus, while Seth's own path to independence was surely a long one, he had plenty of opportunity to practice the arts and affectations of masterhood, in immediate supervision over Manda's labor and presumably over that of his sisters as well. The economic and political foundations of his own claim to independence—and masterhood—had been laid.[93]

By contrast, the only coming of age ritual Sloan recorded for his daughter, Barbara, was a brief note of her marriage, a ritual that we can be sure conferred authority but of a different and far more circumscribed kind. Yeoman daughters did not enjoy a long apprenticeship in the culture of freemen. Instead, their entry into adulthood was most commonly marked by evangelical conversion—the struggle to submit to God's will representing, perhaps, proper prologue to the submission required of Christian wives. Daughters came of age into their mothers' world, the world inside the enclosure, ushered in with a brief ceremony, commemorated with "sider" and perhaps a few "wedding trimens," and characterized by a model of female excellence that made the submission of self the apotheosis of womanhood.[94]

Assumptions about gender, race, and power were reproduced within yeoman households in inevitable conjunction with the material basis of independence. Some, like Barbara Sloan and, in profoundly different ways, Manda, retained the identity of dependents permanently. They represented the foundations of masterhood for those, like Seth, who reproduced the paternal claim to independence and to the public recognition and privileged political position that accompanied it in the slave South.

VII

Independence had powerful meanings for lowcountry yeomen. Not the least was that manifest in the household itself: in the virtually unlimited authority conferred over the property and dependents that lay within the enclosure. Patriarchal prerogatives were deeply embedded in the domestic law of every state in antebellum America, but perhaps nowhere were they so rigorously observed as in South Carolina. In a society in

93. Sloan Journals, April 6, 1859, April 13, 1860.
94. Sloan Journals, August 9, 1860; Mary Davis Brown Diary, July 14, 1859, April 25, 1858, August 11, 1859. The close relationship between conversion and marriage is explored further in Chapter 5.

which the authority of masters over domestic dependents was a matter of paramount political significance, state authorities were seriously disinclined to interfere, limit, or even regulate the power of household heads over their subordinates, familial or otherwise. Within the household, the master's word was virtual law.

Certainly those yeomen who owned slaves enjoyed all the considerable powers conferred on masters. In the law of slavery the household was rendered almost a world apart.[95] But the law of husband and wife was configured around the same conception of the household and its boundaries, and it encoded the same inordinate respect for patriarchal authority. In every aspect of domestic relations, from incest to rape to child custody, and in property law as well, South Carolina's legislators and jurists privileged the power of male heads of household to an extent unparalleled in any other state. In no aspect of the law, however, was the state's particular commitment to coverture and the subordination of women so plainly articulated as in the matter of marriage and divorce.[96]

Alone among the states in antebellum America, South Carolina refused to pass a divorce law.[97] Legislators were summarily dismissive on this point. Petitions for divorce by an act of the legislature were few enough, for petitioners were "'well aware," as one put it, "of the reluctance with which the Legislature interposes in business of this character." But those few that were considered were denied without exception and usually without explanation. On one rare occasion the judiciary committee reiterated the settled "policy of the state to refuse granting a divorce under any circumstances whatsoever," judged that policy "most wise," and indicated its "hope it many never be departed from." And it

95. On the law of slavery, see Charles Sydnor, "Slavery and the Laws," *Journal of Southern History* 6, no. 1 (February 1940), pp. 3–24; Mark V. Tushnet, *The American Law of Slavery, 1810–1860* (Princeton, N.J.: Princeton University Press, 1981). Peter Bardaglio has argued that miscegenation laws were the entering wedge of "state supervision of the household" and of judicial paternalism. South Carolina resisted even this incursion on patriarchal authority, a point that casts some doubt on Bardaglio's larger argument that the maintenance of white racial supremacy was the driving legal force in the antebellum as in the postbellum South. See Peter W. Bardaglio, "Families, Sex, and the Law: The Legal Transformation of the Nineteenth Century Southern Household" (Ph.D. Diss., Stanford University, 1987), pp. 37–106. The quotation is on p. 104.

96. This particular judgment departs from that of Marylynn Salmon, who has argued that South Carolina had "a more liberal standard" than northern states with respect to women's autonomy or status at law. See Salmon, *Women and the Law of Property in Early America* (Chapel Hill: University of North Carolina Press, 1986), p. 48 and passim.

97. J. Nelson Frierson, "Divorce in South Carolina," *North Carolina Law Review* 9 (April 1931), pp. 265–82; Bardaglio, "Families, Sex, and the Law," p. 150; Lawrence T. McDonnell, "Desertion, Divorce, and Class Struggle: Contradictions of Patriarchy in Antebellum South Carolina" (Paper presented to the Annual Meeting of the Southern Historical Association, Houston, November 1985). Although legal historians readily acknowledge the singularity of South Carolina in resisting divorce, convincing analyses remain few. Salmon, for example, simply asserts that its refusal owed to the extent of miscegenation in the state, as if South Carolina differed in this respect from other southern states, all of which permitted divorce. See Salmon, *Women and the Law of Property*, pp. 64–65.

was not, at least until Reconstruction. As Judge John Belton O'Neall put it in 1833 and again in 1848, "The marriage contract is regarded in this state as indissoluble by any human means." Only death could discharge its obligations and legal effect. This view, as he explained, "has received the entire sanction and acquiescence of the Bench, the Bar, the Legislature and the People ever since [1833]. The most distressing cases, justifying divorce even on scriptural grounds, have been again and again presented to the Legislature and they have uniformly refused to annul the marriage tie. Those whom God has joined together, let not man put asunder."[98] The "indissolubility" of the marriage relation effectively removed any meaningful limits on the power husbands exercised over wives, as it was designed to do. The conception of marriage, the respective rights and obligations of husbands and wives, and the brutal relation of domination and subordination that ultimately underlaid it was spelled out again and again when masters' authority over dependents was threatened.

Even "the partial dissolution of the husband's authority over the wife" had to be guarded against, one justice reminded the state. The purpose of the law, another baldly stated, was to "operat[e] restrictively rather than enlarging the rights of married women." And it did. Wives, it seems, had few rights the court was bound to respect. The rights of husbands necessarily took precedence, for on the strength of that principle did the whole domestic government of the state stand or fall. Thus, while a woman had the right to leave her husband if he "ill-treated" her (a legal measure of physical abuse that had to be beyond moderate chastisement) and to gain a legal separation and even alimony in the Court of Equity, if "the husband offer to take her back . . . she is bound to return." If she did not, whether for fear of continued battery or just, as one woman explained, because "she never liked him," she forfeited all rights to alimony, dower, and custody. Legally married women had no will, no subjectivity. If he would have her, she was bound by law to go and suffer his abuse. The only "necessity" justifying separation was the husband's refusal to have her in his—and it was his—house. As the prominent lawyer David McCord bluntly put it, the state had no obligation to protect a woman who would rather "starve than submit."[99] The

98. "Petition of Mary Wilson Praying for Divorce," Petitions to the Legislature, 1821, General Assembly Records, SCDAH; Judiciary Committee Reports, 1821, General Assembly Records; *Boyce* v. *Owens*, Columbia, 1833, in W. R. Hill, *Reports of Cases At Law Argued and Determined in the Court of Appeals of South Carolina* (Columbia, S.C.: Telescope Office, 1834), vol. 1, pp. 8–11; *McCarty* v. *McCarty*, Columbia, 1847, in James A. Strobhart, *Reports of Cases Argued and Determined in the Court of Appeals and Court of Errors of South Carolina* (Columbia, S.C.: A. S. Johnston, 1848) vol. 2, pp. 6–11.

99. *Starr and Cleland* v. *Taylor*, Columbia, January Term, 1828, in D. J. McCord, *Reports of Cases Argued and Determined in the Court of Appeals of South Carolina* (Columbia, S.C.: Doyle E. Sweeny, 1830), vol. 4, pp. 413–417; *McDaniel* v. *Cornwell*, Chester, Fall Term, 1833, in Hill, *Reports of Cases*, vol. 1, pp. 428–32; *Bell and Nealy* v. *Wife*, Laurens, Fall Term, 1829, in

point was submission. In its refusal to contemplate divorce and in the constant vigilance over other intrusions or "dissolutions," the real nature of the marriage relation was revealed. The complementarity of husband and wife, the reciprocity the relation purportedly embodied, was exposed time and again as a gloss on the power relations that constituted its essence and political meaning. Any notion that this brutal power existed only at law is belied by every kind of record of state, church, and personal life.

As Judge Glover put it in one decision rendered in a late antebellum custody case, the law, "looking to the peace and happiness of families and to the best interests of society, places the husband and father at the head of the household." In law and custom both, the husband was accorded "a power of control over all members of his household" and especially his wife, whose "legal existence . . . is suspended" in consequence of "that coercion which subjection implies."[100] And since at law the husband "had possession or custody" of his wife, she could hardly be permitted custody over her children. Women were, as a result, denied even a maternal authority over their infant children. As Glover declared, the state simply could not permit a "divided empire in the government of a family." The husband and father was constituted at law, as he was in practice, "a mild and considerate ruler." If not so tempered he was a ruler nonetheless. With some cause, then, did one advocate of legal reform characterize the antebellum South Carolina household as "a sort of domestic monarchy," and women's status at law as tantamount to "matrimonial slavery."[101]

The analogy was a fitting one. While all domestic relations were important to the social order, it was the peculiar "domestic institution" that placed such an unprecedented premium on the latitude and powers accorded male heads of household in antebellum South Carolina. Divorce was an eminently political matter. As one anonymous essayist wrote in the *Southern Quarterly Review,* "From the society formed by marriage, the whole social and political order in which man is placed is grown." Divorce, he insisted, was a supplication to "pestilent" ideas of "natural rights" and "individual liberty," born of the "revolutionary sensuality and passion" of the Jacobins. As South Carolinians did not need to be told, at least by 1854 when the essay was published, those same

H. Bailey, *Reports of Cases Argued and Determined in the Court of Appeals of South Carolina* (Charleston: A. E. Miller, 1833), vol. 1, pp. 312–14; *Lowden* v. *Moses,* February Term, 1825, in D. J. McCord, *Reports of Cases Argued and Determined in the Court of Appeals of South Carolina* (Columbia, S.C.: Doyle E. Sweeny, 1826), vol. 3, pp. 93–104.

100. *Ex Parte Oliver Hewitt,* Beaufort, 1858, in J. G. G. Richardson, *Reports of Cases at Law Argued and Determined in the Court of Appeals of South Carolina* (Charleston: McCarter and Dawson, 1859), vol. 2, pp. 326–31.

101. *Ex Parte Oliver Hewitt,* in Richardson, *Reports of Cases,* vol. 2; pp. 326–31; Anonymous, "Woman, Physiologically Considered," *Southern Quarterly Review* 2, no. 4 (October 1842), pp. 309, 281.

ideas had effectively called into question the legitimacy of all domestic dependencies and had unleashed a campaign against slavery across the entire western world. "The discipline of the family is that which renders the work of government easy," the essayist wrote. "When that discipline is perfect, the reign of order and virtue in the state is established."[102] Nothing less than the social order of slave society was at stake in marriage and divorce and, more broadly, in the defense of patriarchal prerogatives.

The subordination of women, as of other dependents, could never be perfect, notwithstanding the heroic efforts of the state and the vigilance of the community. Everything prohibited was also performed. Men and women alike effected "irregular practices" in the absence of legal divorce, substituting customary arrangements from separation to bigamy to living as man and wife to, in one startling instance, wife sale. The Middle District yeoman who bought his wife from another man participated in one of the oldest forms of customary divorce, one that baldly revealed the property relation of marriage. This man could not be convinced—even by his minister—that he had done anything wrong. He was presumably accustomed to a society in which human beings were bought and sold every day and in which his Christian identity was not invalidated by the transaction. Other extralegal arrangements were more common. Grand juries regularly registered their concern about "the high and increasing crime of adultery" and about men and women who "outrag[ed] the . . . good order of society by living together as Man and Wife."[103] Clearly men could use such arrangements to liberate themselves from the rigidity of the state's divorce law. But women used them, too, to contest the considerable authority of men within the household, claiming a property in themselves and their bodies that the law did not permit and the community did not sanction. Some women resisted publicly and overtly, as Mrs. Nealy did by refusing to return to a husband whom "she never liked," some by leaving their husbands and taking up with other men, some by committing assault and battery on their husbands. A few transgressed every boundary of lowcountry society by forming domestic partnerships with free black men, as Ellender Horton did to the horror of her St. Peter's Parish neighbors.[104] The cost of such

102. Anonymous, "Marriage and Divorce," *Southern Quarterly Review* 26 (October 1854), pp. 353, 350, 349, 352.

103. "Petition of John Christian Smith Praying for a Divorce," Petitions to the Legislature, 1791, General Assembly Records. For the case of wife sale, see Thomas Memorial Baptist Church, Marlboro District, Minutes, July 1848, SCL; Grand Jury Presentments, Barnwell, Fall Term, 1822, General Assembly Records; Grand Jury Presentments, Orangeburg, April Term, 1826, General Assembly Records; Grand Jury Presentments, Darlington, Fall Term, 1830, General Assembly Records.

104. *Bell* v. *Nealy*, Laurens, Fall Term, 1829, in H. Bailey, *Reports of Cases*, vol. 1, pp. 312–14; Claim of Ellender Horton, Beaufort, SCCR, RG 217, File #8006; "Petition of Marmaduke Jones Seeking Divorce," Petitions to the Legislature, 1847, General Assembly Records. For an example of a woman who deserted her husband, see "Petition of Thomas

rebellion was incredibly high, however, amounting to virtual banishment from the respectable community.

Most women thus resisted in more subtle ways, attempting to use the power of a patriarchal state and church to protect themselves from criminal abuse or to turn their legal nonexistence to momentary commercial advantage, as did the women who functioned as feme sole trader and then pleaded coverture to escape legal liability for contracts or debts.[105] But if their authority within the household was radically circumscribed and if women were forced in marriage to submit to their husbands as to their masters, few alternatives to the household existed for yeoman women. In the rural parishes of the Low Country, as in most of the state, few other social spaces existed within which women could reside and make a living. Even literate, educated, single women such as the Sumter school teacher Mary Hort had few options but to attach themselves, to the households of other men. And as David Gavin, the Colleton planter, observed, the wives of his wealthy neighbors who left their husbands after periods of sustained abuse invariably returned. Although Gavin professed amazement at their behavior, it is not so difficult to understand. They had few choices and even fewer that did not leave them in a more vulnerable position: They could return to their fathers' households if such a possibility existed, or they could make their peace with their husbands. Indeed, Gavin's account raises the possibility that women with means and kin nearby fled their husbands not with the intention of permanent separation but with the express purpose of drawing public attention to their plight and forcing the intervention of kin or community to restrain their husbands. For most yeoman wives, even these limited options ultimately boiled down to one: to leave one man and one household only to submit to the authority of another.[106] Independence was for them, in every sense, inconceivable.

Miller Seeking Divorce," Petitions to the Legislature, 1841, General Assembly Records. For a woman living "in open lewdness, whoredom, and adultery," see *State* v. *Brunson and Miller,* Walterboro, Fall Term, 1830, in Bailey, *Reports of Cases,* vol. 2, pp. 149–51. For the case of a woman who left her husband saying "she drank too much was the reason why she married him," see Gum Branch Baptist Church, Darlington District, Minutes, March 14, 1835.

105. *State* v. *Thomas Brown,* Barnwell County, Clerk of Court Sessions Journal, October 20, 1854, SCDAH; *Bean* v. *Morgan,* Columbia, January Term, 1827, in McCord, *Reports of Cases,* vol. 4, pp. 148–49; *McCarty* v. *McCarty,* Columbia, 1847, in Strobhart, *Reports of Cases,* vol. 2, pp. 6–11. The issue of women's resistance is developed more fully in Chapters 4 and 5. Jane Censer has argued convincingly that married women who appeared before southern courts were compelled to appeal to the protective sensibilities of the jurists and thus to adopt a submissive, compliant, and long-suffering demeanor. See "Petition of Mary Wilson Praying for Divorce," Petitions to the Legislature, 1821, General Assembly Records; Jane Turner Censer, "'Smiling Through Her Tears': Antebellum Southern Women and Divorce," *American Journal of Legal History* 25, no. 1 (January 1981), pp. 24–47.

106. Mary Hort Journal, SCL; Gavin Diary, January 15, 1857, February 6, 1857, February 23, 1857, February 4, 1858; Gum Branch Baptist Church, Darlington District, Minutes, January to August 1854.

The reluctance of antebellum South Carolina legislators and jurists to regulate domestic relations reflected a primary concern with masters' prerogatives under the law of slavery and with the legitimacy of slavery itself. But just as it did in the law of property, establishing the boundary of the household as virtually inviolable, so that concern with masters' prerogatives had far-reaching effects on every aspect of domestic relations law in the state, including that of husband and wife. Although it owed, yet again, primarily to the power and interests of planter masters, yeomen found their prerogatives immeasurably strengthened. Just as jurists and legislators could not disentangle domestic relations—especially slavery and marriage—so yeomen could not separate their power as masters from that of their planter neighbors.

In the daily exercise of power and authority within the household, in the authority conferred on household heads and the subordination demanded of dependents, yeoman farmers not only produced the material basis of independence; they laid claim as well, even in the absence of slaves, to the identity of freemen and masters. In the South Carolina Low Country yeomen were unequivocally masters—at least of the small world within the fence.

chapter 3

Unequal Masters

I

Domestic dependencies had public meanings in the South Carolina Low Country. In the complex world outside the fence where masters met on no man's particular land, yeomen's masterly identity engendered quite contradictory meanings, committing them to independence and the public assertion of their social and political rights even as it wedded them to the relations of power and domestic dependency that supported it.[1] The defense of their own independence implicated yeoman farmers in the political defense of the state's "peculiar" domestic relations.

The yeomanry's position at once empowered and compromised them in their relations with planters, the Low Country's other master class. It incorporated the very values on which yeomen and planters found agreement—that the control of property and dependents alone conferred the rights of freemen and masters—and in doing so provided yeomen unassailable ground on which to extract recognition of the rights of independent men from overweening planters. But by the same logic it legitimized planter prerogatives and left yeomen no firm ground on which to protect their particular interests as small farmers, no ground on

1. In recent years, most historians have focused on the first part of this contradictory dynamic, emphasizing the egalitarian and progressive public meaning of yeoman politics in relation to that of planters. Few, if any, however, have grappled with the public meaning of the yeomanry's domestic relations. For this common view among otherwise quite distinct interpretations, see, for example, Steven Hahn, *The Roots of Southern Populism: Yeoman Farmers and the Transformation of the Georgia Upcountry, 1850–1890* (New York: Oxford University Press, 1983); J. William Harris, *Plain Folk and Gentry in a Slave Society* (Middletown, Conn.: Wesleyan University Press, 1985); Lacy K. Ford, Jr., *Origins of Southern Radicalism: The South Carolina Upcountry, 1800–1860* (New York: Oxford University Press, 1988); Harry L. Watson, "Conflict and Collaboration: Yeomen, Slaveholders, and Politics in the Antebellum South," *Social History* 10, no. 3 (October, 1985), pp. 273–98.

which to contend for equality with those who mastered vastly more property and dependents. In the struggles for authority that inevitably ensued beyond the boundaries of the household, yeoman farmers most often found themselves overmatched. Bound by a set of common assumptions and values engendered in the household, yeomen and planters forged an uneasy alliance that simultaneously buttressed independence and planter power.

II

Equally masters, yeoman and planter heads of household were anything but equals in the South Carolina Low Country. In that region of huge plantations and modest farms, the contradiction of independence and inequality that characterized every part of the slave South was played out in unmistakable terms. For there the widespread ownership of property in land and slaves by adult white men coexisted with a distribution of wealth that left little room for political fictions about white equality or "herrenvolk democracy."[2]

By any calculation, the planter elite in the Low Country controlled a greater proportion of wealth than its counterparts elsewhere in the South. In 1850, when the richest tenth of propertyholders in the plantation districts of the South Carolina Upcountry owned about 55 percent of the real wealth, their lowcountry counterparts owned a staggering 70 percent. Taken together, the top quarter of lowcountry propertyholders claimed about 90 percent of the wealth, while the entire bottom half, in

2. Wealth was distributed more unevenly in the South Carolina Low Country than in any other part of the slave South. But the Low Country, if extreme, was hardly anomalous. For the distribution of wealth even among the free population of the cotton South states was more inegalitarian than in any other part of the rural United States. Had slaves been included in such calculations, moreover, there can be little doubt that the concentration of wealth in the slave South would have equaled and probably surpassed that found in the urban parts of the free-labor North. Historians of the antebellum South have been more reluctant to confront the meaning of inequality than that of independence in relations between yeomen and planters. In that respect, the case of the Low Country is an important one.

For the recent debate over the distribution of wealth, see the following: Gavin Wright, "'Economic Democracy' and the Concentration of Agricultural Wealth in the Cotton South, 1850–1860," *Agricultural History* 44, no. 1 (January 1970), pp. 63–99; Wright, *The Political Economy of the Cotton South: Households, Markets, and Wealth in the Nineteenth Century* (New York: W. W. Norton, 1978); Donghyu Yang, "Notes on the Wealth Distribution of Farm Households in the United States, 1860: A New Look at Two Manuscript Census Samples," *Explorations in Economic History* 21, no. 1 (January 1984), pp. 88–102; Donald Schaefer and Mark Schmitz, "The Parker-Gallman Sample and Wealth Distributions for the Antebellum South: A Reply," *Explorations in Economic History* 22, no. 2 (April 1985), pp. 227–32; Ford, *Origins of Southern Radicalism*, p. 49. On the slave South as a "herrenvolk democracy," see George M. Fredrickson, *The Black Image in the White Mind: The Debate on Afro-American Character and Destiny, 1817–1914* (New York: Harper and Row, 1971), pp. 61–70.

whose ranks the yeomanry were squarely placed, claimed less than 5 percent.[3] (See Table 2.5.)

This social inequality pervaded every aspect of the business of low-country life, rendering yeomen hardly the main actors in the region's economy. In 1850 the wealthiest planters in St. Peter's Parish (those who owned more than 500 acres and 100 slaves) controlled fully half of the improved acreage and owned almost half of the slaves, despite the fact that they constituted a mere 13 percent of farm operators. Yeomen, by contrast, while constituting the majority of farm operators, controlled less than one-eighth of the improved acreage and owned less than one-tenth of the slaves. Their share of the Low Country's productive resources was not, moreover, only limited but shrinking, as well. Inequality in the distribution of wealth was deepening all over the South in the 1850s, and the Low Country was no exception.[4] (See Table 3.1.)

3. For the upcountry figures, see Ford, *Origins of Southern Radicalism*, p. 50. Peter Coclanis's work confirms that St. Peter's Parish fell in the middle range of coastal parishes with respect to the distribution of wealth and was comparable to St. Bartholomew's Parish in Colleton District. See Coclanis, *The Shadow of a Dream: Economic Life and Death in the South Carolina Low Country, 1670–1920* (New York: Oxford University Press, 1989), pp. 152–53. Fabian Linden's calculations imply that the distribution of wealth in the South Carolina Low Country was roughly comparable to that in the leading cotton parishes in Louisiana and that, at least with respect to ownership of land, concentration was more advanced in the Alabama black belt and the Mississippi delta. See Linden, "Economic Democracy in the Slave South: An Appraisal of Some Recent Views," *Journal of Negro History* 31 (April 1946), pp. 140–89. Linden's article was an intervention in a debate about the extent of "economic democracy" in the Old South that extends back to the days of U. B. Phillips. Linden was responding specifically to Frank L. Owsley, whose insistence on "economic democracy" and the social and political power of the yeomanry continues to find its supporters today. For a sampling of both sides of the debate see the following, in addition to Linden: Ulrich B. Phillips, "The Origin and Growth of the Southern Black Belts," in Eugene D. Genovese, ed., *The Slave Economy of the Old South: Selected Essays in Economic and Social History* (Baton Rouge: Louisiana University Press, 1968); Owsley, *Plain folk of the Old South* (Baton Rouge: Louisiana State University Press, 1949); Wright, "'Economic Democracy' and the Concentration of Agricultural Wealth," pp. 63–99, and *Political Economy of the Cotton South*; Ford, *Origins of Southern Radicalism*.

4. Also see Appendix, Table II; Chapter 2, n. 35. The concentration of wealth in real and personal property deepened in the Upcountry as well in the 1850s. See Ford, *Origins of Southern Radicalism*, p. 262. On the cotton South as a whole, see Wright, *Political Economy of the Cotton South*, pp. 29–36, and for evidence of the same trend in other areas of the South, see the following: William L. Barney, "Towards the Civil War: The Dynamics of Change in a Black Belt County," in Orville V. Burton and Robert C. McMath, eds., *Class, Conflict, and Consensus: Antebellum Southern Community Studies* (Westport, Conn.: Greenwood Press, 1982), pp. 147–51; William Barney, *The Secessionist Impulse: Alabama and Mississippi in 1860* (Princeton, N.J.: Princeton University Press, 1974), pp. 38–40; Linden, "Economic Democracy in the Slave South"; James C. Bonner, "Profile of a Late Antebellum Community," *American Historical Review* 49 (July 1948), pp. 663–80; and Roger W. Shugg, *Origins of Class Struggle in Louisiana* (1939; reprint ed., Baton Rouge: Louisiana State University Press, 1968). The major exception appears to have been the Georgia Upcountry, which according to Steven Hahn, "during the 1850s . . . became more of a yeoman stronghold." See Hahn, *The Roots of Southern Populism*, pp. 25, 40–43.

Table 3.1 Control of Land and Slaves by Planters and Farmers,
St. Peter's Parish, Beaufort District, 1850–1860

Category (Imp. Acres)	% of All Farms		% of All Improved Acres		% of All Slaves	
	1850	1860	1850	1860	1850	1860
1–24	9.1	10.2	0.6	0.5	0.2	1.8
25–49	17.8	17.7	2.5	2.1	1.0	1.1
50–99	15.9	12.1	4.1	2.8	2.5	3.3
100–149	9.7	9.9	4.3	3.9	5.0	2.5
Yeoman totals	52.5	49.9	11.5	9.3	8.7	8.7
150–199	6.5	6.2	4.3	3.6	5.1	4.0
200–299	14.2	14.4	12.7	11.5	14.1	13.4
300–499	14.2	11.8	21.7	15.3	27.5	17.4
Planter totals	34.9	32.4	38.7	30.4	46.7	34.8
500+	12.6	12.7	49.8	60.3	44.6	56.5
Great planter totals	12.6	12.7	49.8	60.3	44.6	56.5

Source: Federal Manuscript Census, South Carolina [Beaufort District], Schedules of Slaves and Agriculture, 1850, 1860, NA.

Planters' extraordinary grip on land and slaves meant that, despite their numbers, yeomen were only marginal contributors to the region's staples markets. Short-staple cotton had been heralded in the early nineteenth century as "the poor man's crop." But in the South Carolina Low Country, yeomen produced only about one-tenth of the 1850 cotton crop, while the largest planters alone produced more than two-thirds of it. Indeed, more than 80 percent of the crop was grown on plantations with more than fifty slaves. Rice and long-staple cotton, needless to say, were virtually monopolized by planter producers, and every silky boll and pearly grain was registered in their wealth and income, impressive even by southern standards.[5] (See Table 3.1)

If yeomen based their claims to masterhood on the rights of property and the command of dependents inside the enclosure, then the vastly greater wealth, property, and numbers of dependents that their planter neighbors commanded ensured that outside the household they met on unequal ground. Yeomen were independent men and masters, entitled to the respect and public rights accorded such men in slave society, and

5. See also Appendix, Table III. For the quotation see Marjorie S. Mendenhall, "A History of Agriculture in South Carolina, 1790–1860: An Economic and Social Study," (Ph.D. Diss., University of North Carolina, 1940), pp. 62–63.

Lowcountry yeomen produced a significantly smaller share of the region's staple crops than their upcountry counterparts and, indeed, their counterparts throughout the cotton South, including the alluvial areas studied by Gavin Wright. See Ford, *Origins of Southern Radicalism*, pp. 59, 257; Wright, *Political Economy of the Cotton South*, p. 84.

they insisted on that identity in every exchange with planters. But the planters' equals they were not and could never be, installing the tension between independence and inequality at the very heart of the relations between yeoman and planter men in the Low Country.

III

Outside the household, lowcountry yeomen and their families were tied into complex social networks that extended from their own settlements of folk mostly like them and their few slaves to the neighborhoods beyond, with far more diverse populations of planter families and slaves, free blacks, poor whites of various kinds, and, of course, the merchants and tradesmen in whose establishments all the locals bumped elbows. Yeoman relations with local merchants were no more important a part of such networks than any others; certainly merchants had nothing like the significance they would assume in postemancipation society. But the yeomanry's relations with merchants are more discernible in the historical record, and they reveal a good deal about the tensions that shaped relations with planters and about the gendered public culture of the Low Country within which they were played out.

Stores were important sites of social life in the Low Country, staging functions that went well beyond the buying and selling of goods. Where distinct yeoman settlements were situated in close proximity to planter ones, as they were in the coastal and middle districts of South Carolina, class relations between whites evinced a curious combination of social distance and intimacy. Yeoman and planter men were as likely to meet in local stores as in any of the other few institutions that marked the landscape between households, and stores took on multiple functions in part because of their strategic locations in a rural society.

It is not that there were so many stores. The *Southern Business Directory* listed only twelve steady locations of country stores in Beaufort District outside the town of Beaufort itself, and R. G. Dun and Company listed two more. The proximity, especially for district planters, of town and city markets in Beaufort and Savannah, as well as in Charleston, explains the scarcity of country stores in Beaufort. But yeomen in the upper reaches of St. Peter's Parish were not as likely to take their small cotton crops to Beaufort or Savannah as were planters, and they relied on village and country stores to a greater extent. In fact, at least in the late antebellum period, some Coosawhatchie Swamp farmers conducted their business across the district line in lower Barnwell. In the middle districts where there were few market towns of any size (no interior town in the Low Country had even five hundred inhabitants by the end of the antebellum period), yeomen certainly, along with planters, were even more dependent on the village and country stores located in courthouse villages, at the natural junctions offered by landings, crossroads, bridges, and ferries, and, in later years, at railroad depots.[6] Because such gathering spots were scarce, because there were few other gathering spots, and especially because of their strategic locations, all manner of social and political activities transpired at village and country stores.

The culture the stores sustained was a distinctly homosocial one for reasons that owed mainly to the gender relations of lowcountry households. The vast majority of those who held accounts with merchants and who actually did the marketing were men. That did not change either over time or over space in the rural Low Country, although presumably cities like Charleston and Savannah evinced somewhat different patterns. The general merchandise store and tavern in the vicinity of Hanging Rock in Kershaw District may have been an extreme case. Only 4 of the owner's 161 accounts were with women in the period between 1820 and 1823, and on any given day only men were to be found there, having a drink and making a few purchases. On December 1, 1820, the owner had nine customers, all men; on December 2, he had seven more, also all men. In fact, no woman set foot in the store during the period under consideration until December 6, when Elizabeth Bond came in to buy a quart of whiskey. But the line between taverns and stores was hardly firm anywhere, and the gendered pattern of marketing was not significantly different in established village settings late in the period. Samuel K. Carrigan's customers in his Society Hill store in Darlington District in 1859 were also overwhelmingly men. In December of that year he conducted 172 separate transactions, only 7 of which were with women. Even on the busiest Saturday in December shortly before Christmas, there was not one woman among the eleven people who came to shop and socialize.[7] Country stores were anything but the wom-

6. *Southern Business Directory and General Commercial Advertiser* (Charleston: Walker and James, 1854), vol. 1, pp. 308–09; R. G. Dun and Company, Credit Reporting Ledgers, South Carolina, vol. 3, pp. 115–17, 119–23, 127, 130, 135, 137, and vol. 9, pp. 219, 223, Baker Library, Graduate School of Business, Harvard University; Claim of Richard Taylor, Beaufort, Southern Claims Commission Records (hereafter SCCR), RG 217, File #6795, NA. The petition of citizens of Blackville for incorporation of the town maintained that "the larger portion of the cotton of Barnwell District . . . and also a very considerable portion of the cotton of two other districts . . . is shipped for Charleston" from that point. See "Petition of Citizens of Blackville," Petitions to the Legislature, 1849, General Assembly Records, SCDAH. The evidence on the size of interior market towns is drawn from Coclanis, *Shadow of a Dream*, p. 146.

7. Anonymous, Account Book, Camden and Hanging Rock, Kershaw District, December 1, 1820, December 2, 1820, December 6, 1820 and throughout, SCL. A total of 166 separate accounts are listed for the period 1820–1823 (the full run of the account book); 5 names are unidentifiable by gender, 157 were held in men's names, and 4 in women's names. Samuel K. Carrigan, Sales Book, December 1859, December 17, 1859, SCL, and Samuel K. Carrigan, Day Book, 1859, SCL.

The pattern is confirmed by other records. In the mid-1820s, 109 of the 142 accounts (77 percent) held by the Darlington merchant Elisha Rogers were with men; the pattern holds for other middle district merchants throughout the antebellum period. For the records of Rogers's store, see Inventory of the Estate of Col. Elisha Rogers, Darlington District, Court of Probate, Inventories, Appraisement and Sales Book, October 21, 1826

anly and domesticated terrain they were fast becoming in northern cities.[8] Rather, they were important sites of male sociability, shaped by the
legal arrangements of the household that awarded male heads the property to secure debts and by the social and political prerogatives that such
independent men shared.

While yeoman wives complained of their incarceration within the
household, their husbands indulged manly privileges both trivial and
profound in regular visits to local stores.[9] Country stores commonly
doubled as taverns, and transactions were rarely made without the company of a dram or two, some "segars" or plug tobacco, and a chat about
the usual—the crops, the weather, politics—with whomever happened
in. Indeed, since men did the marketing, they often timed it to coincide
with other male rituals, including sales day, court week, and militia musters, which deepened the connection with drinking and politicking, especially since those were also the occasions on which thinking politicians,
to be sure of a hefty turnout, called "citizens' meetings." It all came
together during militia musters and election seasons, when captains and
politicians, often one and the same man, treated at the local store to
shore up their men's loyalties. It was especially handy when the store
served as the militia headquarters, as Richard Taylor's Barnwell store
did, or, indeed, when it was also the polling station, which was not
infrequently the case in rural lowcountry districts. It was all part, as one
"retired private" put it, of "the Bust-head system."[10] Stores were more
than the sites of economic transactions; they also staged much of the
common political culture of yeomen and planter men, the social rituals
of which inscribed both the independence that constituted their equal
claims to participation and the disparities in wealth and power that constituted their unequal parts.

If the presence of yeomen in lowcountry stores evoked their place in
a common culture of independent men, then their accounts with those
merchants, and the nature of the exchanges, revealed something of how

and January 6, 1827, SCDAH. See also the Inventory of the Estate of Henry W. Oakman,
Barnwell District, Court of Probate, Inventories, Appraisements and Sales Book, February
11, 1821, SCDAH; and Anonymous, Camden Account Books, 1828, 1854–1855, SCL.

8. On the gendering of consumption, see Karen Halttunen, *Confidence Men and Painted
Ladies: A Study of Middle-Class Culture in America, 1830–1870* (New Haven: Yale University
Press, 1982); Susan Porter Benson, *Counter Cultures: Sales Women, Managers, and Customers
in American Department Stores, 1890–1940* (Urbana: University of Illinois Press, 1986),
especially pp. 12–30; Jeanne Boydston, *Home and Work: Housework, Wages, and the Ideology
of Labor in the Early Republic* (New York: Oxford University Press, 1990).

9. See, for example, Mary Davis Brown Diary, April 25, 1857, SCL.

10. On sales day and court week as occasions for "citizens meetings," see, for example,
Darlington Flag, August 14, 1851, March 4, 1852; Claim of Richard Taylor, Beaufort,
SCCR, RG 217, File #6795. The "retired private" made his charge in *Orangeburg Southron*,
July 6, 1859. On the use of stores as polling stations, see *Darlington Flag*, October 7, 1852,
and House of Representatives, Election Returns, 1820–1860, General Assembly Records,
SCDAH. For a few specific examples, see the returns of St. Paul's Parish, Colleton District,
Oct. 13, 1824, and Williamsburg District, Oct. 9, 1838.

that independence coexisted with limited resources. It is difficult to determine precisely what part of the universe of yeoman exchange extant merchant records represented, although it is safe to say they are only fragments of once complex exchange networks. They are suggestive, nonetheless, of the relations yeomen sustained with local merchants and of the ways in which small producers attempted to shape those relations to limit indebtedness and reproduce household independence.[11]

The outlines are visible in the relations Leach Carrigan and Samuel K. Carrigan maintained with the farmers and planters in the vicinity of their Society Hill store in the late 1850s. The Carrigans together ran a cotton-buying and brokerage business as well as a general store. The parts of the business were hardly distinct. Thirty-three people sold Leach Carrigan cotton in 1859, most either in January from one year's crop or in late September, October, November, and December, presumably from the next. The transactions were modest ones as befitted the clientele, the vast majority of whom (twenty-one of the twenty-seven who could be identified in the federal census) were yeoman farmers. Clearly, Leach Carrigan was not the cotton buyer of choice for the area's many substantial planters. In 1859 Carrigan's largest transaction involved only eight bales and the smallest involved less than one, for on October 21 he bought 117 pounds of loose "seed cotton" from Ellerbe Powe; the remainder, although small in quantity, was at least ginned and baled. The method of payment was recorded legibly for twenty-nine of his thirty-three customers. Calvin Rhodes sold Carrigan four bales of cotton on September 22, 1859, bought about four dollars' worth of goods, and walked out with about half the credit in cash and a due bill for the rest. But he was apparently an exception to the rule. The vast majority of the others (twenty-six, to be precise) put most of the credit from cotton sales against the balance on their accounts with Samuel K. Carrigan's store, although they might have taken home a little cash as well.[12] Most of Leach Carrigan's customers, it would seem, sold him their cotton to

11. Exchanges of goods and services between yeoman households are particularly hard to recover. It is entirely possible that they were never recorded in writing. In any case, no diaries or farm books kept by lowcountry or middle country yeomen have come to light by which such transactions could be reconstructed for the historical record.

12. The 33 names were derived from Leach Carrigan's Cotton Book from the legible entries for 1859 and were then traced in Samuel K. Carrigan's Day Book, also in the entries for 1859. See Leach Carrigan, Cotton Book, 2 vols., 1836–1838 and 1849–1863, SCL; Samuel K. Carrigan, Day Book, 1858–1860. The transaction with Ellerbe Powe is in Carrigan, Cotton Book, October 21, 1859; Calvin Rhodes's transaction is in Carrigan, Cotton Book, September 22, 1859.

The yeoman identity of Leach Carrigan's customers was ascertained by compiling a social profile of each on the basis of the entries in the Federal Manuscript Census. Twenty-seven names were positively identified, of which 21 were yeoman farmers of various means: 14 were nonslaveholders and 7 were slaveholders. The data was compiled from the following sources: Federal Manuscript Census, South Carolina [Chesterfield, Darlington, and Marlboro Districts], Schedules of Population, Slaves, and Agriculture, 1860, NA.

settle bills they had accumulated at the store throughout the preceding year.

There was surely nothing unusual about such arrangements. For most rural and small town merchants, about the only way to do business with farmers and planters was on credit. Cash transactions may have been more common in coastal districts than in interior ones like Darlington. Credit reporters for R. G. Dun and Company suggested as much, noting, for example, that Charles Wilcox at Coosawhatchie in Beaufort District did "a careful bus[iness] chiefly for cash." And certainly Beaufort yeomen had more options in marketing their cotton and other surplus goods than Darlington yeomen, perhaps increasing the likelihood that they engaged in cash transactions for store goods with local merchants. But a least some coastal yeomen marketed their cotton with local country merchants as Carrigan's Darlington customers did, and the "cash" business was, in any case, a very murky one. More than one storekeeper pronounced himself in the "cash" business and simultaneously solicited "country produce." T. R. Collins in Orangeburg treated provisions and cash as equivalents, urging locals to "call at Uncle Tom's Corner where you will be certain to get as much for your money, eggs, chickens, Rags, and Raw Hides as you can almost anywhere else." Another Orangeburg storekeeper, F. H. W. Brigsman, announced that after January 1, 1857, he would sell "at Charleston prices and at Charleston terms—i.e. cash" but concluded his ad with the reminder that "all kind of produce [are] taken in exchange at the highest market rates." Merchants seem not to have made a distinction between money and goods, only between "cash" and "credit" sales. In Samuel K. Carrigan's books, cash sales were recorded as those paid for on the spot, whether with money or bartered goods.[13]

Most merchants in the coastal and interior Low Country continued to accept provisions and home-manufactured goods in exchange for store-bought goods to the very end of the antebellum period. Indeed, they not only accepted them but actively solicited them. By all accounts such goods met a regular demand. For while coastal merchants might ship "country produce" on to Charleston to meet city needs, much of it, including butter, beef, and homespun cloth, met rural needs, as well. As a result, yeomen routinely traded provisions (eggs, fowl, butter, corn, beef), swamp and forest products (cypress shingles and lumber), and home-manufactured goods (tallow, hides, and homespun cloth) for the

13. Dun and Company, Credit Reporting Ledgers, South Carolina, Charles Wilcox, March 8, 1858, vol. 3, p. 115; *Orangeburg Southron*, May 21, 1856; Samuel K. Carrigan, Sales Book, 1859, Samuel K. Carrigan, Day Book, 1859. For a provocative interpretation of the meaning of barter in the exchange relations of northern farmers in the early republic, see Michael Merrill, "Cash is Good to Eat: Self-Sufficiency and Exchange in the Rural Economy of the United States," *Radical History Review*, no. 4 (Winter 1977), pp. 42–71.

store-bought goods even the most self-sufficient farm household required.[14]

Better than any other single good, perhaps, homespun cotton cloth embodied the complexity of the yeomanry's exchange relations. Most lowcountry cotton was, of course, sold in the raw and destined for northern and British factories. But all over the Low Country, yeoman wives and daughters held back small amounts of ginned cotton for home manufacture. Most yeoman households did, in fact, contain cards, spinning wheels, and looms, the requisite equipment with which to make the coarse cloth that women sewed into the cotton shirts, pants, overalls, and even coats that their husbands and sons wore most of the time and the cotton dresses and sunbonnets that made up their own workaday clothing. A few widowed women even managed to eke out a living by this traditional craft skill. Yet if women were content with homespun clothes for workdays, few were content with such inelegant attire for Sundays. For that they turned to local merchants, buying all sorts of inexpensive finery, including printed calico, cambric, muslin, and lace trimming. And they paid for it with the proceeds of the cotton crop, with all kinds of petty produce, and, on occasion, with the very homespun that they desired to replace.[15] In a quite literal sense, homespun cloth

14. *Kingstree Star*, October 11, 1860; *Beaufort Enterprise*, September 26, 1860; *Orangeburg Southron*, May 21, 1856, June 11, 1856; *Darlington Flag*, October 7, 1852. For examples of country merchants selling homespun cloth and of customers buying it, see Samuel K. Carrigan, Sales Book, Account of William Edwards, October 31, 1859; Lawton Family Papers, August 26, 1826, December 8, 1826, March 20, 1839 and bills for homespun that extend well into the 1850s, SCL. For evidence of merchants accepting goods for credit, see Anonymous, Account Book, Camden and Hanging Rock, Kershaw District, Account of Elsey Edwards, March 7, 1821; Elisha S. Spencer Papers, [Sumter District] Day Book, September 20, September 21, 1855, SCL; Anonymous, Bluffton General Store, Account Book, Account of E. Molprus, August 7, 1856, SCHS; Samuel K. Carrigan, Sales Book, Account of William Edwards, October 31, 1859.

15. The evidence on household ownership of cloth-making equipment is drawn from the following records: Barnwell County, Court of Probate, Inventories, Appraisements and Sales Book, 1809–1841; Darlington County, Court of Probate, Inventories, Appraisements and Sales Book, 1789–1840, 1844–1853, 1853–1859. For descriptions of yeoman clothes, see the following: Claim of Williamson Jacobs, Marlboro, SCCR, RG 217, File #2248; Frederick Law Olmsted, *The Cotton Kingdom*, ed. Arthur M. Schlesinger (New York: Random House, 1984), pp. 169–72, 180; Olmsted, *A Journey in the Seaboard Slave States with Remarks on their Economy* (New York: Negro Universities Press, 1968), p. 413; Frances Trollope, *Domestic Manners of the Americans,* ed. Donald Smalley (1832; reprint ed., Gloucester, Mass.: Peter Smith, 1968), p. 241. For some examples of yeomen exchanging homespun for factory-produced cloth, see Anonymous, Account Book, Camden and Hanging Rock, Kershaw District, Account of Jane Oram, May 30, 1821 to August 28, 1821; Mary Davis Brown Diary, July 6, 1857, October 9, 1858. An incredible variety of fabric, trimmings, and notions were included in the inventory of country merchants and figured prominently in yeoman store accounts; for a few examples see the following: Inventory of the Estate of Henry W. Oakman, February 11, 1821, and Calven Hubbard, February 1, 1822, both in Barnwell District, Court of Probate, Inventories, Appraisements and Sales Book; Inventory of the Estate of Col. Elisha Rogers, Darlington District, Court of

represented the continuum of self-sufficiency and exchange that constituted yeoman household economy, spoke to the complexity of their
transactions with merchants, and revealed something of the strategies by
which they limited indebtedness.

Yeómen paid off their accounts with local merchants in a variety of
ways, then, including with surplus provisions and household manufacture. But the bulk of credit against their accounts came, as Leach Carrigan's and Samuel K. Carrigan's books confirm, from annual sales of
their small cotton crops. Interior merchants did a steady but modest cash
business, in the Carrigans' case, about 15 percent. Fully 85 percent of the
Carrigans' annual business was for credit, however, and the bulk of that
was paid for with cotton.[16] Yeomen in every part of the Low Country
had good reason to develop stable relations with local merchants, selling
cotton to the same men who extended them credit throughout the year.
If the Carrigans' customers are anything to judge by, that was precisely
the pattern to which they adhered.

William Polson, James Sumner, John Byrd, Wiley Griggs, and William Gainey were all Darlington yeomen of varying means. In 1859 each
sold Leach Carrigan one or two bales of cotton and used most of the
proceeds to pay off bills for the usual variety of store-bought goods they
had purchased during the year: hardware and plantation supplies, including nails and screws, powder and shot, axe handles, bagging, rope,
and guano; provisions, including sugar, coffee, tobacco, whiskey, and
molasses; dry goods, including calico, thread, buttons, hats, shoes, and
suspenders; occasional pharmaceuticals such as "painekillers," asep-
heteda, panegoric, or tonic; and instruments of pleasure including violin
strings, accordions, and "Jews harps."[17] Each of their accounts with the
Carrigans had its own permutations.

The young and quite poor William Polson sold Leach Carrigan what

---

Probate, Inventories, Appraisements and Sales Book, October 21, 1826, and January 6,
1827; Samuel K. Carrigan, Day Book, Account of Daniel McLeod, May 11, 1859.

16. The figure representing the proportion of their business for credit was calculated
from the account summaries entered in the ledger at the end of each month. See Samuel
K. Carrigan, Day Book, January to December, 1859. Further evidence is provided by the
records of a Kershaw merchant. Of his 112 accounts for which settlement can be determined, 90 were settled in cash, 11 in bartered goods, 8 in a combination of cash and goods,
and 3 by note. This store was primarily a tavern, and there is no indication that the
merchant was in the cotton-buying business, both of which would help to explain the high
percentage of accounts settled in cash. Anonymous, Account Book, Camden and Hanging
Rock, Kershaw District, 1821–23.

17. In each of the five cases discussed here and below, the following research method
was employed. The names were derived from Leach Carrigan's Cotton Book from the
1859 accounts and the amount of cotton sold and amount and method of payment determined. Then the names were traced to Samuel K. Carrigan's Day Book for the same year
and the annual balance for each account was tallied. The social profile of each of the five
customers and the size of cotton crop of each (in 1860) was derived from the Federal
Manuscript Census, South Carolina [Darlington and Chesterfield Districts], Schedules of
Population, Slaves, and Agriculture, 1860.

was probably the only bale of cotton he produced in 1859, but the $32.59 he received in payment was still not sufficient to cover his outstanding account of about $34. Nonetheless, Polson put exactly half ($16.20) of the credit "to balance on his account" and walked out of Carrigan's store on December 9 with the other half in cash. It is not clear how he paid the rest, but evidently the debt was carried over into the next calendar year. James Sumner was, by contrast, a considerably older and wealthier farmer than the twenty-two-year-old and newly married Polson. He too sold only one bale of cotton to Carrigan, but he put the entire amount "to credit on his account" and in doing so came close to paying off the balance. But the real difference between Sumner and Polson was that Sumner's one bale represented only a portion of his cotton crop, for at least in 1860 he produced five bales to Polson's one. Sumner, it would seem, sold Leach Carrigan just enough of his cotton to settle the debt at the Society Hill store. And that appears to have been the practice pursued by all but the poorest yeomen in the area. John Byrd and William Gainey, both of whom were small slaveholders, each sold Carrigan only a portion of their crop, took a small amount of the value in cash, and paid the rest "to credit on [their] account[s]." Carrigan carried any leftover balance into the next year at which point, presumably, it was settled with additional cotton sales, with cash from cotton sold elsewhere, or, as in Wiley Grigg's case, "by a note with interest from January last." "Well-off poor men" like Sumner, Byrd, and Gainey either sold the remainder of their cotton to another buyer for cash or maintained similar relations with other area merchants, spreading their modest cotton crops around to secure good will and good credit for the year ahead.[18]

The accounts of Darlington yeomen with Leach Carrigan and Samuel K. Carrigan are not definitive. But they are suggestive of the enormous complexity and modest scale of yeoman relations with local merchants. Cotton was the single most valuable good yeoman farmers had to sell, and they used it judiciously. Price was by no means their only—or even perhaps their primary—concern. The common assumption that local planters ginned and shipped their yeoman neighbors' cotton with

18. For the transactions of William Polson, see Leach Carrigan, Cotton Book, December 9, 1859, and Samuel K. Carrigan, Day Book, February 15, May 18, June 18, July 21, September 8, September 13, September 23, October 13, November 17, December 8, 1859. For James Sumner: Leach Carrigan, Cotton Book, November 3, 1859, and Samuel K. Carrigan, Day Book, January 29, February 5, May 30, 1859. For John Byrd: Leach Carrigan, Cotton Book, October 19, 1859, and Samuel K. Carrigan, Day Book, January 27, February 22, March 8, April 14, May 3, May 21, July 1, July 2, July 22, August 7, August 25, September 9, September 13, September 28, September 30, October 19, October 31, November 5, November 12, November 15, November 19, December 3, December 20, 1859. For William Gainey: Leach Carrigan, Cotton Book, December 12, 1859, and Samuel K. Carrigan, Day Book, February 19, December 12, 1859. For Wiley Griggs: Leach Carrigan, Cotton Book, December 3, 1859, and Samuel K. Carrigan, Day Book, January 13, June 25, July 2, July 16, July 29, August 10, August 25, September 6, September 22, October 1, October 22, October 29, November 8, December 3 or 4, December 22, 1859.

their own is not, in fact, borne out by the evidence, except, of course, in cases in which, like Caleb Coker, another Darlington planter, they ran a cotton brokerage or merchant business as well.[19] Rather, yeomen marketed their cotton through local storekeepers and in that way secured the credit in goods without which they could not have survived the long year between harvests. Their accounts with local merchants thus look like an extension of their particular strategy of household economy. By carefully balancing the production of basic foodstuffs with the marketing of food surpluses and a small cotton crop, they limited indebtedness and made their bid to reproduce independence. As merchant records reveal, that independence entitled yeomen to a place in the public culture of freemen and masters, but the limited means revealed in those same accounts made it entirely unlikely that theirs would be an equal place or that the public culture of freemen would transcend class differences.

IV

The yeomanry's relations with planters, on which that public culture really turned, were mediated not by market values but by a complex of customary and legal arrangements that defied fixed characterization. Indeed, the tension between independence and inequality at the heart of those relations ensured that their basic character was a contested one. Planters may have understood their ties to local yeomen as constituting essentially a patron-client relationship. But yeomen themselves would never have conceded that. They struggled instead to shape something more befitting free men and masters, however unequal in wealth and social standing. Common assumptions about the prerogatives of property and masters' need to discipline dependents, together with the imperatives of republican politics, went a long way toward forging grounds for an accommodation; in the Low Country neither yeomen nor planter masters could ever forget their minority status. But it was an accom-

19. For "toles" charged for ginning cotton and evidence that Coker was not just ginning but buying cotton, see entries in the back of Caleb Coker Plantation Journal, October 31, 1859, November 3, 1859, October 15, 1860, December 29, 1860, November 19, 1861, December 7, 1861, SCL. In some of those cases Coker ginned the cotton for a "tole," but the yeoman owners sold it elsewhere, the pattern suggested by the Carrigan material. Similarly, Peter Wilds, another Darlington planter, packed cotton for local producers, some of them yeomen, and charged for the rope, twine, and service. It is not clear if Wilds was also ginning the cotton, but he was not buying it or handling the marketing of it. See Peter S. Wilds, "Weight of Cotton Bales Packed, 1841," November 2, 1841, November 29, 1841, December 8, 1841, December 10, 1841, Peter S. Wilds Collection, Darlington Historic Commission, Darlington, S.C. I would like to thank John Campbell for bringing the Coker and Wilds material to my attention. The assumption is revealed, for example, in Eugene D. Genovese, "Yeoman Farmers in a Slaveholders' Democracy," *Agricultural History* 49 (April 1975), pp. 331–42.

modation ever unstable, ever on the verge of breaking down over, ironically, precisely the values and assumptions that masters shared.

A peculiar combination of social distance and intimacy characterized the yeomanry's relations with planters in the Low Country. It was one of the ways in which the tensions of independence and inequality were played out and, in some respects at least, contained. For while planters could not remove themselves from the society of their yeoman neighbors whom they met regularly at the store, courthouse, ballot box, and, in some cases, church, they could attempt to limit the occasions and to structure the unavoidable ones into ritualistic and thus more predictable forms. This is precisely what lowcountry planters tried to do, moving in social circles of their own kind except on those public and usually political occasions when forced to admit the local yeomen to the grounds— although never to the house—for July Fourth barbeques, militia dinners, and the like. Both the social distance and the intimacy were authentic, and often simultaneous, parts of the relations that yeomen and planters forged. Both were expressions of a society structured around households at once independent and deeply unequal in terms of the wealth and power they embodied.

At least one lowcountry planter, Frederick Porcher, expressed concern that a dangerous social distance characterized the relations of yeomen and planters in the Low Country and that the independence of yeoman households bred threatening independent political instincts, as well. Such an "excess of independence," the "only evil of slavery," he ruminated in 1854, could undermine the very conditions that the defense of slavery required. Slavery "isolates classes and prevents a healthful sympathy from existing between the poor and the rich," he observed, so that men develop "no sense of mutual dependence." A conservative in the deepest sense of the word, Porcher warned planters to nurture an organic society whose ranks would be held together by very tangible bonds. Only where the "small farmer [finds] a market for the sale of his kitchen stuffs" with his planter neighbors, he insisted, would the proper proslavery sympathy develop among the nonslaveholding classes.[20]

Porcher knew whereof he spoke. His own immediate "social circle" in rural Charleston District was an exclusive one indeed. By his own admission, it was composed entirely of "planter families, all of whom occupied the same social position." In fact, "the line of demarcation between them and the others [was] so distinctly drawn," he recalled in his memoirs, that "of those other people, I knew nothing." Doubtless he exaggerated. But his description of the St. John's Hunting Club, around which the social life of neighborhood planters revolved, made it abundantly clear that even the cultural practices common to yeomen and planter men, such as hunting, inscribed, rather than ameliorated, class distinctions among

20. Frederick Porcher, "Prospects and Policy of the South as They Appear to the Eyes of a Planter," *Southern Quarterly Review*, 10 (October 1854), pp. 431–57.

freemen. Every planter living within ten miles of the club was a member, and not only did that company form exclusive hunting parties but, mounted on horseback and attended by their slaves, they displayed in every possible way their distinction from the local yeomen and other poor men, including slaves, who hunted for subsistence rather than for sport. Porcher and his friends hosted dinners at the clubhouse every month by turn, and on those days, he recalled, visitors were sure to find assembled "together all the gentry of the neighborhood" engaged in conversation about "politics or agriculture." Although they were not invited to hunt or to share the monthly dinners, local yeomen did break bread at the St. John's clubhouse at least once: in November 1831, when Porcher and his pals threw a "public dinner" for three hundred people. Using the clubhouse as "a sort of pantry," they spread out one table to the north "for the expected guests," and around it they arranged another twelve or thirteen tables at which "the people were seated."[21] Even in the common culture of lowcountry freemen, distance and intimacy, independence and inequality, were inscribed and enacted.

But if yeoman farmers did not stand in the kind of organic relation to planters that Porcher desired, neither were they so isolated as he had feared. No lowcountry household was sufficiently autarkic to forgo entirely the petty exchange of goods and services that connected yeoman settlements to planter ones nearby. Those exchanges were, moreover, inextricable from the long-standing and complex social ties of which they were a part. Not the contractual relations of employer and employee, nor those of master and slave, relations between yeomen and planters were rather a historically distinctive case of men equally independent—men, masters, and citizens—and thoroughly unequal. Precisely because they had to accommodate both truths, lowcountry yeomen and planters found themselves in a constant contest over the appropriate interpretation of the social inequality at work between them. There was plenty of room for interpretation.

Yeomen, at least lowcountry ones, did not typically keep account of the numerous petty exchanges that linked them to planter neighbors. The torn and hastily written receipts marked with an "x" and scattered haphazardly among planters' papers provide one obvious reason. But even the fragments in planter accounts evoke relationships so dense they are difficult to recover. At the very least, they suggest that Porcher's fear

21. Samuel Gaillard Stoney, ed., "The Memoirs of Frederick A. Porcher, *South Carolina Historical and Genealogical Magazine* vols. 44-48 (April 1943-January 1947), vol. 44, no. 3 (April 1943), pp. 66–67; vol. 45, no. 3 (July 1944), pp. 32, 36–37; vol. 46, no. 2 (April 1945) pp. 90–92. For an interesting discussion of the "subtext of exclusion" in planters' hunting culture, see Stuart Marks, *Southern Hunting in Black and White: Nature, History, and Ritual in a Carolina Community* (Princeton, N.J.: Princeton University Press, 1991), pp. 1–38. Porcher's experience was hardly unique. Its main outlines are more fully elaborated in William Elliott's famous sportsman stories. See Elliott, *Carolina Sports by Land and Water: Including Incidents of Devil-Fishing, Wild-Cat, Deer and Bear Hunting, Etc.* (1846; reprint ed., New York: Arno Press, 1967).

was misplaced: Yeomen found a ready market for all kinds of surplus produce on lowcountry and middle-country plantations. In both areas, large planters usually failed to attain anything approaching self-sufficiency in foodstuffs. And while they typically met most of their household provisioning needs through bulk purchases from town merchants and factors, there were plenty of occasions on which, caught short, they turned to yeomen neighbors for small amounts of foodstuffs to tide them over. Planters' accounts contain receipts from yeomen for all sorts of foodstuff and materials, grown, raised, hunted, and gathered: corn, bacon, beef, butter, lard, tallow, chickens, ducks, shingles and boards, to name only the most common.[22] Paid for in cash or in credit arranged with local merchants, such transactions might appear straightforward. But the ties between yeomen and planters neither started nor ended there. For if yeomen sold goods to planters, they also sold their skills and services, and, most freighted of all, in some cases they even sold their labor.

Yeomen skilled as blacksmiths, carpenters, and turners plied their trades irregularly on neighboring plantations, and yeoman wives in turn practiced the nursing and midwiving skills peculiar to women for which there was no end of demand among slaves, mistresses, and planter families in general. And in an exchange that was particularly volatile, some yeoman farmers worked as overseers on local plantations while they continued to operate their own farms. Other exchanges pulled even closer to the employer-employee one so at odds with lowcountry notions of social relations, for while the majority of free laborers hired to work on plantations were free blacks or, more commonly, landless whites, it was by no means unheard of for yeomen—and especially yeoman sons— to hire on for the day, month, or season to ditch, build fences and Negro houses, or perform any other task a casual laborer might perform.[23]

22. Such evidence is scattered throughout planter papers, but for a sample see the following: John Riley to Colonel Alexander Lawton for money paid to Redden Tuten, December 16, 1829, and February 14, 1829; receipt of Redden Tuten for payment received from Alexander Norton, November 17, 1841; Estate of Robert Brooks to A. J. Lawton, Administrator, for money paid to Redden Tuten and Charity Tuten, July 2, 1842, April 20, 1842, April 1844, all in Lawton Family Papers. Joseph Palmer Account Book, July 10, 1827, June 17, 1829, Palmer Family Papers, SCL; Receipt of John Threewits for payment received from Richard Singleton for lumber, April 14, 1841, receipt of Chosel Weeks for payment received from Richard Singleton for boards, June 18, 1853 and bill of James Ray to Estate of Richard Singleton for beef and tallow, March 24, 1853, all in Singleton Family Papers, SHC. John Berkley Grimball Diary, receipts for lumber and shingles, vol. 1, February 25, 1833, May 9, 1834, November 18, 1834; vol. 2, January 9, 1837, April 20, 1840, April 10, 1841, April 15, 1842; vol. 3, April 3, 1850, all in Grimball Family Papers, SHC; Charles Cotesworth Pinckney Plantation Book, [partial] Accounts, 1861 and throughout, Charles Cotesworth Pinckney Family Papers, Series II, No. 1, LC.

23. Nehemiah Ginn to William Lawton, Bills for services [sharpening plough, mending wagon, etc], May 23, 1846, to March 16, 1847; January 22, 1847, to September 20, 1847; and throughout, 1842–1847; John Riley to Alexander Lawton, May 30, 1828; Bill of Elisha Wall to William Lawton for payment due Mary Wall for nursing services, January 22,

For their part, planters provided yeomen with more than a market for surplus goods and occasional services. Those exchanges could be compensated with money, goods, and credit, but others, not so easily defined as economic exchanges, were not so easily compensated either. In addition to selling provisions and lending money, hiring and lending out slaves and work animals in explicit exchange for goods and labor, planters also served as security on bonds and as administrators for local yeomen's estates, provided legal and medical advice, dispensed charity to destitute widows and sick neighbors, employed worthy young men as overseers, and interceded with sheriffs and judges on behalf of others.[24] Yeomen may have seen such services as discrete parts of a larger exchange relation, one defined by a rough reciprocity. But planters apparently saw it differently, suggesting by their constant complaints about yeoman "ingratitude" that they were owed something they never received: the allegiance, perhaps, of client to patron. Certainly there was reason enough in both perspectives. The myriad forms that relations between yeomen and planters took in the Low Country proved fertile ground for such incommensurable conceptions of the substance and texture of power.

1829; Receipt of Mary Wall [signed with "X"] for money received for services as midwife, April 24, 1832, all in Lawton Family Papers. John Berkley Grimball Diary, vol. 2, May 2, 1840, October 11, 1846; vol. 3, December 20, 1848, all in Grimball Family Papers. For a few examples of yeoman farmers who worked for local planters as overseers, see the following: Claim of Samuel Crews, Beaufort, SCCR, RG 233; Claim of Edward Middleton, Beaufort, SCCR, RG 217, File #10351; Claim of Abner Smith, Marlboro, SCCR, RG 217, File #593. For a good example of yeomen or their sons providing casual labor on neighborhood plantations, see Anonymous, Fair Mount Plantation Journal, Barnwell District, March 28, 1838, June 11, 1838, January 7, 1840, March 26, 1840, June 20, 1840, June 26, 1840, March 20 to April 17, 1843, SCL.

24. Anonymous, Fair Mount Plantation Journal, March 28, 1838, June 11, 1838, February 18, 1839, January 7, 1840, March 26, 1840, June 20, 1840, November 12, 1840, January 25, 1841, June 14, 1841, August 3, 1841, March 20-April 17, 1843; James Henry Hammond, Memorandum Book, 1855, Account with "Kelly," February 14, 1855-September 1, 1855, James Henry Hammond Papers, in Kenneth Stampp, ed., Records of Antebellum Southern Plantations From the Revolution Through the Civil War, Series A, Part 1, Reel 5; William P. Brookes to James Henry Hammond, Silver Bluff, November 17, 1831, James Henry Hammond Papers, in Stampp, ed., Records of Antebellum Southern Plantations, Reel 6; James Henry Hammond Diary, March 27, 1841, September 4, 1841, June 28, 1842, October 9, 1842, reprinted in Carol Bleser, ed., *Secret and Sacred: The Diaries of James Henry Hammond, a Southern Slaveholder* (New York: Oxford University Press, 1988), pp. 48, 72, 97, 112–13; Drew Gilpin Faust, *James Henry Hammond and the Old South: A Design for Mastery* (Baton Rouge: Louisiana State University Press, 1982), pp. 131–34; John Berkley Grimball Diary, vol. 1, December 7, 1832, July 4, 1834, July 22, 1834, and vol. 3, November 21, 1853; David Gavin Diary, July 12, 1856, August 14, 1856, September 24, 1856, January 8, 1857, February 6, 1857, March 31, 1857, April 7, 1857, February 9, 1861, SHC, and references in footnotes below; John Edwin Fripp Plantation Book, vol. 3, April 1, 1857, April 4, 1857, January 28, 1858, January 29, 1858, John Edwin Fripp Papers, SHC; Charleston District, Court of General Sessions, Bills of Indictment, 1837, No. 14A *State* v. *William Campbell*, SCDAH. For evidence from the Lawton Family Papers, see the references in footnotes, 17, 18, and below.

The problem, however, is hardly apparent in the abstract, for it was precisely the personal nature of the relationships that made them so volatile and difficult to define. Take the case of Redden Tuten and Alexander Lawton. For more than twenty years, from 1824 to the late 1840s at least, Tuten, a yeoman farmer and his wife, Charity Tuten, sold various kinds of foodstuff to Lawton, a planter who belonged to one of the wealthiest families in their St. Peter's Parish neighborhood.[25] Lawton bought food for his own household from the Tutens but also for other households whose affairs he was administering in his capacity as executor of estate—one reason, no doubt, for his assiduous bookkeeping. In December 1829 Lawton paid "Mr Redden Tuten" nine dollars for a beef sold to the estate of the Reverend Brooks; a few months later he paid Tuten for "pease"; in November 1841 he paid Redden Tuten twelve dollars for butter. In December of the same year he paid another eighteen dollars, this time to "Mrs Tuten for butter," and so on until at least 1847.[26]

There was nothing unusual about this relationship except that evidence of it survives. But neither was it so straightforward as it might seem at first glance. For if the Tutens sold Lawton petty produce and were paid, for the most part, in cash, the relations between the yeoman and the planter families were hardly defined by the cash nexus. Alexander Lawton was not just a leading planter in the neighborhood but one of the leading lights of the local Baptist church. He was, in fact, at least for a time, the treasurer of the Black Swamp Baptist Church near the village of Robertville. The Tutens were also Baptists, possibly members of that congregation, as were many of the other local folk, rich and poor, for whom Alexander Lawton served as estate executor. In addition to the Reverend Brooks, to whom the Tutens sold butter, corn, and other goods, Lawton settled the estates of James Francis, Erasmus Swift,

25. In 1824 Redden Tuten owned 50 acres of improved land and 1 slave; in 1850, his 60-year-old widow, Charity, was head of a household that included 50 acres of improved land and 3 slaves. In 1824 Colonel Alexander J. Lawton owned probably 190 improved acres and 36 slaves; in 1850, the 58-year-old planter owned 780 improved acres and 60 slaves. The Tutens were part of an extended kin group of at least six families, all of which lived in St. Peter's Parish and all of which were nonslaveholding or small slaveholding yeoman farmers. Alexander Lawton was part of an extended clan of planters, the wealthiest of whom, in 1824, owned 119 slaves but all of whom owned well over 20 per household. The relationship among Redden and Charity Tuten and Alexander Lawton lasted for more than 30 years. Social profiles were compiled from the following sources: South Carolina Lower Division Tax Returns, [St. Peter's Parish, Beaufort District], 1824, Records of the Comptroller General, SCDAH; Federal Manuscript Census, South Carolina, [Beaufort District] Schedules of Population, Slaves, and Agriculture, 1850.

26. John Riley to Colonel Alexander J. Lawton, December 16, 1829; Bill of John Riley for money "paid Redden Tuten for pease," February 14, 1829; Bill of Redden Tuten for butter, November 17, 1841; Bill of Estate of John A. Corley to Colonel Alexander J. Lawton, for cash paid Mrs. Tuten for butter, December 4, 1841; Account of Alexander J. Lawton with Estate of Robert Brooks, for cash paid Mr. Tuten for lard, March 12, 1847, all in Lawton Family Papers.

and John Dupuis, all local Baptists of extremely modest means.[27] Lawton may not have played that particular role for the Tutens or for the other members of their family with whom he maintained ties, but there can be little doubt that theirs was a relationship configured around the ties of Christian fellowship. When Tuten extended credit to Lawton for goods provided and later called in the debt, when he went down to William Lawton's store in Robertville to use the credit Alexander Lawton had established for him there, those economic exchanges could not be extricated from the larger web of social relations in which they were embedded.[28] No doubt the same was true of Lawton's relationship with Elisha Wall, another local yeoman farmer, whose wife, Mary, was the most skilled midwife and nurse in the neighborhood and on whose services Alexander Lawton regularly called, and of the relationship between his relative William Lawton and the farmer and turner Nehemiah Ginn, who regularly performed odd jobs on another of the Lawtons' plantations.[29] Whether Redden or Charity Tuten and Alexander Lawton would have explained the nature of their relationship in precisely the same way, we will never know. But plenty of evidence exists in other cases to suggest otherwise.

When, on Christmas eve in 1860, the plantation mistress Keziah Brevard sent four pounds of coffee to her neighbor Mrs. Strickland, she viewed herself as engaging in an act of patronage and Christian charity.

27. Alexander Norton rented a pew in Black Swamp Baptist Church in the village of Robertville. It was the wealthiest Baptist church in Beaufort. See Black Swamp Baptist Church, Subscription List, 1847, 1848, and History, 1895, SCL. There is, however, no extant membership list for Black Swamp with which to confirm the Baptist affiliations of Redden and Charity Tuten. Other members of the Tuten clan belonged to Baptist churches in the parish, however, including Mary Tuten, whose husband, Absalom, had a similar exchange relationship with Alexander Lawton. See Black Creek Baptist Church, Minute Book, March 23, 1851, SCL. For inventories of the estates of James Francis, Sr., and Erasmus Swift, see Lawton Family Papers, October 9, 1824, November 18, 1825. Lawton settled John Dupuis's estate in 1833. See Lawton Family Papers, February 21, 1833. For evidence of Dupuis's modest means (he owned land and 8 slaves) see South Carolina Lower Division Tax Returns, [St. Peter's Parish, Beaufort District], 1824, Records of the Comptroller General.

28. John Riley to Colonel Alexander J. Lawton, requesting payment of outstanding bill of Redden Tuten against Estate of Robert Brookes, December 16, 1829, Lawton Family Papers; Bill of Mr. Redden Tuten with Lawton and Norton, Robertville Merchants, May 20, 1825, Lawton Family Papers.

29. John Riley to Alexander Lawton, requesting payment to Mary Wall for nursing services, May 30, 1828 (Mary Wall signed with an "X"); Bill of Elisha Wall against Estate of William H. Lawton, for nursing services of Mary Wall, January 22, 1829; Receipt of Mary Wall for services as midwife, April 24, 1832; Bill of Nehemiah Ginn to William Lawton, for blacksmith-type services, May 23, 1846, to March 16, 1847; January 22, 1847, to September 20, 1847; January 22, 1847 to January 1848, all in Lawton Family Papers. In 1824 Elisha Wall owned 300 acres of land valued at twenty cents per acre (suggesting it was unimproved) and no slaves. See South Carolina Lower Division Tax Returns [St. Peter's Parish, Beaufort District], 1824, Records of the Comptroller General. In 1850, Nehemiah Ginn was a 60-year-old farmer and turner who owned 30 acres of improved land and no slaves. See Federal Manuscript Census, South Carolina, [Beaufort District] Schedules of Population, Slaves, and Agriculture, 1850.

"I feel for poor people who have large families to struggle for," she wrote piously in her journal. "We who are able ought to help them." What Mrs. Strickland thought we can only imagine, but the independent status of her household put her beyond the usual reach of planter intervention even in the guise of charity, and she would have been justified in regarding Brevard's action as part of a more reciprocal exchange. For as Brevard herself noted on that same Christmas eve, "she will pay me eggs for these." Brevard, it seems, wanted it both ways. And, indeed, Mrs. Strickland did regularly sell eggs to Keziah Brevard—and often waited weeks for their accounts to be settled up. When an upcountry yeoman wife accepted an act of charity from a local planter woman, she reputedly stammered, "Well, I will try to do as much for you." Her response was, perhaps, not so unusual. The posture of equality, the lack of deference that southern yeomen apparently adopted in such exchanges, mystified European and Yankee travelers.[30] Planters, however, were not mystified; more often they were angered, and in those explosive moments, captured in diaries and correspondence, is revealed something of their expectations about the proper deportment of yeoman neighbors and the source of their endless disappointment.

David Gavin, a cantankerous and unmarried middle-aged planter in Colleton District, complained incessantly about his plain-folk neighbors. Men like Joel Spell, Richard Waters, and James Pendarvis made too free with his property, expertise, and largesse, he insisted, and were entirely too presumptuous in their dealings with him. Although they paid for the corn they bought, Gavin was never satisfied. After one particular corn deal with Spell in the spring of 1860 for which he extracted a note for security on the debt, Gavin swore that he would "quit selling corn." These "vilains [*sic*] and swindlers," he seethed, "think nothing of *Lies* to get your corn or money, and then abuse and insult you about it." Clearly Spell was withholding something to which Gavin felt entitled, and in another venting of spleen Gavin came closer to articulating it. Richard Waters had been in trouble with the law and had come to Gavin for advice, a community role in which Gavin took inordinate pride. As Gavin put it, I "told him as well as I know." But by the time he recorded the meeting in his diary, he had worked himself into a rage about Waters and his "class" who "loaf about the country, drink, live on credit, swindling, and perhaps stealing." "The dirty scoundrel," Gavin expostulated, "he . . . is ready enough to come to me for advice and assistance to get

30. Keziah Goodwyn Hopkins Brevard Diary, December 12, 1860, December 22, 1860, December 24, 1860, SCL; Mary Moragne, *The Neglected Thread: A Journal from the Calhoun Community, 1836–1842*, ed. Delle Mullen Craven (Columbia, S.C.: University of South Carolina Press, 1951), p. 124. Frances Trollope remarked on southern plain folk's aversion to any appearance of charity. They borrowed necessities "but always in a form that shewed their dignity and freedom," offering, for example, to do work in exchange. "The coarse familiarity, untempered by any shadow of respect which is assumed by the grossest and the lowest in their intercourse with the highest and most refined," was in her view, "a positive evil." Trollope, *Domestic Manners of the Americans*, pp. 119–21. Also see Olmsted, *Cotton Kingdom*, p. 180.

out, but when I want [him] to vote for a decent, intelligent, and respectable man" he is "ready to beat, abuse, and mob me." Clearly Gavin and
Waters had different understandings of what was owed in their relationship. Gavin believed that he could exact a price for his advice and patronage; the price was loyalty and deference. Waters, and presumably
Spell, believed that the exchange entailed no legitimate burdens of clientage.[31]

How such incommensurable expectations could have been sustained,
how reciprocity and patronage could have coexisted in the characteristic
relations of lowcountry yeomen and planters, Gavin inadvertently revealed in an especially difficult moment, when his "near neighbor"
James Pendarvis up and left for Florida. Until the moment Pendarvis
left the neighborhood, Gavin never ceased complaining about him and
about his corn-borrowing habit. "I am getting tired of giving away to
support idleness," he had griped less than a month before, "[h]e and his
son JB owe me now." But after their departure, Gavin was concerned
less about what he was owed than about what he had been given and had
now lost. "I shall feel lonesome many a time for his place looks melan-
choly and it makes me feel so to be about it," he admitted. "I shall need
him in sickness, for he was a good hand in sickness," Gavin went on,
recalling that back in 1857 when he was sick, Pendarvis had "nursed me
or rather visited me as I had previously done him." For that kindness,
one no doubt especially valuable to an unmarried man, Gavin had
"stripped all his fodder and his boys idled about at nothing." Between
David Gavin and James Pendarvis there was a deep personal history and
sense of reciprocal obligation no less authentic than the power and patronage that also bound them. Like many lowcountry yeomen and their
planter neighbors, they had worked out an accommodation that reflected the imperatives of the slave society in which they lived. Some
things mattered more than others, as Gavin conceded. Although Pendarvis "had his faults and so had his wife and children, they were my
only near neighbors, and I do not believe he ever carried on illicit traffick with my negroes." And "that," he noted sadly, "is saying a good deal
for many do it in better circumstances than he was, and are considered
honest."[32] Out of the personal nature of the ties that bound them, out of
their common respect for private property and property in man, and
out of the social and political imperatives of slave society, yeomen and
planters in the South Carolina Low Country forged a workable alliance.

V

Where the characteristic independence of yeomen and planters coexisted with deep social inequality and nurtured contradictory claims and

31. Gavin Diary, May 25, 1860, October 13, 1857, October 25, 1855.
32. Ibid., January 28, 1859, February 9, 1859, February 11, 1859.

expectations, any accommodation reached was bound to be unstable. For reasons both personal and political David Gavin had been constrained from forcing the issue of clientage with Pendarvis and the others. But James Henry Hammond, a newcomer to his Barnwell neighborhood in the 1830s, to the prerogatives of planters, and to the etiquette of relations with his mostly yeoman neighbors, recognized no such constraints. In a standoff that ensued with a particular neighbor, Hammond was not only taught the proper comportment of a planter-politician but in the process confronted the contradiction at the heart of the relationship with yeomen, revealed the ground of its most common collapse, and learned the nature of the customary accommodation.

Hammond was an uncommonly mean man, a despicable character among a historical set that offered great competition for that particular distinction. When he married Catherine Fitzsimmons, this struggling schoolteacher son of an upcountry schoolmaster and college steward came into a great deal of property. He instantly became the planter of preeminent wealth in the vicinity of his Barnwell District plantation.[33] His masterly identity was not so easily acquired. Hammond wielded power with a heavy hand, and, in what was admittedly one of the lesser of his abuses of power, he attempted to exact due submission from a neighbor, John Ransey. From the moment Hammond arrived, he and Ransey contested ownership of a piece of land at the boundary of their respective properties, and in the initial skirmish Hammond demonstrated both his punitive propensities and his failure to grasp the subtleties of yeoman-planter relations.[34] Ten years later the dynamic was fully played out, as Ransey and Hammond locked in mighty struggle over the conflicting imperatives of masters, the power that property conferred, and the relationship it established between planters and their less wealthy, usually yeoman, neighbors.

It was the most ordinary conflict. Ransey had been using the canal around Hammond's mill-dam to get his lumber and other produce to the landing on the river. When challenged by Hammond's overseer, he claimed the customary right to do so based on ten years' use. If yeomen and planters both respected each other's right to virtually unrestricted dominion over the domestic domain within the boundaries of the fence, and if planters were forced to concede yeomen's civil and political rights in the public domain, nothing like a consensus governed relations of those masters on the liminal ground—neither fully public nor yet fully private—between households. Especially in the Low Country, coastal and interior, where large expanses of privately owned but unenclosed land obscured clear distinctions between public and private space,

33. For an outstanding biography of Hammond, see Faust, *James Henry Hammond and the Old South*; on Hammond's standing in his Barnwell neighborhood and his relations with local yeomen, see, especially, pp. 131–34.

34. James Henry Hammond to Mr. Ransey, Silver Bluff, December 24, 1831, Letter Press Book, 1831–1833, Hammond Papers, in Stampp, ed., *Records of Antebellum Southern Plantations*, Series A, Part 1, Reel 3.

struggles such as those between Hammond and Ransey represented perhaps the single greatest fault line in yeoman-planter relations. Outside the fence and its clearly demarcated authority, yeomen and planter masters battled over whose interests would prevail and whose rights would take precedence. Those struggles, which took particular form as conflicts over right-of-way or trespass and, more generally, over common rights and the definition of private property, consumed the courts and the legislature in the antebellum period. And as the legal cases confirmed, yeomen found it hard to resist the prerogatives of private property that planters invoked. Their own considerable prerogatives and privileges rested on precisely those claims. Empowered as property owners and masters of dependents, they confronted men who owned far more property and mastered many more dependents. Yeoman farmers had conceded too much to property to resist effectively its logic. In struggles with planters they found themselves overmatched. As the battle between Ransey and Hammond showed, they had the power to extract recognition, however reluctant, of their identity as freemen and masters; they could not extract equality.

When Ransey countered Hammond's charges of trespassing with claims to customary right-of-way, an outraged Hammond, responding less to the act than to the presumption, insisted that Ransey had only "what is derived from my kindness and indulgence." Ransey, he said, had "convert[ed] into a right what he had begged of me as a favor." The struggle immediately ceased to be about a particular inconvenience and became instead a matter of power and submission. "I must defend my property at every hazard," Hammond declared. "The man who claims such free use of it may soon claim it all and will certainly degrade and disgrace me if I submit to him." Ransey, as it turns out, had little stomach for submission himself.

Hammond's struggle for dominance in this, as in so much else, became his overriding concern. Although he felt like "inflicting personal chastisement" on Ransey, no doubt of the sort with a whip in the public streets that he felt befitted those below him, he was deterred by his own political ambition and the necessity "of avoiding an affray." He opted for symbolic submission instead, demanding that Ransey acknowledge his ownership by agreeing to pay ten cents per year for the right to use the waterway.[35]

---

35. James Henry Hammond to Captain Ransey, Silver Bluff, September 8, 1842, Hammond Papers, in Stampp, ed., *Records of Antebellum Southern Plantations*, Series A, Part 1, Reel 8; James Henry Hammond Diary, September 10, 1842, September 17, 1842, reprinted in Bleser, ed., *Secret and Sacred*, pp. 107–09, 110. Hammond had indulged such instincts in the past. In 1831, in a conflict with a newspaper editor (a man called Daniels), he had refused to honor the man with a challenge to a duel and instead beat him with a whip in the public streets. John M. Huger to James Henry Hammond, Camden, June 15, 1831, Hammond Papers, in Stampp, ed., *Records of Antebellum Southern Plantations*, Series A, Part 1, Reel 6.

Ransey refused to bend the knee. Instead, he insisted on his customary rights, threatened to indict Hammond if he infringed them, and prepared to defend them to the death if necessary. He forced a standoff. Although he chafed at Ransey's "insolence," although he declared he would never "submit to him," Hammond backed down. "He still speaks of having rights," Hammond admitted a few weeks later, but "I told him [they] were of no consequence to me so he did not attempt to enforce them." Ransey had taught Hammond a lesson that would last as long as Hammond's political ambitions. It looked bad to be under indictment when one was standing for election to the Governor's seat, he admitted, and it looked worse "to appear illiberal" in one's dealings with lesser folk.[36]

Hammond never lost his utter contempt for his mostly yeoman neighbors. To him they were "the most ignorant, vulgar, and . . . narrow-minded set of people in the world." And he never ceased to be astonished at the "ingratitude" with which they met his generous patronage. In this respect he was no different from other lowcountry planters, many of whom resented that patronage extended was received as customary right or reciprocal exchange and who were frustrated that their yeoman neighbors would not play their proper part in the patron-client relationship. Hammond's great error was not that he felt as he did but that he expected his yeoman neighbors to concede his view. He had erred grievously in attempting to impose an unambiguous power relation, one that other planters, however unhappily, wisely left ill-defined. Most lowcountry planters left the conceit of reciprocity intact. Belatedly, Hammond learned to dress up contempt in the garb of self-righteous stewardship. "I have . . . descended low to improve them as in duty bound," he wrote of his Barnwell neighbors in 1848.[37]

David Gavin also believed, like Hammond, that yeomen got more than they deserved by way of respect. He even insisted, albeit implausibly, that they used their customary rights and invulnerability as heads of independent households to extract social and political equality. Convinced that his yeoman neighbors were stealing his livestock, Gavin raged about his inability to accuse them publicly or to pursue the wrong-doers. "I have no doubt some democrat, not perhaps having any [cattle], put his political doctrine into practical operation with me," he ranted in early 1860. "For as 'all men are by it equal', and he or they had no beeves and I had, he took mine to be on an equality with me." But what really

36. James Henry Hammond Diary, September 17, 1842, September 30, 1842, October 6, 1842, October 9, 1842, November 16, 1842, all reprinted in Bleser, ed., *Secret and Sacred*, pp. 110–13.

37. James Henry Hammond Diary, July 3, 1841, September 22, 1848, November 17, 1861, reprinted in Bleser, ed., *Secret and Sacred*, pp. 62–64, 189–92, 191. Hammond's contempt was also evident in his published addresses and writings. See, for example, James Henry Hammond, *An Address Delivered Before the South Carolina Institute at its First Annual Fair, 20th November 1849* (Charleston: Walker and James, 1849).

galled Gavin was that "[he] must submit to it." At other times he claimed that his neighbors had compelled compliance with unfair practices such as forcing a rent reduction by threatening "to burn my fence and houses." But in the end, it was their political rights that Gavin, like Hammond, found most intimidating. "These scoundrels who have taken my hogs and beeves, if white (of which I have little doubt) will have the same right to vote as myself," he fumed, "and in all probability created debts and lay taxes on me without paying an part or laying any taxes on themselves. This is Equality."[38] Gavin's insistence that his neighbors had the power to seize his property was more a measure of his exaggerated sense of entitlement than of any ability on their part to claim social equality. But he did not exaggerate when he acknowledged that as independent and enfranchised men they had rights he was bound to respect. Gavin did not like it, and neither did Hammond or, presumably, any other lowcountry planter. Certainly yeomen were ever vigilant against planter disrespect and abuse of power. The independence common to yeoman and planter masters, coupled with the social inequality that characterized their relations in the Low Country, made for a volatile combination indeed.

VI

Where yeomen and planter masters together constituted, as they did in the Low Country, a propertied and enfranchised minority within a dependent and disfranchised majority, their common interests were hard to overlook. But there were conflicts, such as those between Hammond and Gavin and their neighbors, that were difficult to contain. More often than not, the difficulty lay in mediating the claims of men who saw themselves as masters, with all that entailed at home and abroad. The potential for conflict thus resided in the same principles that engendered accommodation. Nowhere was this more patently the case than in the matter of illicit trade with slaves, to which Gavin had pointed in articulating his grudging respect for his neighbor Pendarvis. Nothing, perhaps, revealed so clearly the necessity of good relations between yeomen and planters in the Low Country, and nothing so clearly revealed the instability and even the fragility of those relations, as the specter of local white men trafficking with slaves in stolen goods. In dealing with such conflicts, lowcountry planters simultaneously acknowledged class difference with yeomen and attempted to deny it.

The question of slave discipline and the security of slave property underlay a great many of the conflicts that erupted between yeomen and planters in the Low Country, including those disputes ostensibly over right-of-way, trespass, and the boundaries of private property and mas-

38. Gavin Diary, June 13, 1860, January 24, 1858.

terly authority. But as the struggle between Ralph Elliott and his neighbor Price demonstrates, there was no more volatile issue than that of illegal trade between nonelite whites and slaves, precisely because of its direct connection to slave discipline and thus to the very future of the "peculiar" domestic institution. To David Gavin the trustworthiness of Pendarvis on this score constituted the quintessential characteristic of a good neighbor. His Colleton neighborhood was full of less trustworthy characters, he insisted, "mean democratic white men" who sold liquor to slaves and "who are no better than abolitionists."[39]

Gavin's melodramatic construction of the problem was not singular. From grand juries in virtually every district of the coastal and interior Low Country came similar evaluations of the threat and calls for dire punishment of white offenders. Not surprisingly, such prescriptions followed a chronology of political crisis. Immediately after the Denmark Vesey revolt, during the Nullification Crisis, and throughout the 1850s, indictments flooded the court dockets, vigilantes pursued suspects, and grand juries and groups of citizens beseiged the legislature with demands for more effective surveillance and punishment of offenders.[40] They targeted slaves themselves, foreigners, and all suspicious outsiders. Self-constituted committees such as the "Orangeburg Vigilant Committee" hunted "itinerant Yankees" with dogs and literally rode them out of town on a rail when they found them, as they did with a Yankee nurse working in the local lunatic asylum, putting her, under guard, on the first train to Charleston. Their counterparts in other districts drove out northern women visitors, temperance lecturers, and hawkers and peddlers accused of "abolitionism."[41] But when that Orangeburg Committee drove out one white man who was under suspicion of trading with slaves for stolen guano, they discovered subsequently that "he was not," as they had assumed, "from the land of Yankeedom" but from a neighboring district. Unrepentant at the incursion on the man's rights—they had "ordered him to leave the place in one hour"—"Our vigilants" put out a description of the young man, praying that "should he turn up in any other part of the District, we trust he will be attended to."[42] The turn to suspects not slaves and "not strangers"—that is, to local white men— was a common one. The "Pineville Police Association" of Frederick Porcher's rural Charleston neighborhood was founded in 1823 with the

39. Ibid., October 29, 1860, February 6, 1857, April 11, 1858.

40. The political pattern in the enforcement of the laws against trading with slaves and the calls for stricter penalties can be traced in Grand Jury Presentments, 1820–1865, General Assembly Records, SCDAH. While presentments on this subject proliferated in the 1850s, only one was submitted between 1839 and 1847. See Grand Jury Presentments, Charleston District, May Term, 1846, General Assembly Records. Concern with illicit trade was, moreover, the single issue most frequently addressed by the Grand Juries in this period.

41. *Orangeburg Southron*, April 4, 1860; *Darlington Flag*, March 4, 1852; *Kingstree Star*, March 31, 1859.

42. *Orangeburg Southron*, April 4, 1860.

express purpose of "apprehending or dispersing a gang of desperate Runaways"; by 1839 the association had moved to suppress "all traffick with slaves" and to convict "any individual trading with negroes without a written permission."[43] When political crisis inflamed latent suspicion no white men, not even local yeomen, were immune from planter fury. The facade of trust, so carefully cultivated, burned off in the fire. At those moments, yeoman independence was no match for planter power.

Yet there was no shortage of yeoman farmers among the marauding bands of vigilantes dispensing rough justice in the rural Low Country in the 1830s and 1850s. Proper regulation of slaves was, after all, a matter of critical importance to them as slaveholders in many cases and, more generally, as part of the propertied community invested in the discipline of dependents. Without the support of local yeomen, the planters who typically formed the founding membership of "vigilant" associations would have found themselves obstructed at every turn. But such common concerns with slave discipline not infrequently became divisive. For although yeoman farmers were by no means a particular target of vigilant associations, when local planters raised a posse or formed a committee of public safety it was their interests as owners of large numbers of slaves that they sought to protect.[44] And in such moments all nonelite whites fell under suspicion. Yeomen were not exempt.

Gavin suspected many of his neighbors. Indeed, he insisted that Glen Reeves, Jacob and Reid Utsey, and G. A. T. Johnson, all local farmers, had burned down the cornhouse belonging to Dr. Shuler because Shuler, a local planter, had set them up for indictment by sending his slave Shed onto their property with corn to sell to them in exchange for liquor. Certainly Ralph Elliott had suspected his neighbor Price, and other planters like John Berkley Grimball and James Legaré were so afraid of the possibility that they colluded on land transactions, as one put it, to "prevent the place from falling into other and perhaps unneighbourly hands."[45] There were some yeomen particularly vulnerable to suspicion, like the Charleston District farmer John Broad, who lived in steady violation of the racial proprieties of slave society by having a family with his slave woman and by leaving his property to his heirs "to

43. Pineville Police Association, Secretary's Book, vol. 1, October 2, 1823, April 25, 1839, SCHS. The phrase "not strangers" is from the Branchville Vigilant Association, Minute Book, 10th Article of the Constitution, SCL.

44. The founding membership of the Pineville Police Association included many prominent local planters, including Isaac Porcher, Samuel DuBose, Benjamin Ravenel, Thomas Porcher, Peter Palmer, Henry Ravenel, Joseph Palmer, and other men whose private papers are used in this study. See the Pineville Police Association, Secretary's Book, April 25, 1839. For other evidence of the regulations revealing planter interests, see the following: Branchville Vigilant Association, Minute Book; Anonymous, *Preamble and Regulations of the Savannah River Anti-Slave Traffick Association* (n.p., November 21, 1846), pp. 8–9.

45. Gavin Diary, February 6, 1857; James Legaré to J. Berkley Grimball, December 12, 1857, Grimball Family Papers.

permit them to appropriate their own time and labor to their own use."
Even in 1836, Broad's action had incensed the neighborhood, and the
dispensation of his property had been contested by a local planter.[46] By
the 1850s, however, all kinds of yeomen not guilty of such obvious
transgressions were coming under suspicion, indictment, and vigilante
justice. Actions long indulged as part of the impossibility of perfecting
slave discipline were no longer tolerated.[47]

In the context of the 1850s, minor infractions were perceived as
violating not just slave discipline but the very viability of slavery. "Illicit
traffic with slaves," a group of Barnwell "citizens" insisted, is a "species
of crime more injurious to a slave-holding community than any on which
the Legislature has ever been called to pass." It was an "evil of great
magnitude that pervades . . . the whole state," and it is one, they proclaimed, "which strikes at the vitals of our domestic institution." Nothing
less than the fate of slavery itself was at stake in the discipline of nonslaveholding whites. "Either these men must be put down, or we must
give up our system of servitude," the Charleston Grand Jury declared in
1852.[48] Under such circumstances, yeomen like Richard Taylor did not
stand a chance when suspicious eyes lighted on them. Taylor, a farmer
and storekeeper, was "broke up at Crocketville" in Beaufort District and

46. The struggle over Broad's will and the fate of his slave family can be traced in the
following public documents: *State* v. *James Ferguson, John R. Dangerfield, Daphne et al.,*
Charleston District, Court of General Sessions, Bills of Indictment, No. 1838-11A; "Petition of Dr. Theodore Gaillard," Petitions to the Legislature, 1854, General Assembly
Records; "Petition of Sterling J. Dangerfield and Jane Locklear," Petitions to the Legislature, 1856, General Assembly Records. Credit reporters for R. G. Dun and Company
regularly identified storekeepers engaged in illegal trade with slaves. For an example of
one who was a yeoman farmer and a storekeeper on the side, see the report on William
Harrison, Dun and Company, Credit Reporting Ledgers, South Carolina, vol. 3 [Entries of
June 3, 1856, December 22, 1856, July 6, 1857, March 8, 1858].

47. Lowcountry white men suspected of trading with slaves in stolen goods were not
infrequently in the 1850s framed by planters and then indicted. In one such case Paul
Durant sent his slave Prince to William Campbell's store with a bag of corn, which he
exchanged for a pint of whiskey. Campbell claimed he had been framed by Durant who
had been, Campbell's wife claimed, "in the way of sending his negros to us with tickets and
without tickets. It was this way that thay took us of our Guard." Mrs. Campbell promised
that if they dropped the charges against her husband, "wee will sell the Place as soon as we
can and sell to no negro without a Ticket from Thair master." Campbell was evidently a
very poor man who was jailed despite the intervention of other local planters on his behalf.
See *State* v. *William Campbell,* Charleston District, Court of General Sessions, Bills of Indictment, 1837-No. 14A. Paul Durant was a member of the Pineville Police Association in
1839.

48. "Petition of Citizens of Barnwell District for More Strenuous Punishment of Whites
Convicted of Trafficking with Slaves in the sale of spiritous liquors," Petitions to the
Legislature, 1850, General Assembly Records; Grand Jury Presentments, Charleston District, March Term, 1852, General Assembly Records. Similar sentiments were expressed by
the following grand juries: Grand Jury Presentment, Williamsburg District, Fall Term,
1857; Clarendon, Fall Term, 1857; Sumter District, Fall Term, 1857; Richland District,
Fall Term 1859; Charleston District, January Term, 1859; Kershaw District, Fall Term,
1860, all in General Assembly Records.

forced to move after a run-in with John Tyson, a local planter and a colonel of the militia. He "ordered me to close my store at night to prevent me from dealing with the colored people," Taylor later explained; despite his compliance, he was still "arrested." Taylor's store was the militia headquarters for the area, and once his motives had been impugned, "the people would not patronize my store." Taylor was ruined.[49]

The common interests of yeomen and planters in the policing of slaves thus gave rise to conflict over the planter power unleashed. The planters from Hammond's area of Barnwell District who formed the Savannah River Anti-Slave Traffick Association in the spring of 1846, in attempting to defuse the problem, managed only to demonstrate how intractable it was. First, they tried to justify their association by casting the social threat in melodramatic terms. The man who traffics with slaves in stolen goods, they insisted, is "more potent than the abolitionist." He "seduces [the slave's] affections from his master, renders him unable to endure and insubordinate to discipline, prepares his mind for insurrection, burning and murder, and both ensures a speedy decay and stimulates a violent dissolution of our domestic institutions." They promised to meet such treachery with decisive police measures.

But even as they cast the problem in such ominous terms, they felt compelled to defend themselves against charges circulating in the neighborhood "that ours was a combination to oppress the poor." This they proclaimed a "ridiculous falsehood, circulated by those who are directly and indirectly interested . . . in upholding this infamous traffick with slaves." Declaring it "a calumny upon the poor," they announced their intention not "to oppress any man or class of men, but to preserve the just rights and lawful interests of all." Attempting to invoke the poor man's interest as a propertyholder in the security of slavery—attempting, in other words, to deny class difference and to assert common interests—these planter authors in fact accomplished precisely the opposite. "The poorest man in this community though he possess no slave . . . is as much interested as the largest slaveholder in the purpose of this association," they asserted. "The rich can only lose a portion of their surplus, but the greater part of what the poor man has is at the mercy of the artful villains whom the negro-traffickers are training to plunder all alike; while amid the wreck of property and scenes of violence which must follow the subversion of our slave system, he stands the most defenceless and must be among the earliest victims." The gulf between yeomen—here simply "poor men"—and planters was rarely delineated so baldly as it was in this assertion of common interests. And

49. Claim of Richard Taylor, Beaufort, SCCR, RG 217, File #6795. Other claimants from that area of Beaufort described similar harassment by "Vigilance Committees," or "Committees of Investigation," although not all such claims could be verified. See Claim of John Bradham, Beaufort, SCCR, RG 233, Report #8; Claim of Joseph Rosier, Beaufort, SCCR, File #5671.

although the founders of the association posed as Everyman, insisting half-heartedly that "for ourselves, most of us are far from being wealthy," everything about the association, from the literacy of the statement to the dues levied to the regulations imposed concerning "our negroes," announced to the yeoman farmer that this was a planter organization, devoted to planter interests, that, despite his authentic interest in the security of slave property and the suppression of any threat to property in general, he and his yeoman peers were part of the association's constituency only as another treacherous population to be regulated or mob to be mobilized.[50]

In elaborating the common interests of independent men in slave society, these Barnwell planters revealed the great social gulf that divided yeomen from planters in the South Carolina Low Country. In the 1830s and again in the 1850s, the drive to perfect a system of slave discipline necessarily imperfect and to forge an impenetrable unity among lowcountry freemen put tremendous pressure on the customary relations of yeomen and planters and exposed the contradiction of independence and inequality around which they were arranged.

VII

Planter men were certainly constrained to express their wealth and power in ways compatible with yeoman independence and notions of masterhood. Their wives, however, faced no such constraints. In their dealings with the yeomanry, planter ladies expressed and embodied class privilege and marked the limits of manly independence. If the explosive potential of yeoman-planter relations was largely contained, this was, at least in part, because the contradiction between independence and inequality was played out in gendered terms.

It was among women that the lowcountry class divide was most clearly drawn. Expressed in a deafening silence on the subject of yeoman women in planter ladies' texts, relations between yeoman and planter women registered the particular consequences for free women of a social landscape configured around independent households. They were attenuated relations indeed. With the notable exception of church, few of the occasions of everyday life brought yeoman and planter women into each other's orbit.

Burdened by children and other household responsibilities, yeoman wives complained of the difficulty of maintaining any kind of social ties, even to beloved kinfolk. Men had all kinds of opportunities and reasons to go abroad: processing and marketing crops, doing the household marketing, attending militia drills and musters, and political meetings,

---

50. Anonymous, *Preamble and Regulations of the Savannah River Anti-Slave Traffick Association*, pp. 5–9.

and performing patrol duty. They did not have to seek permission from wives or arrange care for children should duty or pleasure call them off the farm. Some wives, like Mary Davis Brown of York District, recorded their husband's ambits with barely concealed envy. Mrs. Brown loved to go to meeting, but it was her husband, Jackson, and the three eldest children who went to the big camp meeting at Bulix Creek in 1858 although, as she noted, the distance was "so fare" that it had prevented the family from attending a July Fourth "pick nick diner" at the same spot.[51] For yeoman wives like Mary Davis Brown, social life revolved in a much narrower circle around the household. Church, family visiting, and the rituals that attended childbirth provided the most regular occasions for socializing. And even those were few and far between.

The isolation Mary Davis Brown felt was evident as much in her rare delight as in her regular disappointment. "[S]een a great many of my ould friends that i hant seen in a long time," she noted with pleasure in the spring of 1857 after attending the ordination of a preacher. Such entries frequently followed the birth of children (her own or those of her friends), when womanly visiting was customary. It was hard to distinguish the greater source of joy when Mrs. Cain safely gave birth to her baby: "the fine sone [she had] this morning" or "the big diner and fine company of ould ladyes" who gathered around her bed to celebrate the event. More often Mary Davis Brown noted that Jackson had gone off to "coart week" or had taken the older children to the "big corn husking," leaving her at home with the younger ones. But nothing tried her soul like missing church. "[I]ts preachen day but i cant git to go the children is so bad with the cough that i cant leave them," she noted regretfully on November 14, 1858. By November 28 she was still tied to the farm. Willie is still bad, she wrote: "[How] i . . . long to git to preachen." On that day and many others she had to settle for "redding" religious texts like "Christs sermins on the mount."[52]

Brown's frustrations were echoed by scores of lowcountry wives, albeit secondhand, in church investigations of women members' failure to attend Sunday meeting. Many, like Mrs. Brown, simply had sick children at home or lacked the shoes and proper clothes; others found their movements inhibited by more sinister forces. "Sis Wilkerson" told the investigating "committy" of Gum Branch Baptist Church in Darlington District that "she wished to attend Church but she was prevented as was infered by her husband." Sister Mary Spier "sayes that she has not the opertunity to attend as her husband is unfriendly to her." Husbands

51. Mary Davis Brown Diary, September 12, 1858, July 4, 1858.
52. Ibid., April 25, 1857, September 17, 1858, October 12, 1858, October 26, 1858, November 14, 1858, November 28, 1858. Women also seem to have celebrated childbirth with "quiltings." Shortly after Mary Davis Brown's son William Given was born, she noted: "We had a big quilting yesterday theire was near fifty people here and they put out my quilt and had a big singing that night." Each baby's safe arrival was recorded in a quilt. Mary Davis Brown Diary, December 30, 1857, and June 22, 1858.

could simply refuse to let their wives leave the house; they had that power, and even church authorities recognized it.[53] So constrained by duty, distance, and male authority were women's social networks that it is little wonder that some women, like Nancy Cowan's sister Elizabeth Finisher, put their hopes on the next world. "[I] would come to you if i could but William dont want to go there," she wrote Nancy Cowan in August 1846. "I have little hope of ever seeing you in this world of sorrow . . . but press on heavenword [and] we will meet on the happy shore of cannon." It will, she concluded, "be joyful to meet to part no more."[54] To a much greater degree than their men, yeoman women lived in a social world bounded by the fence. Even its most intimate and sisterly parts had to contend with such an impediment. The attenuated character of their relations with local planter ladies was shaped by the same boundaries and constraints.

Yeoman women had little reason to venture into plantation mistresses' social orbit nor the latter into theirs. Little by way of sustained relations typically developed between different classes of free women, judging by the silence on the subject in mistresses' diaries. With the exception of women like Mary Wall, whose midwifery skills were in constant demand on neighboring plantations, yeoman women seem, for the most part, to have left the exchange of labor and goods (even those of their own making) to the men. The one task that might have brought them to the door of the big house was, at least according to the testimony of former slaves, that which men would have found most distasteful: the explicit request for charitable assistance. Perhaps in an attempt to keep dependence running in the gendered channels fit for it by history and nature, yeoman husbands sent their wives to make requests for aid. Such occasions were, however, infrequent, and planter women's ties to non-elite women were, judging by their own accounts, largely confined to those few who fell, usually by reason of poverty, within their household domain.[55] Yeoman women were not prominent among that client population. The material independence of their households precluded the necessity, and the respect accorded the boundaries of such households precluded the practice. For their part, planter women had little reason or inclination to intrude on yeoman households on errands charitable or otherwise, and there is little evidence—virtually none—that they did so.

No less than yeoman women, planter women's social relations and

53. Minute Book, Gum Branch Baptist Church, [Darlington District] March 16, 1844, July 13, 1849, SCL.

54. Elizabeth Finisher to Nancy H. Cowen, August 23, 1846, Nancy H. Cowan Papers, Perkins Library, DU.

55. Poor white women were, on occasion, attached as dependents to plantation households. See, for example, the cases mentioned in the following planter women's diaries: W. Emerson Wilson, ed., *Plantation Life at Rose Hill: The Diaries of Martha Ogle Forman, 1814–1845* (Wilmington: The Historical Society of Delaware 1976), pp. 22, 420; Kate Virginia Cox Logan, *My Confederate Girlhood*, ed. Lily Logan Morrill (New York: Arno Press, 1980), p. 16.

gender identity were configured by the household, its boundaries, and the power relations it embodied. In the complex web of relations that at once subordinated wives to their husbands and conferred on them the irreducible power of a mistress over slaves was the gender identity of planter women situated, and its ideological expression—the southern lady—discursively located.[56] The bonds of sex or ties between women which that identity envisioned were those that bound mistress to slave woman. Whatever religious and social responsibilities planter ladies incurred to the less fortunate were to be fulfilled, as ministers, editors, and almost every other male authority insisted, within their own households with those who stood in explicit relations of legal or customary dependency. Little by way of public benevolence was expected of planter women—indeed, little was permitted—and little was performed.[57] The responsibilities of plantation mistresses did not extend typically to neighboring yeoman households. Yeoman men would hardly have suffered the intrusion lightly even if their wives would have, which is not at all clear.

The exceptions prove the rule. John Berkley Grimball, a prominent Colleton planter, recalled that his mother had taken in a motherless infant whose "destitute condition" had come to her attention. The child, Jane O'Daniel, had, he recalled, "remained in [his mother's] family and under her protection" until she was a young woman, during which time his mother had dressed and educated the girl in a manner "suited to her degree." Jane's parents had been "extremely poor." Precisely what Jane O'Daniel's position had been in the Grimball household he did not say, except to remark that his mother's charity—properly extended within the bounds of the household—preserved the proper distinctions of class and station. The Grimball's Grove Plantation was, evidently, no Mansfield Park and Jane O'Daniel no Fanny Price. Poor girls were not entitled to the rewards of modesty in this lowcountry world. Little wonder yeoman men and women preferred to turn to their church or to the local commissioner of the poor when they faced straitened circumstances. Like the yeoman widow woman who was outraged by the planter lady Eliza Clitherall's treatment of her daughter, those who witnessed ladies' charity evinced little confusion about its meaning. The widow had initially agreed to let Clitherall take her daughter until she was "large

56. On planter women and the southern ideology of womanhood see the following: Elizabeth Fox-Genovese, *Within the Plantation Household: Black and White Women of the Old South* (Chapel Hill: University of North Carolina Press, 1988); Anne Firor Scott, *The Southern Lady: From Pedestal to Politics* (Chicago: University of Chicago Press, 1970); Catherine Clinton, *The Plantation Mistress: Women's World in the Old South* (New York: Pantheon Books, 1982); Jean E. Friedman, *The Enclosed Garden: Women and Community in the Evangelical South, 1830–1900* (Chapel Hill: University of North Carolina Press, 1985); Sarah E. Moss, "'Our Earnest Appeal': The Southern Domestic Novelists and Their Literary Defense of Southern Culture, 1833–1866" (Ph.D. Diss., Washington University, 1989).

57. The matter of women and religion is taken up at greater length in Chapters 4 and 5.

enough to assist her in earning a living." But when she learned that Clitherall had had "the girl baptis'd providential to her own name Susan" and had dressed her in "homespun" (like the slaves?) while her own children wore "calico," she grew enraged and took her daughter home, declaring, as Mrs. Clitherall repeated with utter bewilderment, "that her child was as good as mine."[58] In the slave South as elsewhere in antebellum America, charity exacted its price, and what little of it the Low Country saw served rather to measure than to traverse the class divide between yeoman and planter women.[59]

Planter ladies' social circles did, of course, extend beyond the household, but, with rare exception, they stayed well within class boundaries. When Meta Morris Grimball "had some of the neighbors in to an evening party," the invitation list read like a who's who of planter society in St. Paul's, Colleton. Among planter-class women, great care was exercised to countenance only the right sort. Not content to list the names of her eminent company—Mr. and Mrs. Aiken, Mr. Elliott and wife, Annie Heyward, Emma Manigault, Juliet Elliott, Mrs. Barnwell and her daughter Ann, Mrs. Manigault—Meta Morris Grimball compulsively chronicled their lineage, wealth, and prospects, as well. In one instance, for example, when Mr. Aiken stopped at her house to await some friends who were arriving on "the cars," she conducted the requisite background check on the prospective additions to their circle. "She was a Miss Lowndes and he a rich New York[er]," she noted with evident satisfaction of Aiken's friends, Mr. and Mrs. James. "[H]er mother and father live on Santee in winter where he had a plantation. [T]hey are all rich and high born." Even the parents and grandparents were not spared. "Mrs. Robert Lowndes was a Miss Livingston, the daughter of Mrs. Maturin Livingston who was a Miss Lewis," she went on, "the only child of General Lewis who left a fortune of a Million which Mrs. M. L. on her death divided equally among her nine children thereby giving great satisfaction to all of them." For her part, Meta Morris Grimball wished only and modestly that her son "Berkley could find a nice girl with a little money to get married to." There was scant chance he would marry one without it. Elaborate coming-of-age and courtship rituals, like debutante balls and coming-out parties, coached children's desires into

58. John Berkley Grimball Diary, July 3, 1847, Grimball Family Papers; Eliza Clitherall case is quoted in Fox-Genovese, *Within the Plantation Household*, p. 224.

59. Contrast this approach to charity with that of Suzanne Lebsock in *The Free Women of Petersburg: Status and Culture in a Southern Town, 1748–1860* (New York: W. W. Norton, 1984). Lebsock maintains that, rather than inscribing social power and class difference, charity dispensed by elite women created bonds of sisterhood with "poorer whites" (p. 241 and passim). Such approaches to elite women's charitable activity have been challenged by a number of historians. Perhaps the best treatment is Christine Stansell, *City of Women: Sex and Class in New York, 1789–1860* (New York: Alfred A. Knopf, 1986). See also Lori D. Ginzberg, *Women and the Work of Benevolence: Morality, Politics, and Class in the 19th-Century United States* (New Haven: Yale University Press, 1990).

parental channels and virtually eliminated the possibility that one would marry another "not of the same class."[60]

Even during the Civil War, as the fabric of southern society ripped apart at the seams, lowcountry ladies did not relax their vigilant posture. In fact, the war put their discriminatory skills to the ultimate test. Whereas before the war identities were rendered apparently transparent by personal knowledge or family testimonials, such time-worn methods faced unprecedented challenges from wartime disruptions. As refugees among strangers in inland communities, Mrs. Grimball and her peers struggled to distinguish real ladies from those "uneducated, coarse wom[en]" who only affected the appearance of gentility. Planter society was sufficiently developed all over South Carolina that those forced to move into the middle districts and upcountry areas could usually manage to avoid yeoman neighborhoods. Thus, Emma Holmes, a self-designated Charleston "aristocrat," survived exile in Camden, Kershaw District, largely because of the "good South Carolina people around": the Blandings, DeSaussures, Heywards, Chesnuts, Boykins, and Canteys. Once she and the other displaced Charleston ladies managed to convince the Camden ladies to give up their uncivilized habit of "taking the morning as the most fashionable time for visiting," Camden company suited them well enough for the duration. But Kate Stone was not so lucky when she left Louisiana to refugee in Tyler, Texas. She tried socializing with her yeoman neighbors, but "that was, " as she put it, "too much for me." She offered profound if simple testimony as to the reason. "Their ways," she wrote, "are not our ways." Instead, she had to bide her time until other refugees arrived and she could take up with planter families whose lineage she could verify—like "the Goddards," a good family from "Arkansas who were recommended to us by Julia some time before."[61] To the relief of planter ladies like Kate Stone and

---

60. John Berkley Grimball Diary, January 29, 1847; Meta Morris Grimball Diary, December 15, 1860, both in Grimball Family Papers. The "not of the same class" quotation is from the diary of the upcountry planter woman Mary Moragne. See Delle Mullen Craven, ed., *The Neglected Thread: A Journal From the Calhoun Community, 1836–1842* (Columbia, S.C.: University of South Carolina Press, 1951), pp. 151–52.

See the description of the party attended by Meta Morris Grimball's sons in January 1861. Hosted by Mr. Lewis at Ashepoo "to introduce his daughter," it came closest to the Old South of myth as anything possibly could. It began as a lunch party, after which the young people went riding and rowing on the river. Thirty stayed for "a handsome dinner," and then a band played music and the young folk danced and courted until five in the morning. After a sleepover and a breakfast of eggs, hotcakes, spare ribs, and everything else, the party finally disbanded. Meta Morris Grimball Diary, January 12, 1861, Grimball Family Papers. On courtship and marriage among the planter class, see Steven Stowe, *Intimacy and Power in the Old South: Ritual in the Lives of the Planters* (Baltimore: Johns Hopkins University Press, 1987).

61. Meta Morris Grimball Diary, March 29, 1861, Grimball Family Papers; John F. Marszalek, ed., *The Diary of Miss Emma Holmes* (Baton Rouge: Louisiana State University Press, 1979), pp. 170–74; John Q. Anderson, ed., *Brokenburn: The Journal of Kate Stone, 1861–1868* (Baton Rouge: Louisiana State University Press, 1955), pp. 226–28, 275.

Emma Holmes, "society" continued even in the midst of war. And in war as in peace, the society of planter ladies was a self-consciously elite one in which yeoman women had no appointed place—except, that is, outside.

Indeed, so exclusive was the social world portrayed in ladies' diaries, so self-conscious the discriminatory gaze, that one is compelled to entertain the possibility that the signification of class boundaries was one of planter women's central political roles. Men were, after all, forced on occasion to play the democrat; women faced no such imperative.

Politically ambitious planters like James Henry Hammond learned to conceal contempt and to play their part in front of the local common folk. Like John Berkley Grimball, Frederick Porcher, and many other lowcountry planters, Hammond annually entertained the local "mob" with a public dinner hosted at his expense and on his plantation. "Once a year," a guest recalled, "like a great feudal landlord," Hammond "gave a fete or grand dinner to all the country people about, at which . . . every neighbour, rich or poor, for miles about was present." For that one day, he suffered the presence of his yeoman neighbors, their sons, wives, and daughters. Hammond's wife, Catherine, née Fitzsimons, usually graced such occasions with her presence. What she thought of her husband's entertainment of the local hordes we do not know. But at least some of the meaning of such occasions can be glimpsed in other accounts. One does not have to accept the contemptuous views of Hammond or the patronizing ones of Virginia Clay-Clopton, the lady guest who provided the preceding description, to conjure up the scene. For however the tables were arranged—and there was usually one elevated on a platform or otherwise distinguished as "the head table"—there was little chance that yeomen would be mistaken for planters or, more specifically, yeoman women for planter ladies. "Stiff, prim, and ⁣. . . quaint," was how Virginia Clay-Clopton described them, a generous description compared to Hammond's evocation of the rural masses—"ill-at-ease, if not consciously out of place in Senator Hammond's parlours."[62] Certainly that was Hammond's intent. He wrote quite shamelessly about his "taste" in art, architecture, and household appurtenances, about the distinction he bid for in his Columbia mansion. "Not pride but taste has launched me into these expenses—extravagance it may be," he had noted revealingly during its construction in 1841.[63] But if Catherine Hammond's

62. The description of Hammond's party is from Virginia T. Clay-Clopton, *A Belle of the Fifties: Memoirs of Mrs. Clay of Alabama, Covering Social and Political Life in Washington and the South, 1853–1866*, (1905; reprint ed., New York: Doubleday, Page, 1905), pp. 217–18 and refers to his Redcliffe estate in Edgefield District. See also the descriptions in Faust's biography of Hammond, *James Henry Hammond and the Old South*, p. 131, and in William W. Freehling, *The Road to Disunion: Secessionists at Bay, 1776–1854* (New York: Oxford University Press, 1990), pp. 42–43. For one description of the arrangement of tables at a public dinner hosted by planters, see Stoney, ed., "The Memoirs of William Porcher," vol. 44, no. 3 (April 1943), pp. 66–67.

63. James Henry Hammond Diary, February 25, 1841 reprinted in Bleser, ed., *Secret and Sacred*, pp. 36–37. For an interesting approach to questions of "taste" and the cultural

"taste" was not so crudely bought as that of her arriviste husband, it was, perhaps, only the more evident to those ill-at-ease yeoman women who gathered, awkward and proud, in her home on those hot summer days.

Every aspect of ladyhood was displayed on the body: leisure, luxury, wealth, and refinement. Not even yeoman women's Sunday-best calico dress, hair comb, ribbon, bonnet, and store-bought shoes could disguise untiring labor and limited means. "Stiff, prim, quaint"—respectable— was the best they could summon for Mrs. Hammond's party. In its luxurious materials, in the sophistication of its design, in its perfect fittedness for the occasion, in the sheer time it took to prepare and put on, in everything about the look of the person and the costume, planter women's appearance signified a world of difference. As James Henry Hammond moved among the crowd of local yeomen gathered on his grounds (almost certainly not, as Clay-Clopton said, "in [his] parlours"), pressing the flesh, soliciting votes, promising to attend to the mentioned matter, or pushing his candidate, he simultaneously marked the class divide and ritualistically bridged it. But planter women faced no such contradictory demands. Relieved, although hardly by choice, of the political burden of symbolizing the inclusivity and the coherence of the body politic, they were free, rather, to symbolize and ritually to represent social hierarchy and exclusivity. And every time a planter lady walked into the local church on a Sunday morning, that meaning was communicated.

In distinct contrast to bourgeois gender ideology, which aspired to obscure class in the claims to universality of womanhood and sisterhood, southern gender ideology served, rather, to inscribe class.[64] Ladies played, therefore, a critical political role in the South Carolina Low Country. Mary Boykin Chesnut played that part with all the petty passion of outraged elitism that was its essence.

When her uncle, a state legislator named Alexander Hamilton Boykin, invited "Squire McDonald," a local yeoman, to join Mrs. Chesnut and her husband, U.S. Senator James Chesnut, to smoke and to talk politics at an after-dinner gathering on the piazza of his Kershaw plantation, Mary Chesnut made no effort to conceal her disgust. That "well-digger," she expostulated, with the "mud sticking up through his toes," did not belong among such company. The fawning attention her husband and uncle heaped on the man appalled and angered her. "The raggeder and more squalid the creature, the more polite and softer Mr. Chesnut grows," she noted derisively. Her uncle and her husband may

capital thus acquired, see Pierre Bourdieu, *Distinction: A Social Critique of the Judgment of Taste* (Cambridge: Harvard University Press, 1984).

64. On the bonds of womanhood, the claim to universality, and bourgeois gender ideology, see especially Katherine Kish Sklar, *Catherine Beecher: A Study in American Domesticity* (New Haven: Yale University Press, 1973); Nancy Cott, *The Bonds of Womanhood: 'Woman's Sphere' in New England, 1780–1835* (New Haven: Yale University Press, 1977); Stansell, *City of Women*; Boydston, *Home and Work*.

have been willing to overlook McDonald's plain style and modest means. Mary Boykin Chesnut was not. But then they were frying other fish. For however modest his means, "Squire" McDonald was an influential man in the neighborhood, the descendant of a Revolutionary War hero. Among his circle of yeoman farmers, he commanded respect and, more important, votes. Such distinctions among the broad ranks of the common folk were irrelevant to Mrs. Chesnut. To her, McDonald was no better than a common laborer, "a well-digger." Although Mr. Boykin had not invited the man into the house—he drew the line at the piazza— Mrs. Chesnut thought even that too far to stoop for "democracy," as she disdainfully put it. Her husband and her uncle might feel the need to treat the local plain folk with respect. That was their job. It was not hers. Hers was to measure the distance between the piazza and the parlor in disdainful glances and barely concealed contempt. McDonald's presence, however, she could not contest. She had to grin and bear it. After all, Squire McDonald had a vote, and she did not.[65] By such gender and class distinctions and complexities was the delicate balance of independence and inequality maintained among the small free community of yeomen and planters in the South Carolina Low Country.

65. C. Vann Woodward, ed., *Mary Chesnut's Civil War* (New Haven: Yale University Press, 1981), pp. 204–05. Few pieces of texts (at least of southern women's authorship) have come in for such close scrutiny as this one, which has been harnessed to a number of interpretations of South Carolina politics. For a different analysis see Ford, *Origins of Southern Radicalism*, pp. 372–73.

chapter 4

"Like a Great Family": Nullification Revivals and the Making of Popular Religion in the Low Country

I

One Saturday in January 1854, John Kelly stood up in Gum Branch Baptist Church in rural Darlington District and announced that "his wife Lenore Kelly had left his house." As he stood there, supplicant, before his brethren, Kelly knew what he had begun, knew that he had just invited community intrusion into the most intimate aspect of his domestic affairs. In making the admission—in preempting accusation—he attempted, no doubt, to assert a measure of control over the disciplinary investigation that was sure to follow. And indeed, pained by the news, church elders appointed a "committy" of four to enquire into the trouble between Brother and Sister Kelly and to recommend a course of action. Few could have imagined the depth of trouble that lay ahead. Throughout the spring and summer of 1854, as John and Lenore Kelly, John's kin, and the Gum Branch brethren struggled to contain the forces unleashed among them, the predominantly yeoman congregation gave powerful testimony to a whole set of assumptions and beliefs, usually unarticulated, about the workings of power and authority, domestic and public, in their small corner of the lowcountry world.[1]

In investigating the Kellys, Gum Branch brethren acted only in strict accordance with their covenanted obligation. "[O]ur conduct and con-

---

1. Gum Branch Baptist Church, Darlington District, Minutes, January 15, 1854, SCL. The Kelly family was occasionally referred to as O'Kelly.

versation both in the church and the world, ought to correspond with the sublime and holy system of divine truth," each new member of the Baptist Church pledged, and thus "we feel ourselves bound . . . when cases require such measures, to warn, entreat, exhort, rebuke, and admonish in the spirit of meekness according to the rules of the Gospel." The Kelly case clearly required such measures: Church members sought only to meet their obligation to "carefully maintain a strict gospel discipline," either to "reclaim such as may transgress" or to "put out disorderly persons from our communion."[2] Although they hardly enjoyed the prospect of investigating John Kelly, the leading man among an extended local family of Baptists, the "committy" of four could never have anticipated the disorder about to be visited on their once peaceable community.

The committee initially consisted of minister, deacon, elderly male member, and church clerk. The latter, Willey Kelly, was John Kelly's brother and only one of the many Kellys in the vicinity and among the membership of Gum Branch Baptist Church. Indeed, the Kelly family had been instrumental in the late-eighteenth-century founding of the church, and, according to church history, the congregation had been sustained through a long period of "distress" in the first decade of the nineteenth century only through the heroic efforts of "Brother David Kelly and wife." It was their offspring, John Kelly, Willey Kelly, and the rest, who had fueled the church's growth to the present healthy state of affairs.[3] Mindful of the influence of the Kelly clan, the committee alternately procrastinated, stalled, and agonized over the investigation, proclaiming "the case . . . so delicate a nature and so involved in mystery" as to preclude thorough scrutiny. Finally, after four months, they rendered a judgment worse than any the nervous congregation could have anticipated. Brother Kelly "had committed a crime of uncommon terpitude" [sic] to drive Sister Kelly from his house.[4]

The committee had only two choices. Notwithstanding the unspeakable nature of the crime, they attempted and "failed to effect a reunion of the parties." Unable to reclaim John Kelly, they had to expel him. And it was this eventuality that brought the Gum Branch brethren face-to-face with an explosive contradiction that lay at the heart of the evangelical vision of Christian community. The necessity of expelling husband and exonerating wife pitted the principle of the spiritual equality and moral sovereignty of all individuals directly against the principle of the familial model of Christian social order. Forced to discriminate between two such fundamental precepts, it was inevitable, perhaps, which one they would surrender. Torn, as they put it, between belief in the

2. Beech Branch Baptist Church, Beaufort District, Minutes, 1823, SCL; Mechanicsville Baptist Church, Darlington District, Minutes, 1829, SCL.

3. Gum Branch Baptist Church, Darlington District, Minutes, July 1833.

4. Ibid., "Third Saturday in May, 1854." The committee asked for extensions in February, March, and April and finally reported in May 1854.

honesty of Sister Kelly's testimony and their "great difficulty in believing him [John Kelly] to be guilty"—afraid to disrupt established channels of authority by vindicating wife and excommunicating husband—the committee voted instead to treat them as one marital body and recommended that both Brother and Sister Kelly be excluded from fellowship.[5] The collective failure of nerve was signal; it was, quite simply, impossible to envision evangelical community without the buttress of family relations and their customary hierarchy.

If the committee hoped to contain the damage of the Kelly affair with that apparently equivocal recommendation, they could not have been more mistaken. Willey Kelly insisted that a council be appointed to hear the evidence and rule on the appropriate action. Put before the vote of a local Baptist council composed of five members of the Gum Branch Church and fourteen prominent visitors, including P. K. McIver, Elias Witherspoon, and T. P. Lide, all members of the leading families of the wealthy Welsh Neck Baptist Church in Society Hill, the palpable unfairness of the recommendation proved its undoing. Brother John Kelly "has this day made several admissions which go to show that he has maltreated his wife," the visitors' committee declared in late May. Sister Kelly had not, they found, offered any offense to her husband or her church. She could not be excluded, but John Kelly's behavior had by contrast set him outside the bounds of Christian fellowship. The Gum Branch brethren had no choice, the visitors pronounced; John Kelly had to be excluded.[6]

All hell broke loose in that small country church. The threat to John Kelly's honor as a man and, by extension, to the reputation of the entire Kelly family (John Kelly was its wealthiest member and leading man, a small planter in a yeoman clan) prompted his brother, Willey Kelly, to radical measures. He began with attempts to oust his sister-in-law, Lenore Kelly, from the congregation, confirming that the real offense was the erosion of male authority within the family and community when coverture was cracked and wife elevated, even morally, over husband. Mobilizing "the whole Kelly family . . . Willey Kelly and most of the other members belonging to the family connexion" canvassed the area, urging brethren "to give aid at the next conference in excluding Mrs. O'Kelly from the church." This was, the Kellys threatened, "the only means of saving the church from dismemberment."[7] When plain old politicking failed, largely because the minister refused to reopen the case, Willey Kelly next resorted to falsification of the record. Exploiting his power as church clerk to assert a textual truth where none other could be created, he forged an entry recording a fictional vote that dismissed Sister Kelly from fellowship. Caught red-handed by the minis-

5. Ibid.
6. Ibid.
7. Ibid.

ter, he was unrepentant and, aided by others of his "connexion," insisted again on a vote to exclude Lenore Kelly, warning the members "to beware how they gave their votes . . . as [they] would decide the fate of the church."[8]

Luckily for Lenore Kelly, the Kelly men were not the only ones whose honor was at stake. Having endured eight months of painful trial, the minister, Reverend Culpepper, would take no more. On August 19, when the vote on Sister Kelly was to occur, he issued an ultimatum: If a council was not appointed to restore order and his "character as a man and a Christian minister," he would resign. In the ensuing denouement, a confrontation that smacked more of secular politics than Christian fellowship, the church met to take a vote, and on that day "the Kelly family were able to command a majority . . . in consequence of sickness in several families, and the question was lost." True to his word, the Reverend Mr. Culpepper resigned.[9]

It was this last victory that finally galvanized the rest of the congregation to resist the depredations of the Kelly "connexion." Borrowing a leaf from Willey Kelly's book, the minister's faction deployed secular political tactics, beating the bushes to ensure a majority at a special meeting at which they voted the dismission of the entire Kelly faction. This was radical surgery indeed, involving the exclusion of eleven members of the Kelly family and thirteen of their "accessor[ies] to the disorder," including members of eight other families related to the Kellys by marriage. If the Kelly family had built the Gum Branch Baptist Church, then they were no less surely the cause of its undoing. For restoration of order to the congregation in August of 1854 required the exclusion of more than half of the white membership, a loss only barely recouped by the outbreak of Civil War.[10]

But what of the wronged Lenore Kelly, a figure entirely marginal to the record of the affair? No group of natal kin sprang to her defense during the extended struggle with her husband's family. The public

8. For the forged entry, see ibid., May 20, 1854. The confrontation over the forgery came on July 15, 1854. The forged entry asserted that the church had withdrawn fellowship from Brother John O. Kelly and wife Lenore O. Kelly after the committee had reported that "they had inquired into and laboured with said individuals and found they culd not get a reconcileation between them there being quite a differance in their statements," and as such, fellowship was removed "separately" from Lenore and her husband. The minutes were corrected on July 15, 1854.

9. Ibid., August 19, 1854.

10. Ibid., August 26, 1854. In 1853, the date of the last membership list, Gum Branch had 44 white members, 23 of whom were dismissed over the Kelly dispute. By 1861 the church still had only 55 members. See the membership lists in Gum Branch Baptist Church, Darlington District, Minutes, January 1, 1840, January 15, 1853, February 16, 1861.

Willey Kelly also forged an entry dated September 1, 1854, awarding letters of dismission to himself and 27 others that were intended to testify to their good standing in the Baptist Church and to facilitate membership in another congregation. Other churches were informed not to accept the letters.

humiliation of a married woman—her husband had, after all, committed an unspeakable crime against her person—was not of such consequence, it would seem, as to constitute a threat to her family's reputation
or honor. The Kelly affair, although prompted by her action in leaving
her husband's household, was very clearly not about her; it was, rather, a
contest over male honor waged between factions of men. It was no
coincidence, then, that her social insignificance was textually reproduced in the church account of the affair.

Yet however invisible Lenore Kelly became in the records, it had
been her decisive action in leaving her husband that presented him the
unpleasant task of standing up in church that January day. Although
none among her fellow brethren seemed particularly eager to defend
her rights, her rights had been upheld, albeit belatedly, in ways unim-
aginable in secular court. Lenore Kelly had given no offense to the
Church, the visitors' committee had found, and thus she could not rightly be excluded. The Baptist Church's articulated principle of spiritual
equality—the idea that all people, whatever their worldly status, were
equal in the eyes of God—and the moral accountability that attended it
had provided Lenore Kelly the means to hold her husband accountable,
if not to her, at least to his brethren, and had provided the leverage
required to resist the coercions of his powerful family. Despite eight
months of efforts to disfranchise her, Lenore Kelly had retained her
right to membership in the Gum Branch Baptist Church. And there was
nothing trivial about that.

Lenore Kelly had not been the one to bring her marital troubles to
the attention of her church, however. Perhaps she lacked faith in the
congregation's willingness to believe a wife over a husband; she, above
all others assuredly, knew the power of Willey Kelly and the Kelly clan.
But, more to the point, as a long-standing member of the Baptist Church
she also would have known that even if they found her innocent of any
provocation of her husband's abuse—by no means a certain conclusion
given the standards of submission to which Christian women were held—
the Church posed no real solution. Gum Branch brethren could, and
although under coercion, did hold her husband accountable for his moral
transgression, but when he refused to submit to Gospel discipline their
arsenal was exhausted. They could protect neither the body of the woman
nor her right to support, custody of her children, or any of the other
manifold consequences of her husband's "maltreatment." The only thing
they could protect was her church membership. Moral individualism left
women in precarious dependencies.[11]

Lenore Kelly kept the faith for which she had paid so high a personal
price. But she did not keep her membership in Gum Branch Baptist
Church. Perhaps the shame was too much to bear; perhaps the brethren
blamed her for the crisis unleashed on their little congregation; perhaps

11. The phrase "precarious dependencies" is from Christine Stansell, *City of Women:
Sex and Class in New York, 1789–1860* (New York: Alfred A. Knopf, 1986), p. 1.

her in-laws hounded her out of the neighborhood. Whatever the reason, Lenore Kelly moved away. Six years later she lived in another part of the district, still estranged from her husband, completely propertyless, without a home of her own, a dependent member of another man's household.[12] Perhaps the yeoman farmer and his wife with whom she lived, J. W. Woodham and A. E. Woodham, were her daughter and son-in-law; it is comforting to think so. Lenore Kelly held onto her faith. She had little else to call her own.

II

If the evangelical promise of spiritual equality in general and the recognition of women members as moral individuals in particular proved an explosive issue within the church, those gendered assumptions about power and authority were hardly the only ones traced, tested, and tempered in the heat of the Kelly affair. The prerogatives of and the respect due wealth, social hierarchy, and kinship were no less at work. After all, the measure of justice Lenore Kelly had found in her church had been extracted against the will of the original home committee. It took a committee of wealthy and influential outsiders, men who were indisputably John Kelly's social superiors, to subject him to discipline. Willey Kelly, Reverend Culpepper, Deacon Linton, and Jacob Smith, the four members of the original committee, were not only John Kelly's kin and neighbors; they were also, without exception, his social inferiors, perhaps even his clients. Like the vast majority of the white members of Gum Branch Baptist Church, they were yeoman farmers, men who owned a substantial amount of land and, in three of the four instances, also a handful of slaves. But John Kelly stood apart from them. He was a small planter among a circle of yeoman farmers. He owned significantly more land and twenty-one slaves, a far greater number than any of the original committee or of his extended family who rushed to his defense. Everything about the behavior of the committee—its proceedings, deliberation, and recommendation—articulated a knowing recognition, indeed, a respect for property and wealth, and especially for the influence that customarily accompanied them among discrete local circles of yeomen. Even wealth in the modest proportions of a small planter like John Kelly exacted its due respect, and as such, it points to the way that influence was exercised through the kin-based patronage networks that constituted lowcountry society, secular and sacred.

Nor are such conceptions of power and authority undermined by the

12. In 1860 the 60-year-old Lenore Kelly appeared on the census in the household of J. W. Woodham. Kelly reported no real or personal property. Woodham was listed as a 36-year-old white farmer, with a wife, one slave girl, and a 120-acre farm valued at $2,700. There is no positive indication that Lenore Kelly was related to J. W. Woodham. Federal Manuscript Census, South Carolina [Darlington District], Schedules of Population, Slaves, and Agriculture, 1860, NA.

actions of the visitors' or outsiders' committee. To the contrary, in fact, T. P. Lide, P. K. McIver, and Elias Witherspoon were, by any standards, part of the district's, and indeed the state's, planter elite, and their deliberations and recommendations carried all of the considerable authority that attached to that elevated social position. They could risk the insult to Kelly's manhood and the inversion of gender hierarchy because they stood outside his realm of influence and, perhaps, because they expected the patronage and influence they exercised as a district elite to command the respect, however grudging, of a congregation of yeoman farmers.

The Kelly affair made one thing crystal clear: Even in evangelical community, justice ran in the grooves cut by social power. The church's avowed commitment to the spiritual equality of all believers did have the potential, on the margins, to reconfigure power relations, especially between men and women, and that was of no small consequence to women like Lenore Kelly. But the more dominant historical effect of evangelicalism in the antebellum Low Country was its sacralization of the secular order. In this cultural project, and in its political repercussions, the yeomanry played a central part, their domestic experience, social values, and cultural sensibilities giving particular lowcountry and proslavery shape to the transatlantic and cross-sectional evangelical movement.

For in their churches, yeoman men and women articulated a perspective on the complex world around them, making sense of it both as it was and as it should be: articulating a sort of worldview, if not something so coherent and textually authoritative as an ideology. It found its most common expression in the familial discourse of evangelicalism—in the notion of Christian society as a perfected family—a set of ideas and practices that sanctified the secular experience of yeoman men and women even as it promised to transform that experience. Therein lay the contradictory promise that drew countless numbers into the churches, making them arguably the single most important cultural institution in the Low Country outside of the household itself. As could nothing else in lowcountry political culture, evangelicalism provided the language by which ordinary white men and women understood their world and by which, ultimately, they came to accept the necessity of disunion and new nationhood to preserve it.

III

By the midantebellum period, few South Carolinians would have disputed the contention that evangelical churches were powerful, even dominant, institutions in lowcountry culture and politics. Indeed, one could have described the Low Country, with little exaggeration, as a religious society. Evangelical discourse lent coherence to private experience and public events alike. "My sufficiency is of God," the yeoman woman Mary Davis Brown proclaimed in 1858, while in the summer of 1845 the Governor, out of similar conviction, had proclaimed a day of fasting and prayer to meet "the late awful dispensation of Divine Providence in visiting our land with an unprecedented drought."[13] By the late 1830s, it was already apparent that evangelical religion was fast becoming "a critical weapon in the sectional propaganda battle" and especially in the mobilization of popular proslavery and sectional sentiment. It thus worked at the center not just of private but of public political life as well. Evangelicalism "touched [antebellum] life at more popular points than any other body," including national political parties, one historian has ventured.[14]

It had not always been that way. In the eighteenth and early nineteenth centuries, evangelicals and evangelicalism had been suspect and largely marginal elements in lowcountry society. Although anticipated by a turn-of-the century revival, evangelicalism was not really embraced by planters, planter-politicians, and other prominent men in sufficient numbers to move it from margin to center of lowcountry life until the early 1830s. The timing could not have been more portentous. For as it turns out, the Low Country experienced its greatest revival—and the major drama of planter conversion—in 1831–1833, at the very height of the Nullification Crisis. Having long resisted dissenter religion, lowcountry planters finally embraced—some might say appropriated—the faith of plain folk, women, and slaves at the very moment that they faced the imperative of popular political mobilization. The mature character of antebellum evangelical culture was thereby forged in the midst of the political crisis that set the outlines of the state's political culture down to the Civil War. By the end of the Second Great Awakening, the Low Country had become an evangelical society, one in which distinctions between religious culture and political culture were difficult to discern.

But if planter converts secured the cultural and political legitimacy of

13. Mary Davis Brown Diary, 1858; and passim, SCL; Welsh Neck Baptist Church, Darlington District, Minutes, July 5, 1845, SCL.

14. Drew Gilpin Faust, "Christian Soldiers: The Meaning of Revivalism in the Confederate Army," *Journal of Southern History* 53, no. 1 (February 1987), pp. 63–90; C. C. Goen, *Broken Churches, Broken Nation: Denominational Schism and the Coming of the American Civil War* (Macon, Ga.: Mercer University Press, 1985), pp. 55–56.

The literature on evangelicalism and proslavery ideology is extensive, but for key contributions see William Sumner Jenkins, *Pro-Slavery Thought in the Old South* (Chapel Hill: University of North Carolina Press, 1935); Eugene D. Genovese, *The World the Slaveholders Made: Two Essays in Interpretation* (New York: Vintage Books, 1969); Genovese, *"Slavery Ordained of God": The Southern Slaveholders' View of Biblical History and Modern Politics* (Gettysburg College, 1985); Eugene D. Genovese and Elizabeth Fox-Genovese, "The Religious Ideals of Southern Slave Society," *Georgia Historical Quarterly* 70, no. 1 (Spring 1986), pp. 1–16; Jack P. Maddex, Jr., "'The Southern Apostasy Revisited': The Significance of Proslavery Christianity," *Marxist Perspectives* 2, no. 3 (Fall, 1979), pp. 132–41; Larry E. Tise, *Proslavery: A History of the Defense of Slavery in America, 1701–1840* (Athens, Ga.: University of Georgia Press, 1987).

evangelicalism, they were, with a few notable exceptions, latecomers to the faith. From the establishment of dissenter congregations during the First Great Awakening to the rapid expansion during the Second, yeoman men and women, and with them increasing numbers of slaves, claimed evangelical churches as their institutions. Described loosely as people of "small means," the great majority of white evangelicals in the years preceding and immediately following Anglican disestablishment were, more precisely, yeoman farmers. In 1790, for example, fully two-thirds of South Carolina Baptists owned no slaves, and of the slaveholders, virtually all owned fewer than twenty slaves.[15] The same point is sustained by the membership lists of particular congregations. Yeoman men and women constituted the majority of white members in Welsh Neck Baptist Church in Darlington District in 1775, 1778, 1779, and again in 1814, and likewise in the poorer Mechanicsville church nearby in the same district when its list of members was taken in 1803. As the Welsh Neck records suggest, however, lowcountry evangelicalism had from the outset included all classes, although far from equally, in its ranks. In a discrete number of lowcountry and middle country churches, planters had a foothold early on.[16]

From the very planting of dissenting congregations in the mid-eighteenth century, Baptists and Presbyterians had attracted a few of

15. Joe M. King, *A History of South Carolina Baptists* (Columbia, S.C.: R. L. Bryan Co., 1964), pp. 135–41. See also David Benedict, *A General History of the Baptist Denomination in America and Other Parts* (New York: Lewis Colby and Co., 1848), p. 701; John B. Boles, *The Great Revival in the South, 1787–1805: Origins of the Southern Evangelical Mind* (Lexington: University Press of Kentucky, 1972), pp. 1–4.

16. Welsh Neck Baptist Church, Darlington District, Minutes, Membership List, 1775–1778–1779, and April 2, 1814; Mechanicsville Baptist Church, Darlington District, Minutes, "Saterday before the 2 lords day In August 1803."

Of the members of the Welsh Neck congregation in 1778 who could be identified on the census (21 of 84 members, or 25 percent), 3 were planters (20 or more slaves), one a small planter (10–19 slaves), and 17 were yeomen, 12 of whom were slaveholders and 5 of whom were not. Most (7 of 12) yeoman slaveholders owned fewer than 5 slaves. Of the 1814 congregation, 29 of 66 members, or 44 percent, could be identified; 2 were planters, 5 were small planters, and 12 were yeomen (10 nonslaveholders and 2 slaveholders). In Mechanicsville Baptist Church in 1803, 23 of 105 members could be identified from the census; 1 was a planter, 2 were small planters, and 20 were yeomen, ten of whom were slaveholders and ten nonslaveholders. Again, most yeomen slaveholders (7 of 10) owned five or fewer slaves.

Rates of identification are low because only household heads were listed by name in the federal censuses of 1790 and 1810. As a result, the only women members who could be identified were the few, presumably widows, who were household heads. Rates of identification of men are much higher: 38 percent in Welsh Neck, 1778; 70 percent in Welsh Neck, 1814; and 49 percent in Mechanicsville, 1803. Sources are as follows: *First Census of the United States, 1790*, ed. Ronald Vern Jackson (Bountiful, Utah: Accelerated Indexing Systems, 1978); Population Schedules of the Second Census of the United States, South Carolina [Darlington, Chesterfield, and Marlboro Counties], NA; Population Schedules of the Third Census of the United States, South Carolina [Darlington, Chesterfield, and Marlboro Counties], NA.

colonial South Carolina's richest families. Baptists and Presbyterians from Scotland, England, New England, and Pennsylvania had settled in the Charleston, Pee Dee (or Darlington), and, later, Lower Savannah (or Beaufort) areas in the early years of the colony, building their churches as they built the plantation society around them. Although some communities suffered decline and even extinction later in the century, others prospered, expanding their buildings along with their holdings in land and slaves. Baptist churches in the Pee Dee area and in Beaufort District, built and populated in part by prominent planter families like the Lides, Dargans, and McIvers of Darlington and the Jaudons, Roberts, Bosticks, and Lawtons of Beaufort, gained for lowcountry Baptists a claim to wealth and to a measure of respectability. The same was true of the Presbyterians, who managed to assemble congregations with a few planter members in Charleston, Colleton, Beaufort, Williamsburg, Marion, and Sumter by the opening of the nineteenth century. Methodists could make no such claims to elite patronage. The Baptists "take the rich," Francis Asbury complained in 1804, "and the commonalty and the slaves fall to us." The few of "high position in society" who did attend the preaching of the prominent Methodist minister William Capers, he complained, usually joined the Episcopal Church, which had fewer members but "the prestige of worldly wealth and honor."[17]

Methodist jealousies notwithstanding, the extent and significance of planter evangelicalism can be easily exaggerated in what were, after all, congregations of plain folk, slaves, and women. A handful of prominent families could not alone counteract the more general stigma evangelicalism carried among the elite. Frederick Porcher claimed to speak for his rural Charleston neighborhood when he contrasted "the qualities of the ritual" of the Episcopalian Church in the early nineteenth century, its "calmness and seriousness," with the "wild enthusiasm which frequently disfigures and distorts the religious efforts of those who rely upon the divine afflatus to guide them in their prayers." Pineville planters stuck to Episcopalianism. "A respectable and temperate presbyterian might . . . have won their favour," he reflected, but "a methodist of those times would have created only disgust." The "contortions of body . . . ejaculations of the congregation . . . frantic shouts and gambols of those . . . subjects of religious impressions," combined with the lack of distinction between the laity and the clergy, the "sinner" and the "teacher," ap-

17. Francis Asbury quoted in Boles, *Great Revival*, p. 169; William M. Wightman, *Life of William Capers, D.D.* (Nashville, Tenn.: Southern Methodist Publishing House, 1859), pp. 164–65. For the early history of the Baptist Church, see King, *South Carolina Baptists*, pp. 10–166; for evidence of their early foothold among planters see also Black Swamp Baptist Church, Beaufort District, Historical Sketch, 1895, SCL. On the Presbyterians, see George Howe, D.D., *History of the Presbyterian Church in South Carolina*, 2 vols. (Columbia, S.C.: W. J. Duffie, 1883), 2: 43–44, 347–48; and Hopewell Presbyterian Church, Marian District, Miscellaneous Records, SCL.

pealed only to those of humble means and social associations, Porcher insisted; the refined—his friends and neighbors—were, by contrast, repulsed.[18]

It was not only committed Episcopalians among the planter class who stigmatized evangelicalism as the religion of the poor, however. As late as the 1820s, Richard Fuller, who was to become one of the leading Baptist ministers in the state, refused to join the Baptist Church even though he had been converted by Benjamin Scriven, a prominent Baptist, and joined the Episcopal Church, instead. Baptists were still such a poor congregation in Beaufort at that time, he would later explain, that he could face neither the social stigma nor the small means that would attach to a minister in such an association. "In all social and material advantages the Episcopal Church was so far in advance of all other denominations that nothing but the deepest convictions of personal responsibility . . . could have led to any other church connection," he recalled.[19] Fuller eventually found the strength of his conviction. But despite the presence in their ranks of some prominent planter families, the problem of elite allegiance to the Episcopal Church plagued all evangelical denominations into the early antebellum period.[20]

Planter resistance was, as Porcher suggested, in direct proportion to evangelicalism's plain-folk face, as well as to its deeply suspect appeal to slaves. Plain folk did give shape to early evangelicalism in the coastal and middle country churches, although hardly, at least in social terms, the antislavery shape attributed to it by fearful elite contemporaries. It is true that the promise of spiritual equality introduced radical social possibilities, especially when extended to slaves, and it is certainly the case that slaves could find a message of deliverance—even revolutionary liberty—in the particular Afro-Christianity they created in the biracial churches of the early national South.[21] And it is also true, as Porcher complained, that plain folk found in evangelicalism a social style and self-image, a source of self-respect and self-assertion, with which to counter the superior pose and the customary prerogatives of local planter elites. Methodism, embraced by a nonelite "family in the neighborhood connected by distant relationship with ours," Porcher complained, "ap-

18. Samuel Gaillard Stoney, ed., "The Memoirs of Frederick A. Porcher," *South Carolina Historical and Genealogical Magazine*, vols. 44–48, (April 1943-January 1947), vol. 44, no. 3 (July 1943), pp. 137–44. Quotations are on pp. 141, 142.

19. J. H. Cuthbert, *Life of Richard Fuller, D.D.* (New York: Sheldon and Company, 1879), p. 64.

20. For one indication of the elite congregations of Episcopal churches see A. Toomer Porter, D.D., *Led On! Step by Step: Scenes From Clerical, Military, Educational and Plantation Life in the South, 1828–1898* (New York, 1898), p. 105 and passim.

21. The best study to date on the eighteenth- and early-nineteenth centuries is Sylvia R. Frey, *Water From the Rock: Black Resistance in a Revolutionary Age* (Princeton, N.J.: Princeton University Press, 1991). The definitive study of slave religion in the antebellum South remains Eugene D. Genovese, *Roll, Jordan, Roll: The World the Slaves Made* (New York: Pantheon Books, 1974).

peared to them a panacea for all their woes." Once converted, they lorded it over their richer relatives, seeming to say, he recalled, that they "were in possession of the more valuable spiritual gifts." Certainly evangelicalism had that meaning among the yeomanry and other nonelites. But such matters of self-esteem, no matter how valuable, hardly constituted the "war against the prosperous" that Porcher saw in them—at least not if one considers the actual practice of late-eighteenth-and early-nineteenth-century evangelicalism in local congregations.[22]

The evangelical message was irreducibly one of spiritual equality. But its relation to social equality or status in this world was, even in the early years, deeply contested. For the most part, lowcountry and middle country congregations evinced considerable concern with appropriate secular distinctions, investing them with new religious meaning. Nor was this merely a reflection of planter concerns in any simple sense. For the observation of gender, racial, property, and other distinctions in architecture, ritual, church government, and gospel discipline were no less central to evangelical discourse and practice in Darlington's Mechanicsville Baptist Church, a predominantly yeoman congregation, than in the Welsh Neck Church, with its component of wealthy and influential planter families.

In the first place, free male members jealously guarded their authority against the assumptions of women members, who consistently outnumbered them by a ratio of two to one. In Mechanicsville Baptist Church and Welsh Neck alike, fully two-thirds of the white members were women—and, indeed, in an eerie similarity that persisted throughout the antebellum period, two-thirds of slave members were women as well.[23] In 1804, after an extended discussion, a "quorum" of Mechanicsville members decided that "male members should have the privaledge of praying publickly" but prohibited women from that same expression of faith. Only free male members made that decision, for, from the moment records were kept in Mechanicsville, the "quorum" of members required to transact church business could be constituted only by "male members." As a result, women could not vote for the selection of the minister, exercise gospel discipline of backsliders, officially judge the authenticity of conversion experiences, or admit new members. Most certainly, they could neither preach nor serve as deacon or treasurer or

22. Stoney, ed., "Memoirs of Porcher," *South Carolina Historical and Genealogical Magazine* 44, no. 3 (July 1943), p. 142.

23. According to a membership list from 1803, Mechanicsville had 123 white members, 43 (35 percent) men and 80 (65 percent) women; it also had 278 black members, 49 (32 percent) men and 106 (68 percent) women. See Mechanicsville Baptist Church, Darlington District, Minutes, "Saterday before the 2 lords day In August 1803." According to a composite membership list from 1775, 1778, and 1779, Welsh Neck had 197 white members, 66 (34 percent) men and 131 (66 percent) women. No black members were listed. In 1814 the membership list showed 64 white members, 29 (45 percent) men and 35 (55 percent) women. Again, it listed no black members. See Welsh Neck Baptist Church, Darlington District, Minutes, Membership List, 1775–1778–1779, and April 2, 1814.

in any other formal capacity. Even the collection of charitable contributions observed strict gender boundaries. When "a private collection" was made to pay Brother Fountain's expenses to the association meeting, for example, the congregation was instructed that "the males is to give to Fountain and females to Thomas Conn." Women could not handle money—even that raised among themselves. In every deliberation they made their meaning clear: The "body" of the church might be black and female, but "the mind of the church" was white and male.[24]

Gender did not represent, by any means, the only social difference white male members marked in the churches. They recognized slave and free black members as brothers and sisters in Christ—even acknowledged the calling of slave men to preach, exhort, and dispense discipline among their own.[25] But after the Revolution, no less than before, that spiritual equality coexisted with a faith in the divine status of worldly inequalities, including, perhaps especially, slavery. Lowcountry slaves put their own construction on evangelicalism and, it is fair to say, whatever antislavery potential it evinced there was solely of their making. For their part, however, the white members and leaders of coastal and middle country churches gave no sustenance, official or otherwise, to the antislavery message articulated in England and in the northern states in the aftermath of the Revolution.[26] To the contrary, they struggled against it within the national bodies of their churches as the very death knell of their faith in the region.

The very suggestion that evangelicalism was necessarily or essentially antislavery—an assumption still very much at work in the historical literature—originated outside South Carolina and, for that matter, outside the South. Introduced by resolutions of the national body of, especially, the Methodist Church, it was vociferously rejected by the native-born clerical leadership and was never seriously entertained by the rank-and-file white membership of local congregations, plain-folk, planter, or otherwise. Fleeting enough in the Upper South in the 1780s with respect to white membership, the antislavery moment in southern

24. Mechanicsville [Mount Pleasant] Baptist Church, Darlington District, Minutes, June 19, 1804, "Saturdy before the Second Sunday in April 1704" [1804], July 15, 1815, September 14, 1816, January 7, 1816. For the reference to the male quorum in Welsh Neck, see Welsh Neck Baptist Church, Darlington District, Minutes, May 1, 1814. This was assuredly not a new practice.

25. In 1804, for example, a motion was passed "that Mr. Brockington's Adam shd be set apart as deacons in sd church," Mechanicsville Baptist Church, Darlington District, Minutes, "Saturday before the Second Sunday in April 1704 [1804]."

26. Allan Gallay has argued persuasively that even the earliest and most prominent South Carolina evangelical advocates of the Christian mission to the slaves "[n]ever sought any radical change in the institution." See Gallay, "The Origin of Slaveholders' Paternalism: George Whitefield, the Bryan Family and the Great Awakening in the South," *Journal of Southern History* 53, no. 3 (August, 1987), pp. 390–92. On the insurrectionary and antislavery potential of Afro-Christianity in the post-Revolutionary War period, see Frey, *Water From the Rock*, pp. 284–325.

evangelicalism was virtually nonexistent in the Lower South states; in South Carolina it was aggressively contested and, where it did momentarily surface, quickly suppressed.[27]

The antislavery imperative issued largely from the Methodist Church. But when, in 1784, the Methodist General Conference passed a resolution calling for the emancipation of all slaves owned by church members and prohibiting the further admission of slaveholders to Methodist ranks, they were quickly forced to rescind it in the face of what Bishop Coke identified as "the great opposition that had been given to it" from southern states. Subsequent antislavery resolutions explicitly exempted members from slaveholding states and, in response to the recalcitrance of South Carolina and Virginia Methodists, permitted them not only to own slaves but to buy and sell them as well. Although the very suggestion of an antislavery impetus in evangelicalism sent shock waves through the Low Country and Middle Country and nurtured a deep suspicion of Methodists especially, if by no means exclusively, in the planter elite, lowcountry clerics did everything in their power to distance themselves from such national principles.[28]

By 1804, their unwavering resistance had the desired effect; Methodist resolutions had moved from condemnation of slavery to advocacy of an extensive mission to the slaves, which was presented, quite self-consciously, as an attempt to prove to slaveholders that evangelical Christianity was safe for slavery. Far from censuring slaveholders, preachers were now encouraged "to admonish and exhort all slaves to render due respect and obedience to the commands and interests of their respective masters." And finally, in 1808, a mere twenty-four years after the first antislavery directive, the Methodist General Conference

27. Rachel Klein insists quite rightly on a recognition of "the diverse potentialities of the revival," including antislavery activity in the early national South, and she points to three upcountry ministers who in the late 1790s either preached antislavery or emancipated their slaves; all three had left the state by 1805. But she also confirms that in the South Carolina Backcountry specifically, only small pockets of Quakers "maintained a consistently antislavery stance," and even they had, by 1810, either assimilated or left the state. Her more general argument then, that in the latter half of the eighteenth century "evangelicalism became a vehicle for the expression of antiplanter sentiment among yeomen, and in certain contexts, . . . developed into a critique of slavery itself" does not represent the most central tendency in evangelicalism even in the Upcountry, nor does it establish connection between the yeomanry and the momentary expression of evangelicalism's antislavery potentiality. See Klein, *Unification of a Slave State: The Rise of the Planter Class in the South Carolina Backcountry, 1760–1808* (Chapel Hill: University of North Carolina Press, 1990), pp. 271–76, 284.

28. Coke quoted in H. Shelton Smith, *In His Image But . . . Racism in Southern Religion, 1780–1910* (Durham: Duke University Press, 1972), p. 44; A. M. Shipp, *The History of Methodism in South Carolina* (Nashville, Tenn.: Southern Methodist Publishing House, 1844), pp. 468–69, 474. On planter suspicion of Methodists in particular and evangelicals in general, see Klein, *Unification of a Slave State*, pp. 268–302; Lacy K. Ford, Jr., *Origins of Southern Radicalism: The South Carolina Upcountry, 1800–1860* (New York: Oxford University Press, 1988), pp. 5–37; Frey, *Water From the Rock*, pp. 243–83.

recognized the historical particularity and regional diversity of their own movement and surrendered all control over slavery, authorizing "each annual conference to form their own regulations relative to buying and selling slaves." South Carolina Methodists had never accepted the legitimacy of the antislavery imperative; they had fought it from the outset, and, within the boundaries of their regional association, they had prevailed.[29]

Baptists had an easier time establishing local authority over slavery and slaveholding members, in large measure because of the automony accorded local churches in their system of governance. In the immediate aftermath of the Revolution, the General Assembly of Baptist Churches did pass a resolution condemning slavery but was forced to retract it only two years later. Few white southern Baptists ever supported the position of the General Assembly, and although the resolution of 1785 did engender serious splits within Baptist congregations in frontier Kentucky, in long settled areas like South Carolina no white opposition to slavery emerged at all. Indeed, among the fifteen thousand members of the South Carolina Baptist Association (which encompassed North Carolina and Georgia as well as South Carolina), not one, according to an authorized denominational history, "[l]ifted an official voice against human bondage." At least in South Carolina, where an estimated 40 percent of Baptist ministers were themselves slaveholders, that reaction was hardly surprising. Although they too struggled against the antislavery reputation of evangelicalism—and especially the belief that evangelical principles nurtured insurrectionary ambitions among their slave adherents— they never succored such notions in their own congregations. Like the Methodists, South Carolina Baptists quickly found their best legitimizing strategy in a planter-supported and -directed mission to the slaves, one designed to prove that Christianized slaves better knew their duty to submit.[30] While such strategies only gradually assuaged the suspicions of lowcountry planters, by the end of the revival season of 1831–1833, the endorsement of the mission to the slaves by prominent planters signaled that evangelicals had gained the high ground.[31]

29. Shipp, *History of Methodism in South Carolina*, pp. 468–69; Smith, *In His Image But*, pp. 44–46; Frey, *Water From the Rock*, pp. 243–83; Klein, *Unification of a Slave State*, pp. 268–302.

30. Leah Townsend, *South Carolina Baptists* (Florence, S.C.: Florence Printing Company, 1835), p. 281; Smith, *In His Image But*, pp. 47–55. The Baptist mission to the slaves and its political agenda was delineated first and most fully in Richard Furman's pastoral letter of 1800, "Of Religious and Civil Duties," and again, more fully, in his *Exposition of the Views of the Baptists Relative to the Coloured Population in a Communication to the Governor of South Carolina* (1822; reprint ed., Charleston, 1833). Furman's communiqué was authorized most immediately by the actions of slaves themselves in the recently uncovered Vesey conspiracy. On Furman, see Frey, *Water From the Rock*, pp. 258–62, and on planters' embrace of evangelicalism and the mission to the slaves, see Klein, *Unification of a Slave State*, pp. 268–302.

31. One such prominent lowcountry planter was Colonel Charles C. Pinckney, Sr., of the Combahee River area. In 1829 he threw his considerable weight behind the plantation

These battles—and the victory—were not, however, simply or even primarily official ones. Local lowcountry and middle country congregations were irrevocably caught up in the national and international struggle for the soul of evangelicalism. Although they never wavered in the conviction that their faith was solid on slavery, churches all over the region evinced in the late eighteenth and early nineteenth centuries an increasingly defensive and disciplinary posture on the rights and privileges of slave brethren, registering in the negative the effect of the transatlantic debate. Designed to allay the fears of local skeptics and critics, especially, perhaps, those of local planters, such newly stringent resolutions reflected less a change of heart about the social meaning of spiritual equality than the end of innocence about the privileges of saints and secular status of slaves.

In 1785, the white male membership of Welsh Neck Baptist Church confidently and generously indicated its belief that "truly pious" black brethren "should enjoy the privileges of Saints." The membership gave broad and seemingly untroubled construction to those privileges and to the attendant duties of masters, not only securing to Christian slaves the right to obtain religious knowledge but extending to "those who can read at proper times [the right] to instruct others." Such sanguine acknowledgment, indeed, encouragement, of slave literacy, instruction, and unsupervised assembly—and the unquestioning faith in the compatibility of saints and slaves on which it rested—did not survive the firestorm of postrevolutionary debate. By 1814 the Welsh Neck covenant registered a deep distrust of emergent Afro-Christianity, of the impetus and cover it provided to insurrectionary slaves, and a changed sensibility on the entire subject of slavery and Christianity. They abandoned the unselfconscious reference to our "negro and other slaves" of 1785 and adopted the euphemism "servants," a defensive discursive strategy that fit a new agenda of prohibition and restriction and that marked a nascent proslavery agenda. Its central feature was an aggressive vigilance over slaves' religious meetings, articulated in Welsh Neck as a collective commitment "to restrain them ["servants"] from connecting with sinful assemblies, by using such means as to us may seem best qualified to answer this noble end consistent with the levity of the religon which we profess." The privileges of saints were no longer foremost in their concerns. In Mechanicsville, with a smaller planter contingent and

---

mission movement in the Low Country and used his address to the state Agricultural Society to endorse its goals. By 1833 the movement was gaining ground in the area. He wrote to his son that "some of the planters of both rivers are showing a little anxiety on the subject" of Christianizing slaves and enlisted his son's aid in investigating a prospective missionary with regard "to his qualifications and views both religious and on the slave question." Charles Cotesworth Pinckney, *An Address Delivered in Charleston before the Agricultural Society of South Carolina at Its Anniversary Meeting on Tuesday, the 18th of August, 1829* (Charleston, S.C.: n.p., 1829); C. C. Pinckney, Sr., to C. C. Pinckney, Jr., Charleston, November 18, 1833, Charles Cotesworth Pinckney Family Papers, Series III, Box 12, LC.

a largely yeoman white membership, similar concerns, coupled with a desire to continue evangelizing among the slaves, yielded a compromise of sorts. Particular slaves could be authorized to "hold meetings with the Black Brethren" on the condition that "some of the white Brethren ["the white male members," more precisely] . . . attend with them."[32] Making evangelicalism safe for slavery was by no means the exclusive concern of a handful of planter evangelicals.

The struggle to define and limit the social meaning of spiritual equality engaged the passions and the convictions of the yeoman majority of lowcountry and middle country congregations no less than their few but prominent planter members. This plain-folk religion had always embodied contradictory tendencies born out of simultaneous commitment to spiritual equality and social hierarchy. But as the deliberations of Welsh Neck and Mechanicsville suggest, there was little in the eighteenth- and early-nineteenth-century practice of evangelical plain folk to encourage the suspicion of planter critics that evangelicalism portended a radical inversion of secular social order. With women members as with slave, they had given powerful evidence of their inclination to recognize secular social distinctions and to invest them with religious meaning. For if, as some historians have argued, the predominantly plain-folk membership gave early evangelicalism an antielite and antiestablishment style, then, at least in the South Carolina Low Country, those plain folk were, more precisely, yeoman farmers—hardly the most marginal members of slave society—and their obvious stake in a propertied republic and in the domination of dependents (even if only the women and children in their own households) lent real limits to their challenge to elite authority.[33] Not only were slavery accepted and defended and conventional gender

32. Welsh Neck Baptist Church, Minutes, June 18, 1785, April 2, 1814; Mechanicsville Baptist Church, Minutes, April 13, 1815. The distinctive South Carolina prohibition on the formation of separate slave religious organizations, especially independent black churches, dates from this moment. The ban was not lifted until the last antebellum decade. For the debate over an independent black church in Charleston, see Second Charleston Presbyterian Church, Charleston District, Record of the Building Committee . . . for Erection of the Anson Street Edifice for the Blacks, August 17, 1849, and April 1848, SCL; John B. Adger, "The Religious Instruction of the Colored Population," *Southern Presbyterian Review* 1, no. 11 (September 1847), pp. 139, 150.

33. This argument was made most clearly by Rhys Isaac, whose definition of plain folk was a sketchy one. Isaac referred alternately to "simple folk," "humble neighbors," "yeomen," "small planters," "common people," and "small farmers." Some, he admitted, owned slaves, some had substantial wealth, and most, according to his description, owned land. Thus, although he characterized dissenters loosely as "poor folk," his description seems to refer on the whole to small propertyholders, or what historians would usually call the yeomanry. That "evangelical revolt should have been so restricted in scope" he attributed not to plain folks' own stake in a propertied social order but to "the strength of the gentry's hegemony and . . . the rigidities of the social hierarchy that had slavery at its base." See Rhys Isaac, *The Transformation of Virginia, 1740–1790* (Chapel Hill: University of North Carolina Press, 1982), pp. 147, 150, 163–68, 266; the long quotation is on p. 173. See also Isaac, "Evangelical Revolt: The Nature of the Baptists' Challenge to the Traditional Order in Virginia, 1765–1775," in *William and Mary Quarterly*, 3d series, vol. 31 (July 1974), pp. 345–68.

relations sanctified, but the respect due wealth and property was largely recognized by these men who were themselves independent proper-tyholders in communities composed of mostly propertyless dependents. In congregations with planter members, that respect did, for the most part, mean that male yeomen gave the nod to planters in election or appointment to church office, no doubt as a necessary condition of the patronage and beneficence wealthy church officers could be expected to dispense.[34]

Theirs was not an "egalitarian" Christian worldview. Rather, yeomen—or, more precisely, the men among them—installed their own consider-able prerogatives at the heart of postrevolutionary evangelicalism, lend-ing it a largely conservative and nascent proslavery shape that shored up their own claims to power and authority at home and abroad.[35] In doing so, the yeoman majority congregations of the late eighteenth and early nineteenth centuries prepared fertile ground for the purposeful expan-sion that was to come into the ranks of local "leading men." It hardly makes sense to view proslavery evangelicalism as an "apostasy" (to borrow a fitting phrase) from a purported antislavery essence or to date it, as historians usually do, from planters' antebellum embrace of the faith. Lowcountry evangelicals' commitment to a hierarchical social vision of which slavery was an accepted part has a much longer history and a more complex social location. Such neoabolitionist views only obstruct under-standing of lowcountry evangelicalism and its implication in the region's emergent political culture.[36]

34. In Mechanicsville in 1818, for example, a Brother Lide gave the church a "deed of gift" of two acres of land "which is got a House of Worship thereon." Male members of the same Lide family (James Lide and Hugh Lide) had been prominent on the committee awarded responsibility for building the church. One of the Lide men (which one is not clear) was customarily referred to in church records as "Squr Lide" or "Squire Lide," an obvious recognition of social rank. See Mechanicsville Baptist Church, Minutes, March 7, 1818, April 13, 1815, and September 12, 1818. Welsh Neck charged pew rents as early as 1792, instituting a declining scale of payment as pews moved from front to back. The two front rows on either side of the aisle rented for five pounds per year. Pew rents generated funds for ministers' salaries. See Welsh Neck Baptist Church, Minutes, May 12, 1792; King, *History of South Carolina Baptists,* p. 19.

35. This view contrasts most sharply, of course, with Rhys Isaac's. But it departs as well from the declension theory common in the literature on antebellum evangelicalism, which insists that what began in the mid-eighteenth century as religious revolt against traditional authority and as a vision of equality attractive to plain folk, women, and slaves had, by the 1830s, come to embody that authority and with it a new commitment to slavery and to racial and gender hierarchy within church, family, and society. Evangelicals went, in Don-ald Mathew's view, from "sect to denomination," from "radicals" to "guardians" of south-ern social order. For a sampling of these views see Isaac, *The Transformation of Virginia;* Isaac, "Evangelical Revolt"; Donald G. Mathews, *Religion in the Old South* (Chicago: Univer-sity of Chicago Press, 1977), pp. 97, 149–50; and the overview by John Boles, "Evangelical Dissent to Cultural Dominance," in Charles Reagan Wilson, ed., *Religion in the South* (Jack-son, Miss.: University Press of Mississippi, 1985), pp. 25–26 and passim.

36. The phrase is taken from Maddex, "'The Southern Apostasy' Revisited." It is commonly argued that southern evangelicals, caught in the "contradictions between doc-trine and practice," were forced to compromise their principles to "accommodate the social

IV

The first suggestion of real change came with the Great Revival of 1802–1804. Strongest in backcountry areas of the state, it by no means left the Low Country untouched. The revival spread to the South Carolina Backcountry (or Upcountry) by way of North Carolina and reached its greatest expression in the Lancaster camp meeting of April 1802 and the Waxhaw meeting the following May, which an estimated twelve thousand and thirty-five hundred people respectively attended. As the fires of revival consumed the Upcountry, they cast off sparks, a few of which alighted on the coast. Richard Furman, the Baptist leader, commented at the Waxhaw meeting that he had noticed many people "from the lower part of this state . . . a pretty large proportion [of whom] came under . . . impressions." Since their return to their homes, he went on, "an extraordinary revival has taken place in the congregations to which they belong." At Black Swamp Baptist Church in Beaufort District, for example, twelve hundred people, only "a very small proportion of whom were blacks," attended a three-day outdoor meeting in December 1803. Some had come "a considerable distance." Tents "were pitched on two lines running parallel . . . in the middle and at one end of which a stage was erected" from which "there were five or six sermons delivered on each day and night, besides exhortations in different parts of the camp." A goodly number were converted, the Charleston paper reported, "particularly among the female part of the assembly," and the "interests of morality and piety" advanced.[37] The meeting at Black Swamp and a number of others like it (some called, incidentally, by Presbyterians) extended the influence of evangelicalism within the Low Country. No single revival appears to have transformed community life quite as powerfully, however, as the one led by Reverend Joseph Clay in the town of Beaufort in 1803.

---

and economic realities of southern life." This particular construction belongs to James O. Farmer, Jr., but the view is widespread in the literature on southern religion in the early national and antebellum periods. See Farmer, *The Metaphysical Confederacy: James Henley Thornwell and the Synthesis of Southern Values* (Macon, Ga.: Mercer University Press, 1986), pp. 201–02. For other examples, see Boles, *Great Revival*, p. 194; Dickson D. Bruce, *And They All Sang Hallelujah: Plain-Folk Camp Meeting Religion, 1800–1845* (Knoxville: University of Tennessee Press, 1974), p. 59; and, for a more recent version, Randy Sparks, "'In Bonds of Love': The Search for Order and Discipline Among Mississippi Evangelicals, 1700–1860," (Unpublished paper presented at the Annual Meeting of the American Historical Association, Washington, D.C., December 1992). Even Donald Mathews, who criticizes this neoabolitionist view, inadvertently nurtures it: "[T]he social realities of slavery . . . could not be counterbalanced by religious commitment," he has argued, again as if religious commitment were necessarily antislavery. Mathews, *Religion in the Old South*, pp. 75, 79.

37. Richard Furman quoted in Howe, *Presbyterian Church in South Carolina*, vol. 2, p. 112; *City Gazette and Daily Advertiser*, December 10, 1803. On the revival in the Backcountry, see Klein, *Unification of a Slave State*, pp. 268–302, and Ford, *Origins of Southern Radicalism*, pp. 6–37. On the spread of the revival into South Carolina, see Boles, *Great Revival*, pp. 78–79.

Baptists had established an early foothold in Beaufort and would go on to make it the largest Baptist community in the state by 1847. But when Reverend Clay arrived in 1803, religion there was, according to Reverend Richard Fuller, "in a marked depression." "Religion was very little regarded," the Beaufort planter and resident William Grayson recalled of that prerevival season. "Church going was for the most part confined to women, Sunday was a day of boat-racing, foot-racing, drinking and fighting. . . . Quarter races and cock-fighting were popular amusement. . . . There was much laxity of morals . . . [and] pious people were a great exception." Beaufort, in other words, was not an unusual place. But with Clay's arrival from Savannah, a great change ensued in community sensibility. Church buildings were suddenly too small for the number of worshippers, and although expanded, continued to be "better filled than when of humbler dimensions." "There was a great awakening of religious sentiment among the people," Grayson marvelled years later, and, despite ministers' fears, it was not confined to socially marginal women, slaves, and other dependents. Household heads and prominent citizens, such as the Revolutionary War veteran Colonel Robert Barnwell, embraced Christ and became devout members of evangelical churches. The tone of community culture began to register the change. "The riotous sensuality of the old times had disappeared," Grayson recalled. "If immorality existed it was at least deferential enough to conceal itself from the public eye."[38] No doubt he exaggerated the transformation, but there can be little doubt that the revival of 1803 marked the ascent of evangelicalism in Beaufort as in other areas of the Low Country.

If that ascent was sustained it was, not least, because the revival converted prominent lowcountry ministers to a faith in the efficacy and soundness of the enthusiastic revival style. Notwithstanding a deep concern about the cold state of religion in the Low Country, ministers like Richard Furman, Charleston's leading Baptist, and Edmund Botsford, another leading Baptist, evinced deep suspicion of revival "excesses," such as the famous "bodily exercises" and, especially, to borrow Furman's words, of "the too-great intercourse between sexes in such . . . encampment[s]." Furman was far from alone in his fear that camp-meeting enthusiasm provoked sexual disorder. Indeed, it was a common indictment that the revivalistic preaching and exhortation of camp meetings moved only the weak-minded and emotional—namely, white women and slaves of both sexes—to orgasmic convulsion and liberating conversion. With women already constituting two-thirds of Baptist membership and slaves already outpacing whites in certain congregations, ministers like Furman feared that the revival would only stoke elite

38. Cuthbert, *Life of Fuller*, p. 64; Samuel Gaillard Stoney, ed., "The Autobiography of William John Grayson," *South Carolina Historical and Genealogical Magazine*, vols. 48–51 (July 1947-April 1960), vol. 49, no. 1 (January 1948), pp. 23–40; Howe, *Presbyterian Church in South Carolina*, vol. 2, pp. 64–65; Benedict, *General History of the Baptist Denomination*, p. 711.

fears of evangelical disorder and consign evangelicals permanently to
the periphery of power and influence in South Carolina society. Furman
and Botsford chafed at their fate as the shepherds only of the weak and
dependent. A veritable greediness for white male and influential converts marked their suspicion of camp meeting enthusiasm, and it was
proof of such conversions on which their own conversion to revivalism
turned. At the Waxhaw meeting, Reverend John McGready noted with
relief, not just white women but significant numbers of white men fell
under lasting conviction of sinfulness. McGready was correct. As ministers were just beginning to learn, white men would always convert in
greater numbers in revival settings than in the regular course of church
life. And in the aftermath of revivals, although they would still be outnumbered by women, their share of membership was substantially increased. As the Reverend Mr. Furman put it after his personal attendance at the Waxhaw meeting, while he retained a few reservations, "the
preaching and exhortation of the ministers in general were calculated to
inspire right sentiments and make right impressions."[39] Nothing was
more important for the expansion of evangelicalism in the Low Country
than that it successfully dispel charges of effeminization and general
disorder. In this respect the Great Revival was a critical juncture indeed.

As the report of the Black Swamp revival in the Charleston paper
confirmed, however, evangelicalism still found its appeal "particularly
among the female part of the assembly," and, it might have added,
among others even more socially marginal. If the 1803 revival marked
the ascent of evangelicalism, it would take a great deal more to give it the
social and political legitimacy for which church leaders hungered. It
took, in fact, a revolution in political culture itself.

V

The mature antebellum character of lowcountry evangelicalism was
forged in the heat of the Nullification Crisis. It is that simple, that dramatic, and that complex. A "wave of religious revival . . . swept like a
spring-tide over the Sea Coast" between 1831 and 1833 in the wake, as it

39. Furman quoted in Howe, *Presbyterian Church in South Carolina*, vol. 2, pp. 109, 112.
For a description of bodily exercises, see King, *South Carolina Baptists*, pp. 151–54. On the
gender composition of membership, see also King, *South Carolina Baptists*, pp. 147–48. The
discussion of male converts in revivals is based on analysis of the sex of converts in the four
largest antebellum revivals in one Beaufort Baptist congregation, Beech Branch. Men
constituted 54.9 percent (28/51) in the 1833 revival; 66.7 percent (16/24) in the 1846
revival; 59.1 percent (13/22) in the 1855 revival; and 70.6 percent (12/17) in the 1860
revival. Overall, males constituted 60.5 percent of revival converts when their share of
membership was usually about 45 percent. See Beech Branch Baptist Church, Beaufort
District, Church Book, July 15-July 27, 1833, August 31-September 12, 1846, August 28,
1855, and September 14-23, 1860. Such precise records are not available for the 1803
revival, but contemporary accounts sustain the impression.

turns out, of meetings held by Reverend Daniel Baker in his Savannah church. People had never seen anything like it. Invited to preach in Gillisonville in Beaufort District after word was "noised abroad" of a protracted meeting in his own congregation, Reverend Baker, a Presbyterian, was credited with singlehandedly vanquishing the "great spiritual deadness" that gripped the region.[40] And by many accounts, including the record of conversions in local church records, Daniel Baker, a Presbyterian minister from Savannah, Georgia, was the greatest evangelist in antebellum South Carolina. Certainly the history of the Nullification Revival had his name printed all over it.

The regional scope of the revival was unprecedented. "Oh what blessed meetings we had," Baker recalled in his memoirs of his first Beaufort trip in 1831. "Three times every day did I preach, and night and day to full houses." In Gillisonville, his first meeting in the district, sixty were converted in a matter of days. And that was only the beginning. Next was Grahamville, where, according to Baker, "many of the young and old, the lawyers and planters 'turned to the Lord.' The duelist threw away his pistols, the infidel believed in Christ, political feuds were forgotten and the power of the gospel confessed." These early rural meetings had marked results, not least of which was an invitation to the Reverend Mr. Baker by William Barnwell, a new and prominent convert, to preach in the town of Beaufort. This was by Baker's own admission "the most remarkable" of all his lowcountry meetings. Preaching alternately in Baptist and Episcopal churches—the Presbyterians had no strong presence in the town—Baker and the Beaufort ministers converted seventy souls who joined the Episcopal Church and seventy more of whites "and very many blacks" who joined the Baptists. It was estimated that Baker converted two to three hundred people in Beaufort in that first 1831 season and five hundred more in one twelve-week trip through the Low Country in 1832.[41]

Baker's revival knew no denominational loyalties or district boundaries but quickly swept the coastal parishes and middle districts, answering prayers for "reviving works of grace" at Beech Branch and Black Swamp Baptist churches in rural Beaufort District, at Camden and Barnwell Baptist churches, and at Welsh Neck Baptist Church in Darlington District. On Edisto Island, in Beaufort, Colleton, Williamsburg, Darlington, Richland, and Sumter Districts, Presbyterian churches added to their membership, and in Colleton and Kershaw districts, at least, Methodist records reveal great success.[42] Little of Baker's lowcountry

40. Cuthbert, *Life of Fuller*, p. 67; William Mumford Baker, *The Life and Labours of the Reverend Daniel Baker . . . Prepared By His Son* (1858; reprint ed., Louisville, Ky.: Lost Cause Press, 1961), pp. 133, 144, 155–57.

41. Baker, *Life of Baker*, pp. 155–57, 160–65; Howe, *Presbyterian Church in South Carolina*, vol. 2, pp. 460–66, 556–57.

42. Beech Baptist Church, Beaufort District, Church Book, September 2, 1833; Black Swamp Baptist Church, Beaufort District, Historical Sketch, 1895; First Baptist Church,

success, however, redounded to the benefit of his own Presbyterian church. Of the two to three hundred converted in Beaufort in 1831, it was said that not one joined the Presbyterians, and of the more than five hundred people converted during his 1832 trip, only a small percentage ever joined his own denomination. In Beaufort, to take only one obvious example, Baptists were the chief beneficiaries of Baker's endeavors, for Beaufort had few Presbyterian churches. So unconstrained by denominational loyalties was Baker's mission that one planter who witnessed the October 1832 revival suggested that all denominations contribute to Baker's financial support. It was, this gentleman pleaded, only fair, for "his labors benefit all denominations equally."[43]

The level of interdenominational cooperation evinced during this Nullification Revival was indeed impressive. Although disputes over doctrine and ritual—and especially over baptismal rites and the propriety of infant baptism—fueled intense competition for souls, most ministers acknowledged that in the end, "matters which are least disputed are most essential" in religion. Nor was there any confusion about what was most essential. "Outward morality would not do," one minister thundered, "God says we must be born again." So, dunked or sprinkled, adult or infant, the insistence of all evangelical churches that each new adult member give public testimony of personal experience of Christ's forgiveness and acceptance undergirded revival cooperation and forged a unified movement out of disparate denominations. What really mattered, a Walterboro gentleman concluded after one of Daniel Baker's great revival sermons, was not the fine points of theological distinction but that a preacher could "rivet the attention of the sinner, draw him insensibly to the conclusion that he was a fool—a consumate fool; harrow up his soul, force him to think and lead him to prayer," and ultimately, make him feel that God had lifted the burden of sin from his shoulders and accepted him into the community of the saved.[44] No one, it seemed, quite had Baker's gift.

Camden, Kershaw District, Centennial Address, 1910, SCL; First Barnwell Baptist Church, Barnwell District, Minutes, September 3, 1831, SCL; Welsh Neck Baptist Church, Darlington District, Minutes, October 9, 1832; Camden Station Methodist Church, Kershaw District, Records, 1832, 1833, SCL. For accounts of the extent of the revival see also *Charleston Mercury*, October 29, 1831; Baker, *Life of Baker*, pp. 144, 155–57, 176, 180; and Howe, *Presbyterian Church in South Carolina*, vol. 2, pp. 462–66, 477, 556–57.

43. Baker, *Life of Baker*, pp. 176–85 (quotation on p. 183); Howe, *Presbyterian Church in South Carolina*, vol. 2, p. 556; Cuthbert, *Life of Fuller*, p. 67.

44. Francis Asbury, quoted in Mathews, *Religion in the Old South*, pp. 32–33; Mary Hort Journal, June 28, 1857, SCL; Baker, *Life of Baker*, pp. 184–85. This is not, however, to diminish the significance of denominational struggles over baptism. Daniel Baker, to take an obvious example, was horrified at the refusal of the Baptists to baptize infants. See Daniel Baker, "A Scriptural View of Baptism," in Baker, *Life of Baker*, p. 120. And throughout the antebellum period, as in the 1831–1833 revival, ordinary churchgoers voted with their feet, choosing their denomination (where they had a choice) largely on the basis of baptism rituals. Thus, one woman asked that her name be struck from the Baptist church book because "she believed in infant sprinkling." She joined the Methodists. See Euhaw Baptist Church, Beaufort District, Records, June 26, 1858, SCL.

The success of Baker's Nullification Revival was not, however, simply a matter of the total number of souls, admittedly unprecedented, harvested for God. All souls were clearly not the same. More than anything else, ministers celebrated the conversion of "male adults," or, as Baker put it more precisely, of "heads of families" or households. But even men were not all equally valued, as correspondents made clear in their emphatic reporting of the number of "white persons" among the converted. Slave men, although physiologically male, were here as in secular discourse denied the identity and privileges of masculinity. They lacked the material substance of independence—ownership of property, control over households and dependents, and political rights—that marked men as men in the Low Country. Nor did they exercise any of that power over others that ministers were so desperate to tap. Thus, whether they congratulated themselves, as did the Presbyterian George Howe, because "two-thirds of [their] additions were male" and "included men of eminence in society" or, as Baker did, because they were "chiefly of the young, the refined and the wealthy," what these evangelical leaders really celebrated was their ability to harness the power that such "leading men" exercised over others. Even yeoman men were useful in this respect. But wealthy, influential men were prized above all others, for in addition to their wives and children, they had influence over large number of slaves, and some had even, as the name implied, a reputation for influencing other white men within their local circle.[45] Like slaves, women, no matter how wealthy, had not this capacity. Women embodied dependence. Only once did the Reverend Mr. Baker attribute exemplary power to a woman's conversion, and this in his first Savannah meeting when a "lady who moved in the first circle of society was so much wrought upon that she wept aloud. When this was known," he reported, "it became the subject of much conversation and excited great interest."[46] Notwithstanding, ministers, including Baker, typically took women's conversion for granted, revealing in their vague beliefs in women's natural piety a self-conscious desire to dispel the effeminized image of evangelicalism in which its marginalization was rooted. Elite male converts alone could eradicate the association of evangelical churches with women, slaves, and the common folk, alone could make them legitimate and even powerful institutions in the Low Country. Thus, Baker's "work was remarkable," Richard Fuller would later observe, "not only in the number and soundness of the conversions, but in its triumphs among the higher classes of society." It was Reverend Baker's conversion of influential men such as "W. B. [William Barnwell], two of the E's [Elliotts], and some others [including] RBR [Robert Barnwell Rhett]" in the Nullification Revival that moved evangelicalism from margin to center in Low Country society and political culture. Embraced and patronized by such men, Baker knew, the power of evangelicalism could

45. Baker, *Life of Baker*, pp. 155–57, 160–65; Howe, *Presbyterian Church in South Carolina*, vol. 2, pp. 557, 165–66.
46. Baker, *Life of Baker*, p. 144.

not be contained. "The evangelical party has now the ascendancy in the diocese of South Carolina," he proclaimed in 1833 after three consecutive years of revival, his striking choice of language suggesting a whole other dimension of the lowcountry transformation.[47]

It was one that the anti-Nullifier and Unionist leader James Louis Petigru grasped as early as the fall of 1831. Of all that he had heard and seen across the coastal districts in 1831, he told his fellow Unionist William Elliott, there "was nothing to compare with . . . the Beaufort revival. I suppose by this time the fire has consumed everything in Beaufort that will burn." He soon surrendered hope that "nullification will give way to religion." Nullifiers like Colonel Charles Cotesworth Pinckney had been "vastly devout for six months," he noted sarcastically, "without any visible change in the outer man." Far from dousing the Nullification firestorm sweeping the coastal lowcountry, he concluded despondently the following year, this mania for conversion rather stoked it. "It is like Mahomet's faith," Petigru declared in October 1832. "[T]hey combine war and devotion, and in fact, it seems to me that fanacticism of every kind is on the increase."[48] He had a point, one his "fanatical" opponents did not dispute, although they did cast it in a different light.

The timing of the Nullification Revival was, as Petigru suggested, anything but coincidental, even if the particular psychopolitical dynamics remain difficult to comprehend. It was, assuredly, an explosive historical moment, one redolent with meanings personal and political. Party factions, partisan violence, and political turmoil were the tenor of the day. Reverend Baker knew full well that he walked onto a powder keg in Beaufort, Walterboro, and the innumerable other small lowcountry towns and villages in which he preached in the early 1830s. "[T]here was high political excitement in South Carolina" in 1831, he recalled in his autobiography. "Parties were arrayed against each other, and many persons went armed." One Beaufort Nullifier whom he converted in 1831 confessed that he was on the verge of challenging a Union man to a duel when he was seized by the spirit of God, and now "would be willing to kiss the dust upon the feet of the Union men if they would only come to Christ."[49] Other eyewitnesses, themselves all converts and Nullifiers, told similar tales of violent partisanship prostrate to revivalism, of community unified and distinctions levelled: of religion and politics fused into one system of meaning.

47. Cuthbert, *Life of Fuller*, p. 68; Baker, *Life of Baker*, pp. 188–89. Fuller and other ministers continued to make such distinctions about the value of converts throughout the antebellum period. In 1844, for example, Fuller noted in a letter to a Georgia woman that in his current revival in Beaufort "besides a great many servants, I baptized four most valuable white persons." Cuthbert, *Life of Fuller*, p. 227.

48. James Louis Petigru to William Elliott, November 14, 1831, and James Louis Petigru to Hugh Legaré, October 29, 1832, in James Petigru Carson, ed., *Life, Letters and Speeches of James Louis Petigru, the Union Man of South Carolina* (Washington, D.C.: W. H. Lowdermilk and Co., 1920), pp. 85–86, 103–04.

49. *Life of Baker*, p. 166.

From Walterboro two gentlemen converts reported that the "angry and rancorous . . . spirit of party" that pervaded their town quickly gave way in the course of revival to "harmony, virtue, and piety," and "deadly foes," prepared "to shed a brother's blood . . . on the field of what the world calls 'honor' now are to be found bowing at the same altar . . . perfectly brotherly." From Beaufort, William Grayson reported a similar revolution in community sensibility. "The effect" of the revival on "our little town none can conceive who was not present," he wrote in the *Beaufort Gazette*. "Politics were forgotten. Business stood still—the shops and stores were shut—the schools closed—one subject only appeared to occupy all minds and engross all hearts." Crowds "of all ages and conditions . . . fell prostrate at the foot of the altar . . . animosities long continued were sacrificed, coldness and formality were forgotten, our community," he would say not for the last time, "seemed like one great family."[50]

But if unity was produced where discord and partisan violence had prevailed, then in the representation of these elite Nullifier converts, it was not, as Petigru would have it, because of any unholy marriage between radical religion and radical Nullification politics. Rather, it was because politics gave way entirely before the higher cause. When Baker returned to Walterboro in the fall of 1832, the evangelical victory was complete. "The business of the town ceased," one gentleman reported. "Monday and Tuesday were the days of the general election yet the polls were either not attended, or the voters dropped their votes into the ballot-box and went away." It was nothing short, he concluded, of a "complete revolution . . . in the whole frame of this society and the pure religion of Christ . . . its grand characteristic."[51]

A revolution indeed. On that all lowcountry observers agreed. But Petigru's reading remains a tantalizing one, hardly incompatible with the claims to unity Nullifier converts propagated. The Beaufort Nullifier who professed his willingness to kiss the feet of the Union enemy "if they would only come to Christ" revealed the conviction that God was on his side, that Nullifiers had made the principled religious choice as they had the political one. Unity was still conditional on the embrace of the Nullifier's faith, and political discord ceased only when that convergence was accomplished. Such self-righteous views were expressed, not just by horrified Episcopalians like Petigru, but by other "[f]riend[s] of Religion" in the Low Country, such as the man who wrote to the *Charleston Mercury* to explain that "as a christian [*sic*] and patriot, I cannot support the Union party," or the nameless chairman of the Beaufort State Rights and Free Trade Association (a Nullifier organization) who pressed Governor Hamilton in September 1831 to declare a day of Fasting, Humiliation, and Prayer to enlist God's guidance in "removing the national oppres-

---

50. *Charleston Mercury*, November 12, 1831, November 14, 1831.
51. Reprinted in Baker, *Life of Baker*, p. 180.

sion under which we suffer, and of producing harmony and unanimity of sentiment within the state." Hamilton, although he shared his constituent's goals, was not innocent of the tactic. He designated a day of prayer but in November, intentionally after the city elections, "to avoid," as he put it, "the appearance of being designed for party purposes."[52] Revival religion could and did buttress the Nullifiers' self-representation as the selfless servants of God and Carolina; in the best of all possible words, it sanctified their political claims.

Petigru did not imagine things. There was a marriage of sorts between radical religion and radical politics in key parts of the coastal Low Country. Evangelical revivalism did find its greatest lowcountry expression in Nullification strongholds. It reached its zenith in Beaufort District in 1833, where Unionists were so outnumbered that they did not even run a ticket for the election of delegates to the Nullification convention. And while the individual psychodynamics of elite conversion in the heightened context of the Nullification Crisis remain difficult to grasp, it is equally difficult to overlook the fact that by 1833 many leading Nullifiers had been converted to evangelicalism: Robert Barnwell Rhett (or Barnwell Smith, as he was still sometimes called)—few were more important in Nullifier ranks—but also Robert Barnwell, Stephen Elliott, William Grayson, and Charles Cotesworth Pinckney, to name only an obvious few more.[53] The new convergence of sacred and secular was repeatedly enacted in public political meetings and private correspondence and in the deliberations of local congregations. When the Welsh Neck Baptist Church unanimously took up the Governor's invitation to observe the last day of January 1833 as a "day of Fasting, Humiliation and Prayer to implore the blessing of the *Almighty* on our State and the whole United States, and on the proceedings of the Convention," members quickly revealed the openly sectional and potentially partisan content of their devotion. "Believe in the LORD your God, and you will be established," Brother Dossey preached in what the clerk described as "an appropriate sermon for us," "believe his prophets and you will succeed." Few could have missed the message: "For the Lord had made them rejoice over their enemies, and the fear of God came on all the Kingdoms of the Countries when they heard that the Lord had fought against the enemies of Israel." With the ability to reach thousands of people every Sunday, local churches had a degree of influence on low-

52. *Charleston Mercury*, October 19, 1831, November 10, 1831. On the State Rights and Free Trade Association, see William W. Freehling, *Prelude to Civil War: The Nullification Controversy in South Carolina, 1816–1836* (New York: Harper and Row, 1965), pp. 224–25.

53. William Grayson would become a Unionist and ally of Petigru's in the later antebellum period, but in the 1830s he was an ardent Nullifier and the editor of the Beaufort Gazette, an organ of the cause. See Richard J. Calhoun, ed., *Witness to Sorrow: The Antebellum Autobiography of William J. Grayson* (Columbia, S.C.: University of South Carolina Press, 1990), p. 6.

country political culture that is difficult to overestimate. Their role in the state's deliberations over slavery and the appropriate means of the defense of their peculiar social relations would only increase in the coming years. Little wonder Nullifiers found so much power in evangelicalism. Honor God and he will smite your enemies, preachers promised their congregations. In the tumultuous years of 1831–1833, there was only one way to honor God—but many ways to define your enemies.[54] At another, more prominent, public level, nothing made the point so dramatically, at least as Petigru saw it, as evangelical Nullifiers' efforts to oust the ardent Nullifier but religious skeptic Thomas Cooper from their party. "If they sacrifice Cooper they may do with the State as they please," Petigru brooded in the late fall of 1832, "for very few of our co-religionists have any charity for those who are blind to the light of Calhoun's and McDuffie's revelations."[55] Faced with the unprecedented challenge of popular political mobilization, prominent radical planter politicians had, to Petigru's horror, learned to speak the language of evangelicalism.

By 1833 the new political orthodoxy was married to the new religious orthodoxy, and the "evangelical party" really was in the ascendancy. Evangelicalism and Nullification had simultaneously seized the Low Country's imagination, uniting newly converted planter politicians to their newly enfranchised yeoman constituencies in a set of common institutions with a common discourse. As planters finally embraced the yeomanry's religion in significant numbers, they moved evangelicalism from margin to center of Low Country political culture. Indeed, the mature character of that antebellum political culture was forged out of the same process of appropriation and transformation. In evangelicalism planter politicians found moral and ideological support for their emerging domination of local and regional political culture,[56] a language spoken (at least in dialect) by all classes of South Carolinians and thus an unprecedented political reach. Few forces would prove of such

54. Welsh Neck Baptist Church, Darlington District, Minutes, January 1833, January 31, 1833. The sermon is Chronicles 2:20.

55. James Louis Petigru to Hugh Legaré, October 29, 1832, and November 20, 1833, in Carson, ed., *Life of Petigru*, pp. 103–04, 128–29. See the discussion of Cooper's politics in Freehling, *Prelude to Civil War*, pp. 128–31. Freehling notes the success of evangelicalism among Beaufort planters, but he does not explore the connection with the district's radical politics.

This argument is designed to point only to the importance of the connection between evangelicalism and the popular basis of radical politics in the Low Country and to the origins of that connection in the Nullification Crisis. It does not attempt to argue that evangelicalism always sustained the radical faction. In fact, as will become clear, the opposition of key ministers and churches to the first secession movement was critical to its defeat, their support of the second critical to its success. The connection between evangelicalism and the politics of slavery and secession is pursued further in chapters 6, 7, and 8 below.

56. Rachel Klein has made this point convincingly in her *Unification of a Slave State*, pp. 269–302.

singular significance in the popular politics of the region down to the Civil War. The Low Country, as Petigru had predicted, would never be the same.

VI

When, in his autobiography, William Grayson attempted to convey the revolutionary effects of the Nullification Revivals on community life, he reached for the metaphor he had found so useful in 1831. "The town," he said, "was a great family." It was a fitting metaphor, although not, perhaps, in the unambiguous way he used it. In his construction, the community as family conveyed a powerful sense of social unity, of social distinctions leveled, of sectarian politics submerged. The revival "broke down conventional distinctions," he recalled, "the poor and rich were united as brothers. It erased the lines of sectarian division; the churches of various creeds joined the same services. . . . It opened all hearts and houses; the town" had become "a great family."[57] There was nothing haphazard about Grayson's metaphorical choice. For the familial model of Christian community had already acquired discursive centrality by the 1830s, and it only increased with the deeper and more self-conscious articulation of the ensuing years of expansion and sectional definition. But if the concept of family proved of such utility in evangelical discourse, it did so not because of the unitary and, indeed, romantic, meaning Grayson attributed to it but because of its multivalence.[58] Only one part of evangelicals' familial conception of social order, Grayson's emphasis on unity and community bonds was nonetheless a crucial part.

The revival had transformed the Low Country into an evangelical society; it had broken down some conventional distinctions, not the least of which was rigid class distinction in religious affiliation; most important of all, it had turned evangelical churches into institutions that embraced the lowcountry population in all of its considerable diversity. No other institution—no political party, social club, or militia organization, no school, voluntary society, or newspaper—embraced in its membership all classes of lowcountry society. But the churches did. Within their walls on any given Sunday were to be found in various combinations free and slave, white and black, male and female; yeomen and planters, masters and slaves; planter, yeoman, and slave women; merchants, mechanics, overseers, clerks, and lawyers. No other institution even came close to this social inclusivity except, of course, the household or "family"

57. Stoney, ed., "The Autobiography of Grayson," *South Carolina Historical and Genealogical Magazine* 49, no. 1 (January 1948), pp. 34–35. A more complete version of Grayson's autobiography is now available, although my references are to the earlier published version. See Calhoun, ed., *Witness to Sorrow*.

58. This constitutes the subject of the following chapter.

itself. Popular religion it was by the mid-1830s, and its political location irrevocably changed in consequence. In the antebellum history of the lowcountry yeomanry, few institutions would prove so important and perhaps no other discourse so integral to yeomen's own conception of the imperatives of social order and political culture.

The social composition of the membership of coastal and middle district churches provides clear evidence of the popular reach of evangelicalism[59] and of the continuing centrality of the yeomanry among its diverse circle of fellowship. The issue is less the extent of membership—always difficult to measure—than the actual profile of the members. Estimates of membership in southern evangelical churches range from 10 to 30 percent of the adult white population, with recent evidence confirming the upper end for South Carolina specifically.[60] But evangelical influence extended well beyond formal membership, and not only through its general diffusion into regional culture. In every church, and especially in Baptist ones which permitted membership only by converted adults, formal counts of the membership represented only a portion of those who regularly attended preaching and who were, in many respects, part of the congregation. So, for example, the Quarterly Conference Minutes of the Methodists' Darlington Circuit regularly made distinctions between the number of "communicants" and those "received on trial" but did not count in its membership those who attended preaching but were not yet subject to a work of grace. In all denominations (regardless of their position on pedo-baptism), conversion was a prerequisite to communion, and only communicants were counted as full church members. Children, adolescents, and unconverted adults were never counted in congregational membership reports.[61] In effect, one historian has argued, "nearly every minister preached regularly to congregations three or four times the size of church membership." Richard Furman put it even more forcefully: For every person in the church there were six others who accepted evangeli-

59. While most historians would agree with this assessment, there are some, most notably Bertram Wyatt-Brown, who dissent. In his view, evangelicalism was inherently bourgeois and antithetical to the southern culture of honor, its influence in the South confined to a small group of educated planter elites openly opposed by the largely poor-white antimission Baptists. See Bertram Wyatt-Brown, *Southern Honor: Ethics and Behavior in the Old South* (New York: Oxford University Press, 1982), pp. xv–xviii, and Wyatt-Brown, "The Anti-Mission Movement in the Jacksonian South: A Study in Regional Folk Culture," *Journal of Southern History* 36 (November 1970), pp. 501–29.

60. Mathews, *Religion in the Old South*, pp. 47–48; Bruce, *And They All Sang Hallelujah*, p. 45; Edwin Scott Gaustead, *Historical Atlas of Religion in America* (New York: Harper and Row, 1976), pp. 52–53; Wyatt-Brown, *Southern Honor*, p. xviii. For an indication of the South Carolina figures, in this case drawn from the Upcountry, see Ford, *Origins of Southern Radicalism*, pp. 19–37.

61. Methodist Church, Darlington and Florence Counties, Darlington Circuit, Quarterly Conference Minutes, 1840, SCL; Darlington Presbyterian Church, Darlington District, Minutes, 1845–1853, SCL. Also see Wightman, *Life of Capers*, pp. 116–17.

cal teaching but remained outside the church.[62] Evangelicalism's influence burst the bounds of membership, of individual churches, and even
of organized religion itself.

Notwithstanding the quantitative limitations of membership lists,
they do provide a compelling portrait of evangelical congregations in all
of their gender, racial, and class complexity. No single feature is so
striking as the enduring predominance of women among evangelical
ranks. Ministers rightly worried. Women free and slave dominated the
membership rolls of virtually every church and constituted, without exception, the majority among the aggregate membership of every denomination, whether early in the antebellum period or late. In a sample of
thirty-one churches drawn from Baptist, Primitive Baptist, Methodist,
and Presbyterian congregations and from both the coastal and the interi-
or Low Country, that point was made startlingly clear. With the exception of one Primitive Baptist Church in which women's majority was
quite slight (52 percent), women's share of membership ranged between
58 percent in Methodist churches and 61 percent in Presbyterian ones;
Baptists fell in between, with 60 percent of their members women.
There was, of course, some variation among individual congregations;
some were below that usual proportion of women members, and some—
especially town or urban churches—were well above it. But across denominations, time, and to some extent, space, women represented a
consistent and significant majority of 60 percent of the membership of
evangelical churches. (See Table 4.1.)

Women's share of membership was, moreover, startlingly similar
across the fundamental divide of slavery and freedom. In Baptist
churches six of every ten members, black as well as white, were women;
in Methodist churches, six of every ten white members and more than
five of every ten black members were women; in Presbyterian churches,
more than six of every ten white members and almost six of every ten
black members were women. Clearly, lowcountry evangelicalism shared
with its sectional and national counterparts a distinctly gendered body.
That gendered body was fundamental to the local practice and the regional discourse of evangelicalism. It will hardly do, then, to characterize
the social composition of evangelicalism by its male membership, as historians are still in the habit of doing.[63]

But of course, in lowcountry churches as in the larger society, the

---

62. Goen, *Broken Churches, Broken Nation*, p. 55; Furman quoted in Ford, *Origins of
Southern Radicalism*, p. 24. As Donald Mathews has pointed out, "the quality of the relationship between church members and nonmembers is largely a matter of conjecture." Mathews, *Religion in the Old South*, p. 47. In lowcountry churches it was not uncommon to see
people contributing to the support of the church although not themselves formally members. See, for example, the pew rent records of Midway Presbyterian Church, Williamsburg District, in Presbyterian Church, Miscellaneous Records, vol. 1, SCL.

63. See, for example, Ford, *Origins of Southern Radicalism*, pp. 32–33. Such ungendered
analysis is, however, hardly peculiar to Ford.

female part of the gendered body was further cut through by race and class. Distinctions between free women and slave women and between white women and black women were, clearly, the most obvious lines of division. But class distinctions went well beyond the boundaries marked by race and slave status; poor white, yeoman, and planter-class women hardly constituted a cohesive social group. Gender was thus only one, admittedly crucial, line of social identity in evangelical congregations, one radically cut across by the fault lines of race and class that marked congregations and lent to each denomination its own distinct social character.

Where most African-Americans were also slaves, race marked, imperfectly and incompletely, the single most critical dimension of the class composition of lowcountry churches. Across the region, blacks composed the majority of members in three of four Baptist, two of three Methodist, and four of ten Presbyterian churches. In the coastal parishes, their presence was even more pronounced. In Euhaw Baptist Church in Beaufort District, fully 95 percent of the members were black. In 1860 that quite wealthy congregation had 482 members, only 24 of whom were white. The Euhaw church was a particularly exaggerated case of a general intraregional pattern. In every coastal Baptist and Methodist church for which racial statistics on membership are available and in two of three Presbyterian ones, slaves were in the majority, with shares of membership ranging from a low of 56 percent in the Kingstree Presbyterian Church in Williamsburg District to the unparalleled 95 percent of the Euhaw Baptist Church. There were as well clear denominational patterns within the region. In Baptist churches black membership reached in excess of three-quarters of the aggregate membership (76.5 percent), in Methodist churches nearly half (42.5 percent), and in Presbyterian churches slightly more than one-third (35.5 percent). (See Table 4.2.)

Amid the considerable intraregional and denominational diversity, and the vagaries of individual congregations, however, the biracial character of lowcountry evangelicalism comes resolutely into focus. Almost half the members of evangelical churches in the region were black, and, as the records show, almost all of them were slaves.[64] Out of the commanding presence of black evangelicals, then, does the class composition of the entire evangelical body begin to acquire definition.

As denominational differences in black membership suggest, each denomination developed a distinct social character. Both in the First Great Awakening and in the early years of the Second, Methodists continued to have special appeal to "the poorer of the people"—the slaves

---

64. See Table 4.2. Slaves' share of Methodist membership is underrepresented in the numbers reported in the table as a result of the figures reported for the entire Darlington Circuit. Slaves, however, constituted 7 of every 10 members in the two individual congregations reported. The Methodist average probably lies somewhere between those two returns.

Table 4.1 Gender Composition of Lowcountry Evangelical Churches

A. BAPTIST CHURCHES

Church	White Members			Black Members			All Members		
	No. Members	No. Women	% Women	No. Members	No. Women	% Women	No. Members	No. Women	% Women
Beech Branch, Beaufort (1847)	88	48	54.5	160	89	55.6	248	137	55.2
Euhaw Baptist, Beaufort (1860)*	24	15	62.5	458	282	61.6	482	297	61.6
Kingstree Baptist, Georgetown (1858–61)	43	27	62.8	Not available				Not available	
Dean Swamp, Orangeburg (1821)	60	35	58.3	0	0	—	60	35	58.3
Canaan Baptist, Orangeburg (1856)	61	33	54.1	Not available			Not available		
Bennettsville, Marlboro (1856)*	105	69	65.7	Not available			Not available		
Salem Baptist, Marlboro (1844)	269	161	59.9	Not available			Not available		
Gum Branch, Darlington (1861)	55	33	60.0	Not available			Not available		
Swift Creek, Kershaw (1827–61)	133	78	58.6	375	227	60.5	508	305	60.0
First Columbia, Richland (1833)*	62	36	58.1	Not available			Not available		
Totals	900	535	59.4	993	598	60.2	1298	774	59.6

B. PRIMITIVE BAPTIST CHURCHES

Church	White Members			Black Members			All Members		
	No. Members	No. Women	% Women	No. Members	No. Women	% Women	No. Members	No. Women	% Women
Black Creek, Beaufort (1851)	57	29	50.9	49	26	53.1	106	55	51.9

C. METHODIST CHURCHES

Church	White Members			Black Members			All Members		
	No. Members	No. Women	% Women	No. Members	No. Women	% Women	No. Members	No. Women	% Women
Swallow Savannah, Allendale Circuit (1856)	87	57	65.5	230	128	55.7	317	185	58.4
Caves, Allendale Circuit (1856)	38	27	71.1	Not available			Not available		
Bellingers Chapel, Allendale Circuit (1859)†	23	11	47.8	Not available			Not available		

Gilleth, Allendale Circuit (1856)	59	26	44.1		Not available			Not available	
Darlington Circuit (1840)	52	25	48.1		Not available			Not available	
Camden Station, Kershaw (1860)*	153	99	64.7		Not available			Not available	
Totals	412	245	59.5	230	128	55.7	317	185	58.4
D. PRESBYTERIAN CHURCHES									
John & Wadmalaw Island, Charleston (1829–60)	42	23	54.8		Not available			Not available	
James Island, Charleston (1833)	34	22	64.7	143	88	61.5	177	110	62.1
Second Presbyterian, Charleston (1820–28)*	96	77	80.2		Not available			Not available	
Kingstree, Williamsburg (1856–60)	37	21	56.8	47	34	72.3	84	55	65.5
Orangeburg Presbyterian (1860)*	606	397	65.1	66	42	63.6	672	439	65.3
Darlington Presbyterian (1845–53)	101	55	54.5	61	35	57.8	162	90	55.6
First Presbyterian, Florence, Darlington (1858)*	21	15	71.4	13	7	53.8	34	22	64.7
Mount Zion Presbyterian, Sumter (1835)	115	80	69.6	136	71	52.2	251	151	60.2
Salem, Black River, Sumter (1842)	54	31	57.4	140	63	45.0	194	94	48.5
Great Pee Dee, Marlboro (1857)	28	16	57.1		Not available			Not available	
Bethesda Presbyterian, Kershaw (1857)*	79	59	74.7		Not available			Not available	
First Presbyterian, Columbia, Richland (1818–46)*	339	194	57.2		Not available			Not available	
Totals	1552	990	63.0	606	340	56.1	1574	961	61.1
INTERDENOMINATIONAL TOTALS	2897	1760	60.8	1829	1066	58.3	3189	1920	60.2

Sources: Minutes and Church Books of above listed churches, SCL.

*Town/city churches

†Newly organized

Table 4.2 Racial Composition of Lowcountry Evangelical Churches

A. BAPTIST CHURCHES

Church	Total Members	Black Members	% Black
Beech Branch, Beaufort (1847)	248	160	64.5
Euhaw, Beaufort (1860)	482	458	95.0
Canaan, Orangeburg (1856)	63	2	3.2
Swift Creek, Kershaw (1827–61)	508	375	73.8
Totals	1301	995	76.5

B. PRIMITIVE BAPTIST CHURCHES

Black Creek, Beaufort (1851)	106	49	46.2

C. METHODIST CHURCHES

Swallow Savannah, Allendale Circuit (1856)	317	230	72.6
Darlington, Darlington Circuit (1840)	203	159	78.3
Lynches Creek, Darlington (1824–40)	1425	437	30.7
Totals	1945	826	42.5

D. PRESBYTERIAN CHURCHES

James Island, Charleston (1833)	177	143	80.8
Second Presbyterian, Charleston (1827)	292	125	42.8
Kingstree, Williamsburg (1856–60)	84	47	56.0
Orangeburg Presbyterian, Orangeburg (1860)	672	66	9.8
Darlington Presbyterian, Darlington (1845–53)	162	61	37.7
First Presbyterian, Florence, Darlington (1858)	34	13	38.2
Mount Zion, Sumter (1835)	251	136	54.2
Salem, Black River, Sumter (1842)	194	140	72.2
Bethesda, Kershaw (1851)	81	6	7.4
First Columbia, Richland (1860)	253	34	13.4
Totals	2200	771	35.0
INTERDENOMINATIONAL TOTALS	5552	2641	47.6

Source: Minutes and Church Books of above listed churches, SCL.

and, among whites, the poor whites and yeomen of the Low Country especially. Prominent Methodists such as William Capers submitted with grace, defending their mission to the humble as "the glory of Christ's Gospel that it began at the bottom and worked up."[65] Baptists too claimed most of their members from nonelite ranks but, unlike the Methodists, also claimed some spectacularly wealthy congregations, such as Black Swamp at Robertville in Beaufort District and Welsh Neck in Darlington. The pews and churchyards of Black Swamp Church, reputedly the most elegant Baptist church in the state, shared the great

65. Wightman, *Life of Capers*, pp. 202, 445–46. See also Charles F. Deems, ed., *Annals of Southern Methodism* (Nashville, Tenn.: Stevenson and Owen, 1855), p. 258, on the difficulties Methodists faced in converting Georgetown planters.

planter families of the area with the Episcopalians of St. Helena's.[66] As for the Presbyterians, they boasted the allegiance of planters across the coastal and middle country, and, except on the sea islands where Baptists and Methodists did not develop much of a presence, they had, typically, far fewer slave members than either of the other denominations. Presbyterians were clearly the wealthiest evangelical denomination in the region, and, with their educated clergy, quickly developed a reputation as the most intellectual as well.[67]

Such general denominational reputations were shaped, in large measure, by success among the planter elite. Of 307 lowcountry planters who owned more than 100 slaves (on a single plantation) in 1860, 205, or about two-thirds, were Episcopalian; 44, or about 14 percent, were Presbyterian; 32, or 10 percent, were Methodist; and 26, or 8 percent, were Baptist. Of course denominational choice was not unconstrained. The clerk of Swift Creek Baptist Church in Kershaw District who complained that "the number of white persons attending at the church is inconsiderable . . . although the major portion of persons resident hereabout" identified a common pattern: Denominations typically had distinct local strongholds, individual churches drew their membership from the vicinity of the meetinghouse, and brethren were often neighbors, except of course in towns, where residents could usually choose between denominations. The overrepresentation of planter Episcopalians might well have owed to these urban choices. For those great planters who maintained Charleston residences and who were absentees for a large part of the year were far more likely to exercise their choice in the direction of the Episcopal Church than their counterparts who remained country residents throughout the year. Fully half of Episcopalian planters practiced seasonal absenteeism, while those who belonged to explicitly evangelical churches almost always resided on their estates full time. Perhaps urban life put a greater premium on elite membership in elite churches, while local residence put a greater premium on membership in the churches of one's yeoman and small-planter neighbors.[68] In any case, the allegiances of the so-called "great planters"

---

66. Chalmers Gaston Davidson, *The Last Foray: The South Carolina Planters of 1860; A Sociological Study* (Columbia: University of South Carolina Press, 1971), p. 99. There are photographs of both the Robertville and the Welsh Neck Baptist churches in King, *South Carolina Baptists*, Plates III and IV.

67. James Island Presbyterian Church, Charleston District, Minutes, 1833–1845, SCL; John and Wadmalaw Island Presbyterian Church, Charleston District, Session Minutes, 1856–1911, SCL; Benjamin Morgan Palmer, *The Life and Letters of James Henley Thornwell* (New York: Arno Press, 1969), p. 352; Farmer, *The Metaphysical Confederacy*, p. 201.

68. Swift Creek Baptist Church, Kershaw District, Records, October 11, 1852, SCL. Denominational loyalties and residency patterns of this group of "great planters" was compiled from the biographical sketches in Davidson, *Last Foray*, pp. 170–267. The best evidence for the contiguity of church members' residences and church is that the names recorded on church membership lists usually appear in groups on the Schedule of Population in the Federal Manuscript Census. Church members were, therefore, typically neighbors.

carried considerable—indeed, disproportionate—weight in establishing general social profiles of the various denominations.

Closer to the ground, membership lists of local churches considerably refine the social portrait of lowcountry evangelicalism, especially its white members. Coupled with the information on male and female members' households derived from the manuscript census, lists from a handful of Baptist, Primitive Baptist, and Methodist congregations in fact confirm that, with respect to white membership, lowcountry evangelical churches were still decidedly yeoman institutions.[69] In Beech Branch Baptist Church in 1847, for example (where four of every ten members were white), the white membership was constituted in almost equal proportion by large planters (10.2 percent) who owned upwards of twenty-six slaves; small planters (13.6 percent) who owned more than ten but fewer than twenty-six slaves; and poor whites (11.9 percent) who owned neither land nor slaves. The single largest group of white members—more than half (thirty-two out of fifty-nine, or 54 percent)—came from yeoman households. (See Table 4.3.)

Although every church evinced its own distinctive social profile, the Beech Branch one was far from anomalous. Beech Branch was a rural church, located in Gillisonville (site of one of Baker's first revivals), on the edge of the Coosawhatchie Swamp in the interior of St. Peter's Parish, some distance from the Savannah River and the large rice and long-staple cotton plantations scattered along its front. With only one in ten of its white members owning more than twenty-five slaves and with only one master of more than one hundred, Beech Branch admittedly stood in marked contrast to fabulously wealthy Baptist congregations like the famous Black Swamp Church. That church, located in Robertville near the Savannah river, had many planter members. No membership list survives, but a subscription list for "support of the gospel" in 1848 (which is to say the minister's salary) shows that more than two-thirds (fourteen of twenty-one) of the contributors owned more than twenty-five slaves, and a quarter (five of twenty-one) more than one hundred slaves. Benjamin Bostick, the largest subscriber, alone owned two hundred and sixteen slaves. But Black Swamp was the Baptist showcase,

69. The method used to determine the social composition of the white membership of evangelical churches is as follows: The names of white members, male and female, were derived from church membership lists; then, when possible, they were located in the manuscript census of free population and slaves in the census year closest to the date of the membership list (1850 or 1860) to determine the land and slaveholding status of members' households. The resulting data and the comparisons based on it can only be regarded as approximamations for a number of reasons: coherent and legible membership lists are scarce; rates of census identification vary (from 60% for Beech Branch to 83% for Euhaw); the membership lists appropriate to such an analysis represent the church population in different years (they range from 1847 to 1860) and in different districts (Beaufort and Barnwell). If not rigorous, the information derived is useful, nonetheless, and the yeomanry's share of the white membership sufficiently large in all but one case (Euhaw Baptist in Beaufort District) to sustain the general point.

Table 4.3 Social Composition of the White Membership of Lowcountry Evangelical Churches

Social Group	Beech Branch (1847)		Euhaw Baptist (1860)		Blk. Creek Primitive (1851)		All Baptist		Swallow Savannah (1856)		Caves Methodist (1856)		All Methodist	
	#	%	#	%	#	%	#	%	#	%	#	%	#	%
Planters (own land and 26+ slaves)	6	10.2	4	19.0	1	2.5	10	12.5	10	17.9	0	0.0	10	11.8
Small planters (own land and 10–25 slaves)	8	13.6	9	42.9	6	15.0	17	21.3	5	8.9	3	10.3	8	9.4
Yeomen (own land and 0–9 slaves)	32	54.2	7	33.3	27	67.5	39	48.8	22	39.3	13	44.8	35	41.2
Poor whites (landless and slaveless)	7	11.9	0	0.0	6	15.0	7	8.8	11	19.6	9	31.0	20	23.5
Totals	53	100.0	20	100.0	40	100.0	73	100.0	48	100.0	25	100.0	73	100.0
Not identified	35		4		17				30		9			

Sources: Minutes and Church Books of above listed churches, SCL; Federal Manuscript Census, South Carolina [Beaufort and Barnwell Districts], Schedules of Population and Slaves, 1850, 1860, NA.

boasting its wealthiest congregation and its most ostentatious building.[70] While it undoubtedly had its share of yeoman and poor white members, it was hardly indicative of the general social character of the Baptist Church in the Low Country.

Beech Branch came closest to embodying the general tendency. Euhaw Baptist church, although hardly comparable to Black Swamp, drew more planter members than Beech Branch, in part because of its location at Grahamville in the pinewoods section of Beaufort, which was frequented by planters as a summer retreat. Nonetheless, Euhaw's white membership consisted chiefly of men and women from yeoman (seven of twenty) and small planter households (nine of twenty). Taken together, with one Primitive Baptist Church in which yeoman constituted more than two-thirds of the membership (twenty-seven of forty), the aggregate pattern sustains the image of Beech Branch. Almost half (48.8 percent) of the white membership of those Baptist churches for which such calculations are possible were yeomen; no other single social group—neither small planters nor poor whites—came close to that critical presence. (See Table 4.3.)

Like Baptist churches, Methodist ones included members from all classes of lowcountry society—planters, yeomen, poor whites, and slaves—although in slightly different proportions. The composition of the membership as indicated by the records of two meetings in the Allendale Circuit sustains the methodists' reputation as the shepherds of poor folk and, especially, of slaves. Almost three-quarters of the members in that Beaufort and Barnwell district circuit were black (see Table 4.2), leaving white members in the decided minority. But among that minority white membership, poor whites and yeoman men and women predominated, at least in the two meetings for which membership records survive.

Both Methodist meetings in the Allendale Circuit, Swallow Savannah and Caves, drew their members from Barnwell District; the Baptists seem to have had upper Beaufort pretty much tied up. But like the Beech Branch Baptists, the majority of the white Barnwell Methodists were from yeoman households (about 41 percent). They also had similar proportions of planter members (about 12 percent). The big difference between the two denominations appears to have resided in their disparate appeal to poor whites and small planters. While one Baptist church (Euhaw) had no poor white members but many planters, one Methodist meeting (Caves) had no planters but, at 31 percent, a disproportionate number of poor whites. This was the most significant distinction between lowcountry Methodists and Baptists, judging from extant mem-

70. For the evidence from Beech Branch and Euhaw Baptist Churches, see Table 4.3. For the Black Swamp Church subscription list [1848], see Black Swamp Baptist Church, Beaufort District, Historical Sketches, 1895 and 2 June 1964, SCL. Subscribers' slaveholdings were compiled from the entries in Federal Manuscript Census, South Carolina [St. Peter's Parish, Beaufort District], Slave Schedule, 1850.

bership records. While poor whites constituted only about 9 percent of Baptist membership and small planters about 21 percent, in Methodist meetings those proportions were virtually reversed; 24 percent of members came from poor white households, while only 9 percent came from small planter households. (See Table 4.3.)

The one Primitive Baptist church whose membership lists are accessible confirms the general pattern in the denominational particularity. All classes of lowcountry society were represented in their membership, although in yet another variation on the theme: Four of ten members were slaves, and among the white membership yeomen held a strong majority. As one would expect, the Primitive Baptists attracted few planter members (only about 3 percent) and equal numbers of poor whites and small planters (about 15 percent). Theirs was, however, the yeoman church par excellence, with almost seven of ten (68 percent) white members drawn from that class of lowcountry folk. (See Table 4.3)

After the Second Great Awakening and the powerful revivals of the Nullification years, evangelicalism had indeed been transformed into a faith embraced by all classes of lowcountry society, by both races, and by both sexes. It was, in this respect, truly a popular religion. And although it continued to have disproportionate appeal to the socially marginal and the politically disfranchised, particularly to women and slaves, it reached well beyond them to embrace those white adult men, heads of households, and masters of dependents—yeoman and planter alike—who alone could establish the legitimacy and the centrality of evangelicalism in lowcountry society and political culture.

From this perspective, William Grayson and others of his contemporaries can be excused for portraying lowcountry society in the aftermath of the revivals in familial terms. "A great family," he had said, referring, not unreasonably, to the way in which evangelicalism reached across social divides, bound disparate individuals together outside discrete households, and even over particular antagonisms, social, political and otherwise. Certainly no other institution or set of cultural practices had the same ability to hold lowcountry folk together in one body across the fault lines of gender, race, and class.

And yet Grayson's account flattened, perhaps intentionally, the complex meaning of evangelicalism in the Low Country, and, especially, its familial model of a perfected Christian society. One has only to think of the case of Lenore and John Kelly, the Darlington couple whose own familial troubles introduced this account. For as their experience in Gum Branch Baptist Church made painfully clear, the ties that bound believers into one covenanted community—the family of Christ—drew on the intimate bonds of secular families or households and, in the end, could not do so without recapitulating the hierarchies and relations of power that were integral to them. In an important sense, the familial discourse of evangelicalism sacralized precisely those secular relations within which the power and authority of yeoman men was grounded.

It was this dimension of popular religion—and the related though not identical meaning for planter men—which had such far-reaching consequences in the history of the antebellum Low Country. And in its articulation, in church covenants, rules of governance, gospel discipline, and sectional resolutions, is to be found much otherwise left unsaid about the yeomanry's—men's and women's—understanding of their lowcountry world. For if antebellum lowcountry evangelical churches embraced all manner of folk, then at least with respect to white membership, they were still after the Nullification Revivals what they had always been: decidedly yeoman institutions. The historical aperture they afford is valuable indeed.

chapter 5

"Households of Faith": Gender, Power, and Proslavery Christianity

I

When Daniel Baker held out to tortured sinners a vision of deliverance and sanctuary, he used an image of love and intimacy very close to home. "We are all," he would say of those who had found Jesus, "members of the same household of faith." The perfected image of the family —of household relations consecrated by love, piety, and fellowship— was his model of Christian community. But when he referred to "God the Householder," head of the heavenly household as husbands and fathers were of earthly ones, that pristine image turned to show its fractured, inescapably secular, face.[1]

Baker's metaphor struck a resonant chord with his audience, as it surely was designed to do. For when yeoman converts encoded the household in a familial model of church government, they did not simply echo Baker or other ministers. Rather, they reached for the model of community most concrete and accessible, one rooted in their daily lives and reaffirmed in their experience of conversion and congregation.

The household and the family in their customary lowcountry forms were complicated templates for evangelical society. Indeed, much of the utility of the family metaphor lay in its ability to work meaning in at least two directions simultaneously. On the one hand, it invoked the bonds of love and intimacy that ideally characterized family relations—and extended them to all relations among professing Christians. On the other,

1. Reverend Daniel Baker, *A Series of Revival Sermons* (Georgia: n.p., 1847), pp. 302–03, 318.

it recognized those same family relations or dependencies as they were—and elevated them to sacral status. In the first respect, evangelicals' familial model promised to level or submerge secular distinctions among unrelated believers and to impose new expectations and accountability on relations between family members. In the second, it promised to install the hierarchies and power relations of secular households at the heart of Christian community, to deepen domestic dependencies, and to enhance immeasurably the power of masters at home and abroad.

The contest between the two sets of possibilities was hardly evenly matched. Even in nineteenth-century utopian Christian communities in which the image of society as family was specifically invoked to dissolve hierarchies of class, race, and sex, it was difficult—well-nigh impossible—to cast off patriarchal imperatives and history.[2] In modern slave societies like South Carolina, in which households of women, children, and slaves were governed by men whose authority as masters was recognized in law and custom, such radical inversions were inconceivable. As a metaphor for social order, "the family" was a powerfully legitimating one and, in the nineteenth century as in our own time, a ubiquitous one by virtue of its very polyvalence. But contests over meanings take shape in particular social and political locations, and in the antebellum South Carolina Low Country conservative meanings acquired considerably more discursive force in the hands of yeoman and planter evangelicals.

The evangelical family could not be detached from its secular moorings. When Reverend Baker referred to "God the Householder," he mapped the gendered, racial, and class lines of power and authority in the community of believers just as local congregations articulated and enacted them in their own hierarchical familial order. The implications for regional political culture are not difficult to divine. This was not an evangelicalism that inspired a critique of the state's peculiar domestic institution but one that turned easily, almost effortlessly, to its defense.

II

In imagining Christian community as a family writ large, evangelicals, in one sense at least, simply institutionalized their own experience. Most lowcountry folk converted *en famille*. Across denominations and over the course of the antebellum period, more than seven of ten church members converted in the immediate company of kin or joined congregations in which their kin were already members.[3] During periods of revival

2. For a fascinating treatment of one such utopian community and its struggles with patriarchal relations and assumptions, see Barbara Taylor, *Eve and The New Jerusalem: Socialism and Feminism in the Nineteenth Century* (London: Virago Press, 1983).

3. The extent of family connection by denomination is as follows: Baptist, 74.6 percent; Methodist, 72.1 percent; Presbyterian, 75.7 percent, Family connection was adduced by patronyms in membership lists of the following churches. Any overestimation would be

when churches gained the great majority of their members, the extent of family connection in conversion was even higher. In Beech Branch Baptist Church in Beaufort District, for example, fully three-fourths of the antebellum membership joined during protracted meetings, most of them (63 percent) during four particularly successful meetings in 1833, 1846, 1855, and 1860. In those four revival "seasons" nearly nine of ten converts suffered through the pivotal experience of their spiritual lives with the example and encouragement of kin. Although some had been preceded into the church by other family members, a substantial majority converted at the same time and in the immediate company of kinfolk.[4] Women were slightly more likely to join churches independent of their kinfolk (30 percent of women and 20 percent of men),[5] but in congregations in which more than 70 percent of all converts joined in family groups, it is difficult to discern any clear gender patterns to conversion. In contrast to the pattern found in the Northeast, in the Low

---

more than compensated for by the inability to trace kinship among women members by patronym. See Beech Branch Baptist Church, Beaufort District, Church Book, Membership List, 1847, SCL; Euhaw Baptist Church, Beaufort District, Minutes, Membership List, 1860, SCL; Black Creek Primitive Baptist Church, Beaufort District, Minute Book, Membership List, 1851, SCL; Kingstree Baptist Church, Georgetown District, Church Book, Membership List, 1858–61, SCL; Dean Swamp Baptist Church, Orangeburg District, Historical Sketch (1903), Membership List, 1821, SCL; Canaan Baptist Church, Orangeburg District, Church Book, Membership List, 1856, SCL; Thomas Memorial Baptist Church, Marlboro District, Minutes, Membership List, 1838, SCL; Swift Creek Baptist Church, Kershaw District, Records, Membership List, 1827–61, SCL; Horns Creek Baptist Church, Edgefield District, Church Book, Membership List, 1839, SCL; Gilletts Methodist Church, Allendale Circuit, Beaufort and Barnwell Districts, Church Book, Membership List, 1856, SCL; Caves Methodist Church, Allendale Circuit, Beaufort and Barnwell Districts, Church Book, Membership List, 1856, SCL; Swallow Savannah Methodist Church, Allendale Circuit, Beaufort and Barnwell Districts, Church Book, Membership List, 1856, SCL; Bellinger's Chapel Methodist Church, Beaufort and Barnwell Districts, Church Book, Membership List, 1859, SCL; James Island Presbyterian Church, Charleston District, Minutes, Membership List, 1833, SCL; Darlington Presbyterian Church, Darlington District, Session Minutes and Register, Membership List, 1845–53, SCL; Bethesda Presbyterian Church, Kershaw District, Session Minutes and Records, Membership List, 1857, SCL; Smyrna Presbyterian Church, Marlboro District, Session Minutes and Church Roll, Membership List, 1857, SCL; Salem, Black River Presbyterian Church, Sumter District, Records, vol. II, Membership List, 1842, SCL.

4. Beech Branch Baptist Church, Beaufort District, Church Book, July 15–July 27, 1833, August 31–September 12, 1846, August 28, 1855, September 14–23, 1860. By 1860 all converts had been preceded in church membership by family members. These numbers and those in the previous note stand in sharp contrast to those reported by Mary Ryan for evangelical churches in Oneida County, New York, where between 17 and 54 percent of regular converts and 30 percent of revival converts were preceded by other family members. See Mary P. Ryan, "A Woman's Awakening: Evangelical Religion and the Families of Utica, New York, 1800–1840," *American Quarterly* 30 (Winter 1978), p. 604.

5. Gender patterns in membership were compiled from the same records listed in note 3 above. In Oneida churches, by contrast, according to Ryan, fully 50 percent of women compared to 41 percent of men joined churches independent of kinfolk. Ryan, "Woman's Awakening," p. 604.

Country women did not appear to exert particular influence or agency in the conversion of husbands, fathers, and sons. In one church with twenty-four married couples, wife preceded husband in one-third of the cases, husband preceded wife in one quarter, and in nearly half (ten of twenty-four, or 42 percent), husband and wife confessed their experience and were admitted to fellowship on the same day.[6] Frightening and lonely as the struggle for grace no doubt was, this ritual experience was not one lowcountry evangelicals endured alone.

It was precisely the prospect of family separation by death or distance that drove more than a few individuals into the church. Ministers made the threat of death and the promise of family recongregation in heaven central themes in revival sermons, although in this they clearly followed the lead of the sinners' already converted kinfolk. "My cup of earthly happiness would be full," James Henley Thornwell wrote to his son in 1859, "if you, and Jimmie, and Charlie were only true Christians. You would then be safe for time and eternity." "Fly to Jesus," he begged them, "before it is too late." Converts often responded to the accomplishment of their own salvation with concern for that of their loved ones. Conversion promised eternal life while death threatened eternal separation from those who had not found Jesus. Death pervaded everyday life in the Low Country, moving many to reflect continually, as did one yeoman woman, on "the vanity of earthly things and the shortness of life. Oh think of eternity and be wise," Mary Davis Brown chastened herself.[7] Only the knowledge of loved ones' conversion and expectations of reunion could ease the pain of death and reconcile Christians to this most cruel judgment of God. "Do not," the minister's daughter Genia Brooks begged her unregenerate brother, "die as one who knows no God."[8]

With the death of converted family members, heaven ceased to be simply the place where God lived. Like Daniel Baker, who pledged while still a child to "meet [his] mother in heaven," an eight-year-old South Carolina girl answered in the affirmative her dying brother's question, "Will you come to meet me in heaven?" When her brother passed away, her father prayed that "God would take us to that beautiful holy place, where our Saviour and the baby and Willy are; and where they will never die again."[9] Likewise, the upcountry yeoman woman Elizabeth Finisher grieved over her sister's move to Georgia and, feeling "little hope of ever seeing you in this world of sorrow," implored her to "press on heaven-

6. Swift Creek Baptist Church, Kershaw District, Records, 1827–61.

7. Benjamin Morgan Palmer, ed., *The Life and Letters of James Henley Thornwell* (New York: Arno Press, 1969), p. 442; Mary Davis Brown Diary, December 31, 1855, SCL.

8. Genia Brookes to Walker Brookes, January 28, 1848, Iveson L. Brookes Papers, SCL.

9. Charlotte Richmond to her Mother, n.d., Mary Hort Journal, SCL. The theme of family recongregation is discussed in Jean E. Friedman, *The Enclosed Garden: Women and Community in the Evangelical South, 1830–1900* (Chapel Hill: University of North Carolina Press, 1985), pp. 11, 49; Anne C. Loveland, *Southern Evangelicals and the Social Order, 1800–1860* (Baton Rouge: Louisiana State University Press, 1980), p. 7.

word. We will meet on the happy shore of cannon," and, she consoled herself in terms reminiscent of revival sermons, "that will be joyful to meet to part no more."[10] The specter of death, the instability of family life, and the promise of family recongregation in heaven was a powerful force in the conversion of lowcountry evangelicals, and it was one ministers worked to fever pitch.

"The Character and the Reward of the Earthly Minded," a standard in Daniel Baker's revival sermon repertoire, was exemplary in this respect. "Oh! my soul," he began, "there must be mourning—mourning, at the judgment seat of Christ. Parents and children there must part, must part to meet no more. Husbands and wives there must part; must part to meet no more. . . . Oh! who can bear the idea of being excluded from the dwellings of the blessed," he would go on, "cut off from the society of those whom we loved on earth, and cast down to hell, there to associate with murderers of fathers and murderers of mothers." So Baker tormented his listeners with the all too real prospect of eternal separation from loved ones.[11] In dramatic counterpose to this image of family instability, he held out another path: conversion and eternal life in the "Household of Faith." The efficacy of such sermons and of the familial pressure that accompanied them is evident in family patterns of church membership and in the generational reproduction of membership Baker noted during his second visit to the Low Country. Those he converted, he noted in his memoirs, were, for the most part, "children of the covenant."[12]

As they sought to explain the meaning of conversion and the nature of the new Christian community they had just joined, lowcountry evangelicals, men and women, plain folk and planter, slave and free, reached for the language and experience of family that had brought them safely through the struggle for grace. They had joined the "family of God." "I had become . . . a child of God," William Capers said joyfully, while the yeoman woman Mary Davis Brown reassured herself that should she die, Jesus would be "a God and Father" to her motherless children.[13] To evangelical Christians, conversion represented "new birth" and death the beginning of eternal life. Once born again, they became part of a new social order, one that redefined their relationship to the world and forged an extended family of those chosen by God. "Whosoever hath the mind that is in Christ," Methodist covenants proclaimed, "the same is our brother, and sister, and mother."[14] The religious community to

10. Elizabeth Finisher to Nancy Cowen, August 23, 1846, Nancy H. Cowan Papers, Perkins Library, DU.

11. Baker, *A Series of Revival Sermons*, pp. 185–86.

12. William Mumford Baker, *The Life and Labours of Reverend Daniel Baker . . . Prepared by His Son* (1858; reprint ed., Louisville, Ky.: Lost Cause Press, 1961), pp. 457, 474.

13. William M. Wightman, *Life of William Capers, D.D.* (Nashville, Tenn.: Southern Methodist Publishing House, 1859), p. 82; Mary Davis Brown Diary, July 14, 1859.

14. Albert M. Shipp, *The History of Methodism in South Carolina* (Nashville, Tenn.: Southern Methodist Publishing House, 1884), p. 581. On evangelical community as family, see Friedman, *Enclosed Garden*, p. 49.

which lowcountry folk turned upon conversion institutionalized their own experience of the family of faith.

III

If all believers belonged to one "household of faith" or "family of God," then it was the function of church covenants and rules of government to establish the principles by which such ideals acquired substance. The principles contained contradictory imperatives, however. On the one hand, covenants envisioned perfectly reciprocal relations such as those that prevailed within the natal family, and insisted that in relation to each other members "discharg[e] properly the humble duties of [their] social relations"; on the other, covenants envisioned those reciprocal relations within a hierarchical order and insisted that each member of the evangelical family accept his or her "providentially assigned role."[15] Duty and obligation coexisted uneasily with prerogatives and privilege in the evangelical family.

The first and most important rule to which covenanted members bound themselves was to "walk with each other in all humility and brotherly love." To that end, they promised to use "no greater appellation in addressing one another than brother and sister," and to that expression of spiritual equality they were bound to add the kind of loyalty, mutual respect, tolerance, forgiveness, affection, and support of which such sibling relationships supposedly consisted. Thus, members pledged to "hold [themselves] censurable for evil speaking, either irreverently of God or to the prejudice of our brethren," to guarantee that "not even their weaknesses will we expose to any person out of the church," to seek resolution by "confess[ing] our . . . faults to one another," and, failing that, to attempt reconciliation through gospel discipline before taking recourse to the secular courts.[16]

In this perfected image of brotherly love inhered all kinds of possibilities to reconfigure customary relations. "The man who is careless of his own household is hardly able to take care of the world," James Henley Thornwell, the state's leading Presbyterian minister, philosophized while still a young man, "and the man who loves not his own family can hardly be expected to love the race." Local churches inscribed a similar sensibility in covenants, focusing intently on the responsibilities

---

15. Palmer, *Life of Thornwell,* p. 124; Marilyn J. Westerkamp, "James Henley Thornwell, Pro-Slavery Spokesman within a Calvinist Faith," *South Carolina Historical Magazine* 87, no. 1 (January 1986), p. 53.

16. Beech Branch Baptist Church, Beaufort District, Church Book, Covenant, 1823; Prince Williams Baptist Church, Beaufort District, Record Book, Covenant and Rule No. 8, SCL; Mechanicsville Baptist Church, Darlington District, Minutes, Covenant and Rules No. 9 and No. 12, 1829, SCL. Covenants and rules changed little either over time or across denominations.

of Christian heads of household to their dependents. Parents acknowledged obligations to their children: to "bring them up in the nurture and admonition of the Lord, by giving them wholesome instruction . . . and good example," to "take due care to have them taught to read and to impress on their minds the importance of . . . conforming to the Holy Scriptures," and to restrain them from "vain amusements." In contrast to northeastern churches in which childrearing instructions were addressed quite specifically to mothers, in South Carolina they were addressed to parents jointly.[17] But that covenanted equality of parental responsibility was belied by the rules of gospel discipline, which held fathers, not mothers, chiefly accountable for family morality. Even in their capacity as mothers, women did not share the burden of authority that men assumed as heads of lowcountry households.

By the same token, church covenants consecrated marriage as the bedrock of the family edifice. "Marriage is indeed the natural state of man, having for its authority the highest divine right," one country minister proclaimed, underscoring in the process the asymmetrical character of the husband-wife relation. Thus, although ministers made sermons such as "domestic relations, the duties of Husband and of Wife" regular staples of Sunday preaching in lowcountry churches, covenants focused more resolutely on the obligations of husbands than of wives. Husbands were bound to honor their wives, to provide them sufficient support, and, as with their children, to maintain a proper Christian environment in the household.[18] Children and wives incurred their own burden of Christian obligation in family relations, but covenants evinced far greater concern with paternal power and the obligations of masters.

Strenuous insistence on a master's duties could, as evangelicals were aware, nurture in dependents legitimate expectation of, even entitlement to, support, protection, and respect. Pushed further, it had the potential to reconfigure familial relations, at least on the margins, by providing a dependent leverage against a master's power. Such possibilities, once introduced by the evangelical family model, could hardly be confined to the relations of parents and children or husbands and wives. Slaves were no less part of the family of God, no less brethren, than were those who were free, white, and wealthy or who were themselves heads of households. As masters, Christian men assumed obligations to all of

17. Palmer, *Life of Thornwell*, p. 124; Thomas Memorial Baptist Church, Marlboro District, Minutes, Covenant, 1820. On maternal responsibility for family morality in the Northeast, see Nancy F. Cott, *The Bonds of Womanhood: "Woman's Sphere" in New England, 1780–1835* (New Haven: Yale University Press, 1977), esp. pp. 86, 147, and Mary Ryan, *Cradle of the Middle Class: The Family in Oneida County, New York, 1790–1865* (New York: Cambridge University Press, 1981).

18. Anonymous, *The Old Pine Farm, or The Southern Side, Comprising Loose Sketches From the Experience of a Southern Country Minister* (Charleston: Southern Baptist Publication Society, 1860), pp. 133–34; Robert F. W. Allston to Adele Petigru Allston, Columbia, December 16, 1849, in J. H. Easterby, ed., *The South Carolina Rice Plantation as Revealed in the Papers of R. F. W. Allston* (Chicago: University of Chicago Press, 1945), pp. 98–99.

their domestic dependents—including their slaves. As one prominent Presbyterian missionary put it: "They belong to us. We also belong to them. . . . They live with us, eating from the same store-houses, drinking from the same fountains, dwelling in the same enclosures, forming parts of the same families. . . . They fill the humblest places in our state and society, yet they are not more truly ours, than we are truly theirs." To these other, often more numerous family members, Christian masters had to "avoid acts of cruelty . . . [to] point out . . . the course of duty, [to] open the way for them to receive instruction from a preached Gospel, and [to] supply food and raiment becoming their station, and worthy of the Christian character which we sustain." A formal reciprocity governed the covenanted obligations of masters and slaves in the region's biracial churches. "Masters give unto your servants that which is just and equal; knowing that ye also have a master in heaven," one church covenant instructed. And some lowcountry masters took the message to heart. "Thank God my Family all Black and White are well," the Beaufort Baptist planter, Winborn Lawton, wrote to his son in 1843.[19]

As in all well-regulated families, so in evangelical ones proper government required discipline. It was "absolutely necessary to our peace, prosperity, and the honor of God," the covenant of Prince Williams Baptist Church declared, "to carefully maintain a strict gospel discipline." To that end, the church laid out the rules of government that bound each member to watch "over the walk and conversation of the members, to observe that they keep their places" and, in the event that they did not, "to warn, entreat, rebuke, and admonish in the spirit of meekness according to the rules of the Gospel." The formal rules of government held members to the duties and obligations incumbent on their "place," that "providentially assigned role" in the social order to which Thornwell, for one, attributed such moral significance.[20] If what the Christian community covenants encoded was configured around a series of reciprocal family relations, then the duty each individual incurred was in direct proportion to the rights, prerogatives, and power he or she exercised within the family hierarchy.

The inordinate concern with the duties and obligations of masters displayed in covenants and rules of government was not primarily an interrogation of the power and authority masters exercised in secular households. It was, rather, an acknowledgment of it. Like the society of

19. John B. Adger quoted in James O. Farmer, Jr., *The Metaphysical Confederacy: James Henley Thornwell and the Synthesis of Southern Values* (Macon, Ga.: Mercer University Press, 1986), p. 210; Mechanicsville Baptist Church, Darlington District, Minutes, Covenant and Rule No. 11, 1829; Winborn A. Lawton to Winborn B. Lawton, August 16, 1843, Lawton Family Papers, SCL.

20. Prince Williams Baptist Church, Beaufort District, Record Book, Covenant, 1812; First Barnwell Baptist Church, Barnwell District, Minutes, Covenant, 1858, Euhaw Baptist Church, Beaufort District, Minutes, Covenant and Rule No. 12, 1834; Westerkamp, "James Henley Thornwell," p.

which they were a part, the lowcountry evangelicals who framed the covenants accepted inequalities and dependencies as part of the natural order. They recognized children, wives, and slaves as variably dependent individuals to whom were owed Christian respect, dignity, and a measure of protection, and in so doing they opened up the possibility that relations with father, husband, and master could be renegotiated. But just as they created that possibility, so they virtually foreclosed it by laying the responsibility for dependents' moral welfare precisely in the hands of those whose power it was designed to check. Duty was the Christian face of power, reciprocity the Christian face of inequality.

Even in the covenants and formal rules of gospel discipline, the perfected family evangelicals envisioned was distinctly hierarchical, patriarchal, and proslavery. "We hold that a Christian slave must be submissive, faithful, and obedient," the South Carolina Methodist Conference pronounced in 1836, "for reasons of the same authority with those which oblige wives, fathers, brothers, sisters to fulfill the duties of those relations."[21] Thus did evangelicals invest customary dependencies and inequalities with the sanction of divinity.

IV

If the covenants and rules of gospel discipline nurtured contradictory possibilities in lowcountry evangelicalism, that contest was played out, and the substance of familialism fortified, in the practice of church government within individual congregations. "There is neither Jew nor Greek; there is neither bond nor free; there is neither male nor female; for ye all are one in Christ."[22] So the scriptures set out the dialectic of spiritual equality and the inequalities of everyday life. The tension was evident in the very structure of church government. Free women and slave members were fully recognized within the body of the church; indeed, in most cases, as the great majority of the membership, they constituted its very corporeality. But if the "body" was overwhelmingly black and female, the "mind" was incontrovertibly white and male. Every church body was governed exclusively by a white male head.

This organic order prevailed in every denomination and was institutionalized in the rules of church governance. Ministers and church officers were invariably men, even in Baptist churches where ministers were elected from lay ranks. Free women always outnumbered free men in lowcountry congregations, yet they had no formal right to voice or vote in church affairs, except occasionally in the choice of the permanent minister. Every church adopted some version of Barnwell First Baptist's

---

21. Quoted in Shipp, *History of Methodism*, p. 498.
22. Quoted in George Howe, D.D., *History of the Presbyterian Church in South Carolina*, 2 vols. (Columbia, S.C.: W. J. Duffie, 1883), 2: 595.

Rule No. 7, which stated that "one officer and three male members" were the requisite minimum quorum for the transaction of church business. In theory, then, even slave men were more empowered in church government than women, free or slave. Of course, it was never the intention or the effect of Rule No. 7 to give slave men responsibility equal to free men in church affairs, although in many cases slave men were empowered to serve as deacons, exhorters, and even preachers among the slave membership. Women, including free white women, had not even that delimited domain of authority. Rules governing the gender constitution of quorums put control of church affairs exclusively in the hands of male, and for the most part white male, members; whereas men (in short supply in some congregations) were disciplined for failure to attend business meetings, women, no matter how numerous, did not count. It was men, including slave men in matters concerning slave members, who met in regular business meetings, usually on Saturdays, to sit in judgment on a variety of matters: the authenticity of conversion experiences and the admission of new members; complaints against, investigations of, and discipline of old members; the fitness of candidates to preach; and the election of ministers, deacons, elders, and class leaders. This was the mind of the church at work. But while men were fit to judge all church members, women had no say even over the female part of the church body. They had no say as to who was admitted or expelled, selected to preach, or chosen to represent them in denominational assemblies. And save for rare instances usually involving women members in cases of a sexual nature, women had little or no role in the investigation and discipline of backsliders. In short, they had no part in or power over the rules or the people who enforced them.[23] The church made husband, father, and head of household, whether yeoman or planter, into representative, legislator, and judge.

It is not difficult to understand what yeoman men saw in evangelicalism. Few other institutions could provide such legitimation of their authority and prerogatives within household and polity. And if the organic conception of church government could represent planter members as particularly fit to govern, that was an unhappy effect of its sanctification of secular hierarchy—one in which yeoman men were themselves privileged parties in relation to the great majority of the people in their households, communities, and churches. But if their attraction to evangelicalism is not so difficult to divine, the tremendous numbers of yeo-

23. First Barnwell Baptist Church, Barnwell District, Minutes, 1858, October 6, 1821, February 2, 1828, July 3, 1830, July 30, 1830, October 1, 1831, February 7, 1841, March 6, 1841, May 13, 1857, SCL; First Charleston Baptist Church, Charleston District, "Rules and Regulations of the Coloured Ministers, Elders, and Members," July 1819, SCL. Salem Baptist Church in Marlboro District proved a notable exception. In 1830 it amended its rules to read that "sisters are privileged and requested to vote" in matters of the admission and the exclusion of members. Salem Baptist Church, Marlboro District, Records, March 20, 1830, SCL.

man women drawn to the church is another matter altogether. Here the tension at the heart of familial ideology—between the spiritual equality and moral sovereignty of individual believers and the social inequality and hierarchical conception of rights and duties—found perhaps fullest expression.

V

For yeoman women the promise of spiritual equality was alluring. It meant, at the very least, that women were recognized and could insist on being recognized as morally sovereign individuals to be judged fit for admission and subjected to discipline on the basis of their own actions and merits. In a society in which married women had no independent standing at law or in the polity, that was no small matter.

Although white male members alone judged the authenticity of a women's conversion experience, like all prospective members women had to give testimony of it before the congregation or its designated committee. This moment of authorized female speech was a dramatic one. Only the woman involved could articulate her individual experience, the passing from "death to life," that every evangelical regarded as the central ritual of spiritual life. At that moment, all other relations were stripped away. The woman stood alone, her capacity for redemption judged and asserted equal to that of any man. The significance of the moment was only heightened by its singularity, for this was one of the few acts of public witness permitted women in lowcountry churches.[24] With the admission of every new woman member, those already part of the congregation saw their worthiness affirmed as they did on those infrequent occasions when particularly devout women were commended, usually in obituaries, as "Mother[s] of Israel." Death "found her like a faithful soldier, fully prepared with her armour on," a Charleston minister proclaimed of his recently deceased wife, "childlike and submissive" in the face of death as she had been in that of life's trials. At such moments yeoman women found both recognition of and models for Christian womanhood.[25]

Equally capable of faith, women were held accountable for their

24. For women's public confession of faith and the male committees that judged them see Mechanicsville Baptist Church, Darlington District, Minutes, September 14, 1804, October 19, 1816; First Barnwell Baptist Church, Barnwell District, Minutes, May 31, 1857. For churches' suspicion of female speech see below, but one interesting suggestion of the customary practice is provided by the case of Mrs. Emely Williams, who, when called to answer charges of "heresy" for her adherence to "Campbellits" beliefs, was represented by her husband, who spoke extensively in the third person on her behalf. See Euhaw Baptist Church, Beaufort District, Minutes, April 5, 1835.

25. Swift Creek Baptist Church, Kershaw District, Records, October 11, 1852; First Charleston Baptist Church, Charleston District, Minutes and Burial Register, July 12, 1858; Mechanicsville Baptist Church, Darlington District, Minutes, April 4, 1856.

behavior. When the aptly named Mary Outlaw by "dishonesty . . . obtain[ed] a pair of spectacles," when yeoman woman Sister Carlia Shuman
was charged with drinking too much, when Sister Augeant Condon
"killed a beef which belonged to James Wood," when Charlotte Linton
was caught in "filthy and foolish talking," each paid the price of her
transgressions in public humiliation that started with an investigation
and ended in punishment doled out along a spectrum of severity from
probation to exclusion.[26]

Secular principles of coverture and property did not, for the most
part, deter the church from holding women (including married ones)
responsible for their own bodies and sexual behavior. In fact, congregational discipline of women focused inordinately on sexual transgressions. In a region in which birth control and abortion were not easily or
effectively practiced, women's sexual sins often were evident to the community in the form of "bastard" children. Women were disciplined, as
were the unmarried Sister Hill of Darlington District for violating the
sanctity of marriage by taking "up with a man who had a wife [when] she
was knowing to that fact" and another Darlington Sister, Delight Griggs,
who fulfilled the promise of her name though it involved cheating on
her husband. All of them lent unauthorized meaning to female moral
agency, though few so defiantly as Dicey Suggs. When accused of leaving
her husband, Suggs made no excuse, evinced no "signs of repentance,"
but, taking full responsibility for her actions, declared that she would not
return to him, explaining "that she drank too much was the reason why
she married him." For all such crimes and for others even more troub-
ling to lowcountry congregations—like the rare suggestion of sexual
relations between a white woman and a slave man—women were held to
account by their brethren.[27]

Bastardy was by far the most common sexual charge against women
and the one most easily proven. While paternity went largely undis-
covered and unpunished, hundreds of women, like the unfortunately
named Obedience Bass, found themselves shamed before their brethren
and excommunicated for the crime of "fornication" compounded by the
greater "crime of bastardy." When Sister Catlett was discovered to have
protected her pregnant unmarried sister, Elizabeth Braddock, by refusing to report her to the church, both were excluded.[28] All members had
responsibilities to uphold the familial order upon which the church was

---

26. Gum Branch Baptist Church, Darlington District, Minutes, October 18, 1833, SCL;
Beech Branch Baptist Church, Beaufort District, Church Book, February 9, 1833, January
13, 1838; Welsh Neck Baptist Church, Darlington District, Minutes, October 6, 1827, SCL.

27. Mechanicsville Baptist Church, Darlington District, Minutes, November 16, 1833;
Welsh Neck Baptist Church, Darlington District, Minutes, August 3, 1822; Gum Branch
Baptist Church, Darlington District, Minutes, March 14, 1835; Darlington-Florence Cir-
cuit of the Methodist Church, Minutes, August 10, 1844, SCL.

28. Mechanicsville Baptist Church, Darlington District, Minutes, July 18, 1835; Welsh
Neck Baptist Church, Darlington District, Minutes, January 6, 1844, March 2, 1844.

founded even when it ran against secular familial loyalties, although, as
the Kelly debacle reminds us, ministers, deacons, and white male committees clearly found it easier to hold women to such standards than
men, for whom loyalty to male kin was recognized as a virtue, if not
always a wholly Christian one.

It was not, however, abstract notions of female purity or passionless-
ness that were at issue in "the courts of Jesus Christ" but quite concrete
notions of family relations and duties. Churches commonly referred to
women who lived with men without benefit of marriage as "liv[ing] in
the ordinary way," implying that such practices, although widespread
and natural enough, could not be condoned as Christian. "[N]o person
should be a member of this church without a marriage," the Second
Charleston Presbyterian Church declared.[29] For women as for other
Christians, the paramount task of gospel discipline was to hold individuals
to the "humble duties of their social relations." Thus, ironically it was as
wives, mothers, daughters, mistresses, sisters, even mothers-in-law, that
yeoman women answered for the state of their individual souls. By such
moral accountability did disciplinary committees of yeoman and planter
men give substance to their familial model of Christian community.

Each position in the family carried with it a particular set of duties
and privileges, and it was the neglect of the former and the abuse of the
latter that the church discountenanced. So, for example, when daughters defied parental authority, as Sister Mary Cooper did in marrying
"contrary to the will of her mother," or when three Sumter District
sisters abused their elderly father by depriving him of his share of the
cotton crop from land he had already relinquished into his son-in-law's
control, churches acted decisively. In their view, the parent-child relation was a perfectly reciprocal one, and parental responsibility was to be
met with filial obedience and devotion. Filial duty knew no age limit.
Yeoman men, like those who judged the Sumter District sisters, understandably worried about the potential for neglect and abuse in rural
households as daughterly powers increased in the renegotiations over
property and support that accompanied the aging of parents.[30] Such
inversions—daughters defying mothers and, especially, dominating
fathers—posed an insidious and ever present threat to the integrity of
the family. To be good Christians, women had first to be good daughters. Yeoman women may well have been, indeed were, subordinated to
male authority within the household, but, judging from the range of
infractions church committees investigated, they proved resourceful in
plumbing the limited authority that inhered in their customary familial
roles. No relation was exempt from scrutiny, no infraction too trivial for

29. Second Charleston Presbyterian Church, Charleston District, Record of Session,
October 15, 1825, SCL.
30. Canaan Baptist Church, Orangeburg District, Church Book, December 2, 1839;
Mount Zion Presbyterian Church, Sumter District, Minutes, December 1839, April 2,
1841, SCL.

discipline. The arm of the church reached every corner of family life.[31] Although none escaped regulation, no single relationship carried the burden of Christian example more than that of husband and wife, as the constant battle to police female sexuality indicated.

Women bore undue burdens for family stability in their capacity as wives. They were censured repeatedly for "walking disorderly," as churches typically referred to those who violated some unspecified norm of wifely comportment. In marital conflicts, husbands were often exonerated and wives found culpable even where the husbands admitted, as one Marlboro minister did, that he had been "careless and negligent in his Christian duties" and "wrong in some particulars" in the "unhappy difficulty between himself and his wife." But because his wife had refused his invitation "to return to him and his home," he was retained in membership, although not in his capacity as minister.[32] Forgiveness and an offer of support were incumbent on the husband, obedience and submission, whatever the circumstances (recall Lenore Kelly) on the wife. Those who would conform to the Christian ideal of the good wife accepted strenuous duties and obligations. But those who managed to abide by its strictures bid well to be honored, if only at death, as "Mothers of Israel."

In distinguishing wife from husband in discipline and conversion, churches momentarily cracked the secular edifice of coverture and recognized women as morally sovereign individuals. But by tying spiritual equality to the fulfillment of the particular duties incumbent on their family relations, they virtually ensured that women would not confuse spiritual empowerment with its social expression. Empowered by the promise of spiritual equality genuinely honored in lowcountry churches, recognized as morally sovereign individuals there as nowhere else, yeoman women nonetheless found a peculiar and peculiarly constrained sense of authority in evangelical religion.

It was, of course, possible for lowcountry women to find in spiritual equality and moral individualism the imperative for a transgressive reading of gender relations and women's roles. Women did not always read their lessons straight, as women's historians and feminist literary theorists have pointed out; radical interpretations were always possible. Afro-Christianity made that point powerfully in the antebellum South, for left to read St. Paul for themselves, literate slaves found a radically different interpretation than that offered by their masters. In other parts of the country and in the transatlantic world of nineteenth-century

31. For examples of women disciplined for physical abuse of daughters-in-law and of nieces and sisters for un-Christian speech see Beech Branch Baptist Church, Beaufort District, Church Book, December 10, 1836, February 10, 1844; Thomas Memorial Baptist Church, Marlboro District, Minutes, September 1841.

32. First Columbia Presbyterian Church, Richland District, Session Book, April 14, 1838; Thomas Memorial Baptist Church, Marlboro District, Minutes, May 1848, August 1848, November 1848.

evangelicalism, there were, moreover, numerous examples of breakaway sects that took the notion of women's moral mission to its logical conclusion in the idea of the female messiah.[33] In the rural churches of the South Carolina Low Country, however, such prospects existed in far more limited form.

One Sunday in February 1839 in a Primitive Baptist church in rural Beaufort District, one "Sister Roberts" put her own construction on the notion of ministerial calling and, "styling herself a preacher"—which is to say imitating one, as the clerk contemptuously put it—"seized the pulpit." Whatever imagination and courage went into that act of moral presumption, the violence with which it was suppressed (the force with which the deacon and his cronies physically dragged her from the pulpit disturbed some members) left no doubt as to the place of women preachers in lowcountry churches. "He did what he had to do to prevent her preaching in the pulpit," the deacon said to the apparent satisfaction of the rest of the voting members. And when the church reiterated the rules on preaching and insisted on offering a public explanation of the incident "to prevent mispresentations from going abroad," they revealed a touchiness on the subject of women and gender as on that of slavery, race, and religious practice.[34] In disclaiming the incident to other Baptists in the vicinity and around the state, they sought to protect their reputation by reiterating their commitment to the patriarchal lineage of moral authority.

Sister Roberts's act was stunning in its singularity. In more than sixty churches over the course of more than sixty years, she alone so imagined and presumed. Transgressive interpretations of evangelical womanhood have clearly taken shape within particular historical locations and grids of social power. If they were possible in the South Carolina lowcountry, they were anything but likely. Sister Roberts was excommunicated.

In a society in which evangelical community was modeled on perfected family relations, even modest assumptions of female moral authority met with unflinching opposition. Slave men could be licensed

33. On slave religion see, for example, Eugene D. Genovese, *Roll, Jordan, Roll: The World the Slaves Made* (New York: Pantheon Books, 1974). On female messiahs see the debate over the nineteenth-century Englishwoman Joanna Southcott in E. P. Thompson, *The Making of the English Working Class* (Harmondsworth: Penguin Books, 1963), esp. pp. 411–440; Taylor, *Eve and the New Jerusalem*, esp. pp. 118–83; Joan Wallach Scott, *Gender and the Politics of History* (New York: Columbia University Press, 1988), pp. 68–90. For a striking antebellum American example of female religious leadership, see Jean McMahon Humez, ed., *Gifts of Power: The Writings of Rebecca Jackson, Black Visionary, Shaker Eldress* (Amherst: University of Massachusetts Press, 1981). There is of course a much older Christian tradition of female religious authority and leadership. For a few examples, see Phyllis Mack, *Visionary Women: Ecstatic Prophecy in Seventeenth-Century England* (Berkeley: University of California Press, 1992); Rosemary Radford Reuther, *Religion and Sexism* (New York: Simon and Schuster, 1974); Eleanor McLaughlin and Rosemary Radford Reuther, eds., *Women of Spirit* (New York: Simon and Schuster, 1979).

34. Prince Williams Primitive Baptist Church, Beaufort District, Record Book, February 16, 1839.

regularly to preach and exhort in recognition of their special capacity to
serve fellow slaves; women were accorded no such rights and no such
essential constituency. When Mary Hort, a spinster school teacher in
Sumter District, encouraged a revival that had begun among her female
students, her minister, Reverend DuBose, "took offence," as she put it,
and "reproved me." "Calling it a religious meeting, he spoke of it as
unwomanly, unscriptural, [and he] implied fanacticism. I tried to reason
him out of it," she recorded in her diary (she was only holding evening
prayer meetings with her students), "but he overbore me [telling] me
that nothing has hurt him so much of that sort during his 12 years
ministerial life." Angered and depressed that, in her words, "[m]y hopes
of religious usefulness . . . are gone . . . [still] convinced that I was within
my Christian duty," in the end Mary Hort decided that she owed "submission to my temporary head." In South Carolina women's religious
battles were far less likely to be like those of Sister Roberts's attempt to
"seize the pulpit" than to represent efforts to control an overweening
and unwomanly will. Mary Hort's special relationship with her students
and her obvious devotion to the church did not earn her even the right
to lead young women in prayer and religious conversation. Like another
unmarried middle-aged Charleston woman who called Christ "the
bridegroom," Mary Hort had tried—and failed—to sanctify spinster-
hood through "spiritual usefulness" in the only household she could call
her own.[35] But in the lowcountry household of faith, perhaps because of
women's numerical dominance, any exercise of authority by women,
even in the harmless confines of a girls' school, was perceived as a hereti-
cal challenge to the designated divinity of the "temporary head." The
message was clear: Women were to make their contributions to evangelical community life under the supervision of men and within the confines
of their own households.

In a region in which the secular household, like the church, had a
male head and in which designated divinity descended along the male
line, even the household provided no clear arena of womanly authority
and moral accountability for dependents necessarily fell more heavily on
fathers than on mothers. Mothers were censured on occasion for having
been "very deficient in family government," and parents more generally
for letting their children grow up, as one Methodist church put it, "like a
wild ass's colt." But it was, for the most part, fathers who were held
responsible for lapses in the moral discipline of dependents, including
children. Thus, when a family attempted to transfer membership from
its old church to the First Barnwell Baptist Church in 1834, the wife and
daughter were admitted but the husband excluded on the grounds that
he had "consented to have dancing in his house." His wife lacked the

---

35. Mary Hort Journal, September 21, 1846, SCL; Ann Reid to William Reid, August
29, 1836, Reid Family Papers, Perkins Library, DU. On the matter of licensing slave men to
preach see the case of Adam in the First Barnwell Baptist Church, Barnwell District,
Minutes, April 30, 1830.

authority to permit or to prohibit such ungodly behavior; it was not "her" household in the same sense that it was "his." She could not be held accountable for matters not within her power.[36]

No matter how devout, mothers were no substitute for fathers. "How misterious are the providences of God," the itinerant Baptist preacher William Hill reflected in 1846 when in the home of a yeoman woman who had just lost her husband. "A father who maintained good government in his family is taken, and a weakly mother is left with a large family of children on her hands—mostly boys. Some of them rude and unmanageable." It was not simply the loss of the main provider that Hill bewailed but also the loss of the family's moral and spiritual head (although one does have to wonder just how good family government was under his supervision if the boys were so rude and unmanageable). Given such views and the almost biblical self-representation adopted by at least some evangelical men, it is hardly surprising that women without husbands found themselves subjected to a kind of community patriarchy. Even in the absence of the male head of household, mothers' authority over children was not fully recognized. Instead, other male members of the evangelical community sought to assume it, insisting in one case, for example, that the children of the poor widow Sister Moore be bound out ("put out to work for their living") over her express objections. Because they paid her a meager support, five dollars "for the present," other yeoman and planter men acquired the right to dictate her household affairs in ways they would never have dared had her husband been alive.[37] Even in death, the role of the household head had to be shored up; even as mothers, women found no clearly sanctioned domain of moral authority.

The experience of women in lowcountry, and most likely southern, evangelicalism represents in this respect at least a critical departure from the purportedly national patterns delineated in studies of the northeastern United States. There, as many historians have now argued, women's majority in evangelical churches, their particular agency in bringing their husbands and children to conversion, and the transformation of the household into a bourgeois home secured for them a claim to moral superiority and religious authority in their families and, increasingly, in their communities. As men "abdicated their roles as eighteenth-century heads of households," one historian has written,

36. Welsh Neck Baptist Church, Darlington District, Minutes, August 2, 1823; Darlington Circuit of the Methodist Church, Quarterly Conference Minutes, August 18, 1860; First Barnwell Baptist Church, Barnwell District, Minutes, November 1, 1834.

37. William P. Hill Diary, August 29, 1846, SHC; Welsh Neck Baptist Church, Darlington District, Minutes, January 5, 1833. F. R. Goulding of Savannah wrote to his brother-in-law the minister William R. Reid of Sumter, "[R]eally we are becoming quite the little patriarchs are we not?" and another correspondent, the Reverend Andrew G. Peden, similarly referred to "our wifes and little Benjamins." F. R. Goulding to William R. Reid, March 23, 1840, and Andrew G. Peden to William R. Reid, August 2, 1836, Reid Family Papers.

women "assumed new kinds of moral authority" that served to authorize a wide array of female initiatives and politics, from maternal associations to women's suffrage.[38] Whatever moral authority lowcountry women extracted from evangelicalism was of an entirely different order, however. Lowcountry men had not "abdicated their roles . . . as head of household," and women had not acquired the household sphere and family morality as their own particular domain. Motherhood, even evangelical motherhood, developed quite distinctly from its elevated bourgeois form. The desire to separate children from their mothers, as in the case of the widowed Sister Moore, reveals more than a different approach to charity; it reveals an entirely different, and far less sentimentalized, approach to motherhood itself.

Small wonder, then, that free women found themselves operating within a closely circumscribed arena, either in individual congregations or in larger evangelical communities. In the extension of charity, for example, lowcountry women, especially yeoman and poor white ones, found themselves inscribed almost exclusively in the role of recipients. The vast majority of those who received charity from their congregations—almost 80 percent in one survey of lowcountry churches—were women, mostly widows.[39] But in stark contrast to patterns in the Northeast, in which charitable activity had become a sanctioned, even compulsory, component of middle-class women's religious duty, in lowcountry churches

38. Quote is from Paul Johnson, *A Shopkeeper's Millennium: Society and Revivals in Rochester, New York, 1815–1837* (New York: Hall and Wang, 1978), pp. 107–08. The literature on women and evangelicalism in the free-labor states is now vast, but the interpretive direction I am suggesting is evinced most clearly in the following books: Cott, *Bonds of Womanhood;* Carroll Smith-Rosenberg, *Disorderly Conduct: Visions of Gender in Victorian America* (New York: Oxford University Press, 1985), esp. pp. 109–65; Ryan, *Cradle of the Middle Class*; Mary P. Ryan, "The Power of Women's Networks," in Judith L. Newton, Mary P. Ryan, and Judith Walkowitz, eds., *Sex and Class in Women's History* (Boston: Routledge and Kegan Paul, 1983); Nancy A. Hewitt, *Women's Activism and Social Change: Rochester, New York, 1822-1872* (Ithaca, N.Y.: Cornell University Press, 1984); Lori Ginzberg, *Women and the Work of Benevolence: Morality, Politics, and Class in the 19th-Century United States* (New Haven: Yale University Press, 1990); Ellen Carol DuBois, *Feminism and Suffrage: The Emergence of an Independent Women's Movement in America, 1848–1869* (Ithaca, N.Y.: Cornell University Press, 1978).

39. The gender of charity recipients is based on a survey of poor relief cases in the following eight Baptist congregations and one Methodist circuit: Salem Baptist Church, Marlboro District, Records, May 19, 1821, February 26, 1826, May 16, 1845; Mechanicsville Baptist Church, Darlington District, Minutes, August 12, 1820, February 10, 1821, May 11, 1822, July 10, 1824; Welsh Neck Baptist Church, Darlington District, Minutes, May 31, 1823, June 4, 1825, January 5, 1833, September 3, 1836, March 31, 1838, July 7, 1839, February 28, 1846; Thomas Memorial Baptist Church, Marlboro District, Minutes, January 3, 1855; Gum Branch Baptist Church, Darlington District, Minutes, December 14, 1839, August 19, 1842, May 19, 1848; Beech Branch Baptist Church, Beaufort District, Church Book, April 13, 1839, May 11, 1839; Prince Williams Baptist Church, Beaufort District, Record Book, November 16, 1850, July 15, 1854, December 15, 1855; Black Creek Primitive Baptist Church, Minute Book, 1838; Lynches Creek Circuit of the Methodist Church, Darlington District, Quarterly Conference Minutes, March 19, 1834, SCL. In a substantial majority of these cases (18 of 23), recipients of poor relief were women.

male church members and leaders without exception held the power to dispense or withhold the largesse. Even when elite women had helped to raise the money, as was not infrequently the case, white male members heard the appeals, established need, and allocated the aid in the form of provisions, shelter, employment, and money. "Every lady *must* be interested in the poor and miserable members of her own sex," Sarah Hale had said in 1831, articulating a central axis of womanly identity and class privilege in domestic ideology.[40] For reasons integral to every aspect of the household and gender relations in slave society, planter women were awarded no particular concern for the condition of indigent sisters and claimed none.[41]

Within lowcountry congregations there was, it would seem, no clearly gendered domain of moral authority for women, yeoman or planter, although by virtue of their ability to raise money planter women did play a significantly different role. While they did not acquire any particular power over the yeoman and poor white women in their churches, they contributed centrally to the benevolent capacity of their class as a whole. Evangelical women's organizations did not come into their own in South Carolina until the Civil War, but there were a few pioneering efforts beforehand. Those organizations took the embryonic form of "Female Mite Societies," which is to say they were dedicated to raising money for a variety of purposes, including the education of young ministers, foreign and domestic missions, church improvement, and support of ministers. In mite societies and the occasional "Ladies Fair," planter women donated their time and money to congregations in gifts of elegant bibles, lamps, chairs, stoves, communion plates, handiwork, and cash.[42] Such acts of female benevolence fit comfortably within the established limits of elite women's role and the traditional practices of planter patronage

40. Hale quoted in Cott, *Bonds of Womanhood*, p. 99. On the deepening gender identity of middle-class women in the North and its religious underpinnings, see Cott, *Bonds of Womanhood*, esp. pp. 97–100; Kathryn Kish Sklar, *Catherine Beecher: A Study in American Domesticity* (New Haven: Yale University Press, 1973). On female charitable activity in the North, see Hewitt, *Women's Activism and Social Change*. And for a recent rethinking of gender and class relations and the formation of bourgeois gender ideology in the North, see Stansell, *City of Women*.

41. Contrast the following interpretation with that of Suzanne Lebsock, who has argued that charity dispensed by elite women created bonds of sisterhood with poor or working-class women. Lebsock's interpretation falls squarely within the dominant bourgeois model. See Lebsock, *The Free Women of Petersburg: Status and Culture in a Southern Town, 1784–1860* (New York: W. W. Norton, 1984).

42. The location, history, and activities of four mite societies are to be found in Baptist Church, Female Mite Societies, Mount Moriah, Beaufort and Charleston Districts, Minutes, 1833–44, SCL. The activities of ladies' sewing societies, female benevolent societies, and female missionary societies for the most part conformed to the same patterns. See Welsh Neck Baptist Church, Darlington District, Minutes, June 30, 1832, April 4, 1835, May 6, 1848, March 2, 1850, November 4, 1854; First Columbia Baptist Church, Richland District, Session Book, June 25, 1820; Euhaw Baptist Church, Beaufort District, Minutes, July 15, 1849, December 1851; Bethany Baptist Church, Sumter District, Historical Sketch of Church, August 6, 1970, SCL.

of evangelical institutions. They represented little threat to gender order, especially when, as was almost invariably the case, planter women appointed male relatives as agents, treasurers, and representatives of their associations and surrendered to them control over the resources raised. Despite the significance of their charitable role, then, elite women's benevolent activities were closely constrained in the lowcountry and their organizations remained isolated within particular congregations. No larger denominational or regional bodies were formed as they were in the Northeast and Midwest, and the number of female-sponsored or female-directed benevolent institutions or even charitable events numbered a very few during the entire antebellum period.[43] Such activities and associations, no matter how critical to the evangelical edifice, effectively cemented elite women's ties to the men of their own class. They did not typically nurture in elite women a particular sense of responsibility for their own sex.[44] Few bonds of sex developed between women of different classes and races, never mind notions of a common womanhood or women's culture; nor did women's sense of moral authority seem to sustain any broader claims to a more public or reform-oriented role for women either within or outside the churches. In the Low Country, as in the rural South more generally, morality was still largely a household affair and, as such, a male one.

The distinctiveness of evangelical women's experience in the Low Country, and by extension in the slave South, lies not in its failure to generate a woman's rights movement, for in the Northeast, as we are now learning, evangelicalism proved as powerful an impediment as it did an inducement to the emergence of an abolitionist-woman's rights movement.[45] Rather, it lies in evangelical women's inability to fashion for themselves, as their northern counterparts managed to do, a com-

43. One perhaps singular example of a female-run charitable organization was the Beaufort Female Benevolence Society. Its members met at various churches but operated without "distinction of religious denomination" and with the object of "cementing Christian fellowship among different denominations." See Beaufort Female Benevolent Society, Minute Book, 1814–1861, SCL. There were a few Ladies Fairs reported in the antebellum period. In 1831 the *Charleston Mercury* announced one, "the first of its kind in Charleston," compared it to those then common in New England, and endorsed it in the context of sectional competition for moral distinction. See *Charleston Mercury*, November 10, 1831, and Euhaw Baptist Church, Beaufort District, Minutes, July 15, 1849. In clear contrast to the proliferation of evangelical women's organizations in the Northeast, those cited here and in note 42 above represent all of the organizations of which I found evidence in local church records of lowcountry South Carolina.

44. It is interesting to note that the one elite women's organization formed out of sympathy with "the suffering and destitute condition of many young females" operated independently of any particular evangelical denomination or local church. Indeed, its roots appear to be among Episcopalian women. See Beaufort Female Benevolent Society, Minute Book, "Original Subscription List, 1814."

45. The clearest statement of this view is to be found in Nancy Hewitt, "Feminist Friends: Agrarian Quakers and the Emergence of Women's Rights in America," *Feminist Studies* 12, no. 1 (Spring 1986), pp. 27–49.

mon identity as women, a positive definition of women's nature, and a claim to moral authority in home, church, and community. Bourgeois women admittedly gained moral authority in their families at precisely the moment that the family was losing legitimacy as a model for social organization. But southern women had not even that ambiguous inheritance. They lived in a world in which the household still served as the model for Christian social organization and in which it was resolutely the master's domain.

Piety was expected of southern women, moral superiority even discursively attributed to them, but women's "nature" remained an ambiguous virtue. The very quality of emotional vulnerability that made women more naturally pious than men also made them more vulnerable to temptation; their "natural" submissiveness made them as easily led by Satan as by God. As Reverend Richard Fuller explained to his female flock: "Your sex are oftener nervous than ours; and when this is the case, Satan is very busy. . . . A woman's piety like her life is domestic; and while it is sheltered from those assaults which a man has to encounter in the world, it is on this very account apt to want vigor and sturdiness." Woman's nature did not arm her for the daily battle with Satan. As ministers commonly put it in sermons, "soft effeminacy" was the gendered personification of sin, "manly virtue" its most resolute Christian enemy. In evangelical discourse the irrational element on which corruption fed was always a woman, sin that "Queen, that hag from hell." Despite their constant majority in evangelical churches—or perhaps because of it—and despite their obvious commitment to the faith, women were still seen by ministers and free male church members as unruly, potentially disruptive elements necessarily subject to male authority. In the Low Country women of all classes, including yeoman, continued to bear the mark of both Eve and Mary.[46] Nothing less than the conception of womanhood itself was at issue between northern and southern evangelicalism.

VI

If the promise of spiritual equality and moral sovereignty did not engender claims to social equality in family, church, or community, if it did not provide a sanctioned domain of female moral authority, it did in

46. J. H. Cuthbert, *Life of Richard Fuller, D.D.* (New York: Sheldon and Company, 1879), pp. 126–27; Wightman, *Life of Capers*, pp. 371–72; Palmer, *Life of Thornwell*, pp. 419–20. For a classic treatment of unruly women in the early modern European context see Natalie Zemon Davis, *Society and Culture in Early Modern France* (Stanford, Calif.: Stanford University Press, 1975). On the transformation in the American Northeast of the image of women as unruly—the demise of that image with respect to bourgeois women and its perpetuation as a peculiarly working-class characteristic—see Stansell, *City of Women*, pp. 19–37.

women's hands acquire other social meanings. By imagining perfectly reciprocal relations and duties incumbent on each family member, familialism provided dependents, especially women, a kind of leverage against particular abuses. Yeoman women proved adept at using churches to hold husbands, fathers, and male relatives accountable for the duties of their particular relations—at extracting a measure of protection from the paternalist familial vision of evangelicals.

Church disciplinary committees repeatedly encountered cases that forced them to make uncomfortable moral distinctions between husband and wife. Whether husband was censured and wife exonerated or vice versa, the point remained that married women's identities could not be fully submerged in the marital relation itself. Especially in cases in which wife was elevated over husband, the consequences could be nothing short of explosive. The case of Lenore and John Kelly was exemplary in this regard. But even in less dramatic cases the meaning was anything but mundane. When Mr. and Mrs. Miller applied for letters of dismission to join another church and their home congregation, First Barnwell Baptist, awarded her one while denying the husband for failing to settle his debts before moving out of the neighborhood and for "gaming," the church effectively threatened coverture.[47] By prying apart husband and wife, subjecting each to separate moral judgment, churches opened ground from which women could assert individual identities, convert paternal duties to wifely entitlements (if not rights), and begin to challenge the deep legal dependency that left them almost powerless in the secular courts.

Yeoman women found their best leverage in the principle of reciprocal duties. Evangelical churches reproduced the hierarchy and inequality that originated in secular households and thus legitimated male domination, white supremacy, and the authority of propertied men. But in their insistence that members not simply exercise the privileges of their station but also "discharge properly the humble duties of [their] social relations," they introduced a whole new set of possibilities. In various capacities as wife, sister, and daughter, yeoman women used the "courts of Jesus Christ" to protect their persons and interests against the abuses of husbands, brothers, fathers, and other male relatives.[48] Church committees of white males regularly disciplined their own brethren for a range of violations from adultery, bigamy, and lack of support to wife abuse and violence against other women kin to shady dealing or outright dishonesty in the distribution of family property bequeathed to women. When Allen Dowling was charged with "improper conduct toward his wife and family, abusing his wife and driving off his children," and John Tyler was charged with getting drunk and beating his wife, their respec-

---

47. First Barnwell Baptist Church, Barnwell District, Minutes, July 31, 1824.
48. Palmer, *Life of Thornwell*, p. 124; Kingstree Presbyterian Church, Williamsburg District, Minutes, June 20, 1844, SCL.

tive churches dealt with them harshly: Dowling got six months probation and Tyler was excommunicated.[49]

Whether women themselves stood up in church and made the charges or designated that responsibility to someone else is not, perhaps, the most important question. In either case abusive men were disciplined, the assaulted women received some justice and maybe a measure of protection, and all women, presumably, derived consolation from the recourse provided. In some cases, however, women did take matters resolutely into their own hands, using the disciplinary committees to resolve marital disputes, control abusive husbands, win their right to support, and even enforce dower rights. Sister Char[ity] Smith did what Lenore Kelly could not or would not do: She stood up in Black Creek Baptist Church in Beaufort District one Saturday in 1837 and "brot" her husband "before the church . . . for and [sic] attempt—for which he was excommunicated, the crime being an atrocious one." There certainly was no shortage of unspeakable crimes against women in the South Carolina Low Country. The only surprise is that in evangelical churches women did occasionally manage to hold their husbands answerable before the only court that mattered—a court of their peers. Abuses knew as few bounds as male power itself. Fathers who failed to deliver dowry property put their daughters in a vulnerable position with their new husbands, although one especially assertive daughter, Sister Bowers of Beaufort District, reported her father to the church, whereupon he "made satisfaction to Mr. Bowers [his son-in-law] for the negro sold." Married women had such few property rights that the church might prove crucial in enforcing fair dealing by male kin. When Lazarus Hudson served as estate executor for his brother-in-law, he took the opportunity to get a little for himself on the side. But because he was a church member, his sister, the surviving spouse, took the best recourse available to her and reported his attempt to "wrest unlawful money from a widowed sister."[50]

In looking to gospel discipline, yeoman women like Sister Smith effectively invoked the authority of one set of men—ministers, deacons, church elders and brethren—against another—husbands, fathers, and male kin. The point was not lost on husbands and fathers. One upcountry father whose daughter had recently converted charged that the "preachers [have] run her mad." She, however, saw his response more clearly as resentment over the diminution of his own authority. "He is

49. Lynches Creek Circuit of the Methodist Church, Darlington District, Quarterly Conference Minutes, October 24, 1829; First Barnwell Baptist Church, Barnwell District, Minutes, February 29, 1840.

50. Black Creek Primitive Baptist Church, Beaufort District, Minute Book, 1837; Prince Williams Baptist Church, Beaufort District, Record Book, May 18, 1821; Lynches Creek Circuit of the Methodist Church, Darlington District, Quarterly Conference Minutes, July 14, 1827; Willow Swamp Baptist Church, Orangeburg District, Minutes, November 5, 1819, SCL.

vexed at the opinion he thinks I have imbibed from others," she noted, "and at the impossibility of receiving his own." Resentment occasionally turned to belligerence. Richard Fuller, the great evangelist, was threatened by an irate husband who warned that if Fuller attempted "to visit or baptize anyone in his house, he would shoot him."[51] Women may have only swapped one patriarchal authority for another, but in doing so they used the church as leverage in negotiating the terms of relations with the men in their own families and households. Theirs was a creative deployment of the church's familial vision, one that secured for them a measure of protection. But while such strategies should never be underestimated, one has only to think of Lenore Kelly to recognize their limits.

Mrs. Kelly's experience was not unusual, for crimes against the bodies of women often evolved as struggles between different factions of men. Men were most likely to face discipline when other fathers and husbands believed their interests had been violated. Thus, Brother Jacob Little of Swift Creek Baptist Church was excommunicated when Brother Bowen charged him with an "offense against his [Bowen's] family . . . [by] improper conduct [in] making three distinct attacks upon the chastity of a young girl." It was men's honor and reputation that was at stake in the protection of women's bodies, as one outraged husband suggested in charging his wife's seducer with "invad[ing] the honor and peace of my household."[52] The idea was never entertained that the women had welcomed the advance, or, if it was a sexual assault, that it was honor or self that had been violated. All too often the leverage women acquired came at the cost of their very subjectivity. Without a doubt, yeoman women found more protection for their persons and interests in evangelical than secular society—and certainly more than the slave men or women for whom the church represented no safe harbor despite the official stand on the duties of masters. But if congregations challenged men's right to abuse their power over female dependents, they never challenged their right to wield it.

On the contrary, yeoman heads of households found in familialism powerful confirmation of their identity as masters. Lowcountry churches imposed on yeoman and planter members more onerous responsibilities than those customarily incurred in secular society. But it was precisely in those responsibilities that Christian stewardship inhered and through which it functioned to legitimize the power husbands exerted over wives, masters over slaves, and heads of households over all dependents. Indeed, in tying their fate to those relations, women contributed their part to the legitimation of domestic dependencies and secular hierarchies.

51. Mary E. Moragne, *The Neglected Thread: A Journal from the Calhoun Community, 1836–1842,* ed. Delle Mullen Craven (Columbia, S.C.: University of South Carolina Press, 1951), p. 138; Cuthbert, *Life of Fuller,* pp. 126–27.

52. Swift Creek Baptist Church, Kershaw District, Records, August 22, 1829, and August 28, 1829; First Columbia Presbyterian Church, Richland District, Session Book, June 25, 1841.

Larger commitments than spiritual equality, moral individualism, and the accountability of masters animated the familial ideal of lowcountry evangelicalism. And when such notions ran head on into conflict, as they repeatedly did, with the church's avowed commitment to organic relations and social hierarchy, there was little doubt as to which interests would prevail. A deep respect for patriarchal authority lay at the heart of Christian community in the Low Country.

Precisely because the recognition of women as moral individuals had the potential to reconfigure relations of power between husband and wife, precisely because it could disrupt customary lines of authority within the household and undermine deeply engrained assumptions about coverture, evangelical congregations were vigilant in countering the suspicion that such was their intention. They jealously guarded the prerogatives of masters.

Dependents were expected to conform to their master's will. That was the duty of their relations, even when it conflicted directly with other evangelical injunctions. Slaves, for example, had to have their masters' permission to join a church and, although church attendance was required of all members, if a master objected the slave was exonerated from any charges of sin or backsliding. This was, on the one hand, a necessary recognition of the master's power, but on the other it constituted a Christian injunction in its own right. Obedience was the first duty of the Christian slave. Similarly, ministers expected free married women to conform to their husbands' will. If a woman was cited for failure to attend church but offered by way of explanation that "she had not the opertunity to attend as her husband is unfriendly to her" or that "she wished to attend church but she was prevented as was interfered by her husband," such excuses were considered satisfactory.[53] Women were not encouraged to resist even the most un-Christian of husbands. Submission was a Christian wife's trial and principal duty.

Clearly women were not sovereign individuals in the South Carolina Low Country, nor did the region's churches construct them as such. As Lenore Kelly and countless other women discovered when they sought justice or just refuge in the "household of faith," some things—and some people—mattered more than others. The gender identity yeoman women managed to create out of evangelicalism thus had a fundamentally contradictory character, caught as it was between the churches' promise of spiritual equality and moral sovereignty and their articulated commitment to an organic or familial Christian social order.

The very position of conversion in the female lifecycle evokes the contradiction. Conversion was commonly represented as a rite of passage, a journey through death to rebirth, in fact the submergence of self in the creation of a new self. To be "born again" one had first to be

---

53. Gum Branch Baptist Church, Darlington District, Minutes, November 20, 1847, July 13, 1849, March 16, 1844.

"buried in Christ," just as Christ had to die so all mankind could be saved. One church represented this symbolic inversion sartorially, rejecting the usual badges of mourning, black clothing, as a "custom of the world" inappropriate to the celebration of death and eternal life. Their baptismal candidates thus wore black robes, signs of death, into the river ("Buried with Him by Baptism into Death," as one church put it) and emerged to don white ones, thereby announcing ritual rebirth. They had been born anew and had become members of the family of God.[54] Conversion was, quite literally, a rite of metamorphosis, liminality, self-creation, self-definition. But for women candidates for whom it existed not infrequently in close proximity to age of marriage, conversion was a rite of passage in another sense as well.

As an experience that presaged marriage and motherhood, conversion was also a coming-of-age ritual, one that acquired distinctive emotional and psychological meaning as part of young women's negotiation of the difficult transition from girlhood to womanhood. Mary Davis Brown intimated its meaning to yeoman women. Like a great many southern women, her daughter Eliza Ann experienced conversion and joined the church the year before she married. It was, in her evocation, a fitting ritual with which to mark a woman's entry into adulthood—the successful struggle to submit to God's will being proper prologue to the submission of self demanded of Christian wives. For it consecrated suffering and infused the struggle for the abnegation of self with a higher, even sacral, purpose. "Oh my God, aid and support me in fulfilling the many duties encumbent on me," Mary Davis Brown prayed on her thirty-seventh birthday. "Oh will thou give me a praying heart and a submissive will to all the troubles and trials of this wourld."[55] For yeoman women like Mary Davis Brown and her daughter Eliza Ann, conversion was, like marriage, a contradictory act of self-effacement in the creation of a new, adult, self. All Christians waged a lifelong struggle for submission to God's will, but for women it was waged in relation to the divine master once removed in the person of the household head. The common martial rhetoric of conversion and evangelicalism thus encoded a deeply gendered vision of Christian subjects.

The meaning of Christian womanhood was articulated poignantly by Mary Moragne, the daughter of a small upcountry planter. And although it had obvious elite inflections, it resonated with the interpretation offered by Mary Davis Brown. For Mary Moragne, conversion was, in the most literal sense imaginable, a rehearsal for marriage. Not only did she convert immediately prior to her marriage, but she married the minister who converted her. The connection between the two events was explicit. "A light of love and joy unspeakable" swept over her, she re-

54. First Columbia Baptist Church, Richland District, Session Book, July 11, 1824, April 6, 1833; Mechanicsville Baptist Church, Darlington District, Minutes, Covenant, 1829.

55. Mary Davis Brown Diary, July 14, 1859, April 25, 1858, August 11, 1859.

called. "There, with no witness but my dying uncle, I first spoke of my love to the Saviour." But if romantic love assumed higher and safer purpose when the woman was courted and won by Jesus then it was, in Moragne's telling, because love of Jesus prepared the woman for the inevitable disappointments and trials of marriage. "I would rather be a simple unambitious and loving wife than to be empress of the world!" she declared. "But can it be so now? Can this wild heart be ever tamed to gentle and familiar duties, to know and desire nothing for itself . . . to become a *living sacrifice,* a meek and uncomplaining sacrifice to another's happiness." Hers was a perfectly ghoulish image of Christian womanhood, a burial alive—marriage literally the death of self.[56] Mary Moragne and Mary Davis Brown each in their own way reiterated in chilling measure a view of Christian womanhood inscribed in evangelicalism. The "Mother of Israel," the Charleston Presbyterian Thomas Smyth declared, was one who spent her life "in the quiet discharge of her appropriate duties . . . [in] unselfish and untiring devotion to the interests and comfort of others, especially her family and friends."[57]

Yeoman women flocked to the churches to hear that earthly distinctions meant nothing to God, that all could be saved. What they heard when they got there offered them hope, self-respect, a means of self-assertion, and a model of female excellence that made the submission of self the apotheosis of womanhood. Soldiers in Christ's army, they spent their lives in an active struggle for submission and for a passivity purportedly natural. By the very definition of duty Christian women embraced, they were rendered agents of their own subordination and of the sacralization of domestic dependencies and masterly identity. Such were the meanings and effects of familialism.

VII

The effect went well beyond the relations of free men and women, as indeed such a comprehensive social vision must. A deep self-consciousness on the subject of slavery infused every aspect of the region's political culture and, not least, popular religion. As it did with husband and wife, evangelicalism envisioned for master and slave a perfectly reciprocal relation and a disciplinary practice to enforce it. But although the churches held husbands and fathers, within limits, to the fulfillment of their Christian duties, gospel discipline failed tragically when it came to masters. This failure of will revealed, as did nothing else, the moral bankruptcy and political complicity of a Christianity hostage to the power relations it claimed to reform. Few cultural institutions

56. Moragne, *The Neglected Thread,* pp. 115–16, 118, 235–36.
57. Thomas Smyth, "The Teachings of the Dead," *Southern Presbyterian Review* 10, no. 2 (July 1857), pp. 163–67.

had the social reach of evangelical churches, and in that respect familialism did much of the work of the popular legitimation of slavery.

Biracial and deeply racist, lowcountry evangelical churches simultaneously maintained equality in God's eyes and inequality in man's.
Slaves heard the message of spiritual equality and lent their own meanings to it. That those meanings diverged, often radically, from the ones
offered by white members and ministers was a matter of constant concern in lowcountry congregations.

Try as they might to control slave exhorters, deacons, and preachers
through rules regulating slave assemblies and licensing of spiritual leaders, white church elders knew they fought a losing battle. When they
learned, as the leaders of the First Barnwell Baptist Church did in 1832,
that Frank, a licensed slave preacher, had been delivering a sermon to
slaves on neighborhood plantations in which he proclaimed that "their
principal portion in the world was a peck of corn, a few clothes, and 700
lashes," their greatest fears were confirmed.[58] These waters were so
deep that most church leaders knew not to test them. But in one extraordinary case that exposed the dangerous currents just below the surface
of a formally coherent biracial Christianity, the white officers of Marlboro's Salem Baptist Church investigated a slave accused of stealing
meat and discovered in the process that he did not consider the seizure
of his master's property to constitute a sin. It was not theft, the slave
informed them, but the reappropriation of his own property: A man was
entitled to eat what he had produced. Horrified, this church decided to
get to the bottom of the matter and surveyed slave members to see if
such views were common. They were indeed. What else slaves considered rightfully theirs church members wisely decided not to ask. Similar
conflicts over, especially, the sacrament of marriage and the problem of
the separation of slave husband and wife by sale plagued lowcountry
churches, eluded any settled policy, and provided constant evidence of
the interpretive struggle between slaves and church leaders, between
white and Afro-Christianity.[59]

Such expressions of the distinctive meanings of Afro-Christianity
were disturbing indications of the manifold possibilities that inhered in
evangelical precepts. Slaves took seriously the matter of spiritual equality, some managing even to seize from it a moral authority that could
momentarily invert the master- (or mistress-) slave relationship. When
Mary Moragne was finally converted at her uncle's deathbed, she was
greeted upon her return to the plantation by a number of slave women
who had been praying for her and who now rejoiced in her final passage. Each took the opportunity to share the "theme of her own experience," Moragne recalled. "Such blessings, and prayers, and advice as
they showered upon me." Although she had lived with these women

58. First Barnwell Baptist Church, Barnwell District, Minutes, October 6, 1832.
59. Salem Baptist Church, Marlboro District, Records, September 7, 1831.

much of her life, she was entirely unprepared for their expression of shared experience and for the posture of spiritual intercessors they adopted. "I was struck dumb," she said bluntly. "I felt that I was but a 'babe in Christ' before two old ignorant Africans. God had revealed himself to them," she noted with marked astonishment. "He has chosen the weak things of the world to confound the wise, and when I went away I felt that they too were my sisters." She soon revealed just what that new recognition involved—or, more accurately, what it did not. The slave women took seriously their equality in God's eyes, were convinced of his indifference to secular station, and, as that stunning moment suggested, their faith changed their relations with masters and mistresses. But for Mary Moragne the connection between sacred and secular was not so seamless; sisterhood proved a very limited notion. "Every day of my life I do inly weep and mourn that I am able to do nothing for the souls of these poor creatures," she commented as if the matter were out of her hands. And indeed she thought it was. "Our religion is not sufficiently practical," she explained. "[I]t does not mingle with our daily affairs, but seems rather an abstract principle than a familiar spirit."[60] Few knew better the bitter truth of that observation than the slaves who sought justice in her church or on her father's farm.

The slave women in Mary Moragne's household showed presumption enough in their posture of spiritual equality. But the familial discourse of white evangelicals opened up even more transgressive possibilities, as one extraordinary letter from a lowcountry slave woman to her mistress suggests. The woman, Lavinia, was heartsick. Her son-in-law Jimmy had just left his wife Aggie and taken up with another woman in the quarters, apparently with the permission of the master and mistress. Lavinia wrote to protest the decision and to ask her mistress to intercede on her daughter Aggie's behalf. She wrote as one Christian woman to another. "Dere Missis cant u take Pity on Aggie and use yore influence in stopping this retched bizniss," she began, reminding her mistress that her intervention worked in the past when "u stopped my huzbuns goin to Mas Winbun Lawton by yore pleading and eft." But supplication soon turned to open rebuke as Lavinia demanded to know "My god is this Religion. . . . Do u kall that nigger [Jimmy] a cristian! I call him A son of Belial." In recognition of the lineage of power in the Elliott household, she then turned her sights on her master, instructing him in his responsibility as a Christian head of household to serve as father to all of his dependents. "Oh Mas Elliott kin u allow this! This krewel thing dun in yore yard! . . . My God! My God! Coln wat have u dun. . . . View the matter as u would if they were yore children. Have they not souls as well as wite peple." In Lavinia's eyes the moral question was no different for black than for white. "Do not allow sutch adultery," she warned him, for such a failure of familialism carried dire conse-

60. Moragne, *The Neglected Thread*, pp. 135–36, 212–13.

quences. "This akkounts for the kold state the chuch is in Bekause thar is So much divilnes in it," she wrote. "Were is yore konshence. Pray over it, Massa and see if u kin allow It."[61] Lavinia, for one, found in Christianity and its promise of spiritual equality the wherewithal to challenge her master's and mistress's judgment and in the familial ideology of their common faith she found the leverage with which to hold them accountable—or rather, to try to—for their Christian duties. Slaves may well have "souls as well as wite people," as she reminded her master, but the very fact that she had to remind him suggests just how difficult it was for white evangelicals to contemplate the implications of that admitted principle.

It was the official evangelical position that "the gospel is the same for all men" and that there is "one only Saviour and one only way of life." Yet in every aspect of church life, from architecture to gospel discipline, that message was contravened. It was, for example, widely accepted by all denominations that "it is due to public decency to seat the colored people by themselves, apart from the whites"; thus, despite the fact that slaves constituted on average four of every ten Methodists and Presbyterians and more than seven of every ten Baptists in lowcountry churches, they were seated in special galleries or sheds set aside for "people of color." By 1860 few white Christians would voice disbelief as one eighteenth-century mistress had that "any of my slaves would go to Heaven and I must see them there," but one suspects that many secretly felt as she did.[62] For every time a slave walked into a lowcountry church, the contradiction of spiritual equality was ritually enacted before the whole congregation.

If Mary Moragne and other Christian slaveowners recognized the distance between the ideas and the practice of familialism, slaves themselves were in the best position to know its failures, if not to give them voice. Since slaves were, at least discursively, considered family members and the family the model of all Christian social relations, masters' treatment of slaves was subject to gospel discipline.[63] But here, as nowhere else, the concept of the perfected family utterly collapsed. Slaves found little if any protection within the evangelical vision. On rare occasions

61. Lavinia to "Dear Missis," July 1849, Lawton Family Papers. There are two versions of the letter in the Lawton Papers, one of which appears to be a copy of the original with the spelling significantly corrected. I have quoted from the apparently uncorrected version.

62. Shipp, *History of Methodism*, p. 456; H. Shelton Smith, *In His Image But . . . Racism in Southern Religion, 1780–1910* (Durham, N.C.: Duke University Press, 1972), p. 11. For a few examples of segregated seating, see Euhaw Baptist Church, Beaufort District, Minutes, September 24, 1859; Presbyterian Church Records, Miscellaneous Information, vol. I, SCL.

63. For a formal statement of the reciprocal obligations of masters and slaves, see Charles Colcock Jones's widely distributed tract, *A Catechism For Colored Persons* (Charleston: Observer Office Press, 1834), especially the chapters entitled "Masters' Duties to Servants" and "Servants' Duties to Masters."

masters were investigated for cruelty to their slaves, but if church committees were reluctant to discipline husbands for maltreatment of their
wives, they were just plain afraid to interfere with this relation. Cruelty
and brutality were condemned by evangelical churches, and covenants
bound masters to treat slaves in a fashion becoming "their station."
When faced with masters who shot at runaway slaves, beat slaves for
stealing corn, or even killed their slaves with no provocation, however,
the church typically settled for temporarily suspending the offending
master or lecturing him. Thus, while church disciplinary records over-
flow with cases of slaves compelled to meet their obligations as slaves,
they are practically silent on the reciprocal obligations of Christian
masters.[64]

For free women, children, the sick, and the aged, lowcountry churches
provided at least a measure of protection and support; for lowcountry
slaves, whether men or women, no such safe harbor existed. The failure
of the evangelical community to live up to its familial ideal exposed the
fundamental contradiction at the heart of evangelical ideology. As one
slave with the proud name "Merica" charged in refusing to attend a
disciplinary hearing, "[h]e would not get justice if he were to come."[65]
Nothing about lowcountry evangelical life made spiritual equality incompatible with slavery in the eyes of its white members. Quite the
reverse. In bringing slaves and masters together in one meetinghouse
only to seat them and treat them according to secular rank and station,
evangelical churches afforded white members profound endorsement
of the divine status of secular relations. For the region's yeoman farmers
there could be few more powerful confirmations of masterly identity
than the gendered and racial relations of the lowcountry "household of
faith."

VIII

If the male yeomanry found in evangelicalism a sacred ground for its
own privilege as men and masters, that ground was not without complications. Especially after the 1830s and the influx of planter members,
yeoman found themselves in a predicament in the churches similar to
that encountered in secular society: at once empowered and compromised by their own commitments to property, domestic dependencies,
and the assumptions about public power and authority they sustained.

Church covenants and rules of governance put all white men, yeo-

64. Camden Station Circuit of the Methodist Church, Kershaw District, Quarterly
Conference Minutes, April 18, 1818, SCL; First Columbia Presbyterian Church, Richland
District, Session Book, December 20, 1828; Beech Branch Baptist Church, Beaufort Dis-
trict, Church Book, August 10, 1850; Bethesda Presbyterian Church, Kershaw District,
Session Minutes and Records, July 6, 1859.
65. Gum Branch Baptist Church, Darlington District, Minutes, July 17, 1840.

man and planter, on an equal footing with respect to church government, and indeed yeomen were elected as officers and ministers in lowcountry (especially Baptist and Methodist) congregations. But judging
from the local records, the most prominent roles in church government
went not to yeoman but to planter members. That planter men ascended
to that position of authority and power through election by the majority
of enfranchised members, which is to say by yeoman men, suggests a
much more complex view of the qualities that recommended a man to
leadership than the formally egalitarian structures of church government would indicate.

In both Black Swamp Baptist Church and in the local Methodist
circuit in Beaufort District, for example, yeoman brethren regularly
elected Bosticks and Lawtons, Martins and Tisons, men from local planter families, as deacons, stewards, class leaders, and elders. Benjamin
Bostick, long-standing deacon of Black Swamp Baptist Church, was the
richest man in the congregation, paid the highest pew rent, and topped
every subscription raised during his years in office. In another wealthy
Baptist congregation, Welsh Neck in Society Hill, Darlington District,
yeoman members joined with their planter brethren to elect to church
office men from the McIver, Wilson, and Coker families. These were precisely the men whose subscriptions to the church fund in 1844, the year
a new meetinghouse was built, exceeded those of virtually every other
member of the congregation. Presbyterians in the area drew their leadership from the same class of citizens, and in some cases from the very
same families.[66] But the elevation of the wealthiest members and most
generous patrons was not confined to wealthy congregations, for the
pattern prevailed in relative terms in more modestly endowed churches.
Thus, in 1848 the predominantly yeoman enfranchised members of
Beech Branch Baptist Church in Beaufort District elected Jonas Johnston
their minister. Owner of twenty slaves and a farm valued at two thousand
dollars, Johnston was by no means a wealthy man in lowcountry terms,
but as a small planter in a yeoman church his election constituted leadership by the congregational elite no less surely than did that of Benjamin
Bostick in Black Swamp. Ministers' memoirs, church histories, and records of local congregations all point in a similar direction: conceptions
of who was best suited to leadership reveal an intimate, if murky, relationship among wealth, patronage, and power.[67] That such ideas pre-

66. Black Swamp Baptist Church, Beaufort District, Subscription List, 1847, and History, 1895, SCL; Chalmers Gaston Davidson, *The Last Foray: The South Carolina Planters of
1860: A Sociological Study* (Columbia, S.C.: University of South Carolina Press, 1971),
p. 102; Welsh Neck Baptist Church, Darlington District, Minutes, January 1844 and December 6, 1844; Howe, *Presbyterian Church in South Carolina*, vol. 2, p. 352.

67. Beech Branch Baptist Church, Beaufort District, Church Book, July 8, 1848. The
profile of Jonas Johnson's land and slave holdings was derived from the Federal Manuscript Census, South Carolina [Beaufort District], Schedules of Population, Slaves, and
Agriculture, 1850, NA. For one minister's comments on the election of the "richer brethren," see Wightman, *Life of Capers*, pp. 199–200, and for the perspective from planter

vailed in institutions formally governed by yeoman majorities points to a whole set of assumptions and practices that animated lowcountry politics, for with respect to their internal operations churches were themselves little republics.

It is already perfectly evident that property had its privileges in lowcountry churches and that yeomen respected them. Their own prerogatives after all rested on that foundation. In the regulation of economic transactions between members, disciplinary committees buttressed the rights of propertyholders, establishing a principle of "just" exchange that condemned (although with diminishing conviction) gouging, extortion, and overzealous creditors while upholding, in every instance, just return on money lent or goods exchanged. Even petty crimes against property were dealt with harshly. Although one country minister bemoaned the demise of a "Christian" economy in which "moral obligation" was "superior to all human law," most appear to have embraced what might more accurately be called a moral economy of the propertied. Poor white men took their chances in it, but yeomen were hardly likely to object, at least to the principle of the matter.[68] It is not difficult, however, to see how such principles could have the inadvertent effect of advantaging more propertied members over lesser ones within the body of the church.

The system at work in church government was not a simple endorsement of elite rule. Rather, connections between property and power worked according to a particular logic in the hands of yeoman voters, and the hierarchy to be found among the ranks of white male members reflected anything but a simple politics of deference. In lowcountry churches, slaves were physically segregated from whites and, in some, women from men, but more to the immediate point, there was also a system of pew-renting that imposed a spatial hierarchy among different classes of white men. The practice differed from one denomination to another. Presbyterian churches typically designated a number of pews as "free pews for the poor" and rented the rest, while Baptist churches inverted the practice, designating a specific number (often half) for renting while the rest remained free. Pews were rented on a declining

papers, see John Berkley Grimball on the trustees of Wiltown Presbyterian Church, Colleton District, in John Berkley Grimball Diary, April 22, 1834, Grimball Family Papers, SHC.

68. Anonymous, *Old Pine Farm*, pp. 22, 79. For examples of "just" exchange see Black Creek Primitive Baptist Church, Beaufort District, Minute Book, 1828; Prince Williams Primitive Baptist Church, Beaufort District, Record Book, May 18, 1821; Lynches Creek Circuit of the Methodist Church, Darlington District, Quarterly Conference Minutes, July 14, 1827, March 16, 1839; Target and Holly Hill Methodist Church, Orangeburg District, History, May 4, 1980, "Summary of common disciplinary actions under the categories of 'Pilfering and Stealing'," SCL; Salem Baptist Church, Marlboro District, Records, July 20, 1822, August 15, 1829; Gum Branch Baptist Church, Darlington District, Minutes, July 1829, October 18, 1833, January 18, 1840; Darlington Presbyterian Church, Darlington District, Session Minutes, January 18, 1840.

cost scale from front to back, with the most expensive ones costing as much as forty dollars per year in the 1820s and significally more in later years.[69] In Black Swamp Baptist Church in the 1840s (for which a partial pew map survives) pew-renters were without exception planters of various means. The renter of the cheapest pew owned 22 slaves and of the most expensive 216; but with an average planter member owning 71 slaves it is obvious that those who sat in the rented pews were, in declining order, the wealthiest members of the congregation. Not one yeoman family rented a pew. They sat in the free pews in the back along with mechanics, day laborers, tenants, clerks, shingle-getters, paupers, and any other free person who could not afford to purchase status.[70] Every Sunday when churchgoers entered the meetinghouse and took their seats, they played their part in a choreography of class. Ministers always complained about men lingering too long in the churchyard before services. Whatever else it meant, men's tardiness could well have represented a jostling for position. For if those who entered last were poor men, then they could slip into the back pews unobserved by the wealthy already seated in the front of the church. But if the rich entered last, that created an opportunity for ostentatious procession in clean linen and good boots from the back of the church up the center aisle to their pews in the front. The significance of such spatial hierarchies cannot be underestimated, for it was obvious to all who participated in the weekly ritual that seating order represented the lines of patronage and thus of power in their congregations.[71]

Evangelical churches adopted pew-renting for an obvious reason: The support of the gospel lay entirely in the hands of the membership. Whether it was to pay the minister, support a denominational college, a missionary, a Sabbath school, or finance the building of a new meetinghouse, evangelicals had to raise the money from within their own ranks. And although every member contributed his or her "mite," sometimes "in work" rather than in money, the bulk of the contributions to the support of the church was made by those who could most afford to make

69. For examples of pew-renting arrangements, see Welsh Neck Baptist Church, Darlington District, Minutes, May 31, 1823, January 6, 1827, April 6, 1833, November 4, 1837, June 30, 1849; Euhaw Baptist Church, Beaufort District, Minutes, September 1856; Black Swamp Baptist Church, Beaufort District, Pew Map, Church History, 1895; Second Charleston Presbyterian Church, Charleston District, Record of Session, May 14, 1855; First Columbia Presbyterian Church, Richland District, Session Book, December 1842; Howe, *Presbyterian Church in South Carolina*, vol. 2, pp. 27–28, 594.

70. Black Swamp Baptist Church, Beaufort District, Pew Map, Church History, 1895. There is no precise date on the pew map, but there are other indications in the church history that place it roughly in the 1840s. The social profile of pew-renters was created by matching names to the next census, that is, Federal Manuscript Census, South Carolina [Beaufort District], Schedule of Population, Slaves, and Agriculture, 1850.

71. For a fascinating analysis of just such symbolic politics, see Rhys Isaac, *The Transformation of Virginia, 1740–1790* (Chapel Hill: University of North Carolina Press, 1982).

them, which it to say the planter members.[72] Pew rents were typically used to pay ministers' salaries and to meet debts against the church for building and repairs. It was as patrons of the gospel, then, that pew-renters acquired an enhanced voice in church affairs. In some churches pew-renters who were not members could join with free male members in the election of pastor and elders, and in a few instances pew-renters together held exclusive power in the election of church officers. In one such case, the Second Presbyterian Church of Charleston under the ministry of the Belfast-born and rabidly anti-Catholic minister the Reverend Mr. Thomas Smyth changed the rules of church government with the explicit purpose of raising money. In exchange for assuming responsibility to retire a debt against the church, a select group of gentlemen won total control over its temporal affairs. In elections of church officers, they each held from one to eight votes, distributed according to the amount of money each had subscribed. Pew-holders had only one vote each, and those members who did not rent pews had none at all. The Second Charleston Presbyterian Church was administered in this fashion from 1823 to 1852.[73] This was, admittedly, an extreme case but a revealing one nonetheless. For the relationship between planters' generous patronage and their disproportionate power in church government was everywhere an intimate one, although more complex and interesting when it worked, as it usually did, through the electoral choice of a yeoman majority instead of ministerial fiat.

Rather than resenting planter wealth and the power that accompanied it in evangelical communities, yeomen harnessed it to their own interests, using the franchise to secure the financial health of their churches. Prominent planter church officers like Colonel Alexander Lawton, treasurer of Black Swamp Baptist Church and one of the richest men in St. Peter's Parish in Beaufort District, earned the loyalty of their humbler brethren by generous patronage of the church and by extending their influence as wealthy, literate, and well-connected men on be-

72. The connections are most evident in the records of Black Swamp Baptist Church. There the names of pew-renters, already identified as planters, also appear on the list of subscribers to the building fund raised in 1848 as the most generous subscribers. Of the 18 subscribers who could be identified on the census and whose contributions were listed in descending order from $100 to $5, only 2 could have been yeomen. The remainder were planters who owned from 19 to 216 slaves; more than half of the subscribers owned more than 50 slaves. See Black Swamp Baptist Church, Beaufort District, Subscription List, 1848, and History, 1895; Federal Manuscript Census, South Carolina [Beaufort District], Schedule of Population and Slaves, 1850. For similar class patterns of patronage in a more typical Baptist congregation see Beech Branch Baptist Church where Henry Smart, the second wealthiest member, left the church the single largest legacy it ever received. See Beech Branch Baptist Church, Beaufort District, Church Book, January 1, 1852.

73. Second Charleston Presbyterian Church, Charleston District, Record of Session, April 1837; Howe, *Presbyterian Church in South Carolina*, vol. 2, pp. 27–28, 594; Welsh Neck Baptist Church, Darlington District, Minutes, June 5, 1841; Euhaw Baptist Church, Beaufort District, Minutes, September 1856.

half of less powerful members. Lawton performed numerous services for his mechanic and yeoman brethren, often settling conflicts, collecting debts, estimating property values, arranging estate sales, and performing many other time-consuming tasks incumbent on administrators of estates.[74] Members thus served often rewarded planter patrons with support in election to church office. Eulogized as exemplary Christians for the "discharge of their duties, public and private, and [for] benevolence and kindness to the poor and afflicted," church officers were exemplary in large measure by virtue of "their purse ready to assist," as one obituary put it. A good Christian gentlemen died, as did James Kennedy Douglas of Camden, with many in his debt. In him it was said, "the poor, the widow, and the orphan found a friend and protector." And indeed, benevolent men and women in every congregation earned distinction by supporting poor and afflicted brethren with housing, food, land, money, nurses, doctors' services, and even horses to ride and shoes to wear to preaching.[75]

Yeoman and planter men were anything but equals in lowcountry congregations. There, as elsewhere, yeomen paid the price of their commitment to a social order grounded in the rights of propertied men and the subordination of dependents. But they were not without resources in their negotiations with vastly more propertied planters. For as planters knew all to well, whether in the church or in the republic abroad, their legitimacy as local leaders rested in the hands of yeoman voters. Those voters readily acknowledged that property had its privileges. But in recognizing wealth and status most readily when it was deployed in the interests of the congregation, they also insisted that property had its responsibilities. Through the judicious use of voting power they pushed planters into patronage and the cultivation of local circles of influence and secured for themselves influential patrons in the secular world. These were precisely the kinds of arrangements on which secular political culture turned.[76] The politics of the "household of faith" was instructive beyond its own boundaries.

In the familial ideology of lowcountry evangelicalism, yeoman farm-

74. Evidence of Colonel Lawton's service as administrator of estates is scattered throughout the Lawton Family Papers, but for a few examples see the following bills and receipts for yeoman estate transactions: February 1, 1823, Box 1; April 27, 1825, November 18, 1825, August 1826, Box 2; December 16, 1829, Box 3, all in Lawton Family Papers.

75. Bethesda Presbyterian Church, Kershaw District, Session Minutes and Records, December 18, 1860; Welsh Neck Baptist Church, Darlington District, Minutes, January 16, 1819, October 2, 1819, February 3, 1821, December 16, 1821, August 4, 1838 and throughout.

76. Perhaps for this reason, even nonevangelical planters were careful to establish their reputations as patrons of evangelical churches in their neighborhoods. R. F. W. Allston, the politically astute Georgetown rice planter, was prodded into contributing money for Methodist catechisms and Sunday school hymn books by the reminder that his neighbor had provided poor children of the same church with clothes in which to attend preaching. See Catherine M. Moor to Robert F. W. Allston, July 15, 1859, in Easterby, ed., *The South Carolina Rice Plantation*, p. 161.

ers found profound confirmation of their own masterly identity. The rights of property upheld, domestic dependencies sanctioned, equality constrained to the next world, in their hands Christian community sacralized the secular order of slave society—and with it the power of the planter class. From the Nullification Revivals to the second secession crisis, the "households of faith" that dotted the South Carolina Low Country proved to be critical institutions in the region's political culture, providing both an unimpeachable logic and an unparalleled popular constituency for an increasingly aggressive defense of slavery and the social order it engendered.

chapter 6

Slavery, Gender, and the "Social Fabrick"

I

When yeoman farmers went to town on court day, to a July Fourth barbecue, or an annual militia review and heard prominent politicians such as Robert Barnwell Rhett or James Henry Hammond defend slavery against the calumnies of abolitionists, they probably cheered as vociferously as the planters with whom they rubbed shoulders. For judging by the remains in the written record, those politicians and political theorist invariably rang what were to yeomen a series of familiar notes, embedding the defense of slavery in a social theory that was in many ways simply a more sophisticated version of the familial one yeomen enacted in their churches. Indeed, evangelical arguments replete with their gendered referents figured centrally in even the most secular venue. When push came to shove, lowcountry politicians could find no better defense of slavery than the biblical one. "What God ordains and Christ sanctifies should surely command the respect and toleration of man," James Henry Hammond wrote in 1845 in his now famous letters to the British abolitionist Thomas Clarkson.[1] This was an argument sure to move a yeoman audience. In using it and elaborating it through a broad theory of social relations—and especially through the analogy of marriage and slavery—he and his counterparts bid well to put proslavery discourses on a popular footing. And when they turned them to specifically political ends, as they invariably did in the protracted struggle over South Carolina's fate in the nation, lowcountry politicians

1. James Henry Hammond, "Hammond's Letters on Slavery," in *The Pro-Slavery Argument as Maintained by the Most Distinguished Writers of the Southern States* (1845; reprint ed., Philadelphia: Lippincott, Grambo and Co., 1853), p. 108.

carefully cast their arguments in the same terms, calling yeoman farmers and other freemen to the defense not of slave society narrowly construed but of a conservative Christian republicanism. That particular representation of South Carolina society and politics lay at the heart of popular political culture in the Low Country from the Nullification Crisis to the secession movement in the fall of 1860. The proslavery argument, as intellectual historians have traditionally called it, may have been written by planter elites, but it spoke the language of the white majority, albeit in a different idiom.

II

Republican and proslavery politics already had a long and intimate relationship in South Carolina by the beginning of the antebellum period. Indeed, the vision of the slave republic around which sectional consciousness cohered in the early 1830s had been taking shape in political struggle within the state at least since the constitutional reforms of 1808 and, more alarmingly and visibly, in congressional debate over slavery in the Missouri controversy.[2] But the crucial moment was the Nullification Crisis, when, in the midst of the state's greatest religious revival, South Carolina's antebellum political culture and ideology were forged.

As fire-eater politicians (not a few of whom were, like Robert Barnwell Rhett, newly born again) met the challenge of an unprecedented political mobilization, they embraced the language of evangelicalism and, with it, the faith of its white, primarily yeoman, congregants.[3] Evangelicalism and popular politics were thereafter indissociable in South Carolina. And as the ideological work of slavery took on new urgency in those years, so the defense of slavery, infused with evangelical references, acquired the discursive shape it would maintain until the Civil War. Thus while fire-eaters and moderates would continue to contest

2. Mark D. Kaplanoff, "Charles Pinckney and the American Republican Tradition," in Michael O'Brien and David Moltke-Hansen, eds., *Intellectual Life in Antebellum Charleston* (Knoxville: University of Tennessee Press, 1986), pp. 85–122; Rachel N. Klein, *Unification of a Slave State: The Rise of the Planter Class in the South Carolina Backcountry, 1760–1808* (Chapel Hill: University of North Carolina Press, 1990), esp. pp. 238–68; Mark D. Kaplanoff, "Making the South Solid: Politics and the Structure of Society in South Carolina, 1790–1815" (Ph.D. Diss., Cambridge University, 1979), esp. p. 265.

3. James Petigru Carson, ed., *Life, Letters, and Speeches of James Louis Petigru, the Union Man of South Carolina* (Washington, D.C.: W.H. Lowdermilk and Co., 1920), pp. 85–86, 103–04, 128–29; William Mumford Baker, *The Life and Labours of the Reverend Daniel Baker . . . Prepared by his Son* (1858; reprint ed., Louisville, Ky.: Lost Cause Press, 1961), pp. 133, 155–57, 160–66, 180; Samuel Gaillard Stoney, ed., "The Autobiography of William John Grayson," *South Carolina Historical and Genealogical Magazine*, vols. 48–51 (July 1947-April 1950), 49, no. 1 (January 1948), pp. 33–40. Rhett's conversion is noted in Baker, *Life of Baker*, pp. 188–89. Beech Branch Baptist Church, Beaufort District, Church Book, Sept. 2, 1833, SCL; William W. Freehling, *Prelude to Civil War: The Nullification Controversy in South Carolina, 1816–1836* (New York: Harper and Row, 1965), pp. 73–74.

the particular political uses of proslavery discourses right down to the successful secession campaign of 1860, the representation of the Christian slave republic, forged in the fires of Nullification, was beyond contestation. Proslavery republicanism had become the state religion.

In 1852, in the tense aftermath of the first secession crisis, James Henley Thornwell, minister of the First Presbyterian Church of Columbia and the state's leading Presbyterian spokesman, looked back on the state's struggle for a sectional identity. "We are not alarmists but slavery is implicated in every fibre of southern society," he observed. The world's condemnation of slavery had thus forced southerners into a consideration of the very "nature and organization of society" and "the origin and extent of the rights of man." Southerners had emerged from that philosophical essay, Thornwell concluded with satisfaction, "justified in [their] own consciences" and confident that they had been "eminently conservative in their influence upon the spirit of the age."[4] Evangelicalism, proslavery discourses, and republican politics were inextricably intertwined in antebellum South Carolina.

III

Evangelical ministers did the main work of the proslavery effort, contributing more than half of the tracts ever written in the United States and leaving their imprint clearly on the more secular remainder. In fact, the biblical defense of slavery was the centerpiece of an organic social theory that encompassed far more than the relation of master and slave.[5] To Christian society as family evangelical intellectuals conjoined the metaphor of "a healthful body in which all the limbs and organs perform their appropriate functions without collision or tumult" under the rule of the head. To the Presbyterian minister James Henley Thornwell, the central tenet of that conservative social theory—that "the relation of master and slave stands on the same foot with the other relations of life"—was grounded in scriptural proof. "We find masters exhorted

4. James Henley Thornwell, "Slavery and the Religious Instruction of the Coloured Population," *Southern Presbyterian Review* 4 (July 1850), pp. 110–11.

5. Larry E. Tise, *Proslavery: A History of the Defense of Slavery in America, 1701–1840* (Athens: University of Georgia Press, 1987), esp. p. xvii. For a good introduction to the literature on the biblical defense of slavery see William S. Jenkins, *Pro-Slavery Thought in the Old South* (Gloucester, Mass.: Peter Smith, 1960); Eugene D. Genovese, *The World the Slaveholders Made: Two Essays in Interpretation* (New York: Vintage Books, 1974) and *'Slavery Ordained of God': The Southern Slaveholders' View of Biblical History and Modern Politics* (Gettysburg, Pa.: Gettysburg College, 1985); Drew Gilpin Faust, "Evangelicalism and the Meaning of the Proslavery Argument: The Reverend Thornton Stringfellow of Virginia," *The Virginia Magazine of History and Biography* 85 (January 1977), pp. 3–17; Drew Gilpin Faust, ed., *The Ideology of Slavery: Proslavery Thought in the Antebellum South, 1830–1860* (Baton Rouge: Louisiana State University Press, 1982); Jack P. Maddex, "'The Southern Apostasy' Revisited: The Significance of Proslavery Christianity," *Marxist Perspectives* 2 (Fall 1979), pp. 132–41.

in the same connection with husbands, parents, magistrates," Thornwell among others insisted, "slaves exhorted in the same connection with wives, children and subjects."[6] Their language, too, was familial. Such stitching together of all social relations into the seamless fabric of southern society became the mainstay of proslavery arguments, and it drew proslavery advocates inexorably into a struggle with abolitionists in which the stakes were no less than the nature of society and the republic itself. Thornwell characteristically minced no words: "The parties in this conflict are not merely abolitionists and slaveholders," he railed from the heated perspective of the 1850s. "They are atheists, socialists, communists, red republicans, Jacobins on the one side and the friends of order and regulated freedom on the other." His view of the conflict was widely shared by ministers of every denomination and politicians of both radical and moderate stripe.[7]

It was not only evangelical intellectuals and politicians who were disposed to such a broad construction of the struggle. Lowcountry yeomen too counted themselves among the friends of order and regulated freedom. They were no more drawn to abolitionists' insistence that the "essential equality of men implies a corresponding equality of state" than were their ministers, or to the view that slavery violated the natural equality of man. Slavery was for them in the first instance a moral question, one that could be resolved only on scriptural ground. So when ministers like Thornwell argued that "opposition to slavery has never been the offspring of the Bible" but "of visionary theories of human nature and society—from the misguided reason of man," when they argued, in short, that abolitionists were atheists, yeoman evangelicals

6. Thornwell, "Religious Instruction," p. 134; James Henley Thornwell, "Report on Slavery," *Southern Presbyterian Review* 5 (January 1852), pp. 383–84; Iveson L. Brookes, *A Defense of the South Against the Reproaches and Encroachments of the North* (Hamburg, S.C.: Printed at the Republican Office, 1850), esp. p. 28. See also Iveson L. Brookes, *A Defense of Southern Slavery: Against the Attacks of Henry Clay and Alexander Campbell . . .* (Hamburg, S.C.: Robinson and Carlisle, 1851), pp. 19–20; Thomas Smyth, D.D., *The Sin and the Curse: or, The Union, The True Source of Disunion, and Our Duty in the Present Crisis* (November 1860), reprinted in *Complete Works of Rev. Thomas Smyth, D.D.*, ed., J. William Flinn, 10 vols. (Columbia, S.C.: R.L. Bryan Co., 1908–1912), 7: 544. Similar arguments were used by politicians. See William Harper, "Memoir on Slavery," *Southern Literary Journal* 3, no. 1 (January 1838), pp. 65–75, esp. pp. 68–69; *Southern Literary Journal* 3, no. 2 (February 1838), pp. 81–97, esp. pp. 89–90; *Southern Literary Journal* 3, no. 3, (March 1838), pp. 1–75; *Southern Literary Journal* 3, no. 4 (April 1838), pp. 241–51; *Southern Literary Journal* 3, no. 5 (May 1838), pp. 321–28; Hammond, "Hammond's Letters on Slavery," pp. 125–26, 154–55, 161–63.

7. Thornwell, "Report on Slavery," p. 391. For radical politicians' views, see Hammond, "Hammond's Letters on Slavery," esp. p. 174; Robert Barnwell Rhett, "Address to the People of Beaufort and Colleton Districts Upon the Subject of Abolition," January 15, 1838, Robert Barnwell Rhett Papers, SCL, esp. pp. 6–7. For moderates' views, see Robert Nicholas Olsberg, "A Government of Class and Race: William Henry Trescot and the South Carolina Chivalry, 1860–1865" (Ph.D. Diss., University of South Carolina, 1972), pp. 100–04, 115, 122–23; John Townsend, *The South Alone Should Govern the South* (Charleston: Evans and Cogswell, 1860), pp. 9–10.

were disposed to agree.[8] Everything about local evangelical life in the Low Country, from church covenants to gospel discipline, contradicted the abolitionists' view of the moral imperatives of Christian society.

Throughout the antebellum period and even earlier in South Carolina, ministers and politicians scored the philosophy of natural rights and universal equality as "well-sounding but unmeaning verbiage." As early as 1807 one of the state's leading Baptist ministers, Richard Furman, had offered as "the order of providence that a considerable portion of the Human race must necessarily move in a humble sphere and be generally at the disposal of their fellow men." Thirty years later William Harper, the South Carolina lawyer, judge, politician and fierce defender of slavery, elaborated the point in what became a famous contribution to proslavery literature. "[I]s it not palpably nearer the truth to say that no man was ever born free and that no two men were ever born equal?" he asked. His answer was already, by 1838, a predictable one: "Wealth and poverty . . . strength and weakness . . . ease and labor, power or subjection, make the endless diversity in the condition of man."[9] Politicians and ministers alike struggled to formulate a "Christian Doctrine of Human Rights and Slavery," as the Charleston minister John B. Adger's contribution was titled. "An absolute equality among men . . . neither has existed nor does exist . . . nor is yet anywhere demanded by the Scriptures," Adger insisted, mixing secular and scriptural proof in typically promiscuous fashion.[10]

Instead of natural rights and universal equality, Harper, Adger, Thornwell, and others offered an elaborate theory of providential relations and particular rights that bore striking resemblance to the views articulated in local evangelical congregations. As Adger explained, all human beings did not have identical rights but only the ones that attached to their particular social role. In the Christian republic, wives did not have the rights of husbands, or slaves the rights of masters; rather, "a husband [had] the rights of a husband . . . a father the rights of a father; and a slave, only the rights of a slave." Slaves thus could not claim the rights of citizens. Those were not, Thornwell explained, "essential,"

8. Thornwell, "Religious Instruction," pp. 117–18, 114.

9. Harper, "Memoir on Slavery," *Southern Literary Journal* 3, no. 1 (January 1838), esp. pp. 71, 68; Furman quoted in Tise, *Proslavery*, p. 40. For biographical information on Harper, see Faust, *Ideology of Slavery*, pp. 78–79. See also Whitemarsh B. Seabrook, *An Essay on the Management of Slaves and Especially on Their Religious Instruction* (Charleston: A.E. Miller, 1834), p. 6; John B. Adger, "The Christian Doctrine of Human Rights and Slavery," *Southern Presbyterian Review* 11 (March 1849), esp. pp. 570–71; Whitefoord Smith, *National Sins: A Call to Repentance* . . . (Charleston: n.p., 1849), p. 18; Thornwell, "Religious Instruction," pp. 108–09, 130, 133–36, 140–41, and "Report on Slavery," pp. 387–88, 390–91; Brookes, *Defense of the South*, pp. 8, 19–22, 30, 34; Hammond, "Hammond's Letters on Slavery," pp. 109–10; and James Henry Hammond, *Are Working Men Slaves? The Question Discussed by Senators Hammond, Broderick and Wilson* (n.p., 1858), p. 3.

10. Adger, "Christian Doctrine," pp. 569–71.

meaning that they did not "spring from humanity simply considered, for then they would belong to women and children, but from humanity in such and such relations." Where rights were particular, so were duties, and proslavery theory came complete with its own version of the Golden Rule. "Do unto others," Thornwell explained, did not mean, as abolitionists insisted, that "I am bound to emancipate my slave because if the tables were turned . . . I should covet this boon from him." Rather the Rule required that "we should treat our slaves as we should feel we had a right to be treated if we were slaves ourselves—do right, in other words, as you would claim right." Above all else, then, good Christians must "be content to remain in God's hands, doing their duty in the place he has appointed them." They were not, it is clear, prescribing only to slaves. Religion, the Reverend Whitefoord Smith cautioned, "teaches contentment with the lot in life which Heaven assigns to each." Sophisticated formulations of the "providential status of society's relations" were offered to South Carolinians, but the middle country Baptist minister Iveson Brookes put it simply for the benefit of his congregation. He found no good substitute for the Pauline original: "Let everyman abide in the same calling wherein he was called." Slavery occupied no anomalous category in lowcountry social thought, and its defense became inseparable from that of Christian and conservative social order.[11]

The real measure of the effectiveness of proslavery arguments, as politicians were acutely aware, was the breadth of their social appeal, which explains, no doubt, the wide cast of the philosophical net. For the ideological work of slavery assumed the greatest significance precisely where it confronted the greatest challenge: in holding nonslaveholders and small slaveholders to planters within a common system of meanings and values. In reaching beyond masters and slaves to all relations of southern households, proslavery publicists bid for the loyalties of all white male adults. They repeatedly reminded white southerners of every class that slavery could not be disentangled from other relations of power and privilege and that it represented simply the most extreme and absolute form of the legal and customary dependencies that characterized the Old South—and their own households.

The conjoining of all domestic relations of domination and subordination enabled proslavery spokesmen to tap beliefs about the legitimacy of inequality that went, and sadly still go, so deep in the individual psyche and social structure that for most historians they are unrecognizable as the subject of history. In the dual task of painting the abolitionist

11. Adger, "Christian Doctrine," p. 573. See also Benjamin Morgan Palmer, "Thanksgiving Sermon" (1860), quoted in Thomas Cary Johnson, *The Life and Letters of Benjamin Morgan Palmer* (Richmond, Va.: Presbyterian Committee of Publication, 1906), pp. 212–13; Thornwell, "Religious Instruction," pp. 134–36; Smith, *National Sins*, p. 18; Smyth quoted in E. Brookes Holifield, *The Gentlemen Theologians: American Theology in Southern Culture, 1795–1860* (Durham, N.C.: Duke University Press, 1978), pp. 151–52; Brookes, *Defense of the South*, p. 28.

image of social disorder and their own benevolent and peaceful social order, proslavery spokesmen returned repeatedly to gender relations, exploiting assumptions about the "natural" relations of men and women. On the common ground of gender they sought to ensure that every white man recognized his own investment in the national struggle over slavery.

William Harper early demonstrated the power of that approach, playing the trump card of gender inequality to give the lie to the philosophy of the Declaration of Independence. "[W]hat is the foundation of the bold dogma so confidently announced?" he asked. "Females are human and rational beings. They may be found . . . better qualified to exercise political privileges and to attain the distinctions of society than many men; yet who complains of the order of society by which they are excluded from them?"[12] Who indeed? Not yeoman farmers whose own households and community institutions embodied precisely that principle. The transhistorical subordination of women was presented as incontestable proof that social and political inequality were natural.

In the lexicon of metaphors for slavery, marriage took pride of place, a discursive construction historians have rarely recognized.[13] No other relation was more universally embraced as both natural and divine, and none so readily evoked the stake of enfranchised white men, yeomen and planters alike, in the defense of slave society. By equating the subordination of women with that of slaves, proslavery ministers and politicians attempted to endow slavery with the legitimacy of the family and especially marriage and, not incidentally, to invest the defense of slavery with the survival of customary gender relations.[14] In this sense, the subordination of women bore a great deal of the ideological weight of

12. Harper, "Memoir on Slavery," *Southern Literary Journal* 3, no. 1 (January 1838), pp. 68–69.

13. For use of the marriage metaphor, see the following: Harper, "Memoir on Slavery," *Southern Literary Journal* 3, no. 1 (January 1838), pp. 68–69, 89–90, 165; L.S.M. [Louisa Susannah McCord], "Enfranchisement of Woman" (1852), in Michael O'Brien, ed., *All Clever Men Who Make Their Way: Critical Discourse in the Old South* (Fayetteville: University of Arkansas Press, 1982), pp. 337–56; Richard Fuller, quoted in J. H. Cuthbert, *Life of Richard Fuller, D.D.* (New York: Sheldon and Co., 1879), pp. 194–96; Hammond, "Hammond's Letters on Slavery," pp. 125–26, 154–55; Thornwell, "Report on Slavery," pp. 383–85; William M. Wightman, *Life of William Capers, D.D.* (Nashville, Tenn.: Southern Methodist Publishing House, 1859), p. 296; Thornton Stringfellow, "A Brief Examination of Scripture Testimony on the Institution of Slavery," in Faust, ed., *Ideology of Slavery*, pp. 156–57, 144–45; Henry Hughes, "Treatise on Sociology," in ibid., pp. 262–63; George Fitzhugh, "Southern Thought," in ibid., pp. 291–95, and Fitzhugh, *Cannibals All!: Or, Slaves Without Masters* (1857; reprint ed., Cambridge, Mass.: John Harvard Library, 1960), pp. 95–97.

14. I mean the analogy of women and slaves to be understood specifically as an ideological construction. I do not mean to suggest that white women's legal or social position was analogous to that of slaves. The latter interpretation has been offered in various forms by Anne Firor Scott, *The Southern Lady: From Pedestal to Politics, 1830–1930* (Chicago: University of Chicago Press, 1970), esp. pp. 45–79; Catherine Clinton, *The Plantation Mistress: Woman's World in the Old South* (New York: Pantheon Books, 1982), esp. pp. 16–35.

slavery, providing the most concrete example of how public and private distinctions were confounded in political discourse and culture.

IV

Women's nature and their appropriate social role became, perhaps as never before, a matter of political concern all over the country in the antebellum period. But they assumed added political significance in the South, where their fate was shackled to that of slavery. While southern republican discourse, like its northern variants, had long depended on gendered language and images, the specific analogy of slaves with women, masters with husbands, and slavery with marriage appears, in the late 1830s, to have replaced an older emphasis on the family in general and fathers and children in particular.[15] Perhaps the shift marked the need to put a more modern and benevolent face on familial authority (marriage was, after all, voluntary) as evangelical reformers urged masters to push the institution into conformity with its Christian ideal; it almost certainly reflected a new self-consciousness about gender relations and ideology provoked by the heated contestations of the antebellum period.

In proslavery discourses, religious and secular, the analogy of marriage and slavery functioned in a number of ways, not least of which was to police the boundaries of "women's sphere," glorifying women within it, vilifying them out of it. And while there was some, not insignificant, disagreement over precisely what those boundaries were—over, for example, the innate intelligence of women, the content or curriculum of female education, and women's responsibility in upholding southern civilization—there was also a clear and common sense of what constituted women's proper "sphere," or, at least, what constituted a transgression of it. "Providence . . . and her own endowments mark out the proper province of women," the Reverend Mr. Howe asserted confidently in 1850. "[T]o rule with the hand of power was never designed for her. When she thus unsexes herself she is despised by women and men alike." The references, as if not obvious enough, he laid out explicitly: "When women go about haranguing promiscuous assemblies of men, lecturing in public on infidelity, or religion, or slavery, on war and peace—when they meet together in organized bodies and pass resolu-

15. See the familial metaphors in Richard Furman, *Exposition of the Views of the Baptists Relative to the Coloured Population of the United States* (1823; Charleston, A.E. Miller 1833), p. 10. Also see the discussion in Linda K. Kerber, *Women of the Republic: Intellect and Ideology in Revolutionary America* (Chapel Hill: University of North Carolina Press, 1980); Ruth H. Bloch, "The Gendered Meanings of Virtue in Revolutionary America," *Signs* 13 (Autumn 1987), pp. 37–58; Jean Gunderson, "Independence, Citizenship and the American Revolution," *Signs* 13 (Autumn 1987), pp. 59–77; Christine Stansell, *City of Women: Sex and Class in New York, 1789–1860* (New York: Alfred A. Knopf, 1986), pp. 20–30.

tions about the 'rights of woman,' and claim for her a voice and vote in
the appointment of civil rules, and in the government, she is stepping
forth from her rightful sphere and becomes disgusting and unlovely,
just in proportion as she assumes to be a man." Howe and other ministers and politicians cautioned lowcountry women against the most radical transgressions of women's sphere, but they never neglected the local
agenda. Power tempted in many forms. It is "fit" that women should
recognize their subordination, Reverend Benjamin Morgan Palmer proclaimed, boiling the point down for the benefit of his female audience,
"for anything else would be unnatural, monstrous, and grotesque."[16]
The message could hardly have been lost on lowcountry women of any
class, accustomed as they were to witnessing the chastisement of women
such as Mary Hort and Sister Roberts for far more modest assumptions
of female authority.[17] A great anxiety on the subject of women's nature
and social role suffused proslavery discourses and in the threats and
prescriptions of the proslavery voices the disciplinary intent was clear. So
was the political one. The legitimacy of male authority over women
within the household was a cornerstone of the slavery edifice.

But if the analogy of slavery with marriage reflected a growing self-
consciousness about the contingency of gender relations, there can be no
doubt that it reflected as well the need to put the defense of slavery on
the broadest possible social basis and the utility of the metaphor of

16. George Howe, *The Endowments, Position and Education of Woman* . . . (Columbia,
S.C.: I.C. Morgan, 1850), pp. 10–12; Benjamin Morgan Palmer, *The Family in its Civil and
Churchly Aspects: An Essay in Two Parts* (Richmond: Richmond Presbyterian Committee of
Publication, 1876), p. 69. Although published after the war, Palmer's book was based on
sermons delivered in the antebellum years and includes chapters on "The Authority of
Masters" and "The Subjection of Slaves." For other contributions to the genre see J. Edwin
Spears, "An Address Delivered at the Examination of the Female School of Bennetsville,
June 9, 1859," in Louis Manigault Papers, Perkins Library, DU; John Belton O'Neall, *An
Address on Female Education Delivered at the Request of the Trustees of the Johnson Female Semi-
nary at Anderson, S.C. on Friday, 3rd August, 1849* (Anderson, S.C.: Printed at the Gazette
Office, 1849); William Porcher Miles, *Women "Nobly Planned": How to Educate Our Girls,* in
South Carolina Education Pamphlets, College Addresses 1 (Columbia, S.C.: n.p., n.d.). Although
this chapter focuses on nonfictional discourses, the most expansive claims for the political
significance of women's role and sphere in sustaining southern civilization were offered by
domestic fiction writers. There was little, according to Sarah Moss, however, that rendered
their view of women's sphere incompatible with that presented in texts authored by men.
See Sarah Elizabeth Moss, "'Our Earnest Appeal': The Southern Domestic Novelists and
Their Literary Defense of Southern Culture, 1833–1866," (Ph.D. Diss., Washington University, 1989).

17. Tracts such as that of Reverend George Howe quoted above found yeoman audiences in South Carolina in their original oral form as sermons and commencement addresses. One upcountry yeoman woman, Mary Davis Brown, noted on commencement day
at the female college in her area that "theire is a great crowd of people a gethered theire
and Eliza Ann and Emily Jane [her two eldest daughters] is gone." Mary Davis Brown
Diary, June 30, 1856, SCL. On the purpose of southern women's education see Steven
Stowe, "The Not-So-Cloistered Academy: Elite Women's Education and Family Feeling in
the Old South," in Walter J. Fraser, Jr., et al., eds., *The Web of Southern Social Relations:
Women, Family, and Education* (Athens: University of Georgia Press, 1985), pp. 90–106.

marriage in that unceasing effort. Although ministers continued to use the familial metaphor generally defined, insisting, for example, that "a Christian slave must be submissive, faithful, and obedient for reasons of the same authority with those which oblige husband, wives, fathers, mothers, brothers, sisters, to fulfill the duties of those relations," they increasingly focused on the relation of husbands and wives. In the family, that "model state," Benjamin Morgan Palmer explained, "subjection to law" originated with the authority of man "as the head of the woman." By the time dutiful subjection was prescribed to the "servant," it had "already been exemplified to the child, not only in the headship of the husband, but in the wifely obedience which is its commentary."[18]

The metaphor of marriage had much to recommend it to proslavery ministers and politicians. But it was not without its problems, as they admitted. The most obvious was the matter of volition: Wives' submission was voluntary, while that of slaves was not. Nevertheless, the problem of the analogy of husband and wife was more easily negotiated than that of parent and child. After all, male children grew up to lay claim in adulthood to the prerogatives of husbands, fathers, and masters. Female children, on the other hand, became wives; they remained, like slaves, perpetual children, at least in relation to masters. The rice planter and one-time governor R. F. W. Allston literally enscribed this planter model of romantic love in letters to his wife by addressing them to "my dear child," while one plantation mistress, for her part, thanked the "Heavenly Father" for a husband who had "just such a master will as suits my woman's nature." Females provided the only constant point of reference for naturalizing subordination.[19]

At another level, though, one cannot help but speculate that ideologues found a great deal more psychological satisfaction in likening slaves to women than to children. For the rebelliousness of women, like that of slaves, was a specter only summoned to be banished. Women were "crowned with that sense of dependence out of which submission springs as instinct," Palmer noted, burying the wish in the assertion. But few, including Palmer himself, were willing to trust such important matters to nature or instinct, insisting in addition, though by no means logically, that woman was "ennobled" by her choice to submit. As Palmer put it, "[H]er husband becomes to her a crown and a covering as soon as she sees in him the representative of God in her. . . . Her subjection to [him] takes on a religious character." By insisting that women chose to

18. Wightman, *Life of Capers*, p. 296; Palmer, *The Family*, pp. 10–12, 15, 35–36, 50, 69. The relevant secondary literature on paternalism in the slave South is extensive, but see especially Eugene D. Genovese, *Roll, Jordan, Roll: The World the Slaves Made* (New York: Pantheon Books, 1974).

19. R. F. W. Allston to Mrs. Allston, March 11, June 2, 1850, quoted in William W. Freehling, *The Road to Disunion: Secessionists at Bay, 1776–1854* (New York: Oxford University Press, 1990), pp. 52–53; Gertrude Thomas Diary, July 9, 1852, April 11, 1856, quoted in ibid., p. 53.

submit (a suspect formulation when one considers the options), men were, in effect, denying the personal power they knew women to exercise over them, however temporarily, in romantic and sexual love. Dependence on women was unmanly (even in love), where manhood orbited around the display of independence. Hence, arguments about female submission not only naturalized slavery; they confirmed masculinity.[20] Little wonder that proslavery men went to such lengths to prove that women's subordination was grounded in nature and sanctioned by God. Their hearts were surely in the job.

In their efforts to prove the "natural" subordination of women, moreover, they faced no shortage of materials. Assumptions about "the different mental and moral organization of the sexes" infused southern society and culture, and it was not, as a result, difficult to "prove" that the subordination of women followed nature's directives. "Each [sex] is the best in its place," Palmer reasoned. "The distinction of sex runs through the entire nature of both . . . [and] forbids the comparison between the two."[21] The question of equality was thereby answered in the usual particularistic fashion.

Notions about the different physiological, psychological, and moral constitution of the sexes were clearly not peculiar to the slave South; they had steadily gained currency throughout the western world since at least the late eighteenth century.[22] And while there is always reason for skepticism about separate-but-equal constructions even in their bourgeois form as many historians have pointed out, arguments about the

20. Palmer, *The Family,* pp. 55, 70–71. Other views of the divine origin of female subordination are to be found in the following: Charles Colcock Jones, *The Glory of Woman is the Fear of the Lord* (Philadelphia: William S. Martien, 1847), pp. 17, 22; Thomas Smyth, *Mary Not a Perpetual Virgin, Nor the Mother of God . . . Together with a View of the True Position, Duty and Liberty of a Woman, Under the Gospel Dispensation* (Charleston: B. Jenkins, 1846). For an interesting discussion of the psychological dimensions of manhood and independence in republican discourses, see Elizabeth Colwill, "Transforming Women's Empire: Representations of Women in French Political Culture, 1770–1807 (Ph.D. Diss., State University of New York at Binghamton, 1990).

21. Palmer, *The Family,* pp. 55–56, 28, 30, 36–37, 45, 64. Similar views were expressed in Jones, *The Glory of Woman;* Smyth, *Mary Not a Perpetual Virgin;* Howe, *The Endowments . . . of Woman;* Miles, *Women "Nobly Planned";* O'Neall, *An Address on Female Education;* and, especially, Thomas R. Dew, "On the Characteristic Differences Between the Sexes, and on the Position and Influence of Woman in Society," *Southern Literary Messenger* 1, (May, July, August 1835), 1, (May 1835), pp. 493–512; *Southern Literary Messenger,* 1, (July 1835), pp. 621–32; *Southern Literary Messenger,* 1, (August 1835), pp. 675–91.

22. Thomas Laqueur, *Making Sex: Body and Gender From the Greeks to Freud* (Cambridge, Mass.: Harvard University Press, 1990), esp. pp. 149–92. The literature on the antebellum North is now extensive but for a few key contributions see Nancy F. Cott, *The Bonds of Womanhood: Woman's Sphere in New England, 1780–1835* (New Haven: Yale University Press, 1977); Kathryn Kish Sklar, *Catherine Beecher: A Study in American Domesticity* (New Haven: Yale University Press, 1973); Carroll Smith-Rosenberg, *Disorderly Conduct: Visions of Gender in Victorian America* (New York: Oxford University Press, 1985); Jeanne Boydston, Mary Kelley, and Anne Margolis, eds., *The Limits of Sisterhood: The Beecher Sisters on Women's Rights and Woman's Sphere* (Chapel Hill: University of North Carolina Press, 1988).

complementarity of the sexes in the South put at best a transparent gloss on relations of domination. "Submission . . . will yield all that is incumbent upon the wife," Palmer insisted, as if to prove the point. "Dependence . . . is not her degradation but her glory," and man must learn to distinguish "betwixt subordination and inferiority." The distinction was a handy one for proslavery publicists. As George Fitzhugh noted in characteristically direct fashion, "[M]arriage is too much like slavery not to be involved in its fate."[23]

Marriage did lend itself nicely to comparison with slavery, or rather the proslavery view of marriage did, and lowcountry ministers and politicians were quick to exploit it. God had ordained a position for slaves in the inevitable hierarchy of society, they argued, with particular rights and duties attached to it. Slaves, like women, were fitted by nature to conform comfortably to their place, and slavery, like marriage, was a relationship of "reciprocal interest" that ensured that a "due subordination is preserved between the classes which would otherwise be thrown into sharp antagonism." From their perspective, although not, perhaps, from that of white southern women, marriage was a benign metaphor for slavery. For while the metaphor enshrined male dominance and female subordination, it attempted to cast both in a benevolent light.[24]

Yet the likeness of women and slaves, despite ideological claims, ultimately resided not in the subjects' natural fitness for subordination but in the masters' power to command it. "Is it not natural that a man should be attached to that which is his own?" William Harper queried, wresting benevolence from the self-interest that allegedly secured women and slaves protection from their masters' brutality. "Do not men everywhere contract kind feelings to their dependents?" If women found this an imperfect protection, as Harper inadvertently admitted, slaves surely did too. But the striking feature of the analogy was their common status as "his," as "dependents" who lacked, as Harper said repeatedly, self-ownership. A "freeman" was one who was "master of his own time and action. . . . To submit to a blow would be degrading to a freeman," he wrote, "because he is the protector of himself." But it was "not degrading to a slave—neither is it . . . to a woman."[25] Thus, in proslavery discourses the metaphor of marriage worked in complex ways. It did not, in the last analysis, constrain the masters' boundless power; rather, it confirmed that power by locating the only restraint on the exercise of it in the hands of the masters themselves. The metaphor's multivalence, and

23. Palmer, *The Family*, pp. 49, 36; George Fitzhugh quoted in Dorothy Ann Gay, "The Tangled Skein of Romanticism and Violence in the Old South: The Southern Response to Abolitionism and Feminism, 1830–1861" (Ph.D. Diss., University of North Carolina, 1975), p. 126.

24. Palmer, *The Family*, pp. 35–37, 45, 125, 147–68. For one yeoman woman's heroic struggle for a submissiveness supposedly instinctual, see Mary Davis Brown Diary.

25. Harper, "Memoir on Slavery," *Southern Literary Journal* 3, no. 2, (February 1838), pp. 94, 89–90; *Southern Literary Journal* 3, no. 3, (March 1838), pp. 163–68.

particularly its manipulation of benevolence and power, explains its political efficacy.

In their efforts to impress on ordinary southerners the seamlessness of the social fabric proslavery writers were afforded assistance from the most unlikely of quarters. In the 1830s a handful of Garrisonian abolitionists also came to the conviction that slavery and the subordination of women were inseparable and that conventional gender relations were at stake in the national struggle over slavery. As that radical minority of abolitionists forged its own position in struggle and, indeed, in schism with the mainstream of the antislavery movement, it forever changed the meaning of the analogy of women and slaves by mounting a progressive challenge to its emergent reactionary proslavery construction. Abby Kelley, a committed Garrisonian and a leading figure in the antebellum woman's rights movement, articulated the radical meaning most concretely in acknowledging a debt of gratitude to slaves: "In striving to strike his irons off, we found most surely that we were manacled ourselves." Garrisonians' yoking of the subordination of women and slaves and their public commitment to a dual emancipation proved a perfect foil for proslavery politics.[26]

Although the analogical construction heralded a new political movement of unprecedented sort on American shores, Kelley was hardly the first to use it. Indeed the analogy of marriage and slavery, or "sex slavery," was by the 1830s an established one in western political discourses. Connections between political and domestic revolution—between monarchy and marriage, for example—had been part of radical critiques of illegitimate power in England since at least the late seventeenth century and by the late eighteenth century had become commonplace in both radical and conservative tracts. While British conservatives used images of domestic revolt to conjure up the specter of revolutionary disorder in Jacobin France or, for that matter, in England itself, a handful of radical thinkers extended the critique of illegitimate power from state to family though the concept of "domestic slavery," to use Mary Wollstonecraft's formulation. Even the analogy to black slavery was not original to the

26. Abby Kelley quoted in Blanche Glassman Hersh, *The Slavery of Sex: Feminist-Abolitionists in America* (Urbana: University of Illinois Press, 1978), pp. 20–21. Use of the analogy by first-generation women's rights activists is exemplified in the writings of Sarah Grimké and Angelina Grimké. See Elizabeth Ann Bartlett, ed., *Sarah Grimké: Letters on the Equality of the Sexes and Other Essays* (New Haven: Yale University Press, 1988); and Angelina Grimké, *Letters to Catherine Beecher*, reprinted in *The Feminist Papers: From Adams to de Beauvoir*, ed. Alice S. Rossi (New York: Columbia University Press, 1973), pp. 319–22. The literature on abolitionism and women's rights is now vast, but see Gerda Lerner, *The Grimké Sisters From South Carolina* (New York: Schocken Books, 1967); Ellen C. DuBois, *Feminism and Suffrage: The Emergence of an Independent Women's Movement in America* (Ithaca, N.Y.: Cornell University Press, 1978); Nancy Hewitt, *Women's Activism and Social Change: Rochester, New York, 1822-1872* (Ithaca, N.Y.: Cornell University Press, 1984); Jean Fagan Yellin, *Women and Sisters: The Antislavery Feminists in American Culture* (New Haven: Yale University Press, 1989); Lori D. Ginzberg, *Women and the Work of Benevolence* (New Haven: Yale University Press, 1990).

Garrisonians. For as the antislavery movement had gained momentum in England, "domestic slavery" had acquired new social and political referents and, by the mid-1820s in the hands of Owenites like William Thompson, new meaning in analogies between the unfree status of West Indian slaves and that of British women. From Mary Astell to Mary Wollstonecraft to William Thompson, the history of the radical tradition has been written largely through the efforts of feminist historians and theorists. But although it has not commanded anything like the same scholarly attention, it is abundantly clear that the radical and conservative streams of this tradition developed in tandem and that conservative uses of the analogy were no less deeply entrenched than were radical ones by the middle of the nineteenth century. It is hard to avoid the conclusion, then, that the analogy of marriage and slavery lay at the very center of political discourse in the Atlantic world in the nineteenth century and that the entire contested discourse of antebellum Americans was well developed by the time proslavery South Carolinians and New England abolitionists staked out their positions in the 1830s.[27]

If all men should have "equal rights," more than one South Carolinian had worried since Harper raised the possibility, "then why not women?" That some northern women abolitionists, and some male ones too, asked the same question lent credibility to proslavery threats.[28] The Garrisonians' radical actions in the late 1830s and 1840s lent new fervor and detail to standard comparisons of the natural, divine, and benevolent social order of the slave South and the chaos of the revolutionary North, now embodied in the dual specter of abolitionism and feminism. No more dramatic illustration of the political significance of domestic, and especially gender, relations could have been imagined. South Carolinian politicians exploited it for all it was worth.

It was not difficult for ministers and politicians to convince lowcountry yeomen, among others, that abolitionists really threatened a violent end to Christian society as they knew it. By the late 1830s the connection between Garrisonian abolitionism and women's rights had already found firm root in the American political imagination, planted there by

27. On the British radical tradition, see, for example, the outstanding discussion of "sex slavery" in Barbara Taylor, *Eve and the New Jerusalem: Socialism and Feminism in the Nineteenth Century* (London: Virago Press, 1983), pp. 32–48; Mary Wollstonecraft, *A Vindication of the Rights of Woman*, ed. Carol H. Poston (New York: W. W. Norton, 1988), pp. 5, 45, 51–52, and passim. The point is well developed too in the historical literature on the woman's rights movement in antebellum America. See Hersh, *The Slavery of Sex,* and the other books cited in n. 26 above. By contrast, the literature on proslavery politics and discourses misses the mark. Larry Tise, for example, makes no mention of it at all in a recent and very lengthy treatment of proslavery ideology in the United States. See Tise, *Proslavery.*

28. Quotation from Gay, "Tangled Skein," p. 131; Dew, "On the Characteristic Differences Between the Sexes." The best evidence is the commonplace yoking of abolitionism and feminism, often through ridicule and humor. See *Orangeburg Southron,* June 11, 1856, and February 13, 1860; *Beaufort Enterprise,* October 10, 1860; John L. Mannning to his wife, May 29, 1860, Box V, Folder 172, Williams-Chesnut-Manning Families Papers, SCL.

the uncompromising actions of women like Angelina Grimké. And if Grimké's appearance before a committee of the Massachusetts legislature in 1838 sent shock waves throughout the South, the impression was nowhere so intense as in South Carolina, her native state.[29] But the outraged and fearful response to Garrisonian-feminism was not confined to South Carolina, nor even to the states below the Mason-Dixon line; it was mirrored north of slavery, providing compelling evidence of how deeply gender undergirded conceptions of social and political order.

William Lloyd Garrison was no doubt right when he declared in 1837 that "the proslavery heads and tails of society know not what to do, when *WOMAN* stands forth to plead the cause of her degraded, chain-bound sex." His exultant tone was surely misplaced, however, for he soon discovered, if he did not already know, that similar resistance to female emancipation, much of it issuing from evangelical churches, cut deeply into his political support in the North. Indeed, there was a striking, and even suspicious, resemblance between some of the anti-woman's rights, anti-Garrisonian formulations of conservative northern clergy and proslavery southern versions. When the General Association of Massachusetts (Orthodox) Ministers, in response to Angelina Grimké's highly publicized antislavery lecture tour in 1837, issued a pastoral letter that denounced as "unnatural" any woman who "assumes the place and tone of a man as a public reformer," they may well have provided the script for South Carolinian George Howe's 1850 pontification on the "Endowments [read nature], Position and Education of Woman." Northern resistance to Garrisonians was by no means limited to the ranks of conservative clergymen moreover. In the early 1840s, conflict over the issue of women's rights provoked a split within the ranks of the broader antislavery movement as well.[30] Although their radicalism may have found its limits on the prerogatives of capital, Garrisonian abolitionists and women's rights advocates nonetheless did, as their proslavery adversaries charged, issue ringing challenges to traditional authority and privilege— to chattel property, the church, and, it would seem, most threatening of all, male supremacy.[31]

29. Lerner, *The Grimké Sisters of South Carolina*, pp. 226–42; Yellin, *Women and Sisters*, pp. 29–52.

30. William Lloyd Garrison, quoted in Yellin, *Women and Sisters*, pp. 189, n. 34, 44–51; "From a Pastoral Letter, 'The General Association (Orthodox) to the Churches Under Their Care'" (1837), reprinted in *The Feminist Papers*, ed. Rossi, pp. 305–06; Howe, *The Endowments . . . of Woman*. See also Ronald G. Walters, *The Antislavery Appeal: American Abolitionism After 1830* (New York: W. W. Norton, 1978), pp. 3–18; Tise, *Proslavery*, pp. 261–85; Leonard Richards, *Gentlemen of Property and Standing: Anti-Abolitionist Mobs in the North* (New York: Oxford University Press, 1970), pp. 56–61.

31. Jonathan A. Glickstein, "'Poverty is not Slavery': American Abolitionists and the Competitive Labor Market," in Lewis Perry and Michael Fellman, eds., *Antislavery Reconsidered: New Perspectives on the Abolitionists* (Baton Rouge: Louisiana State University Press, 1979); David Brion Davis, *The Problem of Slavery in the Age of Revolution, 1770–1823* (Ithaca, N.Y.: Cornell University Press, 1975), esp. pp. 435–68.

The radical and emancipatory analogy of women and slaves, the one embraced by Abby Kelley and her abolitionist-women's rights allies, is the one with which we are now most familiar. But it is perhaps the conservative power of the analogy, in its different northern and southern uses, that best captures antebellum meanings. In the South, where the household gave palpable form to the common dependency of women and slaves, the analogy buttressed an aggressive proslavery Christian republicanism. In the North, in contrast, a commitment to customary gender relations did not sustain a proslavery politics, but it did work to conservative effect. For the Free Soil direction of popular antislavery activity in the 1850s appears to have been due, at least in part, to a social conservatism, particularly marked on matters of gender, and a general reluctance to envision the reconstruction of social relations according to liberal principles of equal rights as Garrisonians envisioned them.[32] At the very least, the conflict over gender relations and ideology within even the progressive ranks of northern republicanism helps to explain the centrality and power of gender in proslavery discourses.

It is not so surprising, then, that one of the most powerful and coherent proslavery tracts to come out of South Carolina, a virtual model of conservative reasoning, was written to meet the challenge of the woman suffrage movement. Louisa Susanna Cheves McCord argued in her 1852 article that the "Enfranchisement of Woman" was "but a piece with negro emancipation." Advocates of woman's rights such as Harriet Martineau ("This Wilberforce of women") do southerners a favor, McCord insisted, in standing "exactly where they should be, cheek by jowl with the abolitionists. We thank them, at least, for saving us the trouble of proving this position." Yet prove it she did attempt to do, and the evidence she adduced was an amalgam of by then classic proslavery positions. She began with the usual mocking references to natural rights: "Mounted on Cuffee's shoulders, in rides the Lady. The genius of communism bows them both in, mouthing over Mr. Jefferson's free and equal sentence." She then turned to the inevitable contrast of northern and southern society: Whereas southerners were "conservatives" who had accepted "God-given distinctions of sex and race" and sought reform by working with "Nature's Laws," northerners' unnatural principles inevitably produced unnatural spectacles. Here McCord took an old genre to new depths, calling suffragists those "petticoated despisers of their sex . . . would-be men . . . moral monsters . . . things which nature disclaims." Women on top, the world indeed turned upside down, McCord

---

32. The problem with the analogy of women and slaves, in both its feminist and its proslavery uses, is that it worked to occlude class differences between women (by which both camps invariably meant free white women) and slaves (by which they meant male slaves). Given the centrality of the analogy in antebellum history and its enduring political appeal to feminists, the problem deserves a separate treatment. On the antislavery platform of the Republican party, see Eric Foner, *Free Soil, Free Labor, Free Men: The Ideology of the Republican Party before the Civil War* (New York: Oxford University Press, 1970).

conjured up the most fundamental image of social disorder to demonstrate that reform threatened nothing less than revolution and to remind southerners that where all relations of power were connected, the assault on privilege would not stop short of anarchy—or the threshold of their own households.[33]

In the most literal sense, the subordination of women was at issue in the struggle over slavery. In another sense, the larger question was the social and political status of dependents, men and women alike, and thus the proper parameters of the republican polity. Although the debate was a national one, the conservative South probably had more to gain than the North from the politicization of gender relations in antebellum America.

Nationally the debate over women's emancipation strengthened conservative resolve on a whole range of social and political issues, the most important of which was slavery. In the North, however, it caused division within antislavery ranks, marking for the majority the limits of democratic republican commitment to the rights of man. But in the South, in the absence of any women's movement, ideas about the natural inequality of women contributed not a little to the ideological and political cohesion of the proslavery cause.

No social relation has ever had such difficulty shedding its apparently "natural" character as that between man and woman. Then, as now, unexamined assumptions about natural gender differences and conventions were invoked through language to naturalize other social relations—class and race, for example—organizing difference hierarchically and lending it the cast of immutability and inevitability.[34] That was precisely what proslavery ministers and politicians attempted to do in their association of women and slaves. The philosophy of natural rights foundered everywhere in the western world in the "Age of Revolution" on the shoals of women's right to the status of individual and

---

33. [McCord], "Enfranchisement of Woman," pp. 344, 347, 342; Howe, *Endowments of . . . Woman*, pp. 10–12. Scholarly treatments of McCord include Elizabeth Fox-Genovese, *Within the Plantation Household: Black and White Women of the Old South* (Chapel Hill: University of North Carolina Press, 1988), pp. 242–89; Richard Lounsberry, "Ludibria Rerum Mortalium: Charlestonian Intellectuals and Their Classics," in O'Brien and Moltke-Hansen, eds., *Intellectual Life in Antebellum Charleston*, pp. 325–69. On gender reversal as the classic representation of the world turned upside down, see Natalie Zemon Davis, *Society and Culture in Early Modern France* (Stanford: Stanford University Press, 1965), pp. 124–51.

34. Joan Wallach Scott, *Gender and the Politics of History* (New York: Columbia University Press, 1988), esp. pp. 53–68. Scott's advocacy of poststructuralist linguistic theory has inspired a passionate critical debate. See Joan Wallach Scott, "On Language, Gender, and Working-Class History," *International Labor and Working Class History* 31 (Spring 1987), pp. 1–13; Bryan Palmer, "Response to Joan Scott," ibid., pp. 14–23; Christine Stansell, "A Response to Joan Scott," ibid., pp. 24–29; Anson Rabinbach, "Rationalism and Utopia as Language of Nature: A Note," ibid., pp. 30–36; and Joan Wallach Scott, "A Reply to Criticism," *International Labor and Working Class History* 32 (Fall 1987), pp. 39–45.

citizen.[35] By engaging their adversaries at that point, proslavery politicians put their claims about natural inequality on unshakable ground or, more precisely, on ground few wanted to shake. Their success depended on the social breadth and depth of the commitment to the ideas and conventions they invoked.

It is in this respect, in the effort to find a popular constituency for the defense of slavery, that the gendered arguments acquired explicit political purpose. Proslavery writers' recognition that the social relations of the private sphere profoundly shaped political ideas and actions in the public sphere has critical implications for the political culture of the South Carolina Low Country and especially for the yeoman majority's position within it.

V

Lowcountry yeoman farmers may never have read a sermon by Thornwell or a tract by Harper, but they almost certainly heard a sermon at their local Baptist church by the likes of Reverend Iveson Brookes or a speech at a July Fourth barbecue by a prominent politician like Robert Barnwell Rhett. The gulf between high and low culture was just not that great where evangelical values played such a central role in each. Unlike evangelical intellectuals and planter politicians, lowcountry farmers articulated their political views piecemeal, for example, in framing covenants to govern admission, fellowship, and representation and in the dispensation of gospel discipline in their churches. Nonetheless, when they articulated assumptions about power and authority in the language of familialism, representing Christian society as an extended family replete with paternal head and fixed ranks of dependents, their formulation bore striking resemblance to the organic ideology of published proslavery ministers and politicians. In their Baptist, Methodist, and, less often, Presbyterian congregations the yeoman majority, or rather its enfranchised male members, eschewed any attempt to interpret spiritual equality in social terms, instead assigning privileges and duties according to secular rank, station, and status. In the practice and popular language of evangelicalism male yeomen demonstrated an unequivocal commitment to hierarchical social order and to their own version of the conservative Christian republicanism proslavery discourses promoted. Such

35. Joan B. Landes, *Women and the Public Sphere in the Age of the French Revolution* (Ithaca, N.Y.: Cornell University Press, 1988); Carol Pateman, *The Sexual Contract* (Stanford: Stanford University Press, 1988); Colwill, "Transforming Women's Empire"; Kerber, *Women of the Republic;* Linda K. Kerber, "'History Can Do It No Justice': Women and the Reinterpretation of the American Revolution," in Ronald Hoffman and Peter J. Albert, eds., *Women in the Age of the American Revolution* (Charlottesville: University of Virginia Press, 1989), pp. 3–42.

assumptions about power and authority were not, it is safe to say, peculiar to church members.

When proslavery ministers and politicians insisted on the seamlessness of social relations, and, most prominently, on the integral connection between slavery and marriage, they mined deep veins among the yeomanry. For the hidden assumptions and values that underlay their political choices were forged in the relations that engaged them most directly—with the few slaves they may have owned, but, just as important, with the women and other family dependents they presumed it their natural right to rule. Whether slaveholders or not, yeoman household heads were, as they proudly claimed, masters. Masterhood was a complex identity, literally engendered in independent "freemen" by virtue of their personal domination over the dependents in their own households and confirmed in the exercise of the political rights to which that identity entitled them. Out of the same social matrix—located resolutely in the household and the private sphere—the yeomanry's commitment to slavery was similarly engendered. In representing the defense of slavery as the defense of all kinds of power and privilege, domestic and public, politicians acknowledged and confirmed the yeomanry's masterly identity. In their churches, marketplaces, and electoral districts, as in their households, black-belt yeomen moved as independent and enfranchised men amidst a sea of dependent and disenfranchised people: In the struggle over slavery yeoman farmers understandably saw the struggle to perpetuate their own privilege at home and at the ballot box.

They left persuasive evidence to that effect in the records of their own community institutions. When called upon in 1844 to take a public stand against the antislavery agenda within the national bodies of evangelical churches, lowcountry yeomen evinced no confusion whatsoever but gave unequivocal testimony of their proslavery convictions. The yeoman clerk of Gum Branch Baptist Church in Darlington District, the infamous Willey Kelly, needed no prodding from planter members, ministers, or state denominational leaders in his campaign against the "abolishonest" at the North who had threatened, as he put it, a "division withe Baptists at the South except they free or emmancepate their slaves." Instead, he drew the issue to the attention of his brethren, and, claiming the insult as their own, perceiving it as an attack on the morality of every southern Christian freeman, yeoman members joined with planters and poor white voting members to pass "a resolusion" withholding funds from the Board of Foreign Missions until its representatives dissolved "all connection with abolishionists."[36] More extended discussions and learned resolutions were offered by other lowcountry

36. Gum Branch Baptist Church, Darlington District, Church Book, October 16, 1840, SCL. For the background to this conflict, see C. C. Goen, *Broken Churches, Broken Nation: Denominational Schisms and the Coming of the American Civil War* (Macon, Ga.: Mercer University Press, 1985), pp. 93, 148–49.

churches that appointed planter committees to advise the congregations on the appropriate course of action. But few were as eloquent as the Gum Branch brethren or their clerk, Willey Kelly, whose statement spoke volumes in two lines.

Indeed, whether in brief or at length, the grass-roots embrace of secession over submission—for such was the usual construction of the choice—showed just how fully religion and politics were intertwined in the Low Country. The largely planter committee appointed by the Swift Creek Baptist Church brethren demonstrated as much. They condemned the northern antislavery Baptists' articulated intention to exclude slaveholders or those who condoned slavery from receiving appointments from the Foreign Mission Board as an "outrage up on Southern Rights," as "unconstitutional" and "unjust in denying perfect social and religious equality" and awarding the "nonslave holder . . . a monopoly of privileges." Southerners "with becoming self-respect should refuse" any compact on such terms, they advised. It was a matter of justice in abiding by the constitutional compromise on which the Baptist Church and, they implied, the nation was built. And it was a matter of honor: of honor impugned by the assignation of inferior status and honor served by the refusal to submit. We have "long forborne" such insults, they reminded their fellow congregants; compromise had been tried and adjudged a failure. "For the sake of peace and unity," they urged secession.[37] Though Willey Kelly and the yeoman members of Gum Branch Baptist Church would hardly have explained themselves in such a legalistic fashion, there was nothing in the Swift Creek planter statement that they were likely to dispute. Certainly the end result was the same.

In Swift Creek, Gum Branch, and countless other Baptist churches between 1840 and 1845, the antislavery challenge was met head on by the united ranks of yeomen and planters. The *Charleston Courier*, for one, thought it a portentous moment. "If a union cemented by all the finer influences of the Gospel could not last, what can?" it editorialized in 1845.[38] What, indeed? In Gum Branch Baptist Church in 1840, yeoman stood solidly with planter in defense of slavery. When the final decision to separate from the Baptist General Convention was made a

37. Swift Creek Baptist Church, Kershaw District, Records, April 5, 1845, April 19, 1845, SCL. Abolitionist attempts to exclude slaveholders were met with similar outrage in the following churches: Welsh Neck Baptist Church, Darlington District, Minutes, April 13, 1845, May 31, 1845, SCL; Darlington Circuit of the Methodist Church, Quarterly Conference Minutes, August 10, 1844, SCL; Waccamaw and Conwayborough Circuit of the Methodist Church, Georgetown and Horry Districts, Quarterly Conference Minutes, August 31, 1844, SCL. One Presbyterian church on Johns Island refused to abide by its representatives' decision to remain within the national body, declaring that it had "no longer any attachment to ecclesiastical bodies so inimical to southern institutions or so indifferent to their defense." See George Howe, D.D., *History of the Presbyterian Church in South Carolina*, 2 vols. (Columbia, S.C.: W. J. Duffie, 1883), 2: 457–58.

38. *Charleston Courier* editorial quoted in Goen, *Broken Churches, Broken Nation*, p. 97.

year later, it left not a mark on their record book. They had not awaited instructions from Charleston. Their loyalties had never been in doubt.

Religion and politics, domestic dependencies and their public meanings, marriage and slavery, evangelical Christianity and republicanism—these were inseparable in lowcountry political culture. In this complex of connections as yeoman farmers comprehended them lay the popular basis of proslavery discourses and the conservative Christian republicanism that was one of its components. For viewed in holistic social context—not just in relation to planters but in relation to the slaves and the free white women who together constituted the overwhelming majority of the adult population—yeoman farmers come into focus as part of a small lowcountry minority privileged by the qualifications of republican citizenship.[39] Little wonder that they exhibited a deep commitment to natural hierarchy and inequality even as they cherished equal rights as independent men. The political ideology of yeomen in plantation areas was a contradictory one that defies the common characterization of historians, liberal and left, as egalitarian in impulse.[40] That much Willey Kelly and the other yeoman evangelicals made clear.

Yeomen did indeed press overweening planters for a greater share of power and resources, and they pressed them for recognition of their rights as masters. But they also found common cause with planters in maintaining and policing the class, gender, and racial boundaries of citizenship in the slave republic. In the end, their commitment to the slave regime owed as much to its legitimation of dependence and inequality in the private sphere as to the much-lauded vitality of male independence and formal "democracy" in the public sphere. As good republicans, yeomen appreciated both of Columbia's faces.

As usual, they got more—or less—than they bargained for. For even as it was outlined in proslavery discourses the conservative Christian republic embodied all of the contradictory forces of yeoman-planter relations in the Low Country, binding them as freemen and masters even as it divided them on the same account.

VI

In an age in which the limits of republican inclusivity were being debated all over the nation, South Carolina, and particularly its lowcountry rep-

39. Lacy K. Ford, Jr., "Republics and Democracy: The Parameters of Political Citizenship in Antebellum South Carolina," in *The Meaning of South Carolina History: Essays in Honor of George C. Rogers, Jr.* (Columbia: University of South Carolina Press, 1991), pp. 121–45.

40. Compare the otherwise different interpretations of Lacy K. Ford, Jr., and Steven Hahn. See Ford, *Origins of Southern Radicalism: The South Carolina Upcountry, 1800–1860* (New York: Oxford University Press, 1988), and Hahn, *The Roots of Southern Populism: Yeoman Farmers and the Transformation of the Georgia Upcountry, 1850–1890* (New York: Oxford University Press, 1983).

resentatives, staked out the extreme conservative position, insisting that they alone had remained loyal to the principles of republican—as opposed to democratic—government. It was a common trope of lowcountry proslavery tracts that the only true republic was a slave republic, for only a slave republic maintained the public sphere as a realm of perfect equality. But invariably in republican discourses, independence betrayed its intimacy with dependence, and equality with inequality, and so it was in South Carolina. "[N]o social state without slavery as its basis," the Baptist minister Iveson Brookes offered as if to make the point, "can permanently maintain a republican form of government."[41] Yeoman farmers, like most enfranchised southerners, were aware of what republican independence entailed, and they did not shrink from its exclusionary dimensions. The slave republic was emphatically not a democracy, racial or otherwise, as its lowcountry defenders readily acknowledged in boasting of the restriction of political rights to a privileged few as its distinctive and superior characteristic. It was within this exclusionary conception of the polity that lowcountry yeomen negotiated their place in the region's political culture.

From the earliest skirmishes of the Nullification Crisis, antitariff South Carolinians such as the editorialist "Leonidas" laid claim to a distinctive republicanism. In the North, Leonidas observed in 1828, "liberty is a principle." In the slave South, where free men possessed of "habits of command" had developed a "privileged superiority," liberty is "a privilege, a passion, and a principle." South Carolina's freemen would never consent to be made "the dastard-trampled slaves of wool-weavers and spindle-twirlers." Constituted "freemen" by slavery, they would show themselves, Leonidas predicted, to be the natural guardians of the republic against the corruption of the federal state and its dominant interests.[42]

That slavery did not simply wed southern "freemen" to a passionate defense of liberty but led them to define liberty, freedom, and independence in particular ways was already evident in the insistence of Leonidas that the battle would be met over the right to own slave property. But the distinction between the true republican principles and practices of the slave states and the bastardized ones of the free states continued to be refined and elaborated in sectional struggle throughout the antebellum period.

During the struggle over the abolitionists' congressional petition campaign of 1838, Robert Barnwell Rhett introduced what became an enduring focus on social relations, particularly on the distinction between the antagonistic and antirepublican social relations of the free-labor North and the harmonious and republican ones of the slave-labor

41. Brookes, *A Defense of the South*, esp. pp. 45–46; Speech of General Robert Y. Hayne, *Charleston Mercury*, Feb. 3, 1830; W. C. Dana, *A Sermon Delivered in the Central Presbyterian Church, Charleston, S.C., Nov. 21st, 1860* . . . (Charleston: Evans and Cogswell, 1860).

42. Leonidas, *Charleston Mercury*, July 14, 1828.

South.[43] It was an argument to which proslavery politicians turned increasingly as the sectional struggle deepened and, not incidentally, as the problem of enfranchising dependents fueled restrictionist impulses in northern politics in the 1840s and 1850s. James Henry Hammond, planter, congressman, governor, senator, proslavery publicist, gave it perhaps its most vivid formulation in his writings and speeches from the mid-1840s to the late 1850s.

Like countless others, Hammond drew on longstanding popular evangelical ideas about the natural and divine status of social relations and wedded them to an explicit consideration of the political character of slave society. The result was his contribution to a deeply conservative political theory that embedded the defense of slavery not in scientific racism but in a broader conception of social hierarchy and social order that could be characterized variously as organic or familial.

Slavery everywhere exists in fact if not in name, Hammond reminded his fellow United States Senators in an 1858 debate: "Your whole class of manual laborers and 'operatives,' as you call them, are essentially slaves." To enfranchise slaves as the free labor states were compelled to do threatened a "fearful crisis in republican institutions" and invited revolution at the ballot-box. Using a by then time-tested strategy, Hammond sketched frightful portraits of the festering and explosive class politics of industrial England's cities, whose fate awaited, if it had not already visited, Boston, Philadelphia, and New York. The republic could not long survive such developments without the conservative ballast of the South. For the genius of the southern system, as he presented it, was to have recognized the necessity of enslaving the poor and to have found a race of people "adapted to that purpose." Race was not in his analysis an essential but rather a fortuitous characteristic of the slave labor system. It ensured that the South's dependent classes were confined within households under the governance of a master, where they could be deprived, as were women everywhere, of political rights. "Our slaves do not vote," Hammond pointed out. "In the slaveholding states . . . nearly one half of the whole population, and those the poorest and most ignorant, have no political influence whatever, because they are slaves." The half of the population that did vote were, as a result, if not rich, nonetheless part of a privileged class of independent men "elevated far above the mass." Such men could be trusted, as indeed they must be in a republic, to "preserve a stable and well-ordered government."[44]

As lowcountry discourses long had, Hammond's critique of natural rights and defense of slavery took broad social and increasingly explicit class grounds. Scientific racism may well have acquired more discursive

43. Rhett, "Address to the People of Beaufort," pp. 7–9. Harper adopted a strikingly similar position in "Memoir on Slavery."

44. Hammond, *Are Working Men Slaves?* pp. 3–4; Hammond, "Hammond's Letters on Slavery," esp. pp. 110–11.

prominence in other parts of the South by the 1850s, but in the South Carolina Low Country specifically racial justifications of slavery grounded in scientific proof still took a back seat to broad social justifications grounded in biblical proof. As early as 1802 Governor John Drayton had laid out the essentials of that argument, including the gendered constructions of "natural" difference in which it was typically cast. "Nature," he claimed, "governed by unerring laws which command the oak to be stronger than the willow, the cypress to be taller than the shrub, has at the same time imposed on mankind certain restrictions which can never be overcome. . . ." Then, typically, the benign became horrific: "Some men must by nature be slaves while others will be free." By 1837 in William Harper's hands, the divinity of nature was rendered explicit: "It is the order of nature and of God that the being of superior faculties and knowledge and therefore of superior power should control and dispose of those who are inferior."[45] Refined and elaborated throughout the antebellum period by countless clerical and secular authors, infused even by new racial theories, by the late 1850s there was still no firmer discursive proslavery ground than the biblical, no more popular argument than divine injunctions about the providential status of social inequality.

It is not that race was entirely absent from lowcountry proslavery discourses or that the region's ministers and politicians were blind to the utility of racial justifications. But if scientific racism came in handy, it was hardly necessary to a vigorous defense. Indeed, as one can see in the work of Hammond, Iveson Brookes, or the Virginian T. R. R. Dew for that matter, race and the scientific case for black inferiority functioned usually as secondary proof to the far more powerful biblical case throughout the antebellum period. Thus, for example, Iveson Brookes, a middle country Baptist minister who deployed racial categories more frequently and prominently than most of his coastal and more educated clerical counterparts, still cast his argument in class terms, defending slavery "in the abstract" as "the best condition of the poor . . . to be found anywhere in the world" and as "the only true principle of republicanism" because it deprived the propertyless of political power.[46] The biblical argument and its broad social defense pushed to the extreme in the case for "slavery in the abstract" may well have had particular currency in the South Carolina Low Country, but it is undoubtedly the case that James Henry Hammond and his counterparts, clerical and secular

45. Drayton quoted in Tise, *Proslavery,* p. 38; Harper, "Memoir on Slavery," *Southern Literary Journal* 3, no. 1, (January 1838), p. 73.

46. Brookes, *A Defense of the South,* pp. 16–17, and *A Defense of Southern Slavery,* title page. Dew employed racial categories in his famous tract, but again the analysis was conducted substantively in class terms. Thus he nowhere argued that slavery was necessitated by black inferiority but instead maintained that slavery provided the best conditions for rural laborers, a case he made by comparison with the condition of Polish peasants in postemancipation society. See Thomas Roderick Dew, "Abolition of Negro Slavery," in Faust, ed., *Ideology of Slavery,* p. 56.

alike, were closer discursively to George Fitzhugh than to Josiah Nott or
S. A. Cartwright, whose biblical and physiological "proof" of racial difference and black inferiority respectively failed to secure a popular constituency. Scientific racism was on the rise in antebellum America, of that
there can be no doubt. But it could be argued, and quite plausibly, that
racial theories acquired greater currency more quickly in the free-labor
states than the slave. In the South Carolina Low Country, and indeed in
the South as a whole, they had by no means achieved the ascendancy. In
the Low Country in the late 1850s science yet proved no contest for the
Bible, and race coexisted with class and gender in justifying social hierarchies. There was still no safer or more popular ground on which to
stake the defense of slavery and slavery republicanism than that God
had ordained it along with all the particular hierarchical relations that
constituted organic society. Extend religion, James Henley Thornwell
had proclaimed in 1850, and "you will be consolidating the elements of
your social fabrick."[47]

In Hammond, Rhett, Brookes, Thornwell, and many of the others,
the defense of slavery incorporated a particular conception of republican government. In Hammond's account, for example, slavery was not
simply a system of race relations. Indeed in his view it was above all else a
system of class and labor relations that had become, to the inestimable
benefit of the South, a system of race relations as well. It was that convergence that made the South an exemplary republic—one committed to
manhood suffrage yet able to restrict it to independent men—a herrenvolk democracy, if you will. Hammond's view was hardly idiosyncratic.
"History presents no such combination for republican liberty," Rhett
had boasted in the late 1830s, "than that which exists at the South. The
African for the laborer—the Anglo-Saxon for the master and ruler."
Slavery was the "cornerstone of the republican edifice." As Rhett, Hammond, and numerous other South Carolina politicians and ministers
agreed, the "primitive and patriarchal" social relations of the South prevented the republic from going down the French road of corruption (to
use Thornwell's memorable phrase) from a "representative to a democratic government."[48]

---

47. Thornwell, "Religious Instruction," pp. 140–41. On George Fitzhugh and the de-
fense of slavery in the abstract, see Genovese, *The World the Slaveholders Made*, pp. 118–244.
One of the best discussions of early scientific theories of race, including those of Josiah
Nott and S. A. Cartwright, is Stephen Jay Gould's *The Mismeasure of Man* (New York: W. W.
Norton, 1981), pp. 30–112. On the primacy of the biblical argument, see Drew Gilpin
Faust, *A Sacred Circle: The Dilemma of the Intellectual in the Old South, 1840–1860* (1977;
Philadelphia: University of Pennsylvania Press, 1986), pp. 112–32.

48. Rhett, "Address to the People of Beaufort," p. 13; Hammond, "Hammond's Let-
ters on Slavery," pp. 110–11, 162–63. Barbara Fields has argued that slavery should be
recognized as a system of class relations, notwithstanding racial ideology. See Barbara J.
Fields, "Ideology and Race in American History," in J. Morgan Kousser and James M.
McPherson, eds., *Region, Race, and Reconstruction: Essays in Honor of C. Vann Woodward* (New
York: Oxford University Press, 1982), pp. 143–78; and Barbara J. Fields, "Slavery, Race,

Such explicitly antidemocratic sentiments were not reserved for the private communications of a handful of like-minded conservative extremist intellectuals. Even the pamphlets distributed by the 1860 Association, whose explicit mission was to galvanize popular support for secession, prominently employed the antidemocratic defense of slavery republicanism. At least in the coastal parishes and the middle districts of the state, politicians and aspirants to office asserted openly that the franchise was not the right of all men but the privilege only of free and independent men. They were not loath, that is, to make a republican principle out of exclusion. And while it was always a potentially explosive issue, they articulated this view with some confidence that their largely yeoman constituencies would respond as men empowered by the demarcation of such narrow boundaries to the body politic.[49]

Nor was their confidence unfounded. For notwithstanding historians' usual insistence on the egalitarian political impulses of the southern yeomanry, everything about their households and community institutions conspired to confirm investment in social hierarchy and its political consequences, especially when the restrictive boundaries of the polity were drawn around property and masterhood. In carefully framing their conservative republicanism as a defense of the rights of the propertied against an insurgent class of enfranchised poor, they turned a critique of industrial free-labor society into an apocalyptic vision of a defeated South—a free-labor South in which dependents ruled masters.

The inscription of yeoman farmers as the propertied majority whose interests were at stake in the defense of slavery republicanism constituted a central theme in many lowcountry tracts including, of course, those penned by James Henry Hammond. But few put the case so directly as the Baptist minister Iveson Brookes in his efforts of 1850 and 1851. Apocalyptic scenarios were standard fare among proslavery ministers, however educated and refined. Thornwell was the one who insisted, after all, that "the parties in this conflict are not merely abolitionists and slaveholders, they are atheists, socialists, communists, red republicans, jacobins on the one side and the friends of order and regulated freedom on the other."[50] But it was left to Brookes to sound the grass-roots note. For if the propertied were attuned to the threats of communism in the

and Ideology in the United States of America," *New Left Review* 181 (May/June 1990), pp. 95–118.

49. For a few examples of 1860 Association pamphlets, see Townsend, *The South Alone Should Govern the South,* and *Doom of Slavery in the Union: Its Safety Out of It* (Charleston: Evans and Cogswell, 1860). For other examples including tracts originally delivered as addresses or sermons, see Rhett, "Address to the People of Beaufort"; William Henry Trescot, *Oration Delivered to the Beaufort Volunteer Artillery on July 4, 1850* (Charleston: Press of Walker and James, 1850); James Henley Thornwell, "National Sins: A Fast Day Sermon Preached in the Presbyterian Church . . . November 21, 1860," *Southern Presbyterian Review* 13, no. 4 (January 1861), pp. 649–88; James Henley Thornwell, "State of the Country," in ibid., pp. 860–89.

50. Thornwell, "Religious Instruction," p. 114.

post-1848 world, then the most threatening form in which the specter presented itself to yeoman farmers and the one on which Brookes played was, of course, "agrarianism." Abolitionism was, he admitted, a species of radical heresy related to every other form manifest in the modern world—"Socinianism, Universalism, Deism, Socialism, Fouriourism, Millerism and, perhaps, other isms"—but with the sure touch of the local politician he cast the all-American version in terms designed to boil the blood of farmers. In states in which abolitionists "pervert the great principles of truth and fact [and seek] to carry out the false notions of universal equality, [they] are striking at the very vitals of the social compact, and must unhinge the foundations of law and government," he raged, "and carry agrarianism, mobocracy, and anarchy in their wake." Any nonslaveholding state can carry by law "the agrarian system . . . and divide the capital amongst the rabble" and in doing so, he pointed out, "produc[e] the equalization of condition, which Mr. Jefferson's ultra-sentiment, may by some be construed to make the basis of republicanism." Southerners knew better, he insisted. For such "an antagonistic principle of labor and capital . . . actually contains the elements of agrarianism and anarchy, and proves"—and here the minister was indistinguishable from the political theorist—"that no social state, without slavery as its basis, can permanently maintain a republican form of government."[51]

Yeoman farmers, like modest landowners in rural societies everywhere, were not known for their support of progressive movements that threatened, even rhetorically, a redistribution of landed property and a political insurgency of the dispossessed and dependent.[52] The yeomen in the South Carolina Low Country were no exception, as Brookes, Thornwell, Rhett, Hammond, and the others acknowledged in wedding the defense of slavery and slavery republicanism to the preservation of property rights and social order in all its class, racial, and gender peregrinations.

But if the antidemocratic conception of the Christian slave republic appealed to yeoman farmers in its explicit parameters, then the emphasis on property and the political privileges that attended it cut in another direction simultaneously, imagining relations within the polity between those few men empowered by inclusion. If yeomen could see themselves embraced within this conservative Christian republicanism, as indeed it was intended they should, then it was discernible in the theory and confirmed in practice that they would pay the price of membership.

Not that theorists elaborated the prerogatives of planters as distinct from yeomen. To the contrary, they went to great lengths to avoid even the acknowledgment of social inequality among the propertied and

51. Brookes, *A Defense of the South*, pp. 22, 34, 46.
52. This argument has been made most compellingly by Steven Hahn in *The Roots of Southern Populism*.

enfranchised, casting their restrictive republicanism largely in gendered terms. Thus, proslavery politicians, usually planters, nonetheless claimed to speak simply as "free men" for "free men." Just as all dependencies were deliberately conflated—marriage and slavery, women and slaves, for example—so independence, by contrast, remained brilliantly distinct, the common property, indeed identity, of "free men."[53] But if in so doing they attempted to fudge the meaning of their antidemocratic politics for those included within its parameters, casting it as an equality of "free men," that flattering discursive egalitarianism hardly obscured the political inequality property introduced among those who owned such disparate amounts of it.

VII

Prompted by theories about the complexities of power in modern society, a number of historians, feminists most prominent among them, have joined the recent debate over the proper definition and boundaries of "the political." The stakes are high. As one feminist philosopher put it, "this question about the limits of the political is precisely a political question."[54] In advocating an expanded approach to political history that transgresses the limits of formal politics and confounds conventional distinctions between public and private spheres, they have raised the intriguing possibility of a gendered history of politics.[55]

The history of republican political ideology and culture in the antebellum South may seem a long way from the concerns of contemporary theorists, but it is not so far, perhaps, as it appears at first glance. After all, theories of government and citizenship, in modern republics as in ancient ones, have been grounded in assumptions about the relation of public and private spheres, or civic sphere and household. In Aristotle's *Politics,* for example, according to Jürgen Habermas, "Status in the *polis* was . . . based upon status as the unlimited master of an *oikos.* Moveable

53. This line of analysis is developed more fully in Chapters 7 and 8, but see, for example, Robert Barnwell Smith [R. B. Rhett], "An Address of Sundry Citizens of Colleton District to the People of South Carolina," *Charleston Mercury,* June 18, 1828, and John Townsend, *The South Alone Should Govern the South.*

54. Nancy Fraser, *Unruly Practices: Power, Discourse and Gender in Contemporary Social Theory* (Minneapolis: University of Minnesota Press, 1989), p. 6. Michel Foucault, Jürgen Habermas, and Jacques Derrida are among the most influential of these theorists. For a helpful discussion and critique of their work, see ibid.

55. Scott, *Gender and the Politics of History,* esp. pp. 28–67, and also the series of articles cited in n. 33 above. Studies that exemplify gender analysis of political history include Kerber, *Women of the Republic;* Stansell, *City of Women,* esp. pp. 19–37; Mary P. Ryan, *Women in Public: Between Banners and Ballots, 1825–1880* (Baltimore: Johns Hopkins University Press, 1990); Landes, *Women and the Public Sphere in the Age of the French Revolution;* and Lynn Hunt, *The Family Romance of the French Revolution* (Berkeley: University of California Press, 1992).

wealth and control over labor power were no substitute for being the master of a household and of a family."[56]

In the antebellum South, where the defense of "domestic institutions" and relations were matters of the utmost political significance, one finds compelling reason to eschew conventional historiographical boundaries, particularly those that separate the public from the private sphere and the history of women and gender relations from that of "high" politics. In the Old South, "high" politics *was* the politics of the household, and all relations of power in what we would call the "private sphere," including those of men and women, were inevitably politicized. Indeed, the gender, class, and race relations contained in southern households were, as we have seen, the distinctive social conditions to which proslavery politicians pointed as permitting the South, and the South alone, to retain the proper political arrangements of republican government. For the slave South was commonly represented as the last republic loyal to the principle of government by an exclusive citizen body of independent and equal men.

However inadvertently, that portrait revealed the two faces of republicanism in the antebellum South. The first gazed outward on the public sphere and countenanced a purportedly egalitarian community of enfranchised men. This is the familiar face of slavery republicanism privileged by antebellum politicians and, for the most part, by historians. But to view the political edifice solely from that perspective is to remain captive to the designs of its proslavery architects. For southern men, like other republicans, established their independence and status as citizens in the public sphere through the command of dependents in their households. The modern slave republic was defined above all else, as its defenders never tired of saying, by the boundary that separated the independent and enfranchised minority from the majority of dependent and excluded others. Republicanism thus had another, more conservative, face, one that gazed inward on the private sphere and counte-

---

56. Jürgen Habermas, *The Structural Transformation of the Public Sphere: An Inquiry Into a Category of Bourgeois Society,* trans. Thomas Burger and Frederick Lawrence (Cambridge, Mass.: Harvard University Press, 1989), p. 3. J. G. A. Pocock makes the same point in *The Machiavellian Moment: Florentine Political Thought and the Atlantic Republican Tradition* (Princeton, N.J.: Princeton University Press, 1975), p. 68. Some of these themes have been pursued by Hannah Pitkin, *Fortune Is a Woman: Gender and Politics in the Thought of Niccolo Machiavelli* (Berkeley: University of California Press, 1984); and Pateman, *The Sexual Contract,* esp. p. x. The debate over the republican or liberal character of nineteenth-century political ideology rages on; for the briefest introduction, see Drew McCoy, *The Elusive Republic: Political Economy in Jeffersonian Virginia* (Chapel Hill: University of North Carolina Press, 1980); Joyce Appleby, *Capitalism and a New Social Order: The Republican Vision of the 1790s* (New York: New York University Press, 1984); and Lance Banning, "Jeffersonian Ideology Revisited: Liberal and Classical Ideas in the New American Republic," *William and Mary Quarterly,* 3d series, 43 (January 1986), pp. 3–19.

nanced inequality and relations of power between masters and their dependents: slaves, women, and children.

Any assessment of antebellum southern political culture, and especially of the yeoman-planter relations on which it hinged, must confront the republican edifice whole. This broader perspective is most pressing with respect to the politics of the yeoman majority. As independent proprietors, yeoman farmers were (and knew themselves to be) empowered by the exclusionary boundaries of the public sphere. Their republicanism, no less than that of the planters, was centrally configured around the politics of the household and around the public meaning of domestic dependencies.

In this respect, the South Carolina Low Country provides a dramatic case in point. Nowhere did proslavery republicanism find more momentous expression; nowhere was its social basis more starkly displayed in ways that confound a conventional focus on the public sphere in the interpretation of the yeomanry's politics. In that coastal region of vast rice and cotton plantations, social and political inequality reached staggering proportions. Not only was the great majority of the adult population —slave men and women and free women—propertyless and disfranchised and the political culture thereby defined primarily in terms of those it excluded, but the concentration of wealth in land and slaves was so advanced that it gave decisive shape to relations between yeomen and planters as well as between masters and slaves. Even in the "aristocratic" Low Country yeoman farmers constituted the majority of the adult white male population, and their relations with planters formed a crucial dimension of political life.

But if the Low Country provides a particularly dramatic case, it was by no means an isolated one. All over the slave South, and particularly the black-belt South, social inequality was not comfortably confined between black and white and limited to the private sphere, as those who define slave society primarily in terms of race would argue.[57] Rather, inequality and relations of power took many forms in the South Carolina Low Country and all over the black-belt South where similar social patterns prevailed. They not only gave definitive shape to the public sphere

---

57. See, for example, George Fredrickson, *The Black Image in the White Mind: The Debate on Afro-American Character and Destiny, 1817–1914* (New York: Harper and Row, 1971), p. 61; James Oakes, *The Ruling Race: A History of American Slaveholders* (New York: Alfred A. Knopf, 1982); J. Mills Thornton III, *Politics and Power in a Slave Society: Alabama, 1800–1860* (Baton Rouge: Louisiana State University Press, 1978); J. William Harris, *Plain Folk and Gentry in a Slave Society: White Liberty and Black Slavery in Augusta's Hinterlands* (Middletown, Conn.: Wesleyan University Press, 1985); and Ford, *Origins of Southern Radicalism.* Class analyses include Eugene D. Genovese, *The Political Economy of Slavery: Studies in the Economy and Society of the Slave South* (New York: Vintage, 1965); Genovese, *Roll, Jordan, Roll;* Genovese, "Yeoman Farmers in a Slaveholders' Democracy," *Agricultural History* 49 (April 1975), pp. 331–42; and Hahn, *The Roots of Southern Populism.*

but permeated its boundaries and infused its culture. To confront that pervasive inequality is to raise searching questions about interpretations that locate the yeomanry's politics and their commitment to the slave regime in the purportedly egalitarian public sphere of the slave republic and the "democratic" culture and ideology it engendered. To confront the relations of power in yeoman households, including gender relations, and the political privileges to which they entitled male household heads is to reveal a yeoman republicanism rather more complicated and rather less distinctly egalitarian and "democratic." And it is to offer an interpretation that comports more with the manifest social and political inequality of the black-belt South. Yeomen in the Low Country knew, better than their upcountry peers, that the slave republic was defined by its exclusionary boundaries. But the patterns revealed in the Low Country speak nonetheless to a characteristic of republican political culture all over the South. To train our attention on it is to compel a quite different interpretation of republicanism in the antebellum South from the one that currently prevails. It might even compel another perspective on republicanism in all of its American variations. At the very least it suggests a broader and more interesting view of what constitutes the "political" and thus political history.

chapter 7

Manly Resistance, Slavish Submission, and the Political Culture of the Low Country

---

I

The political history of the lowcountry yeomanry poses more than the ordinary challenges of evidence and analysis. For the contradictions of American republicanism were played out larger than life in that corner of the United States, and they left an indelible mark on the historical record. In the Low Country, the historian is confronted at once with the most apparently "aristocratic" political culture in the nation in the arrogation of political power by a small and fabulously wealthy planter elite and with a political culture as authentically "democratic" as any other in its broad extension of the franchise to all adult free white men. The appearance of yeoman farmers in the political record primarily in the blurry figure of "the people" testifies to the first characteristic; the posturing evident everywhere in the same record to claim the mantle of "the people" testifies to the second. Critical to but barely discernible in the region's politics, yeoman farmers have a political history as important to tell as it is difficult to grasp.

The very impediments to a clear view of popular politics constitute a critical dimension of the region's political culture. Few things speak more directly to the political relations of yeomen and planters than the muffled quality of the popular voice and the blurry corpus of "the people"; few speak more directly to the contradiction between aristocracy and democracy or, more accurately, between inequality and independence within which yeoman voters were located and their political choices framed. The political system of the Low Country was not made in the image of yeoman farmers, endless paens to "Free Men" notwithstanding. It was configured around the interests of planter architects, managers, and officeholders. But yeomen were not irrelevant to the design. As "Free Men," they had political rights planters were bound to respect, or at least acknowledge. And in the necessity of negotiation thereby imposed, in the yeomanry's struggle to hold the political elite accountable to their particular interests—to "the people"—and in planter politicians' attempts to contain them within manageable bounds lay much of the substance of lowcountry political culture.

The political position of the lowcountry yeomanry is not, however, one readily comprehended within the narrow compass of ballot-box politics or in struggles between yeoman and planter voters. If yeomen found themselves overpowered and outmaneuvered by planter politicians—and they most certainly did—they also found themselves privileged by inclusion in a small elite of enfranchised men. Set apart from the mass of disfranchised and dependent others that surrounded them, part of a "democracy" so small and exclusive that membership itself conferred distinction, yeoman farmers had more than passing reason to feel common cause with planters. As freemen and masters in a world in which most were neither, they knew their own freedom to be secured by riveting the unfreedom of others. That was precisely what radical planter politicians counted on in claiming "the people" for disunion.

In this complex position, empowered by a system that also overpowered them, the yeomanry's political choices were forged. To comprehend those choices is to take a broad and, perhaps, unorthodox view of the forces that converged on the ballot-box. For if planter politicians always kept yeomen voters in political view, then neither yeomen nor planters could afford to lose sight, even for a moment, of the hordes of lowcountry folk whose various dependencies and common disfranchisement the politics of masterhood was designed to perpetuate. In this respect, the disfranchised, especially slaves but also the free female disfranchised, played an important political role and have a political history no less properly a part of the grand narrative of sectionalism, disunion, and Civil War than that of the freemen whose martial masculinity helped link yeomen and planters across the fault lines of class, wealth, and power. Yeoman farmers were neither planters' equals nor their dupes, lowcountry political culture was neither "herrenvolk democracy" nor planter "aristocracy." It was, rather, something far more complex— and far closer, for all its peculiarities, to what was known in the antebellum South as republican democracy.

II

Politics in antebellum South Carolina rested constitutionally on the well-known compromise of 1808. But it was in the Nullification movement of the late 1820s and early 1830s that the political culture acquired substantive shape.[1] In what would prove a testing ground of popular politics, a generation of would-be leaders groped their way toward new organizations, strategies, and personal styles fitting to and effective in campaigns to mobilize an expanded citizenry across the entire length and breadth of the state. The political culture they fashioned owed to the old but introduced much that was new, unpredictable, and, at times, seemingly unmanageable. And while some of the elements that would come to define it over the course of the antebellum period, including a periodic resort to political terror and a propensity to cast radical appeals in gendered terms, showed in only protean form during Nullification, there could be no mistaking the major outlines of a political culture that would characterize the Low Country until the fall of 1860, when its final measure was taken.

In the first decade of the nineteenth century, South Carolina entered the vanguard of modern American politics by eliminating property qualifications for voting on white male adults.[2] Introducing what has long been called white manhood suffrage, the state laid the constitutional foundation of democratic republicanism and created the conditions for a truly popular politics.

Or did it? If, as some historians have recently argued, white manhood suffrage put political power in the hands of the white majority, forced planter politicians to adopt positions that resonated with the interests of the yeoman voter, and nurtured a genuine "white man's democracy," then there was also much to sustain the opposite view: that South Carolina was the closest thing to a political "aristocracy" the United States would see in the nineteenth century.[3] Constraints on popular politics and safeguards for planter rule contained in the system of apportioning representation, in property requirements for officeholders, and in legislative control of appointments and elections were also part, indeed were prior part, of the constitutional compromise

1. Notwithstanding the steady barrage of criticism directed against it, the definitive study of Nullification remains William W. Freehling, *Prelude to Civil War: The Nullification Controversy in South Carolina, 1816–1836* (New York: Harper and Row, 1965).

2. By amendment to the constitution of 1808 and passed in 1810. Rachel N. Klein, *Unification of a Slave State: The Rise of the Planter Class in the South Carolina Backcountry, 1760–1808* (Chapel Hill: University of North Carolina Press, 1990), pp. 238–68; Lacy K. Ford, Jr., *Origins of Southern Radicalism: The South Carolina Upcountry, 1800–1860* (New York: Oxford University Press, 1988), pp. 106–08.

3. The first view is articulated most forcefully by Ford, *Origins of Southern Radicalism;* the quotation is on p. 209. The second view is an older one, articulated by Ralph A. Wooster, *The People in Power: Courthouse and Statehouse in the Lower South, 1850–1860* (Knoxville: University of Tennessee Press, 1969), pp. 4–5; and Fletcher M. Green, "Democracy in the Old South," in *Democracy in the Old South and Other Essays by Fletcher M. Green,* ed. J. Isaac Copeland (Nashville, Tenn.: Vanderbilt University Press, 1969), pp. 80, 86, although it is shared in large part in more recent work by Kenneth Greenberg, *Masters and Statesmen: The Political Culture of American Slavery* (Baltimore: John Hopkins University Press, 1985). A more measured version of the aristocracy case is made by Freehling, *Prelude to Civil War,* p. 89 and passim.

of 1808. If white manhood suffrage was the democratic component of democratic republicanism, then in the eyes of much of South Carolina's political elite (and not only the lowcountry part), the impediments to majority rule and the constitutional guarantees of planter dominance were the republican components that distinguished their political culture from that of the free-labor states and, increasingly, the rest of the slave states as well. They had a point, judging from the social character of those the system brought to power. White manhood suffrage might have engendered a white man's democracy, but in the South Carolina Low Country the white man who embodied it was a planter.

Such was the case, although to varying degrees, at every level of political life from parish or district office to the United States Senate. In South Carolina as "perhaps nowhere else in America with the possible exception of Virginia," one historian has argued, "political power remained in the hands of the rich and well born."[4] Yet in no single institution did it matter quite so much who held office as in the state legislature because of the influence that body exercised over federal, state, and local politics. And there, planter dominance of lowcountry representation was virtually complete. Fully 92 percent of state senators from Beaufort, Barnwell, and Darlington districts (a sample of coastal and middle country districts) were planters, as were 72 percent of those who served in the state house of representatives over the course of the antebellum period. (See Table 7.1.) Even the social diversity suggested by the house figures turns out to be more apparent than real. For while the vast majority of lowcountry voters were farmers or planters of various sorts, those legislators who were not planters were, almost without exception, professionals.

In Beaufort's four parishes, for example, most nonplanter representatives were lawyers, with a few factors, medical doctors, one timber dealer, and a handful of planter sons rounding out the group. Except for the planter sons who had still to inherit slaves as personal property, all owned slaves, and most owned between fifteen and twenty. Of the entire group of 147 representatives elected from Beaufort over the course of the antebellum period whose social identity could be determined, none were yeoman farmers, none even small planters—with one intriguing exception. Among that body of planters and wealthy lawyers apparently sat one yeoman farmer, William Garvin, elected in 1836 and again in 1838 to represent St. Peter's Parish in the state house. Resident of a yeoman settlement, a young man, and a modest nonslaveholding farmer whose land in 1850 was valued at only three hundred dollars, Garvin was the exception that proved the rule. His story would make a fascinating one, if it could ever be told.[5]

Matters were not very different in the Middle Country, save that

4. Wooster, *The People in Power*, p. 5.
5. The real propertyholdings, slaveholdings, and professions of legislators were derived from the sources listed for Table 7.1.

Table 7.1 Planter Representation in the State Legislature, 1820–1860

A. STATE HOUSE OF REPRESENTATIVES

Planter Representatives by Decade (percentage)

District	1820–29	1830–39	1840–49	1850–60	Average
Beaufort	87	67	71	59	71
Barnwell	90	86	67	78	77
Darlington	100	67	89	47	70

Number = 252
Total % planters = 72
% Legislators identified = 80

B. STATE SENATE

Beaufort	100	87	100	78	
Barnwell	100	100	100	100	
Darlington	100	100	100	83	

Number = 113
Total % planters = 92
% Legislators identified = 88

Sources: Walter B. Edgar, ed., *Biographical Directory of the South Carolina House of Representatives* (Columbia, S.C.: University of South Carolina Press, 1974), vol. I, pp. 301–85; Federal Manuscript Census, South Carolina [Beaufort, Barnwell, and Darlington Districts], Schedules of Population and Slaves, 1850, 1860; South Carolina Lower Division Tax Returns, 1824, Records of the Comptroller General, SCDAH; N. Louise Bailey et al., *Biographical Directory of the South Carolina Senate, 1776–1985* (Columbia, S.C.: University of South Carolina Press, 1985), vol. 3, 1846–87.

planters had an even tighter lock on the state senate. As in Beaufort, so in the two middle country districts of Barnwell and Darlington, 70 to 77 percent of the representatives were planters. Again, the remainder were drawn overwhelmingly from the ranks of slaveholding professionals. Of the 105 men who represented those two districts in the house between 1820 and 1860, only two were nonslaveholders, and both of these were professionals. Viewed over space and time, the regional pattern is stunning in its clarity: 250 of the 252 men elected to represent those three districts in the state house were substantial planters. Only two were not. One, D. G. Woods of Darlington, was a small planter (he owned twelve slaves and land valued at $2,250); the other, the anomalous William Garvin of St. Peter's Parish in Beaufort District, was by all accounts a yeoman farmer. With respect to the class composition of representation in the state legislature, the Middle Country and the coastal districts were of a lowcountry piece.

There was, however, one apparent difference between interior and coast with respect to representatives. Judging from a comparison of Beaufort and Barnwell in the last antebellum decade, it would seem that middle country legislators were wealthier as a group than their coastal counterparts. The mean value of real property held by Barnwell's representatives in the house was $8,545, an almost exact match with the state median, while that held by Beaufort's representatives varied from a low of $2,937 for the Prince William's delegation to a high of $11,571 for the St. Luke's men. Thus, while there was great variation, the mean value of the real property held by the Beaufort delegation was only $5,854, significantly less than that of Barnwell and below the state median.[6] It would be a mistake to make too much of this, given the range and kind of wealth involved (none of these calculations includes personal property), but it does suggest that the parishes had no monopoly on planter-dominated politics or on returning wealth to represent the people.

Planter influence did not end in the legislature. The planter elite had a virtual monopoly on the governor's office and on congressional seats as well.[7] The extent of their hold on local government was, however, a bit less predictable. It is true that more planters served in local government in South Carolina than anywhere else in the antebellum South. Yet here the pattern was more complicated. For although the median value of the real property holdings of the state's district officials was the highest in the South, and although the figures indicate few yeoman farmers among their ranks (two-thirds of local officials owned more than five thousand dollars of real property), lists of officials appointed and elected also confirm that the odd yeoman farmer could find his way into local office in the Low Country.[8]

Commissioners of roads and bridges are cases in point, although the evidence is fragmentary and only suggestive. Local government in South Carolina was administered largely through a series of commissions, among which none held greater powers than the Commission of Roads and Bridges. Commissioners were selected by the state legislature, and influence over those positions fell within the patronage of the district or parish representative. As a result, the majority of the commissioners of roads were planters with close personal and even kinship ties to legislators. Indeed, many who held that office had either served in the state legislature themselves or would go on to do so.[9] But judging from the

6. Median real wealth of house members was $8,000 in 1850 and $10,000 in 1860; for state senators, it was $11,000 in 1850, and $25,000 in 1860. The figures can be found in Wooster, *The People in Power*, pp. 33–36. Mean real property values of Beaufort and Barnwell legislators were derived from the Federal Manuscript Census, South Carolina [Beaufort and Barnwell Districts], Schedules of Population and Slaves, 1850, 1860, NA.

7. Five of 6 governors in the 1850s owned in excess of 100 slaves and all owned in excess of $150,000 of real property. See Wooster, *The People in Power*, p. 55.

8. For the median real property owned by local officials and for the comparative evidence, see Wooster, *The People in Power*, pp. 99, 104. Wooster's calculations are based only on the office of Commissioner of Roads and include only those who held office in 1860.

9. For the organization of local government in South Carolina, see Ford, *Origins of Southern Radicalism*, pp. 304–6; Wooster, *The People in Power*, pp. 81–106; Emily Bellinger Reynolds and Joan Reynolds Faunt, *The County Offices and Officers of Barnwell County, South Carolina, 1775–1975* (Spartanburg, S.C.: The Reprint Company, 1976). Election of Commissioners of the Poor was given over to the people during the 1830s; selection of all other

composition of the Lower Board of Commissioners of Roads for St. Peter's Parish in Beaufort District in 1824 (one of the few for which records survive), planter legislators occasionally dispensed this political patronage down the social scale. While most of the eleven identifiable members of that parish board were planters, two appear to have been yeoman farmers. One was a slaveholder who owned six slaves and land valued at $225, the other a nonslaveholder who owned only $77 worth of land.[10]

Much the same pattern appears to have prevailed among sheriffs and tax collectors, other local offices of some significance, with planters and small planters dominating the ranks and a few yeoman farmers making appearances. In St. Peter's Parish, for example, only seven men held the office of tax collector during the antebellum period, and of the four whose social identity could be ascertained, only one, Shadrach Wooten, was a yeoman farmer. Wooten, interestingly, held the office between 1826 and 1833, when it was still appointed by the legislature. After 1836, when the office was given over to election by the people, the people of St. Peter's Parish chose substantial planters such as A. M. Ruth.[11]

Yeomen, moreover, appear to have had as good a shot at local office in the coastal parishes as they did in the middle country districts. Among the identifiable tax collectors in Barnwell District, none were yeomen (the most modest officeholder owned thirteen slaves and ten thousand dollars worth of real estate), although two slaveholding yeomen did serve as sheriff between 1841 and 1857.[12] Yeomen made a little better showing in Darlington District, where they constituted two of the five men known to have served as tax collectors, together with two of three sheriffs.[13]

---

selection of all other commissioners remained the prerogative of the legislature. See Ford, *Origins of Southern Radicalism*, p. 305.

10. The Lower Board of Commissioners of Roads for St. Peter's Parish was found in Petitions to the Legislature [Beaufort District], 1824, General Assembly Records, SCDAH; its members were identified in South Carolina Lower Division Tax Returns [St. Peter's Parish, Beaufort District], 1824, Records of the Comptroller General, SCDAH. Of the remaining 9 commissioners, 3 were planters (they owned 23, 25, and 26 slaves respectively), 3 were small planters (they owned 15, 15, and 19 slaves respectively), and 3 were small slaveholders (they owned 3, 6, and 9 slaves respectively).

11. The names of tax collectors from St. Peter's Parish were derived from the Secretary of State Papers, List of District Officers, Beaufort District, 1821–1862, SCDAH. Land and slaveholding profiles were derived from South Carolina Lower Division Tax Returns [St. Peter's Parish, Beaufort District], 1824; Federal Manuscript Census, South Carolina [Beaufort District], Schedules of Population and Slaves, 1850 and 1860.

12. Names of Barnwell sheriffs and tax collectors were derived from Secretary of State Papers, Lists of Officers Appointed and Elected, [Barnwell District], 1839–1898. Profiles of land and slaveholdings were derived from the Federal Manuscript Census, South Carolina [Barnwell District], Schedules of Population and Slaves, 1850 and 1860.

13. Names of Darlington tax collectors and sheriffs were derived from the following: Secretary of State Papers, List of District Officers, Darlington District, 1821–1862; Secretary of State Papers, List of Officers Appointed and Elected [Darlington District], 1839–

It would be a mistake to conclude, however, that the planters' grip on political power in the Low Country slipped in the management of local affairs. For if yeoman farmers occasionally appeared in their neighborhoods in the garb of state authority, they did so—and were known to do so—with the explicit backing of prominent local planters, themselves tied to the state's political leadership. And this was true whether the officeholder was appointed or elected by the people, as the lists of bondholders filed with the secretary of state confirm.[14] Among those who posted bond as security for public funds in the possession of sheriffs and tax collectors, there was always at least one substantial planter and one not infrequently who was or would become a legislator himself. This patronage network did not make yeomen any different from other local officials or, for that matter, from state representatives and senators or from U.S. representatives and senators who were themselves wealthy planters. Every politician in South Carolina, however wealthy, elevated, and apparently secure in his position, was part of a complex system of brokered politics and sponsored office holding—a patron-client network—that came to define the state's political culture.[15] That a few yeomen (and it was a few) found a lowly place in a planter-configured politics only testifies to the resiliency of the system and the confidence of its managers.

Exceptions did prove the rule. With respect to the social composition of those who held office, the state's political system put vastly disproportionate power in planter hands. If white men's democracy implies a rough equality of political influence, access, and power between yeomen and planters, then, it is safe to say, the political culture of the Low Country was of a different character. To the extent that yeomen had a voice in the councils of state, it was barely audible above the planter din.

1898. Land and slaveholdings of local officeholders were derived from Federal Manuscript Census, South Carolina [Darlington District], Schedules of Population and Slaves, 1850 and 1860. No tax list has survived for Darlington District. Land and slaveholdings of those who held office before 1850 could only be derived from the 1850 census and are, as a result, only rough indications.

14. Every public officer had to post bond in varying amounts. Those who secured the bonds are listed in the Secretary of State Papers and provide a good indication of officeholders' patronage networks. In every case, bondholders for sheriffs and tax collectors included, usually in addition to officeholders themselves and a few family members, at least one substantial local planter. See Secretary of State Papers, Public Officers' Bonds, 1847–1861. My observations are based on analysis of the list of bondholders for the offices of sheriff and tax collector in Barnwell and Darlington districts. The social identity of bondholders was derived by matching names to the Federal Manuscript Census, South Carolina [Barnwell and Darlington Districts], Schedules of Population and Slaves, 1850 and 1860. This technique of mapping patronage networks was borrowed from Steven Hahn's *Roots of Southern Populism* (New York: Oxford University Press, 1983), pp. 95–96.

15. One aspect of this system, that involving state legislators, is explored in greater detail below.

III

Planters' hold on power was not a haphazard or incidental result of discrete political contests. It was not produced simply out of the informal practice of politics in the region. Not only were nonplanter officeholders constrained to venues far from the center of political power—notably the state legislature—but planter domination of that body was carefully orchestrated by every arrangement of lowcountry political life, beginning with the state constitution. By apportioning legislative representation on the basis of taxable property as well as white population, the compromise of 1808 had awarded upcountry districts more equitable representation in the legislature while continuing to secure the disproportionate influence of the lowcountry parishes. A compromise passed and thereafter defended only with the connivance of a significant proportion of the upcountry elite, the sectional arrangements of that system of representation had a definite class agenda, as a number of historians have pointed out: to secure planter rule against the potentially leveling effects of white manhood suffrage and government by the majority.[16]

The conflation of sectional and class prerogatives persisted in a messy mix throughout the antebellum period, complicating attempts to build popular political organizations across the state. As radicals struggled to forge new political organizations and alliances that could sustain the Low Country for Nullification in the late 1820s and 1830s, they found themselves confronted time and again with Unionist attempts to exploit long-standing antagonisms between coastal and interior districts over apportionment and the proper limits of popular politics. Thus, in 1830 radical advocates of a convention of the people (Nullifiers' strategy to enact their doctrine into law) were forced to repudiate Unionists' charges that, once assembled and possessed of the power, the people in convention might also be disposed "to abolish the system of Parish representation" and to "destroy the weight of the lower country in the Legislature." But if Unionist charges forced Nullifiers into passionate declarations of faith in the "people of the upper country" and of the honesty and integrity of "every man in the interior," in private they were far less sanguine about their ability to control a mobilized and

16. Klein, *Unification of a Slave State*, pp. 238–68; Mark D. Kaplanoff, "Making the South Solid: Politics and the Structure of Society in South Carolina, 1790–1815" (Ph.D. Diss., Cambridge University, 1976); Ford, *Origins of Southern Radicalism*, pp. 99–144; Chauncey S. Boucher, "Sectionalism, Representation, and the Electoral Question in Ante-Bellum South Carolina," *Washington University Studies* 4, no. 1 (1916), pp. 3–62. For the disproportionate representation of the parishes in the 1820s, See Robert Mills, *Statistics of South Carolina* (1826; reprint ed., Spartanburg, S.C.: The Reprint Company, 1972), p. 211. For the 1840s, see William Gilmore Simms *The Geography of South Carolina* (Charleston; Babcock, 1843), pp. 16–17, 29.

potentially disgruntled electorate.[17] Indeed, so sensitive was the issue, so
threatening to nascent organization, that one political newcomer and
Barnwell Nullifier, James Henry Hammond, took it upon himself to
apprise coastal leaders of the resentment percolating in the Middle
Country against the Charleston style and domination of their party.
"There is still great jealousy of Charleston among the upper Countrymen," he wrote to Governor James Hamilton in the summer of 1831,
and while assuring him that the "tide . . . is telling strongly for us,"
warned that "if the idea is at once taken up that Charleston is arrogating
to herself the lead—good bye." Hammond had reason to worry, for at
least in 1830 anxiety over the reapportionment issue and the challenge
to lowcountry planter power embedded in it had contributed to the
defeat of the Nullifiers' first convention campaign. Radicals learned a
lasting lesson. "We are gone if anything prevents a general and cordial
cooperation from the mountains to the seaboards," Hammond conceded
in 1831.[18]

It was not the last time coastal and interior antagonism would foil
radical attempts to build statewide coalitions. Nor was it the last time that
struggles over reapportionment would frame challenges to planter domination of political life. Certainly the class dimension of the issue goes a
long way toward explaining how the original system survived repeated
assault. For with the exception of one belated concession to the Upcountry in the division of Pendleton District into two election districts in 1851,
the lowcountry parishes successfully staved off the threat of reapportionment and preserved the sectional basis of the planters' legislative
power down to the Civil War. They could not have done it without the
support of upcountry and middle country planters who accepted the
disproportionate representation of the parishes as the price to be paid
for keeping popular political influence within acceptable bounds.[19]

Reliable as it was, however, sectional gerrymandering was not the
only insurance lowcountry planters possessed. Other, more explicit re-
straints on white majority politics were inscribed in the state constitution,
not the least of which were substantial property qualifications for officeholders: qualifications, it is important to add, to which most of the
state's political elite remained committed long after they had been aban-

17. *Charleston Mercury*, May 15, 1830, May 18, 1830. As late as the fall of 1832, according to one pro-Nullification organ, Unionists were still stirring up animosities between the
lowcountry parishes and the interior. See *Winyah Intelligencer*, October 6, 1832. On reapportionment and the convention issue see Chauncey S. Boucher, *The Nullification Controversy in South Carolina* (1916; reprint ed., New York: Greenwood Press, 1968), pp. 88–89.

18. James Henry Hammond to Governor Hamilton, July 28, 1831, James Henry Hammond to P. M. Butler, July 31, 1831, Letter Press Book, 1831–1833, James Henry Hammond Papers, SCL, in Kenneth Stampp, ed., Records of Antebellum Southern Plantations
From the Revolution Through the Civil War, Series A. Part 1, Reel 3.

19. On the struggle over reapportionment and the division of Pendleton, see Ford,
Origins of Southern Radicalism, pp. 281–307.

doned in other southern states.[20] But no single aspect of state politics so enhanced planter power, so marginalized the majority of yeoman voters, and so shaped the distinctive political path onto which South Carolina moved in the 1830s as the legislature's unyielding control over political offices filled almost everywhere else in the country by popular election.

Alone of all the states by the 1830s, South Carolina reserved to the state legislature the right to elect governors, state senators, the majority of state and local officials, and, perhaps most important, presidential electors. No yeoman farmer in the Low Country ever cast a vote directly for Andrew Jackson, James K. Polk, or any other aspirant to the presidency. At the polls, voters elected only U.S. representatives, state legislators, and, by the late 1830s, a handful of local officials, including sheriffs and tax collectors. It amounted, as many historians have pointed out, to a system of legislative government. "It is only on rare occasions, and the rarer the better," the lowcountry planter, politician, and historian William Henry Trescot declared approvingly, "that it is necessary for the people to turn politician."[21]

The few concessions made to extending the boundaries of popular political participation in the state were wrung out of a reluctant legislature only after years of struggle and stonewalling. And on key offices no quarter was ever given. Demands for the popular election of tax collectors came before the legislature repeatedly in the late 1820s and 1830s, for example, and were invariably "postponed" on the grounds of "inexpedien[cy]," usually after little or no discussion. Even in the midst of the Nullifiers' full-throated appeals to the people and charges of elitism leveled at Unionists, radical lowcountry politicians like Robert Barnwell Rhett (still Barnwell Smith) thought the principle of exclusion worth the risk of popular disapproval and joined to kill the initiative. Rhett was nothing if not consistent. While he mastered the mechanisms of popular politics, he never wavered on the necessity of maintaining the limits on it. Indeed, his commitment to retaining state and local offices "free from popular favor or rage" dated from his freshman year in the state legislature, when he had taken a resolute stand against a popularly elected judiciary. Although modest concessions were eventually made on a few local offices, they hardly portended a revolution in political culture, and there were those among the lowcountry elite who would continue to

20. On property qualifications for officeholders, see Wooster, *The People in Power,* pp. 8–9.

21. Trescot quoted in Robert Nicholas Olsberg, "A Government of Class and Race: William Henry Trescot and the South Carolina Chivalry, 1860–1865, (Ph.D. Diss., University of South Carolina, 1972), p. 87. On South Carolina as a system of legislative government, see Wooster, *The People in Power,* pp. 5–9, 49–53, 84–92, 109–15; Green, "Democracy in the Old South," p. 80; James M. Banner, Jr., "The Problem of South Carolina," in Stanley L. Elkins and Eric McKitrick, eds., *The Hofstadter Aegis: A Memorial* (New York: Alfred A. Knopf, 1974), pp. 76–79; Greenberg, *Masters and Statesmen,* pp. 45–61; and Ford, *Origins of Southern Radicalism,* pp. 281–307.

insist that the popular election of tax collector and sheriff marked the demise of South Carolina's true republican system. "Popular elections," "popular self-government and universal suffrage," the crotchety Colleton planter David Gavin snapped, "the most pernicious humbug of a humbug age," nothing other than rule by "the *Sovereign* people, alias mob," "mobocracy alias democracy."[22]

The issue of electing tax collectors and sheriffs marked only skirmishes in the real battle, for the distinctions some made between a republican form of government and a democratic one came to a head in South Carolina over the method of choosing presidential electors. And here no concessions were ever made. In that protracted struggle, reformers and defenders of the status quo alike identified the legislative stranglehold on the electoral college for what it was: class legislation designed to constrain government by the majority, preclude "democracy," and sustain "republicanism"—or, as some called it, "oligarchy" or even "aristocracy." The brief for a conservative and antidemocratic republicanism, regularly indulged in the safe textual environs of journals, private correspondence, and addresses to planter associations, was brought into the full light of day in this defense of legislative prerogative. That so many politicians, without regard to section or partisan affiliation, were willing to voice publicly such ostensibly undemocratic views tells us more than a little about the complexities of political life and the meaning of democratic republicanism in lowcountry South Carolina.

By appropriating the power to select presidential electors and by insisting on that prerogative long after other states had turned to election by the people, South Carolina legislators put the state outside the mainstream of national politics. In doing so, they precluded, and quite self-consciously, the development of the second-party system and the fusion of national and local political issues that historians have identified as the signature of Jacksonian democracy. "The conduct of politics [in South Carolina] was so distinctive as to be markedly different from any other state," one historian of the second-party system has explained. Another, although determined to establish the Old South as the cradle of Jacksonian democracy, still felt compelled to jettison South Carolina as "the one remaining stronghold of the landed aristocracy in the South."[23] If the latter exaggerated the case, the tendency was nonetheless clear.

22. House of Representatives Journal, November 30, 1829, December 15, 1829, November 24, 1830, December 6, 1832, December 14, 1832, General Assembly Records; Rhett quoted in Laura A. White, *Robert Barnwell Rhett: Father of Secession* (Gloucester, Mass.: Peter Smith, 1965), p. 8; David Gavin Diary, May 31, 1856, October 8, 1856, August 8, 1857, SHC.

23. Richard P. McCormick, *The Second American Party System: Party Formation in the Jacksonian Era* (Chapel Hill: University of North Carolina Press, 1966), p. 7; Green, "Democracy in the Old South." On the second-party system and sustained party conflict as the signature characteristics of Jacksonian democracy, see Harry L. Watson, *Jacksonian Politics and Community Conflict: The Emergence of the Second American Party System in Cumberland*

A principled opposition to government by the majority, and the articulated distrust of "the people" that usually accompanied it, were perfectly
legitimate parts of public political discourse in lowcountry South Carolina
throughout the antebellum period. There were many in South Carolina
who publicly proclaimed that they last thing they wanted was "democracy" as they understood it to exist in other southern states. Many, perhaps
even yeoman voters in the rural areas of the coastal and interior lowcountry, were convinced that the undemocratic aspects of the state's political
system constituted its firmest claim to a true republicanism.

Every adult white man—every yeoman farmer and every planter—
possessed the right to vote in antebellum South Carolina. But white
manhood suffrage did not a rough political equality make. A herrenvolk
democracy the South Carolina Low Country surely was not. Yet neither
was it the "aristocracy," the perfected planter regime, some desired to
make it and some historians have declared it. Although no match for the
prerogatives so jealously guarded by their planter counterparts, the
rights of yeoman freemen were anything but illusory. In the constant
tension between "popular" suffrage and elite rule, and in the discourse,
rituals, organizations, and strategies such tension engendered, lay the
substance of the lowcountry's complex and distinctly republican political
culture.

IV

In their endless stream of complaints about the "mobocratic" character
of republicanism in the state and in their periodic demands for further
restrictions on popular politics, even on white manhood suffrage itself,
lowcountry planters and politicians gave eloquent testimony to a crucial
dimension of the region's political culture: the importance of yeoman
voters and the difficulty of managing them.[24]

That dimension of political life took on heightened significance during the late 1820s and early 1830s as Nullifiers and Unionists did battle
for the hearts, minds, and ballots of "the people" and introduced a level
of political organization and mobilization entirely unprecedented in the
state or the Low Country. For along with regular expressions of contempt for the process, politicians on both sides of the divide admitted the

---

County, North Carolina (Baton Rouge: Louisiana State University Press, 1981). Ford dissents
somewhat from this view, arguing that although it did not participate in the second-party
system, South Carolina did evince the "massive popular involvement of the 'common man'
in public life" that was the definitive characteristic of Jacksonian democracy. Ford, *Origins
of Southern Radicalism*, pp. 142–44.

24. For two good examples of lowcountry planters who railed against the "mobocracy"
and who supported property qualifications for voters, see Gavin Diary, January 18, 1858,
May 18, 1861 and passim; and John Berkley Grimball Diary, October 5, 1832, and passim,
Grimball Family Papers, SHC.

political necessity and applied themselves, if unevenly and ambivalently, to it. Nullifiers and Unionists alike struggled with the problem of mobilizing nonelite voters, seeking mechanisms by which to take the temperature of the electorate in their various neighborhoods, parishes, and districts, developing strategies by which to claim the mantle of the people and by which to tar the other party as the people's enemy. They struggled, in other words, for ways to control a potentially unruly electorate. In the Nullification Crisis, the yeoman voter was ever in political view.

When the Nullifier James Henry Hammond penned an editorial in the pages of the *Columbia Southern Times* ridiculing the Unionist congressman James Blair for his undue deference to the "wisdom" of his constituents, he committed a strategic error. For Blair's acute response—that "I am still willing to admit that amongst my constituents are many men 'wiser' (much wiser) than myself and equally honest, and I hope I shall never become so foolish or so vain as to think otherwise"— put Hammond and his cause in an unflattering light and forced him into a hasty retraction and a twice-repeated avowal of respect for the people of Blair's congressional district. Hammond was a quick study. A few months later he was whistling a different editorial tune. "It is the people and the people only who possess the power surely and effectually to arrest and change the current of usurpation and oppression," he wrote in late August 1830. "To them we should appeal when it becomes necessary to make any great political movement." In addition to the obvious pandering, there was in Hammond's statement evidence of a pragmatic lesson learned. It was one that had been taught on the ground.

Since the early part of 1830 Hammond had served as middle country point man for the Nullifiers' campaign, taking instruction on editorial policy mostly from the coastal lowcountry leadership and advising them in turn on strategies calculated to build support among middle country voters. It was a delicate job. As one leading Nullifier, U.S. Senator Robert Y. Hayne, told Hammond, "[E]verything which looks like unnecessary violence [mu]st have the tendency to create reaction, and yet it is extremely difficult to keep up the public feeling at a proper point, and prevent its boiling over." Requested to "obtain the best information you can of the state of public sentiment in the interior," Hammond embraced his role enthusiastically, sending frequent missives on how to "stir up" middle country voters against Unionist judges, urging lowcountry leaders to "follow the [Charleston] lead and get up [State Rights] associations" in the interior, and cautioning them against "mismanagement," especially in the reflexive advancement of coastal lowcountry party men at the expense of middle country candidates.[25]

25. James Henry Hammond, "The Controversy Between General James Blair and James H. Hammond, Esq" [1830], James Henry Hammond Papers, in Kenneth Stampp, ed., Records of Antebellum Southern Plantations, Reel 6; Hammond in the *Columbia Times and State Gazette*, August 26, 1830, quoted in Drew Gilpin Faust, *James Henry Hammond and*

Hammond never lost his contempt for "the people" and the processes of popular politics. After the defeat of the Nullifiers' first convention campaign in 1830, for example, he railed bitterly against "universal suffrage [which] had given a class of people power which they are totally incompetent to exercise." But Hammond was no political fool—or at least not in the ordinary sense. He embraced the necessity of managing the people and, along with the rest of the Nullification leaders and footsoldiers, applied himself to divining the means by which to do so successfully. Like many other ambitious coastal and middle country politicians, Hammond would, for the rest of his political career, veer wildly between unguarded and usually private expressions of disdain for the people—"I despise the mass," he wrote in 1845—and energetic embrace of precisely the behavior he condemned. Although he preferred to stand aloof from the crowd—to stand (rather than run) for office in the old Jeffersonian tradition—he was not above "throwing himself open mouthed on the mob" (his phrase) when circumstances demanded it, as they not infrequently did.[26]

Unionists were no different, although it is arguable that they were slower and less apt students of the new popular politics. Daniel Huger, one of the most prominent lowcountry Unionists, was roundly maligned by Nullifiers, with some reason, as an old "federalist" and his party as one resistant to the principle of "general suffrage." But even he admitted by 1836 that "[a] party no more than a nation can be governed with out reference to the feelings of the governed," and in a letter to James Chesnut of Kershaw District he insisted that the Unionists' candidate of choice be withdrawn in deference to the tastes of the electorate. "Mr. W. is a gentleman and man of understanding," he wrote, "and will have to be told that his acknowledged pretension will, at this moment, interfere with the interests of the party . . . and their integrity."[27] If lowcountry

the Old South: A Design for Mastery (Baton Rouge: Louisiana State University Press, 1982), p. 54; Robert Y. Hayne to James Henry Hammond, Washington, February 25, 1830, in "Letters on the Nullification Movement in South Carolina," *American Historical Review* 6 (July 1901), p. 737; James Hamilton, Jr., to James Henry Hammond, Charleston, June 11, 1831, in "Letters on the Nullification Movement," pp. 746–47; James Henry Hammond to P. M. Butler, Ashville, North Carolina, July 31, 1831, Hammond to Isaac Hayne, July 31, 1831, Hammond to Governor Hamilton, July 28, 1831, all in James Henry Hammond Papers, Letter Press Book, in Stampp, ed., Records of Antebellum Southern Plantations, Reel 3. The *Columbia Southern Times* was the paper in which Nullification leaders placed much of their hope in their effort to carry the Middle Country.

26. *Columbia Times and State Gazette*, October 14, 1830, quoted in Faust, *James Henry Hammond and the Old South*, p. 54; James Henry Hammond Diary, July 3, 1845, February 19, 1846, in Carol Bleser, ed., *Secret and Sacred: The Diaries of James Henry Hammond, A Southern Slaveholder* (New York: Oxford University Press, 1988), pp. 150, 153–54.

27. *Charleston Mercury*, February 8, 1831; D. E. Huger to Colonel James Chesnut, August 20, 1836, Williams-Chesnut-Manning Papers, SCL. James Henry Hammond cast the contest as one between "Republicanism and Federalism in its old form and spirit." See *Columbia Southern Times and Gazette*, November 23, 1830, quoted in Faust, *James Henry Hammond and the Old South*, p. 55. Historians have concurred in the contemporary radical

Unionists conceded the necessity of attending to the will of the people, however, their suspicion of the people and their contempt for the process of wooing them was never far below the surface, impeding efforts at grass-roots organization. "The majority of our folks are citizens such as Rome had in her worst days," James Louis Petigru, another lowcountry Union leader, wrote in 1833 by way of exonerating his party in defeat. "The people" were dupes of "Jacobinal" planters, he insisted, as he had since 1828, representing them as men incapable of independent political judgment whose votes existed only to be bought and sold. He and his allies railed in print against the irresponsibility, even insanity, of radical leaders who used any means to "inflame the minds of the people." One would think they "had been bitten by some mad bull or mad dog," John Townsend proclaimed in the *Charleston Mercury*. Perhaps for this reason the Unionists were slow to deploy organized means to arouse the voters in their interest. As late as August 1832 Unionists were just beginning to raise money to "disseminate information among the people" and to make arrangements to have extra newspapers printed and distributed among the districts. Although they appeared to have had the jump on the radicals in 1830, they could not staunch the flow of moderates into the radical camp, and by 1832, when the final score was tallied, lowcountry Unionists readily conceded the Nullifiers' superiority in courting the mob. "On the sin and gin we were defeated again," Petigru complained to Hugh Legaré, "thus you see we are on the gallop, and how long our demagogues keep the saddle, no one knows." But in the highbrow sour grapes in which defeated Unionists characteristically indulged was embedded a more serious recognition. "They practiced new and unheard of means," Petigru admitted.[28] Although Unionists conceded the necessity, they had failed, in Nullification at least, to match the radicals' mastery of the techniques of a new popular politics.

Much as planter politicians feared, the new politics could not help but create dangerous openings for the expression of usually latent conflict between yeoman and planter voters. For where contests were close and hotly disputed, even planter politicians could not always resist the temptation to play the class card. In 1830, for example, as the first Nullification convention campaign was drawing to a close, Nullifiers played every card in their hand, temporarily heedless of the conse-

identification of coastal and especially Charleston Unionists as Federalists. See Lacy K. Ford, Jr., "James Louis Petigru: The Last South Carolina Federalist," in Michael O'Brien and David Moltke-Hansen, eds., *Intellectual Life in Antebellum Charleston* (Knoxville: University of Tennessee Press, 1986), pp. 152–85.

28. James Louis Petigru to Hugh Legaré, July 15, 1833, James Louis Petigru to William Elliott, August 25, 1831, September 7, 1831, October 3, 1832, all in James Petigru Carson, ed., *Life, Letters, and Speeches of James Louis Petigru, the Union Man of South Carolina* (Washington, D.C.: W. H. Lowdermilk and Co., 1920), pp. 83–84, 85, 98–99; *Charleston Mercury*, September 28, 1830, October 2, 1830; Chapman Levy to William Elliott, Camden, August 27, 1832, Elliott-Gonzales Papers, SHC; James Louis Petigru to Hugh Legaré, October 29, 1832, James L. Petigru Papers, SCL.

quences. So while Robert Hayne was commiserating with James Henry Hammond over the difficulty of keeping the "public feeling at proper point [while] prevent[ing] its boiling over," one lowcountry radical editorialist, "General Suffrage," pointedly charged Daniel Huger, "the head of the Tariff or Anti-State Rights Ticket," with being "the same person who as Representative from St. Andrew's Parish voted, as landlord *against* the extension of the *right* of voting to those citizens whose only fault might be *poverty*." If Huger was indeed that man, General Suffrage closed, "no poor man should vote for him." Nor were Unionists above such moves. Seeing their temporary advantage slip away in the face of the Nullifiers' superior organizing and the collapse of hopes of federal redress in 1831, they too played their hand, accusing the Nullifier governor, Stephen Miller, of "being arrayed against the poor," of "prefer[ring] one rich man's vote to six poor ones." Miller's response— that "I have not found it necessary to make great professions of attachment to the poor," that he left such appeals to "those who have been harder pressed than myself to gain the favor of the people," and that, unlike their "wealthy planter" opponents, Nullifiers sought only to protect "the farmer" from the depredations of the federal government— revealed a great deal about the nature of Nullification politics. The yeomanry's ability to inject its particular concerns into political contests was, predictably, greatest in closely contested legislative elections in which competing factions or parties did bloody battle for the yeoman vote. Planter politicians risked a great deal in exploiting such volatile ground. Indeed, they might well have regretted in leisure what they had so readily done in crisis, for as one legislator noted in 1833, "[A] mean feeling is pervading the house—such as opposition to the aristocracy so called in other words opposed to gentlemen." They reaped what they sowed.[29] At such moments, the tension at the heart of the Low Country's still developing political culture, between planter rule and yeoman voters, was revealed for all to see.

In the new popular politics of the South Carolina Low Country, yeoman farmers clearly did not possess the strength to force a redistribution of political power. The decks were stacked carefully against them. But if they could not secure an equal place with planter voters, they could and did find a recognized place in the exclusive fraternity of freemen that constituted the body politic of the Low Country. And that privileged but unequal position marked every aspect of yeoman politics. The sheer ballot-box power yeomen wielded, their majority part in a small body politic, ensured that while they could not compel planters to yield their particular prerogatives, they could force them to govern in the name of freemen and masters and not just, as many legislators would

29. *Charleston Mercury*, October 6, 1830; Printed Letter of Stephen D. Miller, Governor, Plane Hill, September 9, 1831, Williams-Chesnut-Manning Papers; P. M. Butler to James Henry Hammond, Columbia, December 12, 1833, James Henry Hammond Papers, in Stampp, ed., Records of Antebellum Southern Plantations, Reel 7.

have preferred, in the interest of slaveholders and planters. In this respect, then, yeoman farmers gave fundamental shape to the political culture forged in the crucible of Nullification.

Few things mattered so decisively in the Nullifiers' victory as the success with which they met the challenge of managing the people. And in that victory, few things figured so centrally as their ability to frame Nullification as the only fit response of freemen and thus to present themselves as the embodiment of the people's will. That the Nullification struggle took this discursive shape confirms that in the new political culture the yeoman voter was ever present. And it begins to suggest the ways in which yeoman farmers' limited ability to define their relations with planters also sapped their political will, wedding them to a system that empowered them as freemen and masters even as it subordinated them to wealthier and more powerful members of that exclusive fraternity.

V

As early as 1828 the discursive outlines of the Nullifiers' campaign were already in place. Both the federal threat posed by the tariff and the case for Nullification were cast in terms calculated to speak to the whole of the Low Country's small body politic. Whether they mounted the stump at a militia muster, Fourth of July barbecue, or public state rights meeting, penned an article to the newspaper, or addressed a more elite audience in the state legislature, the region's richest planters and most powerful men spoke simply as "freemen" for "freemen." As "freemen," Robert Barnwell Rhett told a public meeting of "Citizens" at Walterboro Court House in June 1828, "we have proclaimed to the world that such a tariff would be an infringement of our privileges as men." "As a freeman," he declared to his fellow legislators in the same year, "I will not lay the bones of a slave beside those of a free ancestry."[30] In that one word, "freeman," and its opposite, "slave," was encoded a universe of political meanings.

The Nullifiers' posture was designed, in the first instance, to obscure the social divisions within the body politic, to narrow the distance between politicians and the majority of the "citizens," and, not least, to appeal to the majority of the men who marched in militia reviews, stood in sales-day crowds, and filled up the polling lists throughout the rural Low Country. Although most Nullifiers stuck to the vague and malleable term "freemen," some on occasion made their appeal to the yeomanry in more explicit terms. Thus, "One of the People" from Prince George, Winyaw, argued that the tariff "strikes a deadly blow at the prospects of the FARMER AND PLANTER" and insisted that should it stick, "the POOR BUT HONEST YEOMEN of our country must bid adieu to all

30. *Charleston Mercury,* June 18, 1828, August 6, 1829.

independence." Another "One of the People" from Orangeburg claimed to speak for all of the "frugal and industrious . . . farmers" of his district in advocating a nullification convention. Even state leaders were not above such transparent tactics. Congressman Thomas Mitchell of Georgetown District shamelessly courted the "bold yeomanry" of the Pee Dee at a dinner held in his honor at a rural muster house, urging them to "put down that club of Jacobins who, aiming at power under false pretenses, would make you slaves." And, in the General Assembly debates of 1830 over the calling of a convention to nullify the tariff, State Senator Whitemarsh Seabrook of St. John's Colleton moved from railing about the "chains" which Northerners designed to "rivet . . . on the patient and unresisting slaveholder" to insisting that the real issue was the "tribute which they annually receive from the southern yeoman."[31]

Indeed, Seabrook, Rhett, and other leading Nullifiers claimed not only to speak for the people—the yeomanry—but went further, presenting themselves as the embodiment of the people's will. Robert Barnwell Rhett typically posed as the people's servant. "[T]he power [a representative] uses or abuses is the power of his constituents," he declared in an "Address to the Citizens of St. Bartholomew's Parish" in the summer of 1829, and the Governor and First Vice-President of the State Rights and Free Trade Association of South Carolina, James Hamilton, insisted, equally disingenuously, that the party had been called into being by the people. We "rise on the buoyant surface of that glorious enthusiasm of popular feeling which is bearing our State on its resistless current into the haven of security, peace, honor, and imperishable renown," he wrote in the association's first political tract in 1831. But few put the case as baldly as Seabrook, who said simply that "the people" were the legislators' "masters" and who taunted the anticonvention forces in the legislature with the question "[A]re we afraid to trust our masters?"[32] It is one of the more interesting aspects of lowcountry politics that planter politicians were forced to cast their campaigns in terms designed to appeal to precisely the yeoman voters whose influence they struggled so successfully to constrain.

31. *Winyah Intelligencer*, August 28, 1830; *Charleston Mercury*, September 4, 1830; Representative Thomas Mitchell in *Winyah Intelligencer*, May 20, 1829. Mitchell represented the third congressional district and was a moderate on the tariff question in 1829. See Freehling, *Prelude to Civil War*, p. 144. For a biographical sketch of Mitchell, see *Biographical Directory of the American Congress, 1774–1961* (Washington, D.C.: U.S. Government Printing Office, 1961), p. 1342. Seabrook's convention speech is reprinted in *The Debate of the South Carolina Legislature, December 1830, on the Reports of the Committees of Both Houses in Favor of Convention, Etc.* (Columbia, S.C.: S. J. M'Morris, 1831), pp. 9–10. For a biographical sketch of Whitemarsh Seabrook, see N. Louise Bailey, et al., *Biographical Directory of the South Carolina Senate, 1776–1985*, 3 vols. (Columbia, S.C.: University of South Carolina Press), 2: 1434–35.

32. *Charleston Mercury*, August 4, 1829. Hamilton's speech was printed as Political Tract No. 1, *The Proceedings of the First Meeting of the Charleston State Rights and Free Trade Association of South Carolina* (Charleston: E. J. Van Brunt, 1831), p. 4; Seabrook, *Debate of the South Carolina Legislature . . . on Convention*, p. 16.

The image of the lowcountry body politic as one made up simply of "freemen" went beyond forms of address to shape Nullifiers' representation of the federal threat and the urgency of resistance. For if, on occasion, they dwelled on the particular threat the tariff and the related evidences of northern aggression (particularly the American Colonization Society) posed to planters and slaveholders, they usually emphasized the common patrimony of the region's freemen. Robert Barnwell Rhett, who came to run one of the best-managed and most-envied political organizations in the Low Country, pioneered the technique. As he put it in his speech to his constituents at Walterboro Court House, the issue was simple: The tariff was "an infringment on our privileges as men." "If we have the common pride of men or the determination of freemen," he said firmly, "we must resist." Carolina's freemen, he reminded them on another occasion shortly thereafter, noble sons of revolutionary forefathers, were passionately wedded to "their blood-bought heritage of freedom." Such men, he avowed, would never consent to be made the "crushed and trampled slaves" of northern "despots." "Despair we will leave to the weak," he roused them, for "all that to freemen is worth living for is worth dying for." Any other course—a "smiling peace with your insatiable oppressors," "submissive patience" or "impotent resistance"—was a fit response only of women or slaves.[33]

Rhett mastered the genre. His appeals to constituents rarely contained a discordant note. Although a wealthy planter and substantial slaveholder, he posed as just another "freeman." But other radical politicians were not so adept, and in their appeals the image of the body politic as one of equal freemen could and did fracture into its constituent social parts. "Leonidas," for example, pressed the case for immediate state action on Nullification in the pages of the *Charleston Mercury* in the summer of 1828 in terms closely akin to those Rhett deployed on the hustings. "The genius of the southern people," he wrote, was "detestation—inexcisable—inexpressible detestation of tyranny and oppression." The reason too was clear: "Freemen of the Southern States" hold "freedom" "most dear" and "oppression . . . most detestable" "because our system of slavery inevitably led us to scorn the one, as it gave factitious value to the other." Knowing liberty to be a privilege, then, the property only of those who could call themselves "freemen," they would never be made "the dastard-trampled slaves of wool-weavers and spindle-hurlers." But if Leonidas, like Rhett, urged Nullification in defense of the rights of all freemen, he also exposed the unequal terms of that republican bargain. "The man who has owned slaves can never be made a slave," he offered by way of elaboration, by virtue of "the free spirit that has arisen from his habits of command and his privileged superiority." The tension at the heart of Leonidas's brief, between the common privileges of freemen and the particular privileges of planter

33. *Charleston Mercury,* June 18, 1828, August 6, 1829.

freemen, was revealed time and again in radical political discourse. Nullifiers never could seem to decide whether their northern aggressors designed to make slaves of freemen or slaves of slaveholders.[34] Not surprisingly, many tried to have it both ways. In their efforts to do so, to obscure the contradictions, the gendered language of their particular republicanism carried much of the discursive burden.

Encomiums to manhood were so ubiquitous in antebellum political discourse that historians have only recently begun to attend to their meaning and function in discrete settings. Appeals to manly identity and manly duty such as those Leonidas, Rhett, and every other Nullifier made were not so many words tossed into the wind. Rather, they served as touchstones for a whole political culture, encoding a vast array of social references and partisan meanings in a seemingly self-evident, transhistorical, and even natural dichotomy. Radical lowcountry politicians were, fortunately, anything but subtle in their invocations of manhood, making it possible to begin to discern the role such language played in bringing sufficient numbers of yeoman farmers to see the struggle over the tariff as Nullifiers would have it: as a choice between "manly resistance" and womanly or slavish submission.

To begin with, Nullifiers traced the yeomanry's stake in the defense of the state back to the household itself, acutely elaborating the common patrimony of freemen as independence and, of course, as property of various real and personal sorts. "One of our noblest rights, the right of property, has been invaded," "Utensis" claimed in the *Charleston Mercury* as the Nullification convention battle heated up in the pre-election summer of 1830, and it is "a right that freemen can never relinquish without ignominy and disgrace." Those rights of property were, moreover, common to every freeman, as Nullification leaders were careful to point out. "We contend for a government that secures personal liberty and private property against the invasion of aristocratic wealth or democratic despotism," Governor Miller declared in 1830. "What property I have, my wife and children, are the capital—my stock in trade—which I will confide to the honor and moral sense of South Carolina." The next Governor, James Hamilton, was even more explicit. The investment of rich men in "our country" was, he admitted, self-evident. But, he asked, "have we, yea, the poorest and humblest among us, no hostages to give for our loyalty to our country?" His answer: "Yes, if not alone in the life-blood that gushes from our hearts, in our wives and our children, whom the love of manhood has made us swear to protect, and the very sacrament of nature leads us to love, honor, and obey." "[We] are equally interested as citizens—as owners of the soil—as the fathers of families," one radical correspondent bluntly put it, and it remains only to decide whether to "transmit the proud dignity of freedom or the degrading in-

---

34. "Leonidas," *Charleston Mercury*, July 14, 1828. But see as well Whitemarsh Seabrook's speech in *Debate of the South Carolina Legislature . . . on Convention.*

heritance of slavery."[35] Nullifiers invoked gender quite self-consciously to breach the divide between yeoman and planter freemen. As masters of dependents, even if only, or perhaps especially, of wives and children, every freeman was bound to defend his household, his property, against invasion.

The language of "invasion" not only invoked the spatial arrangements of masterhood as yeoman farmers and planters alike understood them in the Low Country but linked the violation of the state and its rights to the violation of the household itself. And indeed, where the state was cast symbolically as a woman, "Carolina," even "Mother Carolina," as "she" invariably was in radical discourse, spatial language led with seeming inexorability to sexual language: from invasion to violation. Governor Miller attempted to rouse South Carolinians with the image of the "monster . . . planting his foot on the threshold of our sacred political edifice." While the state slept in 1828, he said threateningly, "the deed was consummated."[36]

Miller and others left no confusion as to the nature of the deed. References to the "rapacity" of the federal government or northern aggressors proliferated in Nullifiers' tracts and speeches, as did allusions to the state as woman violated and even on occasion to the violation of the presumably male "body politic." The "safety . . . honor . . . character . . . liberty" of "Carolina, Our first and only mother," one correspondent declared, lay "in the hands of her sons." When the sovereign body of the state had "been so insultingly mutilated by the grasping rapacity of an interested majority," he avowed, Carolina's sons knew "a freeman's duty." The freeman's choice was a simple one: There was the "manly course" and the "effeminat[e]" one, or, as Rhett had put it in 1828, "manly resistance" or "impotent submission." To chose "submissive patience" in the face of one's "insatiable oppessors" was thus to be unmanned.[37]

In the corporeal, indeed sexual, language of resistance and submission, lowcountry radicals made a powerful case for Nullification. Every freeman, whether yeoman or planter, counted his household as an inviolable domain and the dependents within it his property, his alone to master. Freemen's duty as sons to protect the state was rooted in hearth and home, in the already acknowledged responsibility to protect their own mothers, wives, and daughters. Nullifiers had their own version of

35. *Charleston Mercury,* June 19, 1830, June 25, 1830, September 18, 1830; Hamilton in *Proceedings of the First Meeting of the Charleston State Rights and Free Trade Association of South Carolina,* pp. 6–7.

36. On Carolina as mother, see, for example, *Charleston Mercury,* July 8, 1828, July 9, 1830. Whitemarsh Seabrook's speech, delivered December 3, 1830, was reprinted in *Debate of the South Carolina Legislature, December 1830,* p. 10.

37. For examples of references to "rapacity," see *Charleston Mercury,* May 8, 1830, May 13, 1830; Seabrook, *Debate of the South Carolina Legislature . . . on Convention,* pp. 6, 19; Hamilton, *Proceedings of the First Meeting of the Charleston State Rights and Free Trade Association,* p. 16; Rhett, *Charleston Mercury,* June 18, 1828.

the family romance. "In our wives and children, whom the vow of manhood has made us swear to protect," Governor Hamilton reminded South Carolinians, lay every freeman's stake in the defense of "our country." The duty to protect Mother Carolina thus moored sectionalism in sexuality, in property in female bodies, in the integrity of the heterosexual male body, and in manhood itself.[38]

The martial manhood Nullifiers sought to mobilize in the interests of the state was grounded in the household and in the prerogatives of masters. It was designed, that is to say, to evoke the interests not simply of planters but of those yeoman freemen on whose votes radical victory would turn. But it was not an egalitarian and democratic regime that radicals advanced through endless paeons to freemen. It was, rather, a hierarchical and republican one. Such terms as "manly independence" and "womanly weakness" served in political tracts and speeches to construct, legitimize, and patrol the boundaries of the republican community, excluding not just women but all those who bore the stigma of dependence. When a politician took the platform at a meeting, muster, or Fourth of July barbecue and claimed to speak as a "freeman," the salutation was not simply an invitation to his largely yeoman audience to regard him as one among equals. It was also an evocation of shared privilege, an invitation to see themselves as part of the elite: as freemen in a society in which the majority was not free. It was, therefore, a constant reminder of their stake in social hierarchy, political exclusivity, and slavery. In rallying yeoman voters under the banner of freemen, radical politicians invoked their privileged place in a system in which the rights of citizens were awarded only to those few who were fully masters of themselves and their dependents. This was an argument with great appeal to lowcountry yeomen. And it goes a long way toward explaining the majority embrace of the Nullifiers' call to political arms.

If radical discourse testified to the significance of the yeoman voter, so too did radical political organization. When the call to arms rang out in 1830–1832, in 1850–1852, and again, finally, in 1860, it was relayed through local militias, the constituent unit of local politics in the Low Country and arguably the single most important site of the yeomanry's part in political culture. In the context of the militia and the political organizations that grew up around it, gendered words and symbols acquired ritual expression; there, the contradictions and tensions occasionally revealed in the discourse were harder to contain. On every radical political occasion, martial manhood and its gendered referent, "The Carolina Fair," were invoked and enacted, the better to pose the issue; resistance or submission.

38. Hamilton, *Proceedings of the First Meeting of the Charleston State Rights and Free Trade Association,* pp. 6–7. Some of these themes are explored, although not in the context of the South, in Andrew Parker, Mary Russo, Doris Sommer et al., *Nationalisms and Sexualities* (New York: Routledge, 1992). The term *family romance* is from Lynn Hunt, *The Family Romance of the French Revolution* (Berkeley: University of California Press, 1992).

VI

Nullifiers early recognized the importance of "publicity," of building a network of political organizations by which their claims to represent the people could be advanced.[39] They turned to the institutions, structures, and rituals that were already available, to the customary public observation of patriotic holidays, and, most important, to the state militia system. In a state in which personal loyalties and personal influence had been and would continue to be a critical dimension of political life, partisan organization did not come easily to either side in the Nullification contest. Even as they convened the first meeting of the State Rights and Free Trade Association of South Carolina in the summer of 1831, some Nullifiers expressed ambivalence about an openly avowed "party" identity, and some complained that they could not get their allies to adhere to party discipline.[40] But while Nullification clearly represented a transitional moment in the state's political culture, it was already apparent by 1830, if not before, that older political forms were becoming infused with new partisan energy and purpose.

As early as 1828, antitariff men seized on the customary observation of patriotic occasions as the perfect opportunity for political organization, although many initially denied their intent. Accused of illegitimate "expedients to ensnare and overawe public feelings" in using the celebration of the battle of New Orleans on January 8 to launch their campaign for Andrew Jackson's presidency, they went to great lengths to deny that "the sanctity of a national occasion . . . [was spoiled] by the excitements of party spirit." As late as 1830, Charleston Unionists continued to express unease with new partisan practices, including the Nullifiers' practice of hosting so-called "public dinners," ostensibly to "honor statesmen" but in effect to advance party purposes.[41] Yet the Unionist who predicted that such ill-advised practices would be "fleeting" could not have been more wrong, for they quickly became part of politics as usual.

39. *Charleston Mercury,* July 9, 1830, July 17, 1830, July 31, 1830. The term *publicity* was not used until 1832, but in 1830 Nullifiers talked of producing "evidences of public sentiment." See *Charleston Mercury,* January 14, 1832, July 31, 1830. For leading Nullifiers' correspondence of political organization, see "Letters on the Nullification Movement," pp. 736–64.

40. For Nullifiers' ambivalent views of "party politics," compare the speeches of Governor James Hamilton, who admitted that the association was in the character of a "political party" and that he had been "elected by a party," with that of Stephen Elliott, who vigorously denied their partisan nature. See *The Proceedings of the First Meeting of the Charleston State Rights and Free Trade Association.* Elliott wrote to his cousin William Elliott (a Unionist) in 1830 complaining that "our party we cannot persuade to vote 'en masse'—We do not seem to understand in this state the absolute necessity of waiving all personal feeling in a contest for principle." Stephen Elliott to William Elliott, Charleston, July 27, 1830, Elliott-Gonzales Papers.

41. *Charleston Mercury,* January 15, 1828, January 25, 1828, June 14, 1830.

What started in 1828 as the seizure of already established patriotic occasions quickly took on a life of its own as Nullifiers sought to create new opportunities for political organization. In 1830 radical papers like the *Beaufort Gazette* openly urged locales to honor their representatives in Congress with public dinners "that the American world [may] know that the terms and the attitude of Carolina in Congress are the terms and the attitudes of Carolina at home." It was not only the rest of the American world that Nullifiers sought to impress with evidence of their strength and unanimity but other South Carolinians. And by 1830, when the convention issue had reached boiling point, radical leaders in virtually every lowcountry district acknowledged that "the character of the time requires frequent meetings of the people" and organized "public dinners," as one planning committee in Stateburg in Sumter District did, to "manifest . . . publicly our . . . fixed determination to *resist* by every means in our power."[42] The time-honored July Fourth celebration had now become the centerpiece of a political season that started in the late spring with dinners honoring state legislators and U.S. representatives and senators and that continued, almost without pause, throughout the summer and into the formal election season in the fall. The state, William Grayson recalled, had become "a great talking and eating machine." There were no fewer than 304 Nullifier-sponsored meetings, celebrations, and dinners in South Carolina from mid-July 1831 to the end of 1832.[43] Out of the customary observation of such national occasions, now openly organized by local "Friends of the State Rights Party," did Nullifiers construct the framework of a statewide political network.

Formal party organization of local initiatives and associations emerged unevenly. Although leaders made efforts to organize a Nullifier press in various parts of the Low Country as early as 1830, it was not until 1831, in the wake of the legislative defeat of their convention campaign that, as one rural Charleston Nullifier recorded, "active measures were set on foot to bring the state to the crisis of Nullification [through the formation] of Associations throughout the state." By 1831, however, Nullifiers had translated their ad hoc apparatus into a formal party organization, the State Rights and Free Trade Association, with branches throughout the Low Country. Thus, at a January 1832 meeting of delegates from all of the local associations, the party leadership could claim that the demand for Nullification"had been expressed first by the people in their District or parish meetings." By such mechanisms

---

42. *Charleston Mercury,* June 21, 1830, August 4, 1830.

43. Richard J. Calhoun, *Witness to Sorrow: The Antebellum Autobiography of William J. Grayson* (Columbia, S.C.: University of South Carolina Press, 1990), p. 119. The calculation is from James Brewer Stewart, "'A Great Talking and Eating Machine': Patriarchy, Mobilization, and the Dynamics of Nullification in South Carolina," *Civil War History* 27 no. 3 (1981), p. 217.

did Nullifiers claim to speak for "the ranks of the great body of our citizens."[44]

Although lowcountry Unionists were forced over their initial objections to attempt similar efforts, they were even slower to organize than the Nullifiers. As late as August 1832 they were just beginning to see the need to raise money to "disseminate information among the people" and to make arrangements to have extra Unionist newspapers printed and distributed among the various coastal and middle country districts. Hence, despite their ability to deny their opponents the two-thirds majority required to get the convention bill through the legislature in 1830, by 1831 the lowcountry Unionist leadership was already conceding defeat. Certainly "the submission party," as Nullifiers had successfully tarred them, found submission a hard sell, especially after their promises of congressional redress were vanquished in early 1831. But whatever else explains it, there can be little doubt that, as James Louis Petigru himself acknowledged, they had been out-organized.[45]

What had been introduced to meet the exigencies of popular politics and statewide organization in a discrete political moment would not soon be undone. Frederick Porcher, the Charleston planter who got his own political start in the 1830 campaign, argued later in life that Nullification ushered in not only a process of "party" formation but a new political generation and a new chapter in lowcountry politics.[46] The contradictory character of that new antebellum politics and the yeomanry's place in it was then already evident in Nullifier organizations and meetings. At the State Rights and Free Trade–sponsored meetings and at the July Fourth celebrations and public dinners that marked them, yeomen and planters came together as freemen, as citizens, as constituent parts of a single body politic. The very rituals of political life, the dinners, parades,

44. *Charleston Mercury*, June 18, 1830; Robert Y. Hayne to James Henry Hammond, Washington, February 25, 1830, in "Letters on the Nullification Movement," p. 737; Samuel Gailliard Stoney, ed., "The Memoirs of Frederick A. Porcher," *South Carolina Historical and Genealogical Magazine*, vols. 44–48 (April 1943-January 1947) 46, no. 2, (April 1945), pp. 90–92; James Hamilton, Jr., to James Henry Hammond, Charleston, February 5, 1831, in "Letters on the Nullification Movement," p. 741. In January 1832, local branches of the State Rights and Free Trade Association sent 108 delegates to the statewide meeting. See *Charleston Mercury*, January 14, 1832.

45. Chapman Levy to William Elliott, August 27, 1832, Elliott Gonzales Papers; James Louis Petigru to Hugh Legaré, October 19, 1832, James Louis Petigru Papers. Historians have generally supported Petigru's conclusion that Unionists were out-organized and out-maneuvered by the Nullifiers. See, for example, Freehling, *Prelude to Civil War*, pp. 227–44; Ford, *Origins of Southern Radicalism*, pp. 130–31; Boucher, *Nullification Controversy in South Carolina*, pp. 119-64.

46. Stoney, ed., "Memoirs of Porcher," *South Carolina Historical and Genealogical Magazine* 46, no. 1 (January 1945) pp. 33–38, 46, no. 3 (July 1945), pp. 141–43. Most contemporary historians have reached the same conclusion about Nullification as a watershed in South Carolina's political culture. See, for example, Freehling, *Prelude to Civil War;* Faust, *James Henry Hammond and the Old South*, pp. 39–57; Stewart, "A Great Talking and Eating Machine"; Ford, *Origins of Southern Radicalism*, pp. 99–144.

toasts, and banners that celebrated freemen's common franchise, also enacted the inequality, the hierarchy, that characterized the relations of yeoman freemen and planters.

VII

It could hardly have been otherwise, discursive claims notwithstanding. For every part of the Nullifiers' nascent organization built upon the structure provided by the state militia system. No other institution was so critical and none played such a central role in the local politics that persisted after the crisis had passed. As a state-mandated and -funded system that embraced all adult freemen, that organized them in discrete local beats or companies bound into battalions, district regiments, cross-district brigades and state divisions, that required them to muster regularly and subjected them to annual review by the Governor, the militia's organizational merits were obvious. Even in rural coastal parishes like Prince William's in Beaufort District, militia musters brought out hundreds of people, and radical politicians proved especially quick in divining the possibilities.[47]

An extraordinary number of state-rights meetings, and public political meetings of every sort, took place on muster grounds. Where in each parish, as one lowcountry man pointed out, "everybody musters and everybody votes," politicians and aspirants to office had long recognized the opportunity presented. It was the foolish man indeed who, aspiring to office or attempting to hold onto it, failed to show up at the muster ground where "people are gathered together" to "mak[e] interest for himself." In Nullification, an old political practice was turned to new and heightened partisan ends, and militia musters and regimental reviews became a key site of popular political mobilization, especially for radical politicians.[48]

Given the opportunities such occasions provided, it is hardly surprising that some radicals, such as James Henry Hammond and Frederick

47. For the estimates of numbers at the Prince William's muster, see the *Winyah Intelligencer,* July 28, 1830. On the organization of the militia system in South Carolina, see Benjamin Elliott and Martin Strobel, *The Militia System of South Carolina . . . to 17th of December, 1834* (Charleston: A. E. Miller, 1835), pp. 158–60; *The Militia and Patrol Laws of South Carolina to December, 1859* (Columbia, S. C.: R. W. Gibbes, State Printer, 1860), pp. 5–6; Jean Martin Flynn, *The Militia in Antebellum South Carolina Society* (Spartanburg, S. C.: The Reprint Company, 1991), pp. 105–13. On Nullifiers' particular adeptness at deploying the militia system, see also Ford, *Origins of Southern Radicalism,* p. 304.

48. James Louis Petigru in Carson, ed., *Life of Petigru,* p. 70; James Harley to Lewis Malone Ayers, September 17, 1808, Lewis Malone Ayers Papers, SHC, in Stampp, ed., *Records of Antebellum Southern Plantations,* Series A, Part II, Reel 11; John Berkley Grimball Diary, December 29, 1832, Grimball Family Papers. Militia musters continued to be a prime site of organization on sectional issues. In 1838 Grimball went to muster and discovered "an anti-abolition meeting" in progress on muster grounds. See Grimball Diary, February 12, 1838, Grimball Family Papers.

Porcher, made their entry into political life through the militia system. Militia officers possessed considerable political influence. That is why Hammond sought election first as lieutenant colonel of a Barnwell troop and then appointment as aide-de-camp for Governor Hamilton in Barnwell District in 1832. He quickly recognized the relationship between martial display, local influence, and political authority, reluctantly paying twenty dollars out of his own pocket for "a good bass drum" for "his men" in 1833, ordering his captain to attend parade with him at the regimental review "in your uniform, as I wish to make as much display as possible," and urging attendance with the reminder that "by coming you will do much for the cause." Hammond's cause, inseparable from Nullification, was his own political advancement, and ascent through the military ranks remained an essential part of his "design for mastery." In 1841, when seeking legislative election as brigadier general of the Third Brigade, he explained why he put so much stock in military title and office. "I desire it for many small reasons. I am fond of the military, it would carry me in an agreeable manner on my reviews through a part of the State where I should very much like to go, it would give me additional influence, it would change my title of which I am very sick, and altho' militia titles are of no consequence, since they will stick to us, we had as well have the highest." He sought command of the Third Division, he added, to confirm that, although a resident of Columbia, he preferred "for many reasons to remain a citizen of Barnwell, and . . . this command is desirable as demonstrating this fact." That Hammond admitted aspirations to either the U.S. Senate or the governorship in those years reveals as well how the geographical scope of his militia ambitions and authority grew in proportion to his political ambitions and the expanding geographical area they embraced; any canvass for Governor or U.S. Senator would take him far beyond his original local turf in Barnwell District.[49]

Hammond's design was a savvy one. Militia officers had long exercised considerable political influence through the combination of access, display, patronage, and camaraderie that together could engender loyalty, esprit de corps, and even the tendency to vote in company blocks.

49. James Henry Hammond to Captain U. M. Robert, Barnwell, February 5, 1833, James Henry Hammond Papers, in Stampp, ed., Records of Antebellum Southern Plantations, Reel 6; James Henry Hammond to B. H. Smalter, Silver Bluff, April 5, 1833, Letter Press Book, James Henry Hammond Papers, in Stampp, ed., Records of Antebellum Southern Plantations, Reel 3; James Henry Hammond Diary, February 8, 1841, May 8, 1841, in Bleser, ed., Secret and Sacred, pp. 29–30, 54–58. Hammond was acutely aware of the theatrical elements of both militia review and local politics. "We had a grand military display," he noted of the gubernatorial review in 1841. "It was a pageant, theatrical as every thing he [Governor J. P. Richardson] does is, and saved from being ridiculous only by those who consented to act it," including himself and McDuffie. Hammond Diary, December 15, 1841, in Bleser, ed., Secret and Sacred, p. 83. On Hammond's launching of his political career in Nullification, see Faust, James Henry Hammond and the Old South, pp. 39–57.

As early as 1808, in the first testings of white manhood suffrage in South Carolina, one Barnwell militia captain and aspiring politician, John Blalock, promised to throw his influence to Lewis Malone Ayers, a Barnwell planter running for election to the state legislature. "I have been using my Exertions in the supporting of your Election, which . . . will Be warmly supported at our election ground," he wrote Ayers, "[f]or my Company gennarally votes as I recommend." And demonstrating the quid pro quo politics that was the hallmark of the Low Country and its circles of local leading men, he solicited Ayers's "intrust at your election ground . . . with your friends" on behalf of his own candidacy. Nullification politics may have been a step removed from the days when a militia captain would march his men to the polls and oversee their vote, viva voce style, but the kind of political influence Blalock promised Ayers, the promise that his company "will vote for you to a man," was relevant indeed in the Nullification contest.[50] Straw polls taken at musters testified to the importance of the beat company as the basic unit of local politics and confirmed the pattern of block voting that Blalock and Ayers had pointed to fifteen years before.

Militia units tended to vote overwhelmingly in one direction or the other. At one muster in Sumter District, at "Captain Low's muster ground," there were one hundred men in attendance "when Col. Moses, at the end of his speech, proposed that all for a Convention should say with him now." According to the *Sumter Gazette,* not more than "a half dozen opposed." Precisely the opposite result was reached at another Sumter militia meeting at Captain Levy Rhame's muster ground. On that occasion, "a considerable number of citizens from Claremont and Clarendon Counties in Sumter District [had] convened . . . to elect a Colonel of the Sumter Regiment, [when] a desire was expressed to ascertain the sense of the people assembled on the subject of Convention and Nullification." When Captain Rhame introduced resolutions "strenuously oppos[ing] the call of a Convention, the Nullification of the Acts of Congress, or the dismemberment of the Union," there was reputedly only "one dissenting voice" among the 131 men present. Where "election grounds" or polls were located on muster grounds, as they so often were in the rural Low Country, the connection between militia organization, officers' authority, and yeoman politics was riveted even tighter.[51]

Frederick Porcher gave the best description of the workings of this

---

50. John Blalock to Lewis Malone Ayers, Esq., August 22, 1808, and John Blalock to Lewis Malone Ars [*sic*], Esq., September 20, 1806, Lewis Malone Ayers Papers, in Stampp, ed., Records of Antebellum Southern Plantations, Reel 11.

51. *Sumter Gazette* article reprinted in *Charleston Mercury,* September 14, 1830. The other Sumter meeting is reported in the *Charleston Mercury,* September 13, 1830. In the rural Low Country, where meeting places were few and far between, churches, stores, private homes, and muster grounds or muster houses were the most common poll locations. See the list of poll locations and managers for the 1830 election in the House of Representatives Journal, December 17, 1829, General Assembly Records.

new system. In 1832 he had coveted the nomination of "his party," the Nullifiers, for St. John's, Berkeley, Charleston District. But despite the fact that older customs by which it was "considered discourteous to oppose a sitting member" had generally "give[n] way before the exigency of the political crisis," he still did not hold out much hope of getting the nomination. "I had no personal strength," he explained. Young though he was, however, Porcher was already in the process of acquiring that personal strength, for just the year before he had been elected captain of the beat company at the lower end of his parish and had thereby, as he put it, "commence[d] this course of public life." "Now, being one of the Captains of Militia," he noted, "I was a sort of chief of Police in the Parish" and had gained, in addition to that authority, an unprecedented "opportunity for social intercourse." "As the men came from a distance to muster I took care that a dinner should always be provided for the occasion," he explained, and Porcher's generous patronage of his men was soon returned in kind. As he angled the following year for the nomination, his reputation among his men proved critical. In the canvass of 1832, he recalled, "public meetings were held and dinners given at Begin Church, these being the rendezvous of the Lower and Upper Beat Companies of the parish," and "I was," he added, "always expected to speak at them." He did well. "I was frequently told by some of the lower class as I used to call them that I had given them pleasure," he chortled. And although he denied that he "ever asked anyone in any class to give me a vote," it was at these militia-based meetings and dinners, paid for by planter hosts, that Porcher and other planter politicians courted and won the support of yeoman voters, the lowcountry's "lower class." By such means, a wedding of the region's customary style of personal politics to a new partisan discipline through the militia system, were local politics and popular politics entwined. Porcher won not only the nomination but the election as well.[52] Along the way, he revealed the mechanics and substance of the new patron-client political culture while making clear its debts to the old.

As Porcher's experience reveals, the militia system lent more than a formal structure and venue to lowcountry politics. It also illuminated the character of the new political culture Nullification was willy-nilly creating. Like the structure of the militia itself, the meetings and dinners organized by local state-rights associations brought yeomen and planters together as freemen, as citizen soldiers, and then arranged them hierarchically, as planter officers and yeoman troops, as planter politicians and yeoman voters. In the symbols, rituals, and arrangements of those occasions the contradictory character of lowcountry politics was played out for all to see. So was the yeomanry's particular place within it— masters of small worlds in a region of great planters.

52. Stoney, ed., "Memoirs of Porcher," *South Carolina Historical and Genealogical Magazine* 46, no. 2 (April 1945), pp. 81–83, 46, no. 3 (July 1945) pp. 141–43, 150–51.

One lowcountry correspondent articulated the political virtues of the militia system well before the Nullification Crisis placed a new burden on it. "Is not the idea of a common cause and of common danger the strongest ligament by which you can hold men together in a state of society?" "Argus" wrote to the *Winyah Intelligencer.* "Are not wealth and luxury and effeminancy calculated to destroy all national spirit?" To the classical republican virtues of a citizen militia, he added another, militia discipline, which brings "a concourse of men together, embodying them as it were into one mass and accustoming them to move by a common impulse."[53] It was precisely such a "common impulse" that radical politicians attempted to harness: discursively in endless appeals to "Freemen," urgings to "manly resistance," and references to vulnerable womanhood, real and symbolic, and ritualistically, in the coming together of yeomen and planters to meet, parade, deliberate, break bread, and vote, usually in the presence of a female audience. For women spectators were indispensable parts of militia rituals: without them there was no one to witness, authorize, and validate the martial manhood that was the signature of all freemen.[54]

Rural politicians could not count on having at their meetings—as the Charleston State Rights Association did at its big ball in 1831—an "eighteen foot high Palmetto Tree with a rattlesnake coiled at its foot" as an "emblem of state." They could not easily muster eighteen hundred people, including army and militia officers in "full uniform" and hundreds of "ladies [with] Palmetto leaves in their headresses," as evidence of the "patriotic spirit of the fair of Carolina." But they did have their own more modest gendered symbols of martial masculinity and the will to resist.[55] For every militia muster and state-rights meeting or dinner included, with rare exception, women participants, the better, one can only presume, to anchor manhood, to provide concrete referents for it, and to hold particular men to their duty as patriots.

In "1832, during the Nullification contest," the editor of the *Orangeburg Southron* recalled in 1856, "the ladies" of the district had presented a flag to the Orangeburg troop. By now, however, that flag was no more than a "relic," and so the editor urged "our friends the ladies" to make another. There was, he flattered them, "no better monitor to keep the men mindful of their duty when on drill and parade." But the ladies' political role extended beyond the provision of appropriate emblems of male duty. When the troops marched out into the village the young ladies, "heaven bless them, turned out in full force to behold them as they passed in review." "As the fair ones stood and gazed upon that moving mass of mounted men," one witness insisted, the men took

53. *Winyah Intelligencer,* February 20, 1819.
54. For a wonderfully evocative analysis of the martial rhetoric and rituals of Nullification politics, albeit one that does not explore the role of women or gender, see Stewart, "A Great Talking and Eating Machine."
55. *Charleston Mercury,* March 5, 1831; *Winyah Intelligencer,* June 12, 1830.

on a new aspect, "crests erect and bold front"; they marched as if returned from a "hard fought field, the heroes of a well earned victory."[56]
Women were thus in their very persons symbols of freemen's common
patrimony and their obligation to preserve it intact for the next generation. Masculinity could be defined only by its opposite—action by passivity, dark by fair, heroes by adoring women—and every militia parade
and review, no matter how modest, enacted this gendered choreography. "To the Fair Sex of Carolina" went one volunteer toast at an early
radical dinner in Walterboro, "worthy of the admiration and protection of patriots and freemen." Urged to "decorate the altar of liberty," to
remind Carolina freemen that they "would not that their fathers or
brothers be slaves," free women, although disfranchised, were recruited
nonetheless as "patriots" and partisans and ascribed a critical role in the
theatre of lowcountry politics.[57]

But if Nullifiers' rituals brought yeoman and planter freemen together in one citizen body and symbolized their common identity in a
gendered politics, it also arranged those freemen in a distinct hierarchy
that gave the lie to any claims about equality. Not only was the militia by
definition a hierarchial organization; that hierarchy replicated in military form of address, uniform, and authority the social inequality between yeomen and planters. Nor was that ever far from view. In the
"resplendent" uniforms of the officers, which seemed at times to constitute planter men's main interest in militia appointment, in the arrangement of troops for parades in descending order of distinction, and in the
financing and spatial arrangements of the dinners in which such occasions culminated, planters' social and political power was vividly on display. At one state-rights dinner in Charleston, as John Berkley Grimball
described it, "the more respectable part of the company were on the
stage," elevated above the multitudes. At another, this one sponsored by
the Free Trade and State Rights Party of St. John's Berkeley and designed to "impress not only our own people but the state," about three
hundred sat down to dinner at the local planters' hunting club, with the
invited and distinguished guests and speakers at a head table spread
"directly north" of the clubhouse and "the people" at twelve or thirteen
other tables that "radiated from it." In such settings, where planter
politicians and militia officers, often one and the same man, sat on

56. *Orangeburg Southron*, May 21, 1856.
57. *Charleston Mercury*, July 10, 1829, August 4, 1830, July 4, 1832. At one Fourth of
July celebration at Barnwell Court House, the "ladies . . . graced the company with their
personal attendance" during the militia exercises, at the oration (by James Henry Hammond), and at the dinner that followed at "'Patterson's residence." A toast was raised to
"[t]he heroines of '76 [who] parted with their sons for the cause of freedom; and the Fair of
1832 [who] are rallying their husbands and brothers to the standard of Nullification." See
Charleston Mercury, July 12, 1832. At the Charleston celebration the same year, the "State
Rights Ladies" played a more explicit role. "Escorted by the Cadet Riflemen, Irish volun-
teers, and Jackson guards," they presented "a Standard" to "the Young Men's State Rights
and Free Trade Association." See *Charleston Mercury*, July 6, 1832.

"elevated platforms" with the yeoman farmers and militia men on whose votes they depended arranged below them, the symbols, rituals, and general theatrics of lowcountry politics proved a good indication of the substance.[58] Empowered by inclusion in the ranks of freemen, yeoman farmers were simultaneously subordinated to the greater power of planter freemen. Such was the nature of the body politic and the political culture Nullification produced.

VIII

Yeomen may not have been planters' equals, but planter politicians' ability to secure their vote was critical to radical success in the election of 1832. And as Frederick Porcher's nascent political career showed, no site or institution of local politics was so important as the militia in the efforts of parish and district leading men to win over and get out the yeoman vote for the State Rights party. Indeed, election results suggest as much. The patterns of block voting evinced in straw polls of beat companies in the rural Low Country in 1830 offer one explanation of perhaps the most pronounced feature of the electoral returns in 1832: the inverse relationship between voter turnout and the size of Nullifiers' margin of victory.

Nullifiers won decisively in 1832. They won everywhere in the coastal Low Country except in the always anomalous Horry and in Williamsburg, where the contest ended in a dead heat; they prevailed everywhere in the interior districts with the exception of Darlington. In the coastal Low Country, they did lose a number of parishes, notably in Charleston (St. James, Goose Creek, and Christ Church), Georgetown (Prince George, Winyaw), and Colleton (St. George, Dorchester), but they swept many more parishes, especially in Colleton and Beaufort. Those last two districts had been in the van of the Nullification movement since 1828, and as early as 1830, shocked at the predominance of "Jacobinal planters" and "insurging people," Unionists had conceded defeat.[59] Their calculus was correct. Nullifiers won fully 100 percent of the vote in two of three parishes (St. Bartholomew's and St. Paul's) in

58. John Berkley Grimball Diary, September 6, 1832, Grimball Family Papers; Stoney, ed., "Memoirs of Porcher," *South Carolina Historical and Genealogical Magazine* 46, no. 2 (April 1945), pp. 90–92; *Charleston Mercury*, October 29, 1828. For the ordering of military parades, see *Charleston Mercury*, July 12, 1832, and July 18, 1832. And for an insightful analysis of parades and politics, see Susan G. Davis, *Parades and Power: Street Theater in Nineteenth-Century Philadelphia* (Berkeley: University of California Press, 1986).

59. James Louis Petigru to William Grayson, 1830, James Louis Petigru to William Elliott, Charleston, August 25, 1831, November 14, 1831, in Carson, ed., *Life of Petigru*, pp. 80–81, 83–84; William Elliott to Ann Elliott, Columbia, December 5, 1831, Elliott-Gonzales Papers. For the evidence on early radical sentiment in Beaufort, see, for example, the reports of political dinners in the *Charleston Mercury*, July 16, 1829, July 17, 1830; for Colleton, see *Charleston Mercury*, July 4, 1828, October 30, 1828, July 13, 1830.

Colleton and in two of four parishes (St. Peter's and Prince William's) in Beaufort. In Charleston, although they lost two parishes, they swept three others, winning 100 percent of the vote in St. Andrew's, St. John's Colleton, and St. Stephen's, in addition to the solid majorities they racked up in the city and three other rural parishes. (See Table 7.2.)

In the interior districts, the Nullifiers' victory was not apparent so early, but it was, in the end, no less impressive. The pre-electoral political season in 1830 had revealed hard fought battles in Barnwell, Orangeburg, and Sumter especially, and as late as December 1831 James Henry Hammond still described his Barnwell neighborhood as "a submission part of the country."[60] But even in Barnwell, Nullifiers won a solid 65 percent of the vote and, although they did lose Darlington by a good margin (Unionists won 58 percent of the vote), together with one part of Sumter District (Clarendon), they won the other part of Sumter (Claremont) quite handily and routed the opposition in Orangeburg with an overwhelming 91 percent of the vote. With the exception, then, of a few pockets of Unionist strength in the parishes and in Darlington District, the Low Country in 1832 was solid Nullifier territory. As one leader of the lowcountry Unionists, James Louis Petigru, sighed, "Things have turned out as fools wished and wise men expected."[61]

Far more interesting than the Nullifiers' victory and the clear evidence of their success among yeoman voters is the striking pattern displayed in those election results. In every parish and district in the election of 1832, voter turnout was lowest where Nullifiers' margin of victory was greatest and highest where the outcome was most closely

60. James Henry Hammond to Honorable George McDuffie, Silver Bluff, December 18, 1831, Letter Press Book, 1831–1833, James Henry Hammond Papers, in Stampp, ed., Records of Antebellum Southern Plantations, Reel 3. For evidence of the battle in the Middle Country, see Charleston Mercury, September 13, 1830. For particular districts see the following: on Orangeburg, Charleston Mercury, September 4, 1830; on Sumter, Charleston Mercury, July 16, 1830, September 9, 1830, September 10, 1830; on Barnwell, H. G. Longstreet to James Henry Hammond, Pin Corner, September 7, 1832, James Henry Hammond Papers, in Stampp, ed., Records of Antebellum Southern Plantations, Reel 6, and Charleston Mercury, July 14, 1829, July 12, 1830, July 14, 1830, September 20, 1830, September 24, 1830.

61. James Louis Petigru to Hugh Legaré, Charleston, October 29, 1832, in Carson, ed., Life of Petigru, pp. 102–03. So decisive was their victory in the Low Country that Unionist leaders didn't even run a ticket for convention elections in many parishes and districts later in the fall and tried to convince upcountry Unionists to boycott the convention. See "Circular of the Union Party's Committee of Correspondence for Charleston," Charleston, November 2, 1832, in "Letters on the Nullification Movement," pp. 749–50. For commentary on this decision and an accounting of the election results by district, see James Louis Petigru to Hugh Legaré, Charleston, October 29, 1832, in Carson, ed., Life of Petigru, pp. 102–4. In December he wrote Hugh Legaré that they ran no ticket in the "low-country nor in any of the districts above but those where we had a decided majority." Petigru to Hugh Legaré, December 21, 1832, in Carson, ed., Life of Petigru, p. 112. On the decisiveness of Unionists' defeat, see also Benjamin G. Allston to William Elliott, St. Luke's, December 21, 1832, Elliott-Gonzales Papers. It is important to note here that the statistics provided refer to the popular vote. The battle for legislative seats is a distinct question.

Table 7.2 Voter Turnout and Voting in the Lowcountry's
Nullification Election of 1832

District/Parish	No. of Eligible Voter	% Participation	% for Nullification
A. COASTAL DISTRICTS			
Charleston District			
St. Philip's and St. Michael's	3,152	87.7	54.4
Charleston Neck	607	na	na
St. Andrew's	92	43.5	100.0
St. John's, Colleton	143	49.7	100.0
St. James, Goosecreek	353	84.7	40.8
St. John's, Berkeley	209	99.5	66.8
St. Stephen's	111	54.1	100.0
Christ Church	162	79.0	39.1
St. James, Santee	89	89.9	76.3
St. Thomas and St. Dennis	46	115.2	69.8
District totals	4,694	78.9	54.8
Georgetown District			
All Saints	na	na	75.0
Prince George, Winyaw	na	na	49.9
District totals	531	95.9	56.6
Horry District	677	62.2	13.8
Beaufort District			
St. Peter's	472	37.7	100.0
St. Helena	229	70.0	75.9
St. Luke's	245	94.3	71.0
Prince William's	366	43.7	100.0
District totals	1,312	55.4	85.6
Colleton District			
St. Bartholomew's	na	na	100.0
St. Paul's	na	na	100.0
St. George, Dorchester	na	na	29.3
District totals	1,158	55.7	67.1
Williamsburg	589	96.1	50.0
LOW COUNTRY TOTALS	9,231	71.2	56.5
B. MIDDLE COUNTRY DISTRICTS			
Barnwell District	2,020	84.0	64.9
Orangeburg District			
Orange	na	na	90.9
St. Matthew's	na	na	90.8
District totals	1,504	105.4	90.9
Sumter District			
Clarendon	na	na	42.9
Claremont	na	na	62.5
District totals	1,901	92.5	55.9
Darlington District	1,339	89.2	41.6
Marlboro District	838	32.3	100.0
Marion District	1,409	86.7	63.2
MIDDLE COUNTRY TOTALS	9,011	85.8	65.5

Sources: Fifth Census; or Enumeration of the Inhabitants of the United States, 1830 (Washington, D.C.: Duff Green, 1832), p. 94; Chauncey S. Boucher, *The Nullification Controversy in South Carolina* (1916; reprint ed. Westport, Conn.: Greenwood Press, 1968), p. 203.

contested. The lowest voter turnout in the entire Low Country was to be found in St. Peter's Parish in Beaufort District, where Nullifiers won 100 percent of the vote but where only 38 percent of eligible voters turned out at the polls. The same was true in Prince William's in Beaufort District, and in the other mostly Charleston parishes in which Nullifiers won 100 percent of the vote. Conversely, where Unionists gave Nullifiers a run for their money, in Williamsburg where they actually prevailed, or in Georgetown where Nullifiers won by a small margin (56 percent), voter turnout was extraordinarily high, reaching 96 percent in both instances. Even in St. John's, Berkeley, where the Nullifiers' "majority was very decided," the contest had been a heated one and virtually every eligible voter (99.5 percent) had exercised his privilege at the ballot-box. "It was the largest [vote] ever known in the parish," Porcher would recall years later, and indeed he was right.[62] In middle country districts where contests were, for the most part, harder fought and margins of victory smaller, voter turnout rates were, on average, higher, although the same general pattern held. Thus, in Marlboro, where Nullifiers won 100 percent of the vote, only 32 percent of eligible voters appeared at the polls, while in Sumter, where Nullifiers barely pulled it out, voter participation rates reached 93 percent. The only real exception was Orangeburg, where Nullifiers won handily (they received 91 percent of the vote) but voters also turned out in impressive numbers. There, (vote early, vote often) 105 percent of eligible voters cast ballots in the 1832 election, raising interesting questions about the management of the polls. There was one other place, the Charleston parish of St. Thomas and St. Dennis, in which voter turnout rates exceeded the number of eligible voters (115 percent), but the disparity is easier to explain, and it helps to make sense of the general pattern as well. (See Table 7.2)

Especially in the coastal parishes where, as both Unionists and Nullifiers admitted, it was possible to take the sense of the electorate with some accuracy well before election day, the correlation between Nullifiers' domination of particular parishes and the low voter turnout rate suggests the success with which local leading men could organize the electorate, bringing out those favorable to their cause and convincing the rest of the futility of opposition.[63] Electorates were small in the parishes. Most were not so small as in St. Thomas and St. Dennis which had only 46 eligible voters, but even more typical places like the Beaufort parishes, which ranged from 229 eligible voters in St. Helena to 472

62. Stoney, ed., "Memoirs of Porcher," *South Carolina Historical and Genealogical Magazine* 46, no. 3 (July 1945), pp. 141–43.

63. Perhaps the greatest evidence of this lies in the number of candidates whose elections were uncontested. According to J. P. Ochenkowski, excluding Charleston, 7 of 15 rural parishes had uncontested elections in 1832. See Ochenkowski, "The Origins of Nullification in South Carolina," *South Carolina Historical Magazine* 83, no. 2 (April 1982), p. 149.

in St. Peter's, hardly came close to the unwieldy electorates politicians faced in the middle country districts.[64] In such settings, where appeals might need to be made only to a couple of hundred voters and sometimes fewer, local leading men could, and apparently did, create networks of "personal influence," that valuable commodity Frederick Porcher feared he lacked in 1832. And often they created those networks precisely through the militia loyalites and quid pro quo with leading men in other parts of the parish or district that Blalock and Ayer had described in the early part of the century and that Porcher had cultivated with such effect in his successful bid for office in 1832.

In later life Porcher recalled how the system worked, not only for him but for his party in other parts of Charleston District. His own strength emanated almost entirely from his local base in the beat company of which he was captain. He developed it through a careful course of patronage and "social intercourse" with his men, as well as by organizing numerous dinners, meetings, and parades at Begin Church, the "rendezvous of the lower and upper Beat Companies of the Parish." Other men were pursuing the same course in their neighborhoods, however, and so "our party seldom made Black Oak the scene of their operations" as "about there lived Mr. Samuel DuBose and Dr. Ravenel with their large and well merited influence," and Isaac M. Dwight "who is indefatigably active in the case of the Union party." Rather, Porcher wrote, his party "visited the St. Stephen muster field," lending its influence to allies in that neighboring parish. By the time of the election, the Nullifiers' stength was so overwhelming in St. Stephen's that "the Union party made no struggle" there, instead moving every "person with property qualifications into our parish [St. John's, Berkeley] to vote there in aid of their party." Nullifiers used the same strategy themselves in other Charleston parishes, "abandon[ing] St. James, Goose Creek to the Union party," for example, and shifting all of their "party" resident in that parish but with "property qualifications in St. John's" into St. John's, Colleton to cast their vote.[65] Thus did Porcher explain how some parishes had voter turnouts in excess of the number of eligible voters. Clearly, planter and yeoman freemen possessed, in some sense, a different franchise. But beyond that, in pointing out how localized Nullifiers' strength was even within small parishes, how they were forced to "abandon" parts of their own parish where other, Unionist leading men held sway, and how they took what planter votes they could from hopeless

64. Eligible numbers of voters were calculated from *Fifth Census; or the Enumeration of the Inhabitants of the United States; 1830* (Washington, D.C.: Duff Green, 1832), p. 94. Numbers were arrived at by counting all adult white men age 20 and over, and deducting one-ninth of the total for the age category 20–29 to eliminate those who had not reached the age of 21, the legal voting age.

65. Stoney, ed., "Memoirs of Porcher," *South Carolina Historical and Genealogical Magazine* 46, no. 3 (July 1945), pp. 141–43.

parishes to winnable ones, Porcher mapped out an electoral strategy configured centrally around local leading men and their discrete circles of personal influence.[66]

He did more. In characterizing the election of 1832 as a key moment in the formation of a new political culture, Porcher showed how the old patron-client politics had become harnessed to a new party discipline and the requirements of a new popular politics. In this respect, the election of 1832 made manifest the essential character of the political culture that would prevail throughout the rest of the antebellum period and of the yeomanry's position within it. And a contradictory position it was in which the ordinary yeoman voter found himself in 1832: his praises as patriot sung, his power constrained; his stake as freeman and master invoked, his position as lesser master enacted; his ballot courted by planter patrons, his electoral choices limited to planter candidates. Out of that contradictory position did yeoman farmers make their political choices in 1832, and the majority took their stand for Nullification.

Nullifiers had calculated wisely in casting the battle over the tariff as one over hearth and home, over the right of the yeoman freeman to enjoy his property and rule his household without threat of invasion or violation. But Nullifiers did not create the yeomanry's stake in slave society and the exclusive republic of freemen; they only recognized it, invoked it, and exploited it. In the context of the Low Country, where most adults were dependents subject to the authority of masters, yeomen sought to defend their own considerable prerogatives—private and public, domestic and political—against a federal government that would make them slaves. If that politics served the interests of planters, if it buttressed planters' disproportionate power within the state, it was a price yeomen were willing to pay. "Manly resistance," most lowcountry yeomen decided in 1832, was the only fit posture of freemen and masters.

66. Evidence to support this emphasis on the importance of local leading men is presented in Ochenkowski, "The Origins of Nullification in South Carolina." Ochenkowski's thesis, that the Nullification controversy involved no broader issues of slavery and slave society—his critique of William W. Freehling's *Prelude to Civil War*—is not, however, convincing in light of the debate in the Low Country, nor is his conclusion that "support for Nullification depended on the opinion of the local squire" (p. 152). Such a view, deduced from electoral returns, fails to consider the process by which local leading men cultivated popular support and thus tends to eviscerate yeoman politics and political history more generally.

chapter 8

"To Repel the Invaders at the Threshold"

I

On December 17, 1860, the South Carolina secession convention assembled in the state capitol's First Baptist Church to write the Ordinance of Secession that rent the Union asunder. In sheltering under the eaves of evangelicalism, delegates sought divine sanction for the revolutionary act they were about to commit, and they sought no less to unite the people of the state for the struggle that lay ahead.

That concern for unity was hardly new. It had plagued radical politicians since the first great challenge of popular political mobilization in Nullification, and it had plagued them—and eluded them—in their first attempt to take the state out of the Union in 1851.[1] At no point, however, in that long history had the challenge of securing the yeoman majority ever acquired the significance it took on in the struggle from which the state had just emerged. In meeting that challenge and in carrying the state for secession in the fall of 1860, radicals had drawn on an arsenal of political techniques built up over the course of the antebellum period: customary methods of constraining popular participation and suppressing opposition combined with full-throated appeals to freemen to defend their common patrimony and to repel the invaders at the threshold.

---

1. On Nullification, see William W. Freehling, *Prelude to Civil War: The Nullification Controversy in South Carolina* (New York: Harper and Row, 1965) and Chapter 7 above. On the secession movement of 1850–1852, see John Barnwell, *Love of Order: South Carolina's First Secession Crisis* (Chapel Hill: University of North Carolina Press, 1982); and Chauncey Samuel Boucher, "The Secession and Co-Operation Movements in South Carolina, 1848 to 1852," *Washington University Studies* 5, no. 2 (April 1918), pp. 67–138.

Yet it was not business as usual in the Low Country in the elections of 1860, for the question of yeoman loyalty to the slave regime inspired anxiety of unprecedented proportions in radical politicians. This time the radicals left nothing to chance. Their intensification of customary practices amounted to a critical new dimension of the region's political culture. In their drive to win the hearts and minds of the yeomanry, politicians harnessed as never before the power and sanction of popular religion—hence the symbolic politics of the Secession Convention; most important, they sought to mobilize yeoman voters by extending the militia apparatus of the state into a dense network of local vigilant associations and minute men organizations. In this they succeeded beyond their own expectations and perhaps even beyond their own desires. For the predominantly yeoman members of lowcountry vigilant associations played their part in the fall elections with uncontrollable intensity, unleashing a campaign of political terror across the face of the Low Country. With few exceptions, the region's yeoman farmers not only supported the cause of secession and disunion, they made it their own.

II

The entire election year 1860 was one long unbroken political season in the South Carolina Low Country; indeed, in many ways it was simply the culmination of a two-year campaign that had been precipitated in 1858 by the struggle over the admission of Kansas to the Union.[2] Nothing, however, could compare to the level of political mobilization witnessed in the countryside between the spring and the late fall of 1860 as radical advocates of separate state secession did battle with moderate advocates of cooperative southern action at every courthouse village and local muster ground. At those public meetings, radical politicians made their case to the rural electorate in by then predictable terms, adapting the discourse of freemen to the exigencies of the political moment and to their own sharply secessionist ends.

The essentials of the case had been laid out by Robert Barnwell Rhett, James Henry Hammond, and countless other political leaders at various points since the late 1820s. Although Hammond ultimately retreated from the precipice of disunion to which he had done as much as any man to bring the state, his insistence on the superiority of the slave republic, on the disfranchisement of its "mud-sill" class, and the

2. On the secession crisis in South Carolina, see Steven A. Channing, *Crisis of Fear: Secession in South Carolina* (New York: W. W. Norton, 1970); Harold S. Schultz, *Nationalism and Sectionalism in South Carolina, 1852–1860* (Durham N.C.: Duke University Press, 1950). On the upcountry campaign, see Lacy K. Ford, Jr., *Origins of Southern Radicalism: The South Carolina Upcountry, 1800-1860* (New York: Oxford University Press, 1988), pp. 338–73; on the national context of the sectional conflict, see David M. Potter, *The Impending Crisis, 1848–1861* (New York: Harper and Row, 1976).

attendant conservatism of its enfranchised men continued to undergird arguments about the ordinary freeman's stake in the defense of slave society. When Hammond rehearsed the litany once again in 1858 in a Senate speech on the admission of Kansas, the editor of the *Charleston Mercury* defended his views and extracted the politically salient point for the down-home audience. "The free white man here stands above and superior belonging to the master ruling class," he reminded his readers. "He has every reason to make property secure and to perpetuate justice and freedom amongst those of his class."[3]

Between 1858 and 1860 such obvious bids for yeoman support assumed almost frenzied proportions, with radical politicians taking the stump at one public meeting after another to insist that the unity of the nonslaveholder and the slaveholder was never in doubt and that "there is a principle involved in this contest as important to one of these classes as the other." In the same breath, they urged those present to "inform every man (the nonslaveholder as well as the slaveholder) of the deep and vital interests that are involved in our slavery institutions."[4] Those "vital interests" were carefully detailed, as they long had been, to gloss over obvious differences between the yeoman majority and the planter elite. On the hustings, the "rights of slavery" and of slaveholders became the "rights of the South," and, even more explicitly, the "rights of freemen" to the constitutional "protection of person and property" against the "tampering thieves of abolition." "He who will not protect his property will soon have none to protect," Mr. Oliver Williams, a former representative of St. Bartholomew's Parish, warned at a meeting in Colleton District in May 1860.[5] And as always, yeomen were reminded of the obvious: that in property rights lay their claim to masterhood and its

3. For Hammond's speech, see *Charleston Mercury*, March 8, 1858, and for the editor's formulation, *Charleston Mercury*, July 5, 1858. Hammond delivered this "mud-sill" speech on a few other occasions, including at a public dinner in Edgefield District in the summer of 1858, and it also provided the basis of his published pamphlet, *Are Working Men Slaves?* For the Edgefield speech, see *Charleston Mercury*, July 26, 1858, and for the pamphlet, James Henry Hammond, *Are Working Men Slaves? The Question Discussed by Senators Hammond, Broderick and Wilson* (n.p., 1858). On Hammond's retreat from secession, see his speeches and the letters and editorials in the *Charleston Mercury*, August 2, 1858, November 2, 1858, November 4, 1858, November 10, 1858, November 12, 1858, November 16, 1858, November 18, 1858, December 24, 1858, January 12, 1859, January 14, 1859, January 21, 1859, January 28, 1859, February 10, 1859, February 21, 1859, February 25, 1859, March 2, 1859. In 1861 Hammond recalled the events of recent years and attempted to justify his own Unionist posture. See James Henry Hammond Diary, April 16, 1861, to October 23, 1861, in Carol Bleser, ed., *Secret and Sacred: The Diaries of James Henry Hammond, a Southern Slaveholder* (New York: Oxford University Press, 1988), 272–328. See also Drew Gilpin Faust, *James Henry Hammond and the Old South: A Design for Mastery* (Baton Rouge: Louisiana State University Press, 1982), pp. 330–59.

4. *Charleston Mercury*, November 13, 1860, November 12, 1860.

5. *Charleston Mercury*, May 10, 1860, May 25, 1860. Walter B. Edgar, ed., *Biographical Directory of the South Carolina House of Representatives* (Columbia, S. C.: University of South Carolina Press), vol. 1, p. 380.

prerogatives, domestic and public. Images of invasion and violation abounded. "To detect every vile intruder upon our peace," John Townsend said resolutely, was a "freeman's duty to [his] family and the state." There was only one choice, as radicals had long insisted—"whether we should live as slaves or freemen"—and for freemen, only one honorable response. "Evade the crisis we cannot," Robert Barnwell Rhett thundered in October 1860. "[We must] breast it like men and freemen."[6] But the issue was no longer one simply of resistance. This time, Rhett and others insisted, the only fit choice of freemen was dissolution of the Union.

Robert Barnwell Rhett and other radicals had been urging resistance and even secession in similar terms for more than a decade. There was nothing new in that. What was new in the spring of 1860 was the widespread adoption of the same themes and disunionist agenda by moderate men who had opposed separate state secession in 1851, had argued for the greater security of slave property within the Union in the decade following, and who in some cases had personal records of cautioning the state against precipitate action that dated back to Nullification. The headlong rush of coastal and middle country moderates into secessionist ranks was precipitated above all by the debacle of the national Democratic Party convention in Charleston in May 1860, when moderates' hopes of securing constitutional guarantees for slavery in the territories were vanquished and most southern delegations, including that of South Carolina, walked out. What little faith South Carolinians retained in national party solutions was virtually obliterated, and the prospects of the first fully sectional "black Republican" president loomed ever larger on the political horizon.[7] As calls for political unity resounded from public meetings across the state in the aftermath of the Democratic convention, arguments long particular to radical separate state secessionists were heard on every side.

John Townsend epitomized the new political moment and its old political discourse. A planter politician from Edisto Island, Colleton District, Townsend was a fixture of the moderate faction in lowcountry politics. He had opposed Nullification in 1832, had actively opposed

6. *Charleston Mercury,* October 31, 1860, November 13, 1860, October 12, 1860.

7. The *Charleston Mercury* editor represented the secession of southern delegates as among "the most important [events] which have taken place since the Revolution of 1776. The last party pretending to be a national party is broken up . . . a practical separation has already taken place in religious societies, churches, and parties." *Charleston Mercury,* May 1, 1860. One lowcountry planter politician later recalled that in May 1860 the Democratic Party was "broken into fragments" and that black Republican victory was rendered all but inevitable. Lewis Morris Grimball to Elizabeth Grimball, November 27, 1860, Grimball Family Papers, SHC. Calls for political unity picked up immediately after the walkout. See, for example, *Charleston Mercury,* May 8, 1860, May 14, 1860. For a fuller discussion of these developments, see Channing, *Crisis of Fear,* p. 237; Chauncey Samuel Boucher, "South Carolina and the South on the Eve of Secession, 1852–1860," *Washington University Studies* 6, no. 2 (April 1919), pp. 128–44.

separate state secession in 1851, and did not come out for unconditional secession until after the defeat of the state's national Democrats at the Charleston convention in May 1860.[8] But when he did, he lent to the cause an unprecedented level of publicity through the distribution of his stump speeches under the auspices of the newly established 1860 Association. According to a printed circular soliciting members, the 1860 Association had been formed in September 1860 by "several gentlemen of Charleston" concerned about "the position of the South in the event of the accession of Mr. Lincoln and the Republican party to power." Their purposes were explicitly propagandistic: to "exchange information and views with other leading men in the South . . . to prepare the Slave States to meet the impending crisis"; to prepare, print, and distribute tracts, pamphlets, and other printed materials throughout the slave states "to awaken them to a conviction of their danger and to urge the necessity of resisting Northern and Federal aggression"; and to help their own state establish "an effective military organization." Their aims were also explicitly secessionist. They disparaged efforts afoot in the North to "soothe and conciliate the South" and advocated only one course of resistance—immediate "Southern independence."[9] Seeking unity within the South but first and foremost within the state, they distributed a number of pamphlets, six in all, among which no other figured so prominently or was so widely circulated as John Townsend's "Tract No. 1," *The South Alone Should Govern the South and African Slavery Should Be Controlled by Those Only Who Are Friendly to It.* "Read and send to your Neighbor," the pamphlet cover urged.[10]

As befitted a pamphlet designed to galvanize popular support for

8. William Elliott, the Beaufort planter, sportsman, writer, and politician, was another such man who followed this political path to advocacy of secession in the second half of 1860. See the account of Elliott's career offered by his wife. Mrs. Elliott to Caroline, n.d. [1860], Elliott-Gonzales Papers, SHC; and A. H. Seabrook to William Elliott, Rest Park, November 14, 1860, Elliott-Gonzales Papers.

9. Printed Circular, Robert N. Gourdin, Chairman of the Executive Committee, to Honorable R. F. W. Allston, November 19, 1860, 1860 Association, SCL. On the 1860 Association, see *Charleston Mercury*, October 19, 1860; May Spencer Ringold, "Robert Newman Gourdin and the '1860 Association'," *Georgia Historical Quarterly* 55 (1971), pp. 501–09; John Roberson, "The 1860 Association: Catalyst of Secession" (Paper presented at the Citadel Conference, Charleston, April 11, 1987); Channing, *Crisis of Fear*, pp. 262–63; Eric H. Walther, *The Fire-Eaters* (Baton Rouge: Louisiana State University Press, 1992), pp. 220–22.

10. John Townsend, *The South Alone Should Govern the South and African Slavery Should Be Controlled By Those Only Who Are Friendly to It*, 3d ed. (Charleston: Evans and Cogswell, 1860). Townsend's pamphlet sold out in one month after its September publication, and by mid-November the second edition was sold out, too. Townsend also authored the fourth pamphlet published and distributed by the 1860 Association. See John Townsend, *Doom of Slavery in the Union, Its Safety Out of It*, 2d ed. (Charleston: Evans and Cogswell, 1860). For comparison with his moderate views in the first secession crisis, see Townsend, *The Southern States, Their Present Peril and Their Certain Remedy* (Charleston: Edward C. Councell, 1850). I would like to thank Craig Simpson for providing me with a complete set of the publications of the 1860 Association.

secession, Townsend's had originated in the oral political culture of the Low Country, first in a report to his constituents on the proceedings of the Columbia convention of the state's Democrats to which he had been a delegate in May 1860 and then as an address at a public meeting in June.[11] As a result, his brief about the necessity of secession in anticipation of the inevitable victory of "Black Republicanism" in the presidential election—the common currency of political discourse in 1860—was crafted with yeoman farmers squarely in view, as indeed they must have been at the rural Charleston meetings at which he first articulated his position.

By the late spring of 1860 John Townsend the moderate had become John Townsend the fire-eater and one of the most belligerent critics of his own former position. "The Union is lost," he said bluntly, in *The South Alone*. Borrowing from the radical canon, he disparaged "the croakings of political hacks about 'Revolution'" and their "womanly fears of 'Disunion.'" "This is disunion," he bellowed. "This is revolution," and it required only "manly and resolute ACTION" to realize the "deliverance" of the South. Mobilizing lowcountry men to "ACTION" was precisely Townsend's purpose, and to that end he reprised, on the one hand, the history of "the rule of abolitionism" and the "scum" whom *"universal suffrage"* had thrown up in the North and, on the other, the superiority of the slave republic and the privileges all freemen enjoyed within it.[12] His was an extended disquisition on the unity of rural nonslaveholder and slaveholder around the interests of property, franchise, manhood, and racial distinction, that complex of prerogatives that in the South Carolina Low Country together constituted the yeomanry's customary and legal claim to masterhood.

Once converted to the cause, Townsend proved a canny student of the radical genre. In bidding openly for the support of the ordinary rural freeman, he disdained not one of the extant arguments and added to the usual litany of covert threats. He went for the jugular. "Can a free people with their families and property to protect, and having under keeping so sensitive an institution as that of African slavery consent to have interests so precious to them tampered with by the crude experiments of a crazy and impracticable fanaticism?" he asked breathlessly, hitting yeomen and planters alike right where they lived. But amid references to property and dependents, familial and otherwise, and to racial distinction—"this Union was formed by men for the white race, for white men and their posterity"—Townsend also confronted the issue of yeoman loyalty head-on. What, he asked, were the chances that abolitionists were correct, that the "nonslaveholders of the South" could be "detach[ed] . . . from all alliance with the slaveholders?" To demonstrate the utter fallacy of that position was the sine qua non of Townsend's call

---

11. *Charleston Mercury*, September 5, 1860.
12. Townsend, *The South Alone Should Govern the South*, pp. 8–9, 16.

for united action, and in *The Doom of Slavery,* his second pamphlet, as well as in *The South Alone,* he went to great lengths to elaborate the effects of emancipation on "the non-slaveholding portion of our citizens" and the loss "to the non-slaveholder equally with the largest slaveholder" of the "important privileges" conferred by slavery. Among those privileges he listed political ones prominently: the right to militia duty, to serve on juries, to testify in court, and "to cast his vote equally with the largest slaveholder in the choice of his rulers." "In no country in the world," Townsend concluded, "does the poor white man whether slaveholder or non-slaveholder occupy so enviable a position as in the slaveholding states of the South." These propertied poor men, these yeoman farmers, could be counted on, if only to preserve their own privilege. In calling on all freemen to defend "an injured South . . . the peace and prosperity of their homes . . . the security of their property . . . and the cherished safety of their wives and daughters and sons," Townsend and many others carefully nurtured the unity of the body politic.[13]

Thus it was, predictably, in gendered terms that Townsend and other secessionists issued the call to arms. "The 'UNIONIST' of the South is the SUBMISSIONIST," Townsend proclaimed, and no man at all. "If *fears* unmans them now," he taunted, "when is *manhood* and *courage* to take their place?" Those who were true men, however, would repudiate "the contempt for our manhood" Black Republicans had shown. These "MEN of the South" would "set aside womanly fears of disunion" in favor of "manly and resolute action." Thus the call rang out: "The aid of every loyal son is now needed to defend the rights and honor of his political mother, where nestles the home of his wife and children, and where is deposited all his property for their support."[14] As patriotic sons, as fathers, as heads of households, as white men, as propertied men—as masters—yeoman freemen were called in 1860 to defend their world.

III

In the abandonment of the usual reserve with which planter politicians approached the matter of class difference and the political loyalty of the majority of voters, one thing was clear: Loud assertions of unity belied tremendous anxiety. Public expressions of confidence notwithstanding, lowcountry secessionists worried. Daniel Hamilton, U.S. Marshal for Charleston and a correspondent of U.S. Senator William Porcher Miles, minced no words. When the battle comes in earnest, he wrote to Miles, "you will find an element of great weakness in our own non-slaveholding

13. Townsend, *The South Alone Should Govern the South,* pp. 9–10, 13, 22; Townsend, *The Doom of Slavery in the Union,* p. 22.

14. Townsend, *The Doom of Slavery in the Union,* pp. 27, 29, 26; Townsend, *The South Alone Should Govern the South,* pp. 40, 9.

population," adding, at a later date, "I mistrust our own people more than I fear all of the efforts of the abolitionists." Like Hamilton, there were many in the Low Country who did not share Miles's faith "in the common sense of the people of the South" and who, resolving to leave nothing to chance this time, were spurred to ever greater efforts, propagandistic and martial, to convince as many as they could and to suppress the rest.[15]

The problem, as many lowcountry secessionists perceived it, was historical. The example of 1852 was ever before their eyes. Despite apparent leads over the cooperationist opposition in the legislature in 1850 and into the spring of 1851, advocates of separate state secession had failed in their first effort to take the state out of the Union. They were roundly defeated in the Middle Country especially and, ominously, in the midst of a hard-fought campaign in which the interests of the "poor man" in slavery and secession had been centrally debated.[16] Responding to constant cooperationist charges that secession was "the rich men's cause," that "poor men" were being made to fight the rich men's "battle while they [the rich] reclined at home in luxurious ease," middle country radicals had pulled out all the stops in their bid for majority support.[17]

Answering the question of who was urging secession, the editor of the *Darlington Flag*, a paper gotten up in March 1851 specifically to advance the radical cause, denied that "it is any particular class or sex" and went on to "remind the good people of the state that *Carolina expects every man, woman, and child to do their duty, in this, her time of trial.*" To that end, the paper and its correspondents appealed to the yeomanry's interest as masters in southern secession, adverted with unusual frequency to the specter of racial war, and even attempted to recruit nonvoters and especially women to lend their influence to the secession cause. "The

15. D. H. Hamilton to William Porcher Miles, January 23, 1860, and February 2, 1860, William Porcher Miles Papers, SHC. The slaveholders and nonslaveholders of the South "have equal rights and privileges—one fate," the editor of the *Charleston Mercury* insisted in October 1860, confirming in the extended attempt to convince his readers that a great anxiety attended the issue. *Charleston Mercury*, October 31, 1860. Historian Steven Channing, by contrast, regards such concerns as exclusive to the upcountry areas of the state. See Channing, *Crisis of Fear*, pp. 254–56. For similar anxieties during the secession crisis in Georgia, see Michael P. Johnson, *Toward a Patriarchal Republic: The Secession of Georgia* (Baton Rouge: Louisiana State University Press, 1977).

16. On the closeness of the contest in the Middle Country and on the process by which the cooperationists regained ground, see the following commentary from newspapers and the personal papers of local political leaders: John L. Manning to Mrs. Manning, September 21, 1851, J. L. Manning to Wife, September 24, 1851, Box V, Folder 139, Williams-Chesnut-Manning Families Papers, SCL; James Henry Hammond Diary, December 27, 1850, March 9, 1851, May 25, 1851, October 14, 1851, November 8, 1851, December 6, 1851, in Bleser, ed., *Secret and Sacred*, pp. 222–24, 230, 231–32, 237–39, 243–46; *Darlington Flag*, June 25, 1851, July 2, 1851. As late as September 1, 1851, William Elliott, the Beaufort Unionist, was bewailing the cooperationists' lack of organization in the state, although by this point even the editor of the *Darlington Flag* had conceded significant cooperationist support in his district. See William Elliott to Wife, September 1, 1851, Elliott-Gonzales Papers.

17. *Darlington Flag*, July 16, 1851.

poor man has as much at stake [in slavery] as he who is possessed of hundreds of negroes," one state legislator assured his constituents through the pages of the *Flag*. "He has his *all* at stake," his person, his property, his wife and children. Invoking the perennial example of "St. Domingo," he added the specter of racial war to the specter of agrarianism and female emancipation already conjured. "These two races cannot live together on terms of equality," the editor threatened; bringing that threat to the poor man's doorstep, he urged him to "meet this danger upon the threshold." So heated had the contest become in the Middle Country by the spring of 1851 that hardly a "planter" was to be found anywhere—at least anyone who would own up to representing the planter on the stump or in the columns of the paper. Everybody claimed to speak as and for "the farmer."[18]

This development, unprecedented even in Nullification, proved just how far radicals had been pushed beyond the boundaries of the usual conversation between political operatives into a serious contest for the support of the yeomanry—and even for the support of those disfranchised parties who could influence them. Thus, under the banner headline "To the Freemen of Darlington," the editor of the *Flag* insisted at great length that the call for secession issued alike from "the palaces of the wealthy and the humble cottages of the poor." It was uttered "by the politician . . . and the sunburnt yeoman," even "by the grave matron, as she surveyed with pride her group of boys soon to grow up and take their position as independent freemen of an independent State or the degraded vassals of a dependent province; and by the youthful maiden, who would prefer to see her brothers and lover slaughtered in a contest for equal rights, than living and submitting to an acknowledged wrong." In the intense contest over secession in the Middle Country in 1850 and 1851, the class divide in the body politic had been opened up in ways previously unimagined and the body social politicized, with dangerous consequences.[19] For, far from producing the unity which they so loudly asserted, the radicals failed in Darlington, and drastically in the Middle Country in general, managing to carry only Orangeburg District and losing every other.[20]

18. *Darlington Flag*, September 25, 1851, March 5, 1851. For correspondents who claimed to speak as "farmers," see *Darlington Flag*, August 6, 1851, August 14, 1851.

19. *Darlington Flag*, April 9, 1851, May 28, 1851. At least a few Darlington women took up the invitation to political participation, one reacting with outrage to the Unionist Benjamin Perry's charge that "ladies [are] generally in favor of the Union." "The impulses of the women of Carolina have ever condemned submision to wrong in those they loved," this woman proclaimed, "AND THEY DO AT THIS DAY." Submissionists make poor husbands, another woman wrote. The editor made political hay out of this opportunity to urge men to be men, reminding them "Brave gentlemen of Carolina, see that your arms be bright! The *ladies* call upon you to resist your oppression—Who can falter at such a call?" *Darlington Flag*, August 14, 1851.

20. For the electoral returns in October 1851, see *Darlington Flag*, October 6, 1851, October 23, 1851; Boucher, "The Secession and Co-Operation Movements in South Carolina," p. 128. On radical defeat in the first secession crisis, see, in addition, Barnwell, *Love of*

There were many lessons in that defeat, and radicals studiously attempted to learn them. The closer the contest, the more dangerously the breaches between yeomen and planters and nonslaveholders and slaveholders had been opened up, to the ultimate disadvantage, it seemed, of radical advocates of separate state secession. It was precisely this outcome, and perhaps its spread to the coastal parishes, that secessionists guarded against so vigilantly in 1860. For even as cries for unity echoed across the Low Country, politicians continued to agitate class issues and to struggle over who represented the interests of the majority of rural voters. Despite the criticism of radical and moderate leaders and the disgust even of lowcountry political managers, divisions between yeomen and planters assumed pivotal proportions in congressional contests, such as that between Colonel W. A. Owens, General Louis Malone Ayer, Jr., and George P. Elliott to replace Lawrence Keitt in the Third District in 1860;[21] in state senate races, such as that between Edward B. Bryan and none other than John Townsend in St. John's, Colleton in 1858;[22] and in the debate over the wisdom of reopening the slave trade, which proved the hobby of a significant minority of politicians from 1856 until well past secession.[23] "Sympathy in our parish for the poor and op-

---

Order, pp. 155–90. In Orangeburg, the Richland District planter Wade Hampton noted, "both candidates are secession," and the cooperationists had been on the defensive throughout the entire campaign. Wade Hampton, Jr., to James Chesnut, Jr., June 5, 1852, Box V, Folder 140, Williams-Chesnut-Manning Families Papers.

21. Ayers was accused by Owens of supporting the popular election of presidential electors and thus of sowing divisiveness between classes and sections. His unsoundness on the parish system was used by his opponents to cast doubt on his secessionist credentials. Elliott was introduced (thoroughly disingenuously) as the candidate of the "farmers" by a number of lowcountry political managers disgusted by and fearful of the tone of the original campaign. On that point, see W. H. Trescot to William Porcher Miles, November 8, 1859, William Porcher Miles Papers. The contest can be followed in the *Charleston Mercury*, February 29, 1859, March 24, 1859, March 30, 1859, April 6, 1859, July 19, 1859, July 20, 1859, August 8, 1859, August 25, 1859, August 30, 1859, September 1, 1859, September 15, 1859, September 21, 1859, September 26, 1859, September 27, 1859, October 13, 1859. The issue was still being exploited in the fall of 1860, when George Elliott opposed reform in a speech in Orangeburg District before the "solid and intelligent yeomanry of the Country." *Charleston Mercury*, September 7, 1860.

22. Class issues surfaced in a number of ways in this contest. Each candidate accused the other of disrespect for the people, and Townsend, particularly, postured as the defender of the people's political rights against Bryan, whom he accused of opposition to universal suffrage and of having publicly advocated the introduction of a property requirement for the franchise. Townsend, in addition, opposed the reopening of the slave trade, a position which, according to some, cost him the election. See Carrie Elliott to William Elliott, October 17, 1858, Elliott-Gonzales Papers. The Bryan-Townsend contest can be followed in the *Charleston Mercury*, September 16, 1858, September 25, 1858, September 26, 1858, October 6, 1858, October 8, 1858, October 11, 1858, October 28, 1858.

23. Those who advocated reopening the African slave trade were regularly accused of seeking to "array classes against each other" by arguments such as that offered by Williams Middleton that "possession of negros in our country is fast becoming a mere aristocratic privilege." For the charges, see *Charleston Mercury*, July 28, 1858. Middleton is quoted in Channing, *Crisis of Fear*, p. 149. The effect on nonslaveholders and the divisiveness of the

pressed is periodical and spasmodic," the planter P. C. Grimball observed scathingly and accurately during the Bryan-Townsend fight.[24]
But periodic or not, disingenuous or not, as lowcountry radicals knew all
too well, the agitation of class divisions did not usually bode well for their
side.

Little wonder that in 1860, a growing body of lowcountry secessionists attempted to put the stop to such divisive politics and used newly
powerful means to do so. Certainly the formation of the 1860 Association and the publication and wide dissemination of tracts like John
Townsend's were important steps. So, especially, was the publication of
J.D.B. DeBow's pamphlet *The Interest in Slavery of the Southern Nonslaveholder,* which Robert N. Gourdin, the founder of the Association,
had directly commissioned in early October 1860. Clearly, lowcountry
moderates-turned-secessionists worried, as Hamilton had, that nonslaveholders were one of the "weakest links" in their chain; thus they
made the task of securing nonslaveholders' loyalty—or at least their
compliance—to secession a primary propagandistic and organizational
goal. While much of the concern about nonslaveholders' interest focused, as did Leonidas Spratt's idiosyncratic pamphlet "The Philosophy
of Secession," on the small but growing urban white working class of
Charleston, DeBow's focus on the interests of yeoman farmers suggested
that lowcountry politicians never rested entirely easy about the loyalty of
rural propertied nonslaveholders, either.[25]

In the heated political environment of 1860, even such extensive
propagandistic efforts were not sufficient. In the campaign to win the
heart and minds of freemen, anxious radical leaders turned not only to

---

issue were central concerns in the debate. See, for example, *Charleston Mercury,* July 28,
1858, August 6, 1858, February 1, 1859, April 12, 1859, October 5, 1859, February 4,
1860; *Orangeburg Southron,* March 14, 1860, March 21, 1860. For secessionists' fear of the
issue as a dangerously divisive one, see Robert Barnwell Rhett to James Chesnut, October
17, 1859, Williams-Chesnut-Manning Families Papers; Robert N. Gourdin to William Porcher Miles, November 28, 1856, and W. H. Trescot to William Porcher Miles, February 8,
1859, William Porcher Miles Papers. For a full treatment of the issue, see Ronald T.
Takaki, *A Pro-Slavery Crusade: The Agitation to Reopen the African Slave Trade* (New York:
Free Press, 1971).

24. P. C. Grimball, in *Charleston Mercury,* October 7, 1858.

25. J. D. B. DeBow, *The Interest in Slavery of the Southern Nonslaveholder, The Right of
Peaceful Secession, Slavery in the Bible,* 1860 Association, Tract No. 5 (Charleston: Evans and
Cogswell, 1860); Leonidas W. Spratt, *The Philosophy of Secession: A Southern View*
(Charleston: n. pub., February 13, 1861). On Gourdin's commissioning of DeBow's pamphlet, see Walther, *The Fire-Eaters,* pp. 220–22. Spratt deplored the growing power of
white "mechanics" to constrain "the rights of masters to employ their slaves in any works
they might wish for" and worried that "this town of Charleston, at the very heart of slavery,
may become a fortress against it." His solution was, among other things, to reopen the slave
trade. See Spratt, *Philosophy of Secession,* p. 4. For a fascinating treatment of white mechanics' growing influence in Charleston in 1860 precisely as a result of this concern to forge a
new political unity, see Michael P. Johnson and James L. Roark, *Black Masters: A Free Family
of Color in the Old South* (New York: W. W. Norton, 1984), pp. 233–87.

the usual institutions of political culture but to others whose legitimacy rested in precisely their distance from the hustle and compromise of electoral politics. In this respect, none were so crucial as the ministry and the evangelical church. And while the significance of ministers' support for secession in 1860 cannot be measured, it was the foolish politician—and historian—who underestimated it, particularly in its influence on yeoman voters.

IV

The political role of evangelicalism had been part of the radical creed in South Carolina since Nullification. As one anonymous writer put it in 1851, sermons "tend, even more than mere political harangues . . . to encourage the hope and the resolution of our people, in waging unceasing war against the enemies of their institutions."[26] In 1860, as in 1832 and 1851, radical leaders looked to evangelical ministers to bear much of the burden of forging popular political unity. But, as they had learned in the first secession crisis, evangelical influence could work just as powerfully against their cause. For although the state's leading ministers were ardent in defense of slavery, southern rights, and the superiority of the Christian republic of slavery, many had stopped short of endorsing separate state secession in 1851, and some, including James Henley Thornwell, had spoken out against it.

  Thornwell's position evoked the divisiveness that attended the idea of secession, particularly in middle country districts, in 1851. He did not dismiss the threat to slavery posed by the Compromise of 1850, and he defended the right of secession in no uncertain terms. "When the issue is forced upon us of submitting to a government hopelessly perverted from its ends and aiming at the destruction of our own interests," he declared, "it will be our duty, as it is our right, to provide for ourselves." But, in his judgment, that decisive moment had not yet arrived, and he had not yet, as he put it, fully "dispair[ed] of the Republick." Thus, while "South Carolina seem[ed] bent upon secession," and "many of [its] clergy [seemed] as rash and violent as the rashest of their hearers," Thornwell refused to throw his considerable authority behind "single-handed secession," instead denouncing it as "recommended by not a single consideration . . . of wisdom, patriotism, or honor."[27] Nor was Thornwell alone among the clergy in this moderate and cooperationist posture.[28]

26. Anonymous, "Review of National Fast Day Sermons, 1850," *Southern Quarterly Review*, new series, vol. 3, no. 6 (April 1851), p. 555.

27. James Henley Thornwell, "Critical Notice," *Southern Presbyterian Review* 4, no. 3 (January 1851), pp. 450–51; James Henley Thornwell to Dr. R. J. Breckinridge, March 28, 1851, reprinted in Benjamin Morgan Palmer, ed., *Life and Letters of James Henley Thornwell* (New York: Arno Press, 1969), pp. 476–77.

28. Bishop William Capers of the Methodist Church South and William Barnwell, an evangelical Episcopalian bishop, both opposed separate state secession in 1851. See Barn-

The example of Nullification remained a powerfully alluring one to radical politicians. Then, as no one could ever forget, revivalism had made of the state a "great family," to recall William Grayson's phrase. But evangelical influence had not worked to that effect in the first secession crisis. Rather, it had mirrored, and perhaps even exacerbated, the divisions that existed among the electorate. Although no one could say with any certainty just what the political price of evangelical caution was in 1851, it was clear by 1860 that radical leaders had to have God on their side.

Indeed, by 1860 virtually every prominent minister in the coastal and the interior Low Country stood squarely for disunion. Even Thornwell, the man who had, a decade before, declared the "prospect of disunion . . . one I cannot contemplate without absolute horror," stood "heart and hand with the state in her move." "I believe that we have done right," he declared firmly in December 1860. "I do not see any other course that was left to us."[29] In contrast to 1851, most ministers went the full distance with separate state secession in 1860, deploying their unparalleled influence and access through the pulpit, the press, and the obligatory blessings at public meetings to proselytize the cause to ordinary folks in every parish and district in the coastal and the interior Low Country. In the process, they did more than their share to forge the political unity on which secessionists' agenda turned. Judging from the scattered comments of lowcountry churchgoers and one of the few remaining Unionists, ministers' support may have made all the difference.

That was precisely what the state's radical governor, William Gist, counted on when, following a national tradition dating back at least to the Revolution, he appointed November 21, 1860, a day of "fasting, humiliation, and prayer." The date was significant, coming just two weeks before elections for delegates to the state Secession Convention. Gist's purpose was clear. He wished to encourage "the clergy and people of all denominations in this state to assemble at their respective places of worship, to implore the direction and blessing of Almighty God in this our hour of difficulty, and to give us *one heart and one mind* to oppose by all just and proper means, every encroachment upon our rights."[30] By

---

well, *Love of Order*, p. 136. A notable exception, however, was the Reverend Mr. Iveson Brookes, a Baptist minister from the Middle Country, who supported secession in 1850 and 1851. In a sermon later published and widely distributed, Brookes insisted that if the South failed to extract guarantees of political equality, it should create "a separate nationality" through "peaceful secession if possible." Iveson L. Brookes, *A Defence of the South Against the Reproaches and Incroachments of the North* (Hamburg, S.C.: Printed at the Republican Office, 1850), p. 41 and passim.

29. James Henley Thornwell to Reverend Dr. Hooper, March 8, 1850, James Henley Thornwell to Reverend Mr. Douglas, December 31, 1860, reprinted in Palmer, ed., *Life and Letters of Thornwell,* pp. 477–78, 485–86.

30. The Governor's message was printed in *Orangeburg Southron,* November 14, 1860; Reverend Thomas Smyth, D. D., *The Sin and the Curse; or, The Union, the True Source of Disunion, and Our Duty in the Present Crisis,* (November 1860), reprinted in *Complete Works of Reverend Thomas Smyth, D. D.,* ed. J. William Flinn, 10 vols. (Columbia: R. L. Bryan Co.,

all accounts, ministers delivered. On November 21, as on many occasions in the months immediately preceding, yeoman farmers and their families packed into the churches to hear their ministers' passionate endorsements of secession as the requisite and righteous course. In attacking the God-ordained institution of slavery, one minister after another thundered, northerners had violated the constitutional compact on which the nation was founded. Separation of church and state notwithstanding, none retreated from the issue at hand. The question, Reverend Charles Dana of Charleston insisted, was straightforward: Would South Carolinians permit "a foreign and hostile government to rule over them?" His answer, "The South Alone Should Govern the South," directly echoed John Townsend's political pamphlet, exemplified the nexus of religion and politics in 1860, and, together with numerous similar answers, immeasurably advanced the cause of secession.[31]

But ministers did much more. In assuring their predominately yeoman congregations that the "course that this state is at present pursuing is the Christian one," they lent secession a legitimacy that no politician could confer. They lent it, that is to say, the sanction of divinity. "I speak to you in God's name and for God," the Reverend Mr. Thomas Smyth told his Charleston congregation. "The cause of the South is a righteous cause," one after another lowcountry minister intoned from the pulpit; it is the one "that God approves of."[32] No political arguments could have been more more persuasive with the people than those which put God squarely on the side of slavery, southern rights, and secession. "God is on our side," lowcountry South Carolinians were to console themselves when the full consequences of their actions began to crowd in on them in the early months of the war.

By December 1860, the Reverend Mr. Thornwell, like many evangelical South Carolinians, was at peace with his decision. "The rumours about mob law are totally and meanly false," he wrote to one out-of-state correspondent. "The internal condition of our society never was sounder and healthier." "The whole State," he concluded in an eerie echo of Grayson's comment almost three decades before, "is like a family."[33] To

1910), 7: 537. On the national tradition of Fast Day Sermons, see Mitchell Snay, "The Southern Clergy and the Sanctification of Slavery" (Paper presented at the Annual Meeting of the Organization of American Historians, 1987). Snay points out that in the North such calls were issued, not by the secular government, but by the governing bodies of the denominations.

31. Reverend W. C. Dana, *A Sermon Delivered in the Central Presbyterian Church, Charleston, S.C., November 21st, 1860 . . .* (Charleston: Evans and Cogswell, 1860), pp. 6, 8. Other Fast Day Sermons included James Henley Thornwell, "National Sins: A Fast Day Sermon Preached in the Presbyterian Church, Columbia, Wednesday, November 21, 1860," *Southern Presbyterian Review* 13, no. 4 (January 1861), pp. 649–88; and Smyth, *The Sin and The Curse.*

32. Reverend D. A. Lafar, "Sermon Delivered in the Laurel Street Chapel," in *Charleston Mercury,* November 18, 1860; Smyth, *The Sin and the Curse,* p. 549.

33. James Henley Thornwell to Reverend Mr. Douglas, December 31, 1860, reprinted in Palmer, ed., *Life and Letters of Thornwell,* pp. 485–86.

the extent that what he said was true—and Thornwell exaggerated only in part—ministers and evangelicalism had done much to bring that condition about. For, as historians of the French Revolution have recently reminded us, the kind of cultural power evangelicals possessed was critical to every revolutionary movement. Recognizing that to be the case, South Carolina's radical leaders had wisely and with unprecedented self-consciousness wrapped themselves in the cloak of evangelicalism in the months preceding the legislative elections and the election of convention delegates. In arranging for fast day sermons, soliciting ministers' blessings at every political meeting, giving prominence to the biblical defense of slavery in political speeches, and repeatedly invoking the schism of the national churches as foretellings of the fate of the Union—even in invoking God at the polls and inaugurating the Secession Convention in a Baptist church—they had attempted to appropriate to their cause every available symbol of religious authority.[34]

It was a winning political move. The influence of prominent ministers like James Henley Thornwell reached many ordinary men and women in the rural Low Country. In ways not entirely recoverable, although occasionally glimpsed, however, it was the local ministers, the men who took the pulpit every Sunday and spoke to thousands of yeoman men and women, who played the critical role. Mary Hort, a schoolteacher in Sumter District, testified to the fact that the pronouncements of the state evangelical leadership registered at the local level, for it was Thornwell that she credited in her decision to cancel a subscription to The *Presbyterian*, a national denominational publication, because of its "partial spirit" against South Carolina. "Dr. T. has quite convinced me," she noted in her diary in the late fall of 1860. But it was her local minister, Mr. McQueen, who came to visit and "sate a long time talking politics chiefly," whom she credited with reconciling her to secession.[35]

There was no division between religion and politics in the fall of 1860, either in the sermons and publications of prominent ministers or in the pulpits and pews of rural meeting houses. The yeoman churchgoers who had mustered, drunk, and argued politics with the best of them throughout the antebellum period joined vigilant associations and minute men organizations with the best of them in 1860, emboldened by their ministers' assurances that theirs was the course "God approves of." As they had done for so long, yeoman farmers and their families found in evangelicalism a profound reassurance of the sanctity of slavery, of

34. On the argument by analogy from the schism of the national bodies of religious denominations to the Union itself, see *Charleston Mercury*, March 29, 1859, December 8, 1859. The Synod of South Carolina issued a justification of the schism of the Presbyterian Church dated November 29, 1860, in which it declared its belief "that the people of South Carolina are called on to imitate their revolutionary forefathers and stand up for their rights." See F. D. Jones and W. H. Mills, eds., *History of the Presbyterian Church in South Carolina Since 1850* (Columbia, S.C.: R. L. Bryan Co., 1926), p. 74. On candidates' invocation of God's blessing at the polls, see "Address of Colonel E. Jenkins, to the People of St. Paul's Parish, at the Polls, 6th December," *Charleston Mercury*, December 14, 1860.

35. Mary Hort Journal, October 21, 1860, December 31, 1860, January 10, 1861, SCL.

the Christian mission of the slave republic in an increasingly atheistic world, and, in the fall of 1860, of the necessity of secession to the preservation of a Christian future. In the records of more than sixty lowcountry churches, not one critical voice can be detected. There can be no more powerful testimony to the popular political unity that had for so long eluded radicals. At least in the Low Country, evangelical South Carolina did indeed speak with "one mind and one heart." James Louis Petigru, the venerable spokesman of Unionism, for one, believed it made all the difference.[36]

V

When James Henley Thornwell assured his out-of-state correspondent that rumors of "mob law" in South Carolina were greatly exaggerated, he revealed either his own naiveté or the depth of his commitment to the making of a southern Confederacy. For although religion was one powerful part of the arsenal of radical popular politics in 1860, if yeoman farmers and other non-elite voters were moved by ministers' sanctification of secession, they were also moved by politicians' intensification of more customary forms of political mobilization—including and especially the militia.

Concerns about the military preparedness of the state had waxed and waned over the course of the decade in conjunction with the fortunes of secessionists. But after John Brown's raid on Harper's Ferry, Virginia, in October 1859, long-simmering plans for military buildup acquired a new immediacy. Calls to reform the militia system, increase the military budget, and stockpile armaments flooded the press and occupied the attention of state officials, giving martial substance to the usual discursive claims about the "need of some surer protection to our homes and firesides."[37] In purportedly responding to a fear of imminent invasion, such charges ended up producing it.

The process could be seen in every parish and district in the Low

36. James Petigru Carson, ed., *Life, Letters, and Speeches of James Louis Petigru, the Union Man of South Carolina* (Washington, D. C.: W. H. Lowdermilk and Co., 1920), pp. 370–71. The judgment about the support for secession in lowcountry churches derives from the records of the more than 60 churches listed in Chapters 4 and 5. For evidence of the full participation of yeoman churchgoers in the manly political culture of the Low Country, see the following: Beech Branch Baptist Church, Beaufort District, Church Book, May 7, 1836, November 12, 1836, October 9, 1840, March 10, 1860, SCL; Euhaw Baptist Church, Beaufort District, Minutes, June 25, 1859, SCL; Prince Williams Baptist Church, Record Book, January 15, 1848, SCL; Horns Creek Baptist Church, Edgefield District, Church Book, May 1853, SCL; Target Methodist Church, Holly Hill, Orangeburg District, *Historical Sketch*, p. 4, SCL.

37. *Charleston Mercury*, July 16, 1860. For other calls for reform of the militia system and military buildup, see *Charleston Mercury*, April 8, 1859, December 19, 1859, October 2, 1860, October 16, 1860.

Country in 1859 and 1860. At one public meeting after another, local leaders issued urgent calls for the formation of vigilant committees and committees of public safety to "guard and protect the safety of our homes" from the hordes of "suspicious persons" who moved at will among them. "I am for trusting no one here on earth but ourselves," "Vigilance" proclaimed in the *Charleston Mercury*, in November 1859. But by the time they had done whipping up their audiences with countless images of "foreign and domestic enemies," of local illegal traders who tampered with slaves, of foot-peddlers, book agents, and all kinds of strangers whose "true purpose is to murder, to burn, [and] to ruin," the sense of danger was so palpable that it was difficult to tell just who constituted "ourselves" and who the "murderous . . . Abolition emissaries." And after a few months of witnessing the parade of such enemies before the community, few could resist the argument that the issue really was "*Defence of Home*" and that, as one "Slave Owner" stated, it "is a matter that takes precedence of every other consideration, and is antecedent in men's minds to the formality and technicality of law." Once again the defense of the "sovereignty of the State" had been conflated with the defense "of families and . . . their home[s]" and the ordinary freeman moved to take action against the intrusions of the general government by the more literal prospect of the invasion of his household.[38]

By the early months of 1860, calls for the "establishment . . . of Vigilant Societies" had been answered in every parish and district in the state.[39] Formed out of Southern Rights Associations and organized around local beat companies, those vigilant committees riveted ever more tightly the nexus of popular politics and militia organization that had long characterized the political culture of the Low Country.[40] In doing so, they succeeded to an unprecedented degree in their customary purpose of mobilizing yeoman voters. For as the membership of the St. Peter's Parish, Beaufort District, committee confirmed, yeoman farmers were prominent not just in the ranks but in the leadership of vigilance committees. On January 12, when "citizens" of the parish responded to the call to a meeting at George Goettee's Silver Hill store to enact "resolutions . . . for our mutual safety and protection," it was a local minister, Reverend Henry Shuman, and a militia captain, William Speakes, who

38. *Charleston Mercury*, November 11, 1850, November 23, 1859, January 20, 1860; *Kingstree Star*, October 11, 1860.

39. *Charleston Mercury*, November 23, 1859. For evidence of the formation of various local committees, see for example, Brancheville Vigilant Association, and Detective Police, Minute Book, 1860–1863 [Orangeburg District], SCL; *Charleston Mercury*, November 21, 1860 [a Barnwell Committee], January 20, 1860 [St. John's, Berkeley, Charleston], January 12, 1860 [St. Peter's Parish, Beaufort], November 26, 1859 [Williamsburg District]; *Orangeburg Southron*, April 4, 1860 [Orangeburg District]. See also the discussion in Channing, *Crisis of Fear*, pp. 18–38.

40. On the organization of vigilant committees out of "each respective Beat," see the report of the St. John's, Berkeley [Charleston] Committee, *Charleston Mercury*, January 20, 1860.

worked up the crowd with references to "travelling agents and peddlars [and other] . . . secret emmisaries from the North." And when it came time to select "a Vigilant Committee for the purpose of affording protection," among the seventeen "gentlemen" appointed who could be identified (out of a total of twenty-four), eight were definitely yeoman farmers, and at least another six probably were as well.[41] In the campaign of summary justice and political surveillance that vigilantes like the St. Peter's ones unleashed on the Low Country in the ensuing year, yeoman farmers took a leading role.

At one level, of course, there was nothing new about such radical tactics. Southern rights associations had multiplied across the state in the first secession crisis, too, and had then, as in 1859 and 1860, used vigilance committees to exploit fears of enemies within and to "unite the people" of the state and the South, as one association put it, "in an efficient course of action, for the protection of their rights, or the redress of their wrongs." In 1850 to 1852, however, vigilantes on the lookout for "offenders against our peace and institutions" had hounded, harassed, and punished the usual suspects: slaves, free blacks, poor whites suspected of trading illegally with slaves, and any "stranger who appears amongst us whose objects are not well known."[42] By 1860, however, the activities of lowcountry vigilance committees had grown more summary, more brutal, and ever more focused on members of their own communities. The constitution of the Brancheville Vigilant Association and Detective Police, written in 1860, empowered its members not only to "chastise" any "negro found with a general pass" but "to inflict such punishment as they deem proper" on "persons not strangers or now residents" whose "conduct shall constitute an offense known to be punishable by law."[43] In the heated atmosphere of 1860, the definition of offense proved expansive indeed, and vigilance committees took on an ever more aggressive role in policing their own communities.

41. For the membership of the St. Peter's Vigilant Committee see the report of the meeting in the *Charleston Mercury*, January 12, 1860. The social identity of the members was derived from cross referencing members' names to the Federal Manuscript Census. Of the 17 members positively identified on the census, 8 were yeomen (5 nonslaveholders and 3 slaveholders), 2 were small planters and 1 the son of such a man, 4 were planters, 1 a planter son, and 1 a medical doctor. See the Federal Manuscript Census, South Carolina [Beaufort District, St. Peter's Parish], Schedules of Population, Slaves, and Agriculture, 1860, NA.

42. Association of Claremont Election County for the Defence of Southern Rights, October 22, 1850, SCL; F. H. Elmore, Wade Hampton, F. W. Pickens, General Committee of Safety, Printed Circular, Columbia, August 11, 1849, Williams-Chesnut-Manning Families Papers, Box V, Folder 135. For the organization of and the police and political activities of vigilant committees in one district in the 1850–52 secession crisis, see *Darlington Flag*, March 12, 1851, May 14, 1851, June 18, 1851, July 30, 1851, September 18, 1851, October 2, 1851, November 13, 1851, March 4, 1852.

43. Brancheville Vigilant Association and Detective Police, Minute Book, November 17, 1860.

What started out in 1859 as a witch hunt against incendiary strangers whipped up lowcountry communities into a frenzy of fear and excitement, as indeed it was designed to do. One after another, vigilance committees paraded corporeal proof of abolitionists' murderous designs before their neighbors in the persons of hapless northern piano-turners, tutors, nurses, peddlers, book agents, patent medicine hustlers, and other "strangers from the North," often apprehended at train stations before they even set foot in the neighborhood. The rough justice vigilantes dispensed to such unfortunates turned increasingly brutal and increasingly public. Not content to put him on the next train out of town after they apprehended the twenty-five-year-old T. A. Salvo, "an iron-legged abolitionist, a piano-tuner by trade and insurrectionist by practice," the Vigilant Committee of Blackville in Barnwell District shaved "one half of his head," applied "a thick coat of tar and . . . a liberal supply of feathers," and "then carried [him] through town on a rail, greatly to the amusement and delight of the inhabitants." Here and in many other cases of men and women being seized, shaven, tarred and feathered, hunted with dogs, and so badly beaten that they "bore the marks of most inhuman treatment," the yeoman and planter vigilantes turned their police activities into public spectacles and their districts into theaters of political terror. In so doing they created precisely the sense of imminent danger they were ostensibly formed to allay. By the fall of 1860 it was, as one Barnwell correspondent observed, "hardly possible" to comprehend "the excitement which prevails in all our country districts."[44]

Indeed, in the opinion of some local elites, including avid secessionists, vigilantes had provoked altogether too much excitement among the people. The popular political possibilities created by such extensive mobilization did prove difficult to control, and instead of forging a much needed unity seemed instead at times to open dangerous class divisions. When, for example, the largely yeoman vigilant committee of the Boggy Swamp section of Williamsburg District moved to rid "the community" of two northern abolitionists who "have been for some time teaching school in the district," their actions necessarily cast suspicion on the political integrity of the teachers' planter employers. Stung by the charges, those prominent members of the community were moved to publicly "deny that we have protected Northern abolitionists," to assert their "sound southern principles," and, after they insisted on standing up for the unfortunate teachers, to stand down a force of what was reported at anywhere from twenty to one hundred "armed men." As was not infrequently the case, the actions of a discrete group of neighbor-

44. *Charleston Mercury*, November 23, 1860, November 21, 1860, December 17, 1859. The T. A. Salvo episode is reported in the *Charleston Mercury*, November 21, 1859. For other reports of brutal treatment of suspected abolitionists, see *Orangeburg Southron*, April 4, 1860, April 11, 1860; *Kingstree Star*, March 31, 1859; *Charleston Mercury*, November 21, 1860, November 23, 1860.

hood vigilantes had expanded into a paramilitary mob. Despite the planter employers' demand that the teachers be exonerated and themselves "set right before the community," the Williamsburg vigilantes prevailed and forcibly expelled the teachers from the district, an action, the editor of the *Charleston Mercury* reluctantly acknowledged, "that the community, with a few exceptions approved." Clearly, the respect and trust the Williamsburg planters regarded as "due to us and our position as slaveholders" was no longer forthcoming in late 1859.[45]

The lesson was noted far from the original Williamsburg neighborhood in which it had been first taught. Faced with this overwhelming evidence of popular support for vigilante justice, anxious members of the political elite abandoned their earlier calls for caution. Although on December 5, 1859, the editor of the *Charleston Mercury* had expressed concern about the "irregular" justice discharged by "irresponsible and disorganized bodies" and had called instead for the formation of committees of safety "comprised of the *older and more discreet men*" of the respective communities, by January 6, 1860 he had backed off entirely and now advertised his conviction that "there is good reason for the establishment of Committees of Vigilance and Safety, and work for them to do." To do otherwise was to face the fate of Captain D. E. Gordon, the Williamsburg militia captain, whose troops "refuse[d] to muster under [him] on account of the stand he took in favor" of the purportedly abolitionist schoolteachers.[46]

By early 1860 it was apparent to the members of the political elite that they had lost control of the forces they had unleashed. Unable to control the popular committees of vigilance that had spread like wildfire across the Low Country, they could attempt only to harness their considerable political energy. And in the months of unceasing political agitation that led up to the legislative elections of October 8, 1860, vigilance committees proved critical to the secessionists' cause, advancing it on two fronts simultaneously: continuing the process of radical popular mobilization and suppressing any vestiges of dissent. Their contribution to the great unanimity secessionists were to claim in October owed as much to the latter as to the former. For by the time yeoman vigilantes had finished working their districts into a frenzy of political excitement against suspicious outsiders, the definition of suspicious character extended to anyone, including their own neighbors, not sufficiently enthusiastic about resistance—or, as the elections approached, about secession. In October 1860 yeoman farmers went to the polls in an atmosphere of what can only be called political terror. And it was one largely of their own creation.

45. *Charleston Mercury,* November 26, 1859, November 30, 1859, December 22, 1859, January 6, 1860.
46. *Charleston Mercury,* December 5, 1859, January 6, 1860.

VI

In the legislative elections of October 8, 1860, South Carolina's radical leaders finally achieved unity on secession. Long-time fire-eaters and former moderates alike crowed over the new harmony in the body politic. "[I]t is a complete landsturm, a general rising of the people," William Gilmore Simms insisted, while Lawrence Keitt gloated that the incoming legislature was "tremendously, out and out secession." As the Secession Convention prepared to meet in Columbia on December 17, John Berkley Grimball paused to recognize the historical moment, confident about the revolutionary act about to be taken. "The people have . . . with unexampled unanimity resolved to secede," he noted in his diary, "and to dare any consequence that may follow the act."[47] This revolution, Grimball, Simms, and others insisted, was driven by "the people." It was, in every sense, a popular revolution.

Although the radicals' claim were clearly self-serving, election returns in fact support the assertion that the state and its yeoman majority were solid for secession in the fall of 1860. In both the October 8 election of representatives to the state assembly and in the December 6 election of delegates to the Secession Convention, secessionists were everywhere victorious.[48] Neither in the state as a whole nor in the Low Country more specifically was there any evidence of the sectional divisions that had plagued the cause in 1851. Middle country districts proved as enthusiastic as coastal parishes, and in October 1860 the Low Country finally presented a unified political face to the state and the nation.

Nor was that united front simply a product of a constrained popular politics, although in the time-honored traditions of lowcountry political culture, customary tactics of "managing the people" can hardly be underestimated. There were, for example, a few Beaufort yeomen who claimed long after the Civil War that the unanimity on secession in their districts had been produced less by enthusiasm than by the careful narrowing—indeed, elimination—of political choice. There was "no opposition ticket in this section," William Harvey, a farmer from St. Peter's Parish, insisted. Men there simply "could not vote for the union." Harvey did not say if he referred to the legislative or to the secession convention elections; perhaps he did not even remember. But his charges, repeated by a handful of other lowcountry yeomen, certainly would have been true of the convention elections in which more than half of

47. William Gilmore Simms and Lawrence Keitt quoted in Channing, *Crisis of Fear,* pp. 251, 245; John Berkley Grimball Diary, vol. 3, December 17, 1860, Grimball Family Papers.

48. Channing, *Crisis of Fear,* p. 284; Boucher, "South Carolina and the South on the Eve of Secession," p. 143; Ralph Wooster, *The Secession Conventions of the South* (Princeton, N.J.: Princeton University Press, 1962), pp. 14–15; Laura A. White, *Robert Barnwell Rhett: Father of Secession* (Gloucester, Mass.: Peter Smith, 1965), pp. 181–86.

the candidates in the rural parishes ran uncontested. And it is also true, as Josiah Johnson of Beaufort charged, that "the ordinance of secession was not submitted to the vote of the people in this state for ratification."[49] Yet, while there is certainly a good deal of truth in these charges, it is by no means obvious that, given the choice of opposition to secession, the majority of yeoman farmers would have exercised it. The evidence from yeoman neighborhoods, including those in William Harvey's Coosawhatchie Swamp settlement in St. Peter's Parish, Beaufort, suggests precisely the opposite, suggests just how few pockets of resistance to secession remained in the Low Country by October 1860.[50]

In their districts, lowcountry yeomen reported to officials of the Southern Claims Commission after the Civil War, the "prevalent sentiment" was for secession or "all for the rebellion." And this seems to have been in fact the case. For even those few farmers who claimed to have been Unionists during the war either admitted that they had been carried along for a time by the passion for secession or emphasized their isolation within their own communities. Richard Taylor, a farmer and storekeeper from St. Peter's Parish, claimed, for example, that his neighbors had refused to patronize his store "on account of my political opinion, there being too few Union men right about there," and insisted that he had been "broke up at Crocketville"—literally run out of the neighborhood—because of his lack of enthusiasm for secession. Taylor did not find any more amenable surroundings in the Coosawhatchie Swamp settlement of the parish to which he relocated. There, too, he pointed out, secession feeling "ran so high" that he was afraid even to abstain from voting and showed up at the polls to throw suspicious neighbors off his trail. John Herndon, a self-proclaimed Unionist from Marlboro District, reported the same kind of popular passion for secession among his church brethren. They refused "to speak to me or notice me," he recalled, until they accomplished their goal and drove him out of the church.[51] As Taylor, Herndon, and others implied, the great majority of lowcountry yeomen not only supported secession enthusi-

49. Claim of William Harvey, Beaufort, Southern Claims Commission Records [hereafter SCCR], RG 217, File #6796, NA; Josiah Johnson quoted in Claim of Mary B. Tuten, Beaufort, SCCR, RG 217, File #9390; Wooster, *Secession Conventions of the South*, pp. 15–25, 256–66. For other comments on the absence of political choice, see Claim of Joseph Rosier [Rozier], Beaufort, SCCR, RG 217, File #5671; Claim of William J. Peeples, Beaufort, SCCR, RG 233; Claim of Felix W. Tuten, Beaufort, SCCR, RG 233; Claim of Abner Ginn, Beaufort, SCCR, RG 217, File #10076.

50. The records of the Southern Claims Commission themselves point to such a conclusion, for commissioners were hard-pressed in the 1870s to identify more than handful of white Unionists in the area. In Beaufort, for example, most of the awards of compensation went to former slaves.

51. Jasper T. Tuten from Claim of William M. Peeples, Beaufort, SCCR, RG 233; Claim of Richard A. Taylor, Beaufort, SCCR, RG 217, File #6795; Claim of John P. Herndon, Marlboro, SCCR, RG 217, File #267. See also the comments of Charles Brandt and Felix Tuten, in Claim of Charles Brandt, Barnwell, SCCR, RG 217, File #7988, Claim of Felix Tuten, Beaufort, SCCR, RG 233.

astically but acted decisively to discipline the holdouts among their own class. The constraints on political choice were not, it would seem, the doings only of the local elite. Not content to provide support to secessionist candidates through the mere casting of the ballot, a good number of lowcountry yeomen seized more assertive positions as leaders of local vigilance committees and thus, in 1860, as key political operatives of the secessionist movement.

From strangers to local poor whites suspected of illegal trading with slaves, the epidemic of suspicion that vigilantes unleashed across the Low Country in 1859 and 1860 moved inexorably into the heart of the yeoman community, justifying a climate of surveillance that took an increasingly political direction as the October elections approached.[52] The treatment meted out to John N. Smith, a fifty-four year old farmer and a long-time resident of the Coosawhatchie Swamp section of St. Peter's Parish, exemplifies the point. When in September 1860 Smith sheltered a free black woman and her children who had recently been robbed and driven from their home by the local Silver Hill Vigilant Committee, Smith himself, charged with harboring not a lone woman and her children "but a large gang of free negroes, known as the Knight family, comprising some thirty in number," quickly became an object of the committee's paramilitary justice. On September 26, fifteen "gentlemen" members of the Vigilant Committee paid a visit to John Smith and gave him an ultimatum: He had forty-eight hours to get the "negros" off his place or they would be forcibly removed. Smith was incensed. Like that other lowcountry farmer, Price, with whom the planter son Ralph Elliott had tangled, John Smith insisted on the inviolability of his household and on his rights as master within it. Like Price, he resisted the intruders, declaring that he "would not suffer the Committee to enter his place—threatening violence to any that should attempt to do so, and stating that he would protect the negros." But if Smith acted out of the same masterly identity as had Price, the situation could not have been more different. At least four and probably more of the vigilantes who

---

52. For a few examples of the increasing focus on local white suspects, and especially on those suspected of trading illegally with slaves, see *Charleston Mercury,* January 20, 1860, July 3, 1860; *Orangeburg Southron,* April 4, 1860; Brancheville Vigilant Association and Detective Police [Orangeburg], Minute Book, Third Saturday in December, 1860. By 1860 illegal trading was presented by grand juries across the Low Country as tantamount to abolition. See Grand Jury Presentments, Williamsburg District, Fall Term, 1857, General Assembly Records, SCDAH; Grand Jury Presentments, Charleston District, January Term, 1859, General Assembly Records; Grand Jury Presentments, Richland District, Fall Term, 1859, General Assembly Records; Grand Jury Presentments, Kershaw District, Fall Term, 1860, General Assembly Records. So severe had penalties become for those convicted of trading with slaves (a second conviction was "punishable by whipping") that, according to one correspondent, "Cincinnatus," it became the central issue in the 1858 elections in Williamsburg: "this is all the people seem to care about," he wrote—that "the negro trader shall not be whipped." The laws, some worried, were "calculated to widen the breach between the slaveholder and nonslaveholder and do no practical good." *Charleston Mercury,* July 14, 1858.

presumed to discipline him—William Hadwin, Henry Folk, George W. Smith, and J. D. Nix—were his near neighbors in the Coosawhatchie Swamp settlement and were, moreover, yeoman farmers like him.[53]

In the explosive atmosphere of the fall of 1860, as the Low Country geared up for battle, nonconformity such as that exhibited by John Smith in his "notorious" relationship with the Knight family invariably took on overtones of political dissension, and even Smith's identity as a respectable yeoman farmer no longer provided any protection. The case against Smith quickly escalated. Charging Smith initially with protecting free negroes, the vigilantes soon put it around the neighborhood that "Smith had repeatedly declared himself opposed to slavery," had "threatened to arm the negroes against their masters," and had declared his conviction that "Scripture did not recognize slavery," that he "did not believe it was right," and that "if there was war he would fight for no man's negros." Indeed, provoked as he so obviously was, it is conceivable that Smith did rage publicly against his neighbors and their coercive political orthodoxy. But if that was true, he only fueled their fire. For by the time they were done, Smith not only stood accused, as someone recalled years later, of being an "abolitionist," but his two adult sons had been implicated in his crimes and their households had also come under attack. By the end, Smith and his sons faced a veritable lynch mob headed by the original vigilantes. With the entire community arrayed against them, they had not a chance. Visited twice by the mob, the Smiths managed to hold it off once. On the second try, however, a force of armed men launched an attack against John Smith's household and succeeded in seizing Smith bodily and taking him under guard of the local militia captain and "twenty five armed men" to the railroad depot. There, Smith was expelled from the state with the threat that if he or any "male member of his family" returned "he [would] be hung." Smith paid an incredibly high price for his political independence—for his insistence, even in 1860, on asserting his rights as a freeman and a master. He paid with his livelihood and very nearly with his life. That the price was extracted by other yeoman farmers, men who had known him, in some instances, for all of his life, was a powerfully symbolic foreshadowing of the Confederacy's destruction of precisely the masterly preroga-

53. The John Smith episode is recounted in the *Charleston Mercury*, September 26, 1860; and in the Claim of Joseph Rosier, SCCR, RG 217, File #5671. For the membership and yeomen composition of the Silver Hill Vigilant Committee, see note 41 above. That Hadwin, Folk, George Smith, and Nix were near neighbors of John N. Smith is deduced from the location of their households in close proximity to each other on the 1860 census. See Federal Manuscript Census, South Carolina [Beaufort District, St. Peters's Parish], Schedule of Population, 1860. It is worth noting that John Smith may have been moved to protect the woman and her children because they were threatened with reenslavement. The reenslavement crisis that originated in the demands of Charleston's white mechanics reached critical proportions in 1860. For a full discussion, see Johnson and Roark, *Black Masters*, pp. 233–87.

tives it was founded to preserve.[54] It is no small irony that a secession movement got up to repel the invaders at the threshold and that called yeoman farmers to decisive revolutionary action in defense of their households and dependents became itself an agent of invasion and of the abrogation of masters' prerogatives. And it is no small part of that irony that the shock troops were yeoman farmers.

In the shorter term, however, the summary justice meted out to John N. Smith sent a powerful political message across his lowcountry community, and it was one that extended right up to door of the polls. In disciplining Smith, the yeoman vigilantes of Silver Hill did the two things expected of good political operatives: they brought out the vote on their side and suppressed it on the other. Their success in mobilizing yeoman voters was just as evident in the mob that went after Smith as it was at the polls a few weeks later in the secessionists' landslide victory. But their treatment of Smith proved a powerful caution as well to the remaining few still not passionate about the cause.

In Beaufort and in other areas of the Low Country, men were made to feel, as one vigilante boasted, that "eyes are upon [them] which [they] cannot evade, and that hands are ready to be laid upon [them] at any hour of the day and night." That police atmosphere had direct political consequences. By October 1860 the "blue cockade" of vigilance committee members and minute men was "everywhere in evidence." A sartorial symbol of the will to resist, it signaled disloyalty in those who refused to wear it as surely as it signaled the loyalty of those who wore it proudly. As a symbol of their refusal to submit "to the election of a Black Republican President . . . to the destruction of our property and the ruin of our land," the "Constitution of the Minute Men for the Defence of Southern Rights" proclaimed, "each member shall wear habitually upon the left side of his hat a blue cockade." Those "too craven in spirit and too dull of perception . . . too timid . . . to feel our wrongs and . . . see our danger," only those unmanly men would be seen without it.[55] By the fall of 1860, there was no middle ground. If you were not with them you were against them, and every man's position was immediately apparent in the wearing of the blue cockade.

Such was the mood that prevailed in the legislative elections and at the polls where members of vigilance committees served as managers of elections. While "four or five years before the election for secession," one resident of St. Peter's Parish recalled after the war, "men could speak their sentiments and did do it freely and fought about it," by 1860, a man "with a public reputation for unionism . . . would not have been allowed to live here." Such was the popular groundswell of support for

54. *Charleston Mercury,* September 26, 1860; Claim of Joseph Rosier, SCCR, RG 217, File #5671.
55. *Charleston Mercury,* November 21, 1860; "Constitution of Minute Men for the Defence of Southern Rights," Richland District, October 7, 1860, SCL.

secession, such the threatening presence of vigilantes, that men were not only afraid to speak out against secession but were afraid to vote against it—were even, on occasion, afraid not to vote for it. "We had to be very quiet," Charles Brandt said of the Unionists in his Barnwell neighborhood, for they were "too few in numbers . . . and the secessionists were too overbearing." In John Smith's Coosawhatchie Swamp settlement, the "feeling ran so high," one farmer remembered, that "I could not abstain from voting." Instead, he said, "the poll being near my house and there being no Union ticket, I put a blank vote in the box." In testifying to the fate of the minority of yeoman farmers, these latter-day Unionists testified as well to the political disposition of the majority. As Lawrence McKenzie described it, he left his neighborhood on election day "to keep from voting and from being annoyed by those who would vote for it and would be after [me] to do the same thing." But his neighbors were not fooled, and on his return they confronted him, saying, "Well, Lawrence, we have today voted South Carolina out of the Union and you did not help us."[56]

The vigilantes and the local political operatives had done their job. By the fall of 1860 the yeoman majority was mobilized as never before, the last few pockets of resistance were effectively suppressed, and the Low Country stood solidly for secession. To the region's yeoman farmers goes much of the credit—and the historical responsibility—for that dubious accomplishment.

VII

The Secession Convention that began its work in the First Baptist Church of Columbia, arrayed in the symbolism of evangelicalism, finished it in more secular surroundings, in Institute Hall in Charleston, arrayed in the gendered symbolism that had served the cause so well. There, on the evening of December 20, delegates rose one after another to sign the Ordinance of Secession, amid an audience of three thousand and a profusion of "blue cockades, flags of all descriptions, bunting," and all manner of insignia. A few emblems of state took pride of place in representations of the occasion. Above the elevated stage where the male delegates sat was a huge banner on which was figured an erect palmetto tree with a rattlesnake coiled around its trunk to convey, as every South Carolinian knew, the state's deadly ability to strike after a preliminary warning. On either side of that phallic image, in alcoves and galleries also elevated above the stage, were female witnesses, symbolic and real:

56. Minute Men, Saluda Association, Minutes, December 8, 1860; Claim of Felix W. Tuten, Beaufort, SCCR, RG 233; Claim of Ezekiel Stokes, Beaufort, SCCR, RG 217, File #6662; Claim of Charles Brandt, Barnwell, SCCR, RG 217, File #7798; Claim of Richard A. Taylor, Beaufort, SCCR, RG 217, File #6795; Claim of Lawrence McKenzie, Beaufort, SCCR, RG 233.

The Secession Convention, Signing the Ordinance of Secession, Charleston, S.C., 1860.

in the alcoves, statues of female figures rendered in classical form, and in the balconies on either side, selected groups of ladies, embodiments of Carolina [see illustration]. As the representative freemen below proved their manhood by avenging the "honor" of South Carolina, "[our] insulted mother," they did so under the watchful eye of representatives of those female dependents who had for so long rendered Carolina's vulnerability real and her virtue the concern of every husband and father. In signing the Ordinance of Secession, in declaring themselves "ready to uphold her independence and her dignity before the world," the delegates, and every freeman who elected them, acted as masters—in defense of the state against a rapacious federal government and in defense of their households and dependents against Black Republicans and their murderous emissaries.[57]

Planters and their ladies dominated that elegant occasion in Institute Hall and, no doubt to a lesser extent, the many other celebrations that took place that night in muster houses, courthouse squares, meeting-houses, and plantation houses throughout the Low Country. Yeomen were not planters' equals, not even in this, the climactic moment of freemen's common struggle for political independence. But as freemen in a world of dependents, they shared, nonetheless, in the politics those gendered symbols evoked: in a definition of manhood rooted in the inviolability of the household, the command of dependents, and the public prerogatives manhood conferred. When they struck for independence in the fall of 1860, when they contributed their part to tearing the Union asunder, lowcountry yeoman farmers acted in defense of their own identity, as masters of small worlds.

57. *Charleston Mercury,* December 21, 1860, September 21, 1859; Wooster, *Secession Conventions of the South,* p. 22. The description of Institute Hall and discussion of the arrangement of bodies and symbols is based on a reading of a pen-and-ink drawing of the signing of the Secession Ordinance by A. Grinevald. The drawing was used as the cover illustration for the sheet music of "The Palmetto State Song," written by George O. Robinson (Charleston: Henry Siegling, 1861). I would like to thank the staff of the South Caroliniana Library for locating this illustration.

Appendix

The data presented in the tables II–IV following, as well as in many of the tables in the text, were drawn from the Federal Manuscript Census for St. Peter's Parish, Beaufort District, South Carolina, in 1850 and 1860. The universe included all households appearing on the Schedule of Free Population (Schedule I) in each census year (491 and 540 households respectively). I recorded the age, sex, race, occupation, birthplace, and propertyholdings of the household head and spouse (if the latter was present) and the age, sex, race, and occupation (if reported) of other household members.[1] I then linked the household heads to the Schedule of Agriculture (Schedule IV) if they owned or operated farms, and compiled data on the characteristics of individual farm units: on the number of improved and unimproved acres, the farm value, the crop and livestock production, and the value of machinery and household manufactures. Finally, if the household head was a slaveholder, I used the Schedule of Slaves (Schedule II) to record the number, age, sex, and color (black or mulatto) of the slaves owned, thus enabling me to analyze the composition of slaveholdings.

Absenteeism and multiple holdings among some lowcountry planters presented problems for data collection and record linkage. Although absentee plantation owners did not normally appear on the Schedule of Free Population (because they did not live in the parish), their plantations were reported on the Schedule of Agriculture under the name of a resident manager (because their plantations were in the parish). In 1850 the census taker usually noted for whom the manager worked; as a result, I was able to separate the holdings of owners and managers by creating "dummy" households under the name of the absentee planter.[2] In 1860, however, the census taker generally failed to distinguish the manager from the owner, and so plantation size holdings necessarily

1. Except for the spouse, relations of kinship among household members are not recorded in the manuscript census for 1850 or 1860. Nonetheless, reasonable estimates can be made on the basis of age, sex, color, and especially surname.

2. The "dummy" households would only include the name of the absentee planter and the data derived from the Schedules of Slaves and Agriculture.

Table I Racial Composition of the Lowcountry Population, 1820–1860

	1820			1850			1860		
	White	*Black*	*% Black*	*White*	*Black*	*% Black*	*White*	*Black*	*% Black*
Coastal districts									
Beaufort	4,679	27,520	85.5	5,947	32,858	84.7	6,714	33,339	83.2
Charleston	19,376	60,836	75.8	24,580	48,225	66.2	29,188	40,912	58.4
Colleton	4,341	22,063	83.6	7,403	32,102	81.7	9,255	32,661	77.9
Georgetown	1,830	15,773	89.6	2,193	18,454	89.4	3,013	18,292	85.9
Horry	3,568	1,457	29.0	5,522	2,124	27.8	5,564	2,398	43.1
Coastal totals	33,794	127,649	79.1	45,645	133,763	74.6	53,734	127,602	70.4
Middle districts									
Barnwell	8,162	6,588	44.7	12,289	14,319	53.8	12,702	18,041	58.7
Darlington	6,407	4,542	41.5	6,747	10,083	59.9	8,432	11,929	58.6
Marion	6,652	3,549	34.8	9,781	7,626	43.8	11,007	10,183	48.1
Orangeburg	6,760	8,893	56.8	8,120	15,462	65.6	8,108	16,788	67.4
Sumter	8,844	16,525	65.1	9,813	23,407	70.5	6,857	17,002	71.3
Williamsburg	2,795	5,921	67.9	3,902	8,545	68.6	5,187	10,302	66.5
Middle Country totals	39,620	46,018	53.7	50,652	79,442	61.1	52,293	84,245	61.7
ALL LOW COUNTRY	73,414	173,667	70.3	96,297	213,205	68.9	106,027	211,847	66.6

Table II Distribution of Wealth among Free Household
Heads, St. Peter's Parish, Beaufort District, 1860
(by decile of real and personal property wealth)

Decile	Total Value of Wealth	% Share of Wealth	Mean Wealth
Top decile	$4,687,470	67.3	$85,227
Second	1,274,200	18.3	23,167
Third	548,017	7.9	9,964
Fourth	251,104	3.6	4,566
Fifth	117,350	1.7	2,134
Sixth	51,055	0.7	928
Seventh	21,745	0.3	395
Eighth	8,635	0.1	157
Ninth	2,995	0.1	54
Tenth	275	0.0	5
Totals	$6,962,846	100.0	$12,752

Number = 546
Missing = 40

were recorded under the name of the manager. Such instances were duly noted and introduced limited error into findings about the distribution of wealth, land, and slaves and about the operations of farms and plantations.

To examine the production patterns of plantations and farms more fully, I constructed what is known as a "self-sufficiency index." This index represents an estimate (a very rough estimate, in my view) of foodstuffs available for consumption by household members, free and slave, and is thus an indication of whether agricultural units could have supplied themselves with the basic necessities. The index was determined by first converging all grain and vegetable crops into corn-equivalents on the basis of nutritional content, then subtracting the requirements for seed and livestock feed, and, last, dividing the residual by the total number of adults plus two-thirds of the number of children and the elderly in the household.[3] The results, found in Table 2.9, show the

3. For free household members, I considered as an adult any male or female between the ages of 16 and 60. For slave household members, I considered as an adult any male or female between the ages of 14 and 60. To calculate the corn-equivalents of various food crops, I adopted the conversion ratios and seeding estimates used by Roger L. Ransom and Richard Sutch, *One Kind of Freedom: The Economic Consequences of Emancipation* (New York: Cambridge University Press, 1977), pp. 244–53, and Roger L. Ransom and Richard Sutch, "Debt Peonage in the Cotton South After the Civil War," *Journal of Economic History* 32 (September 1972), p. 660, note 44. I estimated subsistence requirements of 20 bushels of corn per adult; additional bushels per capita thus represent a surplus. Also see Steven Hahn, *The Roots of Southern Populism: Yeoman Farmers and the Transformation of the Georgia Upcountry, 1850–1890* (New York: Oxford University Press, 1983), pp. 293–94; Lacy K. Ford, Jr., *Origins of Southern Radicalism: The South Carolina Upcountry, 1800–1860* (New York: Oxford University Press, 1988), pp. 54–56.

Table III Farms and Plantations in St. Peter's Parish, Beaufort District, 1850–1860 (mean values)

		1–24	25–49	50–99	100–149	150–199	200–299	300–499	500+
						Category (Imp. Acres)			
No. of farms	1850	28	55	49	30	20	44	44	39
	1860	31	54	37	30	19	44	36	54
% All farms	1850	9.1	17.8	15.9	9.7	6.5	14.2	14.2	12.6
	1860	10.2	17.7	12.1	9.9	6.2	14.4	11.8	17.7
No. of improved acres	1850	16.2	34.9	63.0	108.0	159.8	217.6	370.6	959.7
	1860	16.2	33.3	64.1	110.7	162.6	223.8	363.6	954.1
% Improved acres	1850	0.6	2.5	4.1	4.3	4.3	12.7	21.7	49.8
	1860	0.5	2.1	2.8	3.9	3.6	11.5	15.3	60.3
No. of slaves	1850	0.7	1.6	4.6	15.0	22.8	28.5	55.8	101.9
	1860	4.1	1.4	6.1	5.7	14.3	21.0	34.3	71.5
% Own slaves	1850	17.9	30.9	61.2	83.3	90.0	95.5	100.0	100.0
	1860	22.6	27.8	64.9	63.3	89.5	93.2	86.1	85.2
% All slaves	1850	0.2	1.0	2.5	5.0	5.1	14.1	27.5	44.6
	1860	1.8	1.1	3.3	2.5	4.0	13.4	17.4	56.5
Rice production*	1850	411.1	1438.0	2016.3	4138.8	52410.0	67208.1	304996.8	157288.7
	1860	5.6	30.4	2393.8	108.7	806.9	1642.3	4783.5	17503.3
% Grow rice	1850	46.4	45.5	53.1	63.3	70.0	75.0	68.2	79.5
	1860	32.3	55.6	48.6	60.0	73.7	72.7	66.7	72.2
% All rice	1850	0.1	0.3	0.4	0.5	4.4	12.4	56.2	25.7
	1860	0.0	0.1	6.7	0.3	1.2	5.6	13.3	72.8
Cotton production (bales)	1850	0.6	1.5	2.3	7.3	8.0	9.6	19.9	99.5
	1860	0.2	1.1	4.1	9.2	15.1	13.6	28.3	110.4
% Grow cotton	1850	46.4	60.0	77.6	66.7	75.0	63.6	65.9	84.6
	1860	16.1	48.1	75.7	90.0	84.2	84.1	72.2	79.6
% All cotton	1850	0.3	1.4	2.0	3.7	2.8	7.3	15.2	67.4
	1860	0.1	0.7	1.8	3.3	3.4	7.1	12.3	71.3

	Year								
Unimproved acres (no.)	1850	177.7	237.8	323.5	578.3	732.1	1085.1	1097.6	2618.0
	1860	100.1	277.4	1066.3	403.3	438.7	803.0	704.2	2596.6
Corn production (bu.)	1850	137.7	193.7	246.0	431.7	377.5	502.3	619.9	1469.2
	1860	135.5	207.7	315.4	447.7	581.6	656.8	627.8	1714.8
Sweet potatoes (bu.)	1850	106.3	118.6	156.6	343.3	367.5	389.8	561.6	2125.6
	1860	82.1	284.0	125.7	245.2	328.9	402.5	601.4	1753.7
Peas & beans (bu.)	1850	1.0	1.5	3.8	6.8	11.0	13.7	20.4	64.2
	1860	9.0	3.7	3.5	16.2	12.9	21.9	24.4	81.0
Horses (no.)	1850	1.3	1.9	2.6	3.3	2.9	4.2	4.6	6.6
	1860	1.4	1.7	2.2	3.2	2.8	3.3	3.1	6.1
Mules (no.)	1850	0.1	0.1	0.2	0.8	0.7	2.0	2.4	6.6
	1860	0.5	0.2	0.5	0.8	2.0	2.1	3.3	10.4
Oxen (no.)	1850	0.0	0.0	0.2	0.3	0.5	1.0	2.2	5.0
	1860	0.0	0.1	0.0	0.0	0.5	0.8	1.0	3.7
Milchcows (no.)	1850	4.4	7.2	7.7	13.0	10.0	18.3	17.4	31.2
	1860	6.1	5.8	7.2	9.9	8.3	11.1	9.7	23.2
Cattle (no.)	1850	9.3	16.9	17.0	32.3	25.2	48.3	42.5	71.6
	1860	6.7	6.7	11.2	14.1	15.1	19.1	17.2	39.0
Swine (no.)	1850	14.8	27.9	41.7	48.5	38.8	56.7	52.8	83.8
	1860	14.2	15.6	19.3	26.7	30.0	28.0	37.2	64.1
Sheep (no.)	1850	2.8	3.5	6.3	11.9	13.3	18.8	24.5	55.6
	1860	3.5	2.3	3.5	8.4	6.9	9.8	12.5	37.4
Wool (lbs)	1850	1.1	6.0	10.4	22.3	26.1	21.5	49.0	87.2
	1860	17.2	30.6	47.6	62.7	72.7	93.4	138.9	267.4
Butter (lbs)	1850	5.6	12.9	7.8	19.5	31.5	42.1	44.7	115.8
	1860	24.0	24.0	30.0	60.5	65.5	92.8	102.1	209.0
Household mfgs. ($)	1850	10.1	9.1	9.5	12.7	12.1	12.7	15.6	37.5
	1860	6.0	10.5	9.3	35.5	25.3	22.9	20.7	94.3
Value of farm ($)	1850	207.1	386.0	592.9	1610.0	2865.0	5050.0	13230.7	23743.6
	1860	407.4	951.1	2102.7	3423.3	5999.3	8814.8	25375.0	51090.7
Value of machinery ($)	1850	36.9	28.7	47.0	114.2	130.3	463.6	1657.8	1289.7
	1860	26.9	30.6	70.1	117.7	372.9	292.5	1979.6	2189.0

*See Appendix above.

Table IV Persistence Rates of Household Heads and Kin, St. Peter's Parish, Beaufort District, 1850–1860 (by category of farm size)

| | Category (imp. acres) | | | | | | | | | |
	0	1–24	25–49	50–99	100–149	150–199	200–299	300–499	500+	Totals
No. households, 1850	210	28	55	49	30	20	44	44	39	519
No. persist, 1860	43	10	12	14	13	8	19	18	18	155
% Persist	20.5	35.7	21.8	28.6	43.3	40.0	43.2	40.9	46.2	29.9
No. of kin, 1860*	141	21	46	42	26	17	37	41	33	404
% Kin persist†	67.1	75.0	83.6	85.7	86.7	85.0	84.1	93.2	84.6	77.8

*Denotes the number of housholds in 1850 for which there is a houshold head with the same surname in 1860. This is intended to provide an indication of the persistence of family groups. Although household heads with the same surname are not necessarily related, this table does not account for relatives with different surnames.

†Denotes percentage of households in 1850 for which there is a household head with the same surname in 1860.

percentage of farms and plantations in different acreage categories that raised grain surpluses.

The production of rice as both a market and a subsistence crop complicated the process of constructing the index. To begin with, I had to convert "rough" rice (the crop reported on the census returns) into "clean" rice before I could convert the rice into corn-equivalents.[4] I then had to estimate the proportion of the rice crop sold on the market and the proportion used for household consumption. Accordingly, I assumed that farmers with fewer than 150 improved acres and fewer than ten slaves consumed 100 percent of the rice they grew, while farmers and planters with 150 or more acres and ten or more slaves consumed only 10 percent of it.[5]

Some of the data presented in the text were derived from the only extant tax list for the antebellum period, that for 1824. It includes land values, land quality, and slaveholdings of taxpayers and is used in full.

4. I used the formula of 162 pounds of rough rice=100 pounds of clean rice as determined by Victor H. Olmsted, *Rice Crop of the United States, 1712–1911,* U.S.D.A. Bureau of Statistics, Circular No. 34 (Washington, D. C.: Government Printing Office, 1912), p. 4. See also Peter A. Coclanis, *The Shadow of A Dream: Economic Life and Death in the South Carolina Low Country, 1670–1920* (New York: Oxford University Press, 1989), p. 117.

5. I assumed that yeoman farmers consumed all of their rice crop because of the small quantities and the low quality of the rice they grew and because they did not own the milling equipment necessary to prepare the harvested rice adequately for market. On the other hand, I assumed that planters grew rice chiefly for the market because of the much larger quantities and the higher quality of the rice they grew. Even so, I ran sensitivity tests for plantations, calculating that anywhere from none to 20 percent of the rice crop would be consumed by household members, and found there to be no discernible difference in the self-sufficiency rates. I thank Professor Peter Coclanis of the University of North Carolina for his valuable advice.

Index